The Hard Disk Companion

The Hard Disk Companion

Peter Norton
Robert Jourdain

Brady
New York

BRADY

Simon & Schuster, Inc.
Gulf + Western Building
One Gulf + Western Plaza
New York, New York 10023

Distributed by Prentice Hall Trade

Manufactured in the United States of America

10 9 8 7 6 5 4 3 2

Library of Congress Cataloging-in-Publication Data

Jourdain, Robert, 1950–
    The hard disk companion.

    Includes index.
    1. File organization (Computer science)
2. Magnetic disks. I. Norton, Peter, 1943–
II. Title.
QA76.9.F5J68   1988   004.5′6   88-3176
ISBN 0-13-383761-0

Contents

Acknowledgments

We'd like to extend thanks to innumerable anonymous voices at the ends of technical support lines, who explained the intricacies of various hardware and software products and who sometimes went well beyond the call of duty in offering tips and advice. Many thanks also to the folks at Brady Books—Terry Anderson, Michael Mellin, Charles Levine, Meagan Calogeras, and Geraldine Ivins—for abundant editorial assistance and unflagging support.

Trademarks

1-2-3	Lotus Development Corporation
1DIR+	Bourbaki Inc.
Awesome I/O Card	CSSL, Inc.
Back-it	Gazelle Systems
Backup Master	Intersecting Concepts, Inc.
Bernoulli Box	Iomega Corp
Breakthru 286	Personal Computer Support Group
CD-I	Sony/Phillips
Command Plus	ESP Software Systems Inc.
CopyII PC	Central Point Software Inc.
Corefast	CORE International
Cubit	SoftLogic Solutions, Inc.
Data Pac	Tandon Computer Corporation
Dayflo	Dayflo Software
Disk Mechanic	MLI Microsystems
Disk Optimizer	SoftLogic Solutions, Inc.
Disk Technician	Prime Solutions Inc.
Disk Tool Kit	Morgan Computing
DPATH+Plus	Personal Business Solutions
Dub-14	Golden Bow Systems
DV-I	RCA
Electra-Find	O'Neill Software
Fastback	Fifth Generation Systems
FILE-LOK	Qualtec Systems
FilePaq	SDA Associates

FilePath	SDA Associates
Flash	Software Masters
HardCard	Plus Development Corporation
HARDPREP	Storage Dimensions
Hercules Card	Hercules Computer Technology
HFORMAT	Kolod Research Inc.
HOPTIMUM	Kolod Research Inc.
Hot!	Executive Systems, Inc.
HTEST	Kolod Research Inc.
IBM PC, PC/XT, PC AT	International Business Machines Corporation
JDISKETTE	Tall Tree Corp.
KeepTrackPlus	The Finot Group
Mace Utilities	Paul Mace Software
Macintosh	Apple Computer
Megafunction Board	Tecmar Inc.
Metro	Lotus Development Corporation
MTM 80-8000 Tape Subsystem	Emerald Systems Corp.
Norton Commander	Peter Norton Computing
Norton Utilities	Peter Norton Computing
Novo Drive 1000	Kapak Designs
OS/2	International Business Machines Corporation
PC-LOK	Qualtec Systems
PC Tools	Central Point Software, Inc.
ProKey	Rose Software
PS/2	International Business Machines Corporation
QDOS II	Gazelle Systems
QuickUnErase	Peter Norton Computing
SafePark	Prime Solutions Inc.
SafetyNet	WestLake Data
SDADEL	SDA Associates
Series 1800 Expandable Jukebox	Cygnet Systems
SideKick and SideKickPlus	Borland International
Silencer	PC Cooling Systems
SmartKey	Software Research Technologies
SmartPath	Software Research Technologies
SpeedStor	Storage Dimensions
Squish	SunDog Software Corp.
SQZ	Turner Hall Publishing
SUPERDRV	AST
SuperKey	Borland International
TheEMCEE	Command Software Systems, Inc.
ThinkTank	Living Videotext
Transpc	Microcomputer Memories Inc.

Turbo-Cool	PC Cooling Systems
Unerase	Peter Norton Computing
Vfeature Deluxe	Golden Bow Systems
Videotrax	Alpha Micro
Word Perfect	Word Perfect Corporation
WordStar	Micropro
X2C	ABMComputer Systems
XTREE	Executive Systems, Inc.
Zoo Keeper	Polaris Software

Limits of Liability and Disclaimer of Warranty

Introduction

What? A *whole* book about hard disks? But hard disks are just big floppies, right? Wrong. A hard disk is the control center of your machine. If it is organized, *you* are organized. If it isn't, you are in big trouble. People who understand their hard disks make them the foundation for enhancing speed and productivity in all their work.

If you doubt the importance of hard disks, scan any computer magazine. You'll be overwhelmed by articles and advertisements on hard disk topics: unformat programs, disk caching, defragmenters, full track buffers, removable media, disk repair utilities, file archiving, image backups, tree design, system configurations, nonvolatile RAM disks, streaming tape backup units, super-high-density floppies, voice-coil actuators, cylinder densities, Bernoulli boxes, interleave optimization, transfer rates, backup utilities, DOS buffers, data compression, hardcards, unerase utilities, high-capacity drives, plated media, seek times, DOS partitions, low-level formatting, multiple drive installation, DOS shells, optical disks, security hardware, file searching, disk housekeeping, head crashes, Trojan horses, disk repairs, operating environments, PC/T, MTBF, ESDI, XCOPY, QIC, MFM, VD-I, SUBST, SCSI, WORM, RLL . . . and on it goes.

We cover all these topics in this book—and much more. You need only a basic understanding of DOS to follow our discussions; no technical knowledge is required. Newcomers to computers will be exposed to a wealth of new ideas. And more advanced readers will see how these all fit together. For example, we bring together every important disk optimization technique in one chapter and discuss the tradeoffs. We sort through myriad hardware features and explain how to choose among them. We also compare the ins and outs of various backup systems. Our goal is to give you a strong grasp of concepts that will serve you well for the years ahead amid constantly changing technology.

We've made every attempt to keep up with the latest IBM introductions. Throughout the book you'll find information on the PS/2 machines. We've also described important changes in DOS 3.3. In general, we've done all we can to help you make decisions for the future, particularly in view of the introduction of IBM's new multitasking operating system, OS/2.

By the time you reach the back cover of this book, you'll be able to make effective, forward-looking purchase decisions; you'll handle routine hardware installation and configuration on your own; DOS and application software will be easier to use; you'll be able to monitor your work and that of others; your disk will run much faster than it does now; you'll have a nearly effortless backup system for your data; you'll be able to avert many dangers to your data, including some kinds of "crashes"; and when disasters occur, you'll be able to recover as much of your data as is physically possible.

Many of these benefits arise through utility software—often quite inexpensive. Because software is constantly changing, we've avoided recommending particular products. Indeed, we believe that any kind of comparative review would be inappropriate because products that performed best when this book was written may have long since been surpassed. Computer magazines are the best place to find up-to-date recommendations (*PC Magazine* gives especially detailed reviews).

We *do* mention many specific products in passing, however. Cited as examples, they often were chosen for a unique feature. Please don't construe every mention as a recommendation, and don't think that omitted products are under par. It's up to you to take the concepts you learn here and make your own decisions. Still, for those who want to look closer at the products named here, we've included an appendix giving manufacturers' addresses and phone numbers.

We hope you enjoy this book. If you absorb most of the information in it, you'll be well on your way to true *power user* status. And that's a good feeling. Not only can you strut your stuff at cocktail parties, but when you ask your computer to do something, it will actually obey. Nothing is quite like knowing what you're doing.

Peter Norton
Robert Jourdain

Chapter 1

Much More Than A Giant Floppy

Once upon a time not long ago, a 10-megabyte hard disk carried as high a price as the computer in which it worked. When the exasperation of working with floppies became too much to bear, people were willing to part with $2,000 and more for a small hard disk. Because time is money, it was clear that those fractions of a minute lost to swapping diskettes and waiting for floppy drives could add up to hours each week.

Then prices dropped. Tremendous excitement ensued when one company released a 10-megabyte drive for *only* $1,000. Soon the IBM PC AT was introduced, and suddenly a 20-megabyte drive was considered standard. Ten-megabyte drives plunged below the $1,000 mark, and the higher capacity drives soon followed. Today, over half of all installed PCs have hard drives, including virtually all AT-class machines. Few PS/2 computers will be sold without one.

Hard disk prices fell just in time, for the balance between "primary" and "secondary" storage was threatened. Traditionally, **secondary storage** (disk storage) has held about ten times as much data as **primary storage** (random-access memory). The ratio was five to one on the first PCs—320K floppy disks served 64K of RAM. But as memory chip prices dropped and many users installed the full 640K allowed by MS-DOS, system memory overtook disk capacity. The computer could generate files larger than it could store! A 20-megabyte disk restores a healthy balance of about thirty to one.

Considering the grief floppy disks have visited upon us over the years, it's no wonder that we regard hard disks as a solution to the floppy disk's failings. We think of hard disks as *giant, speedy floppies* that spare us the indignities of shuffling dozens of diskettes in and out of drives, losing data when a diskette fills, duplicating files repeatedly to keep them handy, and waiting and waiting and waiting as the floppy disk drives grind on and on.

A hard disk is much more than a giant floppy; rather it can serve as the foundation for a system of software and procedures that greatly enhance organization and productivity. Consider the following benefits.

Ease-of-use A hard disk can bring together a mixture of DOS features and software utilities that simplify work and shield the user from the intricacies of DOS and complicated software designs. A network of menus, batch files, and keyboard macros can perform complicated tasks that would otherwise require hours of training. A few keystrokes may instantly reconfigure the machine and switch from one task to another.

Productivity Greater ease-of-use instantly increases productivity, partly because work proceeds more quickly and partly because fewer time-consuming errors are made. Productivity also rises because software works more quickly with a hard disk.

Manageability A large hard disk lets you combine all of your work into one system. Large data sets may be shared and integrated by software. Work can be easily cataloged and archived, and access to files can be monitored and controlled.

These benefits don't come without effort. You need to understand your computer and DOS pretty well to be able to set up a high-productivity system. There are dangers attendant in having all your work on one fragile disk, managed by a complicated web of software. To avoid trouble, here's what you must learn:

Learn to buy the right equipment and software for your needs. The selections you make limit your options. Even if your hard disk purchase is already complete, you need to understand the technical issues so that you can identify and eliminate performance bottlenecks in your system. Without a clear understanding, you can easily squander hundreds, or even thousands, of dollars.

Learn to optimize hard disk performance. Without constant maintenance, hard disks run slower and slower as the directory tree grows and more files are added. Some disks are crippled through mistakes made during installation. With only a little utility software, you can triple the speed of most poorly maintained disks.

Learn to manage memory. The 640K limit on system memory will plague millions of users for years to come. Owners of PCs and XTs as well as many owners of AT clones won't be able to use OS/2, which allows more memory. Unfortunately, many of the productivity gains made possible by hard disks rely upon memory-consuming utilities. Hard disk management and memory management go hand in hand.

Learn to lay out the directory tree and its files intelligently. Many hard disk owners set up extremely inefficient directory trees. Work is hindered; vast amounts of disk space are wasted; and the disk is slowed. A well-ordered directory tree catalogs your work and speeds up DOS.

Learn to monitor the state of the disk. With time, it's easy to lose track of a hard disk's contents. Periodic housecleaning, tree maintenance, and file cataloging see to it that work *stays* organized.

Learn to make backups effortlessly. A good backup system does its work quickly and reliably. A bad backup system may take much *more* time and afford much *less* protection. Backups should not be approached as an afterthought. You must devote time to planning an easy-to-use, largely automatic scheme. After making this investment, you'll be free of backup anxiety forever.

Learn to deter disasters. When you use a hard disk, you put all your eggs in one basket. *You must watch that basket!* You can prolong the life of your disk drive and detect when a drive is malfunctioning. Certain measures can protect you from various user errors, such as accidental erasures or reformatting. And special software can protect data from unauthorized access.

Learn to recover from disasters. Many disk "toolkits" let you recover damaged or erased files. There's much more available than simple "unerase" programs. Utilities can repair damaged format markings, directories, and other non-file information on the disk. In some cases they can bring a "crashed" disk back to life.

We aim to teach you all these skills in the eight chapters that follow. As with so much in computerdom, there's often a circularity in the explanations. You can't understand chickens until you understand eggs, which of course requires a thorough knowledge of chickens. We've begun the book with a technical chapter (Chapter 2). It's not technical in the sense that it requires a knowledge of engineering or computer programming. But those who aren't technically inclined may find it a bit dry. Nonetheless, we recommend that you read it. Chapters 7 (optimization) and 9 (data recovery) are especially technical; you won't be able to follow them without having digested most of the information in Chapter 2.

Chapters 3 and 4, respectively, cover buying and installing hard disk drives. If you already own a drive, you can safely skip them. But it's a good idea to read at least the beginning of Chapter 3, which discusses how much disk capacity you'll likely need. Upcoming software requires much larger files, and many hard disk owners will be in for a rude awakening when they realize how inadequate their current drives are. There are also discussions of various hard disk options (removable media, hard disk cards, and so on) that

will be of interest to many readers who may someday add a second
hard drive to their machines.

Those who just want to use their machines without worrying
about how they work will also find that Chapters 5 (Organizing
Your Files), 6 (Navigating the Disk), and 8 (Backups Without Pain)
call for little technical background.

Let's take a brief look at the contents of each chapter.

Inside Hard Disk Technology

Chapter 2 guides you through the bewildering array of hardware
options. The sophisticated buyer doesn't march into a shop and ask
for a "hard disk." There are too many choices in quality and performance to leave to the salesperson's discretion. Open any computer
magazine and you'll find ads touting "RLL," "plated media," "track
buffers," and "voice-coil actuators." You'll also find a confusing
(and often dishonest) range of performance claims. We'll guide you
through this maze. We also take a glimpse at the future as we examine high-density floppies, laser disks, and bubble memories. Although our crystal ball is cloudy—like anyone else's—we try to
show where the big changes in price and performance may take
place during the late 1980s and early 1990s.

What, Where, and How to Buy

Chapter 3 begins with a lengthy discussion of how to estimate disk
capacity requirements. You may be appalled at how much capacity
is required to support new operating systems and software technologies, such as desktop publishing. We look at the many hard disk
options: ordinary internal and external drives, hardcards, removable
media, and high-capacity drives. Finally, we go through the steps to
making a carefree purchase, including choosing a vendor, negotiat-
ing terms for return and repair, interpreting warranties, and returning defective merchandise.

Installation and Setup

Chapter 4 deals with installing a drive, formatting it, and setting up
the computer to accommodate it. You'll learn the intricacies of installing the various types of disk drives and related components,

such as power supplies and ROM chips. We show how to format a drive at low and high level and how to partition it for multiple operating systems. We devote special attention to high-capacity drives that have trouble working with DOS. We discuss utilities that can create huge DOS partitions or combine two disks into one logical drive.

Organizing Your Files

Most hard disk owners arrange their files and the directory tree haphazardly. As a result, files are lost or accidentally erased; software runs more slowly; and disk space is wasted. We show how to design an efficient directory tree and periodically maintain it. Various file-maintenance utilities are covered, including file compressors, file searchers, and file catalogs.

Navigating the Disk

Having thousands of files on one disk requires an elaborate directory tree that complicates all DOS operations. As you create ever more elaborate software configurations, maneuvering about the disk becomes complicated and tiresome. To simplify DOS operations and automate complex software interactions, we'll show you how to use DOS shells, operating environments, menuing systems, security systems, batch files, and keyboard macros. In evaluating the options, we place special emphasis on managing scarce memory.

Optimizing Speed and Productivity

Chapter 7 tackles the difficult topic of getting a hard disk to run quickly and keeping it that way. Hard disks seem incredibly quick to those who have used only floppies. Heavy use slows hard disks, however. Many users believe that fast disk access requires expensive hardware. In fact, a well-optimized "slow" hard disk can outrun a neglected "fast" hard disk. There are many tricks to the trade, of which purchase decisions are just a part. We'll show you how to adjust the disk format and file layout to optimize DOS. And we'll examine an array of inexpensive utility programs that speed disk access. If your hard disk is poorly maintained now, you may be able to *quintuple* its speed in some applications.

Backups Without Pain

The need for backups generates much more anxiety than action. Backups are widely neglected because, when done badly, they take a lot of work and result in much confusion. We'll show you how to organize and schedule a backup system that exactly fits your needs. We survey the myriad ways that you can lose data and the six kinds of backup that guard against them. All backup media are covered, and we give special attention to selecting and using streaming tape units. We also discuss the full range of backup software offerings and the many pitfalls you should look out for.

Surviving Hard Disk Disasters

Finally, Chapter 9 leads you through the *valley of death.* Here the dead are files, which can be corrupted, scrambled, or annihilated in more ways than you can imagine. We look at what goes wrong with files and how to reclaim them. Our discussion takes us to file-recovery programs, disk editors and toolkits, unerase utilities, and programs that can resurrect an accidentally reformatted disk. We try to cultivate an appreciation of the *limitations* of these utilities. If you don't read our chapter on backups closely, you'll want to memorize this one.

If this looks like a lot to cover, we assure you that it *is* a lot. But mastering this information will take you far toward becoming a true *power user.* You'll be able to think through your options, . . . solve problems, . . . greatly increase your disk's performance, . . . make backups in seconds, . . . automate procedures—in a word, turn your machine into a roaring *powerhouse.*

Chapter 2

Inside Hard Disk Technology

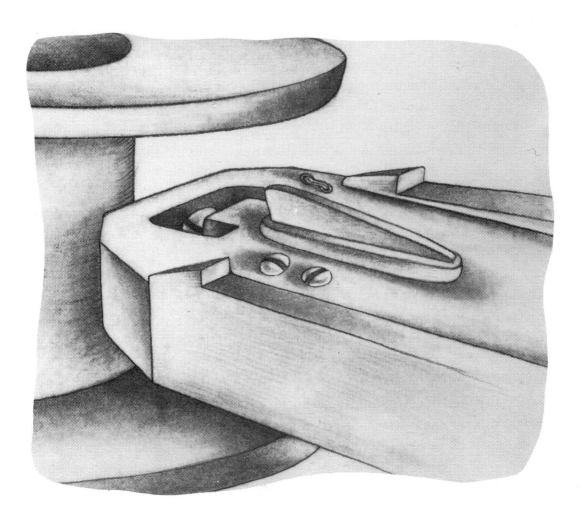

This chapter covers the essentials of hard disk design and function. Although you can live a happy and useful life without this knowledge, you'll find it invaluable when you must sort through manufacturers' specifications, advertising claims, news reports, and unfriendly hardware documentation. You'll also need to know a bit about the technology to understand our discussion in Chapter 7 on optimizing your hard disk's performance. Besides, the technical stuff is rather fun, and we promise not to journey too deep into the woods.

An Overview

Few people have ever seen a hard disk. Unlike floppies, delicate hard disks must be permanently enclosed in a protective aluminum shell. All that's visible is a *hard disk drive*—a metal box with some circuitry on it. There's no easy way to get inside the box to view the rotating disk; to open the drive is to fatally contaminate it. Drives may be opened only in **clean rooms**, where workers wear surgical garb and all dust is filtered from the air. Some disks are enclosed in removable cartridges that are inserted into the drive, but most are non-removable. IBM invented small non-removable drives and informally dubbed them **Winchester drives** (apparently because the drive's code number matched the model number of a popular Winchester rifle).

Tracks, sectors, and heads

For all its impressive armor, a hard disk isn't terribly different from the lowly floppy disk. Data is recorded as magnetic patterns written in circles around the hub of the disk. Each of the concentric circles makes up a **track**, and each track is divided into a number of equal segments called **sectors**. A **read/write head** moves from the outer edge of the disk toward the hub, stopping over the track containing the information the computer needs. Once in position, the head waits for the correct sector of the track to revolve to it, and then it reads or writes data as the sector passes beneath. Figure 2-1 diagrams this scheme.

Differences between floppies and hard disks

Hard disks are distinguished from floppies by the high densities at which data is recorded on the disk surface and by the high speed at which they operate. While a standard 360K-floppy disk holds 40 tracks, hard disks of the same diameter may have over 1,000. And they may pack up to four times as much data onto each track. Such high data densities require a very small read/write head positioned very close to the disk surface. Any flexibility in the disk would make it bounce up and strike the read/write head. And so the disks are made *hard* using rigid aluminum plates coated with a magnetic material.

Figure 2-1 **Data access**

Hard disks are also famed for their speed. While a floppy disk drive turns at 300 or 360 revolutions per minute, most hard disks spin at 3,600 rpm. Also, hard disk drives move their read/write heads from track to track several times faster than floppy drives. Such high performance requires extremely precise machining and assembly.

To increase the drive's capacity, most hard disk drives actually contain two or more disks. The disks, referred to as **platters**, are mounted around an axle called the **spindle**. All platters turn together. The motor that turns the platters may be built into the spindle, or it may reside below the spindle as a **pancake motor**.

Platters

Both sides of a platter hold data. Because it would be impractical for a single read/write head to serve all platter sides, each platter side has its own head. The heads are ganged together on a comb-like armature that moves all of the heads in tandem, as shown in Figure 2-2. The accuracy of this mechanism is astounding. The platters and heads must interleave precisely at every track position, with each head positioned only 1/100,000 of an inch from the platter surface. This precise geometry is maintained as the lightweight heads rapidly shunt back and forth over the heavy gyrating platters. High-tech indeed!

The heads are able to stay so close to the platters without touching because they actually *fly* over the surface on a cushion of air created by the disk's rotation. The heads slowly lift off when the drive starts up, and they gently land when power is shut off and the platters grind to a halt. The heads rest against the disk surface when power is off.

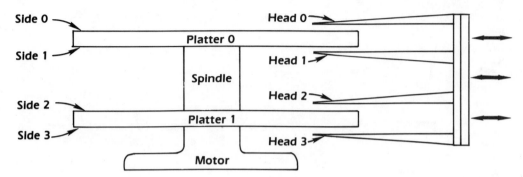

Figure 2-2 **Heads and platters**

Disk controllers

Most disk drives are accompanied by a **controller card** that plugs into one of the computer's card slots. When data is read from the disk surface, it passes from the heads through the disk-drive circuitry onto the controller card electronics. As we'll see later, not all hard disks require a separate controller card to intermediate between drive and computer. But all drives operating in IBM PCs, ATs, and some PS/2s require some kind of adapter that takes up a slot on the computer's motherboard.

Data sent from the disk surface to the controller card arrives at a buffer—a small patch of memory acting as a temporary holding area for data. Once the data transfers to the buffer, the controller card sends a signal to the computer's **central processing unit** (CPU)—the 8088, 80286, or 80386 chip at the heart of any IBM personal computer. The signal tells the CPU to begin moving the data into the computer's own memory chips.

DMA

The data is moved by one of two techniques. In the IBM AT and PS/2 machines, the CPU does the job itself. But IBM PCs and XTs use **direct memory access (DMA)**. DMA relies on a special chip that shifts the data directly from the controller to memory in a single step, rather than through the two-step process of moving it first to the CPU and then to system memory. PCs and XTs use DMA because their 8088 CPUs cannot keep up with a hard disk's data transfer rate.

DOS buffers

The data goes into system memory (RAM) in areas set aside as **DOS buffers**. The number of buffers may be set by the user as we'll see later. Each buffer holds one disk sector, which in DOS contains a 512-byte swatch of a file. Typically, computers equipped with a hard disk run with twenty buffers. As a file is read, its sectors fill the buffers; once all buffers are occupied, a sector transfers to the buffer least recently accessed by a program, overwriting that buffer's con-

tents. In the last step on the journey, DOS extracts data from the
buffers and lays it down at particular memory locations requested
by application software. Figure 2-3 shows the path taken by data.

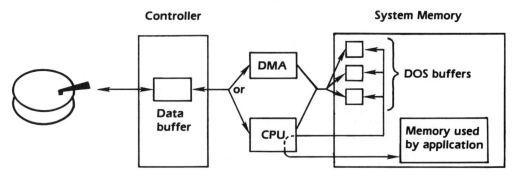

Figure 2-3 **The path taken by data**

When the computer *writes* data on a disk, the entire process is
reversed. An application program tells DOS where to find data in
memory. DOS moves it to its buffers and then transfers it to the
holding buffer on the hard disk controller. Then the disk controller
begins writing, specifying the sector on the track on the platter
side to receive the data, sending commands to the disk drive that
move the read/write head into position. Then the drive electronics
take over, carefully monitoring the disk surface for exactly the right
moment to begin. At that moment, the head emits a stream of magnetic pulses that encode the data in a line along the disk surface.

Writing data

The Disk Surface

A disk is uniformly covered with a **medium** that holds the data.
DOS lays out the data in 512-byte sequences called **sectors**, but, in
fact, an operating system may impose any organization upon the
disk it chooses. We look only at DOS in this section; the general
principles we discuss apply to any common microcomputer operating system.

Flux Changes

The surface of a hard disk contains magnetized particles of metal.
Each particle has a north and south pole, just like larger magnets. A
read/write head can apply a magnetic field to a tiny group of these

particles, reversing their polarity, so that what was north becomes south, or vice-versa. The smallest area of disk surface that can hold one of these **flux changes** constitutes a **magnetic domain**. Thousands of domains taken together make up a track. As the disk spins beneath the head, the head constantly changes the polarity of its magnetic field, creating a sequence of polarity changes on the disk.

Data encoding

All information in computers is stored as patterns of "1s" and "0s," "Yeses" and "Nos," "Ons" and "Offs." For example, when you type the letter "A" in a document, the character is subsequently stored on disk in the pattern **On**-Off-Off-Off-Off-Off-**On**-Off. These are the eight **bits** that make up a byte of data. (The pattern, incidentally, is arbitrary; it is part of the **ASCII standard**, making it an **ASCII character**.) When the character is written to the disk, the read/write head rhythmically changes its polarity to transfer the pattern to a sequence of eight magnetic domains along a track. A change in polarity indicates an "On" (a binary 1), and a lack of a change indicates an "Off" (a binary 0).

When a drive reads back the data, it essentially reverses the process. The head passively hovers over the disk surface, and, as the tiny magnets that make up the magnetic domains pass beneath, they ever so slightly influence the head's magnetic field. Circuitry on the disk drive greatly amplifies these slight perturbations into patterns of "Ons" and "Offs" that are fed into the computer's memory chips.

Data density

Even a floppy disk can pack a staggering number of these magnetic domains ("Ons" and "Offs") onto one track—well over 30,000 domains—enough to hold two screens of text (25 rows of 80 characters, with eight domains per character). Hard disks write at least 10,000 domains *per inch* of track. If you consider that hard drives rotate at 3,600 revolutions per minute, you'll realize that the read/write head is working very quickly indeed. At least 5 million domains pass under a read/write head in a second.

Magnetic Media

If you were curious (and unwise) enough to open your disk drive with a screwdriver, inside you'd find either platters covered with the familiar reddish-brown iron oxide coating of floppy disks or bright shiny platters reminiscent of chrome auto bumpers. The first would typify **coated media**, and the second, **plated media**. In either case, not far below the surface is a finely machined aluminum

blank upon which the medium is applied. The surface is what matters, though.

Until recently, most IBM microcomputer drives were made with
coated oxide, including the drives IBM built into the IBM XT and
AT. Some forty years old, the technology is well understood. The
oxide coating is little more than rust particles held in place by a
binding agent. The coating is relatively easy to apply at the precise
and regular thickness required. Plated media, on the other hand,
are made by applying pure metal to the aluminum blank, either by
vapor deposition or by a technique called **sputtering**. Because
working with vaporized metal is difficult, the industry took many
years to arrive at techniques that produce near-perfect disk surfaces
at a reasonable cost. Today, plated media are reserved mostly for
drives of high capacity, high speed, and high price.

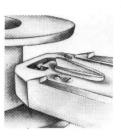

An oxide coating is roughly ten times thicker than a plated surface (which is but a few millionths of an inch), and it holds much
larger magnetic particles. So much binding agent is required in oxide coatings that the magnetic particles are held relatively far apart.
In plated media, on the other hand, the particles are packed against
one another. The absence of a binding agent makes the coating
much thinner, and often plated media are called **thin-film media**.
Even though the oxide coating for hard disks is denser than that for
standard floppy disks, it still cannot pack as many magnetic domains on the disk surface as plated media can.

Coated vs. plated
media

While coated media can hold up to 20,000 magnetic domains on
an inch of track, plated media have exceeded 50,000 domains in
laboratory prototypes. Even higher densities may be achieved by
perpendicular recording, in which the magnetic domains extend
from the disk surface inward rather than end-to-end along the
track. As disks move toward higher and higher data densities, there
is an inexorable trend toward plated media.

Head Crashes

Plated media have another advantage: They are extremely hard,
making them resistant to **head crashes**. Most users have heard
of a head crash or at least know that a disk can "crash," but few
understand what a crash is. The origin of the term is unclear.
The first experimental hard disk drives were giant contraptions
with mammoth platters rotated by powerful motors. A mishap

in the laboratory would cause the drive literally to tear itself to pieces. These calamitous events may have given rise to the term "crash."

These days a disk crash is a much more genteel affair. Severe vibrations or a mechanical failure cause a read/write head to strike the surface of an oxide-coated platter and cut a tiny furrow in the medium. The momentum of the spinning platters adds considerable energy to the collision. Where a head cuts, data can no longer be held, and if it is a place where data has been recorded, the data is lost. Worse, particles of magnetic material are loosened, freeing them to roam inside the drive. These particles may be much larger than the gap that separates the heads and platter surfaces; when a head hits one, it may fly up, crash back down, and damage more data. Sometimes the particles adhere to the head and interfere with the head's magnetic field.

Bad sectors

Sometimes DOS can write upon a lightly damaged point on the disk and the new data is successfully preserved. But when the damage is more severe, with a deep gouge made in the coating, data won't hold at all. The disk has developed a **bad sector**. DOS issues the message "Error reading drive X:" or "Sector not found reading drive X:" when it encounters these gaps in the data. To repair the damage, the sectors must be placed off bounds from DOS's use. Some software utilities perform this service (as we'll see in Chapter 9). Or you can back up all your files, reformat the disk, and then restore the files, including the backups you (presumably) made of the files that were damaged. The damaged area will be marked off-bounds during reformatting. We'll discuss these techniques in detail in Chapter 9, Surviving Hard Disk Disasters.

Severe crashes

When a head crash occurs over the outermost tracks, the damage can be much more serious. These tracks contain special DOS files, the disk's main directory, and information about disk space allocation. If the heads dive into this data, DOS will not be able to read from the disk at all, and all data will effectively be "lost," even though every byte remains intact elsewhere on the platters. This is the most feared of all types of head crash. There *are* ways to get some kinds of data back from the disk but only through great effort and expense (we'll discuss these techniques in Chapter 9 also). Because the read/write heads spend a good deal of time hovering over these outer tracks, head crashes of this kind are relatively common.

For all but the saintly, a hard disk crash is cause for fury and vituperation. "The maker is incompetent; the dealer is a cheat; the consultant is a quack." Remember that when the first IBM PC was released, small Winchester hard disk drives were barely a viable mass-market technology. The rate of technical progress has been remarkable, and quality rises year after year, even as prices fall. Besides, if the disk crashes and data is lost, the real cause for anger is clear: The owner has neglected to make backups.

Engineers are working on other kinds of disk media more resistant to head-crash damage. A particularly promising technology, developed by 3M Company, is called **SRR**, for **stretch-surface recording**, in which a special magnetic-coated film is applied to an aluminum blank with raised rims at the outer edge and center hole. The film is *stretched* between the rims so that the magnetic surface hangs slightly above the surface of the disk. As the head flies above the medium, the air cushion pushes a "dimple" into the surface. When the head crashes onto the surface, the medium can much better absorb the force, and it imparts much less energy to the head. Laboratory prototypes show recording densities almost as high as those for plated media.

Although many people call any hard disk failure a "crash," much can go wrong that has nothing to do with damage to the medium. Electronic components can fail; the motor that drives the platters can burn out, or the actuator that moves the read/write heads can shift out of alignment. And an actual crash can lead to a different kind of problem: The head itself may become contaminated or damaged. Contamination usually occurs in drives with iron oxide coatings; the soft coating material adheres to the read/write heads, causing errors. Plated media, on the other hand, are so hard that they can smash the delicate heads. In either case, the drive must go in for repairs, and this often means total loss of data.

Often **soft errors** occur. In these errors, the hardware is intact, but data is unsuccessfully read or written. **Hard errors**, on the other hand, are those in which the data has been physically mangled or the equipment is malfunctioning. Soft errors sometimes occur when a power surge passes through the circuitry, or when the bearings that support the platters begin to wear, causing a platter to wobble slightly so that it pulls away from the head's magnetic field. The controller can usually recover from a soft error simply by trying to read or write the data again. IBM controllers automatically try ten times before reporting an error to DOS. DOS in turn tries reading or writing data three times before it gives up and displays an error message. So a total of thirty tries may be made. In Chapter 9 we'll see how software can keep an eye on soft error rates and warn you about impending disk failure.

Crash-resistant designs

Failures that aren't crashes

Soft and Hard Errors

Sectors

Although it's possible to lay out data in one long sequence along the entire circumference of a track, generally it's not done this way. Instead, the disk is divided into **sectors** like so many pie slices, and accordingly the tracks are divided into pieces. These pieces of track are themselves commonly called "sectors," so that an expression like "a bad sector" means that only a part of one track has gone bad, not a whole slice of the disk.

Formatting levels

The sectors are created when the disk is formatted. Actually, formatting proceeds in two stages: low-level and high-level formatting. Low-level formatting defines the sectors, laying down a sequence of special codes that tell the controller where a sector begins. Then it writes special identification numbers so that each sector has its own label (the controller knows the track number by virtue of having moved the heads to that position).

Standard 360K floppy disks are usually formatted in nine sectors; the AT's 1.2-megabyte floppy drives have fifteen; and the 720K and 1.44-megabyte 3½-inch floppies in the PS/2 line have nine and eighteen sectors, respectively. Most hard disks have seventeen sectors per track. The number of sectors is set by the operating system for its own purposes. The physically uniform disk surface can be magnetically cut up in any pattern.

There is something about the word "sector" that encourages people to think of disk sectors as little wedges of data written at regular intervals along the disk surface. This conception is wrong, though. The read/write head projects only one magnetic field onto the disk, and so it can read and write only one magnetic domain at each position along a track. Accordingly, the data is written as a single thin line.

Sector size

DOS, which fits 512 bytes of data into each sector, applies this sector size to hard disks as well as floppies. Of course, tracks along the outer edge of a disk are much longer than inner tracks, and they could hold a lot more data—but they don't. Operating systems are complicated creatures, and one further complication DOS avoids is having different numbers of sectors on different tracks. The result is a good deal of wasted disk space. (Actually, some drives do vary the number of sectors per track. For example, on some 40-megabyte hardcards, Plus Development Corporation puts 28 sectors on inner tracks and 34 sectors on outer tracks. But the extra sectors are electronically represented as belonging to separate tracks so that DOS "sees" a disk in which all tracks have the same number of sectors.)

We'll see later that some high-capacity hard disks use 1,024- or 2,048-byte sectors. But larger sectors don't in themselves lead to higher data densities. Fewer large sectors fit on a track. The amount of data that can be written is limited by the speed at which the heads can make flux changes and by the minimum amount of magnetic medium required to store a flux change.

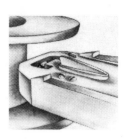

Cylinders

When no more data can be crammed onto the side of a disk, the main approach to higher disk drive capacity is by adding more platters. Drives in the 10- to 40-megabyte range tend to have two platters; high-capacity drives may have six or more. The sides of the platters are numbered starting from 0, with the first platter holding sides 0 and 1, the second platter holding sides 2 and 3, and so on.

Because the read/write heads move in tandem across the platter surfaces, all heads are positioned at a given track at any one time. Because individual files tend to become scattered around the disk surfaces, it would be preferable for the heads to move independently. As one head reads from one track, another head could shift over to the track at which a file continues. But the mechanics would be prohibitively expensive.

How DOS fills the disk

To make the best of this situation, DOS tries to fit as much of a file as possible into all tracks at a given head position. For example, were DOS to record a new file starting from track 15, it would first fill all of track 15 on sides 0 and 1, then would continue at track 15 on the next platter with sides 2 and 3. Only when all tracks numbered 15 are filled would DOS initiate the time-consuming task of moving the read-write heads to track 16, where it would go on writing the file from side 0.

Taking all platter sides together, all tracks numbered 15 are called "cylinder 15." The concept is easy to grasp, because a cylinder would be formed if you joined the tracks from side to side, as Figure 2-4 shows. You will often see the term "cylinder" instead of "track" in hard disk documentation, and logically they are often interchangeable. The 10-megabyte hard disk in an IBM XT has 306 cylinders; an AT's 20-megabyte disk has 615. This is precisely the same as saying that a side of a platter in an XT has 306 tracks and an AT, 615.

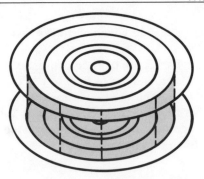

Figure 2-4 **A cylinder**

Cylinder density

An important concept is **cylinder density**. Unlike **track density**, which tells how many concentric tracks fit along an inch of a disk's radius, the cylinder density gives the *number of sectors* held in a cylinder. It is the number of sectors per track multiplied by the number of platter sides. Disks with a high cylinder density are desirable because they can fit a large file into fewer cylinders. Thus, fewer head seeks are needed to read the file, and the drive performs more quickly. Manufacturers increase cylinder density either by creating drives with more platters or by using media and electronics that can achieve greater data densities, allowing more sectors on a track.

Interleave

The rate at which data passes beneath a read/write head doesn't necessarily equal the rate at which the computer can read or write data. There are limits to how fast various circuits can move data. The disk controller transfers data between the disk surface and an internal holding buffer, and then either the CPU or DMA (direct memory access) chips move the data between the controller's buffer and system RAM. The platters are spinning at 60 rotations per second (3,600 rpm), moving seventeen sectors under the read/write heads with each revolution. At 512 bytes of data per sector, 522,240 bytes pass beneath the heads in a second. Actually, on a typical disk, about 625,000 bytes can be packed on a track when the track isn't divided into sectors. Because each byte is made of eight bits ("Ons" or "Offs"), roughly five million bits pass beneath a head during a second.

The data-transfer rate

This calculation is the origin of the 5-megabit data-transfer rate attributed to most drives. Many people wrongly believe that the electronics set the transfer rate. Indeed, the electronics must be fast enough to read and write data at the rate it passes by the heads. But faster electronics couldn't transfer data more quickly, because the data couldn't be physically presented to the heads more rapidly without speeding up the drive motor. (Note that "megabits" is abbreviated as **Mb**, "megabytes" as **MB**.)

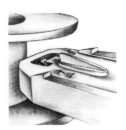

The 5-megabit data-transfer rate doesn't indicate the actual rate at which data is transferred to system memory. When data is read, the disk controller's buffer fills at this rate, but then the read operation must stop until the data is transferred (by CPU or DMA) to DOS buffers. The delay may be prolonged if the CPU then shifts the data elsewhere in memory, perhaps processing it along the way.

Think about what this means from the point of view of the spinning disk. A sector moves under the read/write heads and its data is transferred to the controller buffer. The next sector is coming up in a minuscule fraction of a second, and if the read/write head is to make use of it, the data from the prior sector must be moved out of the buffer and into memory in a big hurry. But most 8088 and 80286 machines cannot make this transfer quickly enough. So the next disk sector flies by without being read. In fact, in an IBM XT, five sectors pass under the head before the controller is ready to read data again. Because ATs run faster, they're ready to read again after only one or two sectors pass by.

If the second sector of a file's data is laid down on the disk surface right next to the first, the sectors are said to be "physically contiguous." Often, this isn't the ideal condition. Because the controller isn't ready to read the second sector when it physically follows the first, the disk must complete an entire revolution before the data passes under the head again. On an XT, the controller is ready to receive data in only a third as much time, wasting precious milliseconds. With the disk turning 60 times per second, waiting two-thirds of a revolution to read the next sector wastes 11 milliseconds. Reading 17 sectors in a row this way squanders 187 milliseconds—nearly a fifth of a second. Disks with four tracks to the cylinder (the most common case) magnify this loss to three-quarters of a second per cylinder. When a file spans many cylinders, you'd be strumming your fingertips waiting for the disk access to end.

Fortunately, there is no intrinsic need for disk drives to operate so inefficiently. On an XT, the file's next sector of data is simply placed six sectors from the first. The read/write head reaches this sector just as the controller becomes ready to receive more data.

Sector contiguity

Figure 2-5 diagrams the sector pattern in a 3:1 interleave. The sectors are no longer *physically* contiguous, but they are *logically* contiguous.

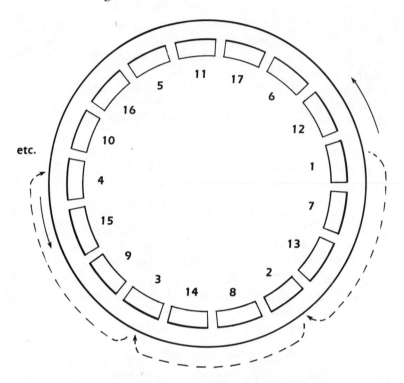

Figure 2-5 **A 3:1 interleave**

The interleave
factor

This logical patterning of sectors is called the disk's **interleave**. Every disk has an interleave factor. On a standard IBM XT, the factor is 6:1, or simply "6." This means that a file continues at every sixth sector. Expressed differently, an "interleave of 6" means that it takes six rotations of the disk to read all data completely from a track. The faster AT uses a 3:1 interleave. A disk in which the data follows the sequence of physical sectors has an interleave of 1:1; all data is read from a track in one turn of the disk. This is the ideal interleave, but it takes a fast 80386 computer to handle it.

A disk's interleave is set when it undergoes **low-level formatting**. (We'll discuss types of formatting in Chapter 4; for now, note that this process breaks up tracks into sectors.) During low-level formatting, each sector is tagged with an identifying number. The numbers may be written in any order, setting the interleave. The

interleave can be changed simply be redoing the format with a different interleave factor so that the sectors are numbered differently.

Read/Write Heads

The smaller a head, and the closer it flies over the disk surface, the
smaller the magnetic domains it can write and hence the more data
it can pack onto the disk. A read/write head resembles a horseshoe
magnet in that it is formed with opposite poles of the magnet facing one another across a narrow gap (Figure 2-6). This gap is made
extremely narrow so that only very small areas of the disk surface
are influenced at any moment as the disk swings by, thus increasing
the data density. Because the head must be large enough to manufacture and manipulate, the gap is much longer than it is wide. The
result is that the magnetic domains are bar-shaped rather than dot-
shaped, and magnetic "fringing" at the edges of the heads extends
the domains quite some distance perpendicular to the tracks.

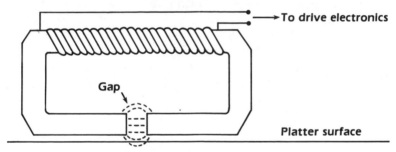

Figure 2-6 **A read/write head**

Although a drive has several read/write heads, only one is in use
at any time. The controller can handle data from only one head at
once. Although more sophisticated circuitry might be able to access data simultaneously on several sides, there would be no point
in doing so, because the real bottleneck in performance occurs in
moving the data between the controller and system memory.

Head Designs

To increase data densities, engineers are designing smaller and
lighter heads. These improvements are also desirable because
smaller and lighter heads are less likely to cause serious damage

during head crashes. Manufacturers are increasingly using **Whitney** technology, a suspension system for very light heads. Such drives may use **mini-monolithic** heads to achieve densities of 1,000 tracks per inch (compare it to the 10,000 domains per inch written *along* the tracks in an ordinary drive).

Researchers are also working on "composite heads," which achieve 1500 tracks per inch, and "thin-film" heads that can exceed 2000 tracks per inch. The latter, a leading-edge technology, relies on vapor-deposition techniques employed in integrated-circuit manufacture to mold extremely complex and fine head geometries. For some years, IBM has applied this technology to mainframe hard disks.

Head Actuators

A **head actuator** moves the read/write heads back and forth over the platter surfaces. Two kinds of actuators are in common use— **stepper-motor actuators** and **voice-coil actuators**. The latter type is faster, sturdier, quieter—and more expensive. The hard disks sold with the IBM XT are of the stepper variety, as are nearly all add-on disks for IBM PCs. The faster disks that come with 80286 and 80386 machines often use voice-coil technology. Let's look at stepper actuators first.

Stepper motor actuators

A stepper motor is a special kind of motor that rotates a few degrees at a time, in little *steps*. It can be made to rotate a precise number of steps in either direction. By converting these steps into linear motion by a **stepper band**, the motor can drive read/write heads back and forth. Floppy disk drives use stepper actuators. Each step of the mechanism moves the heads one track, creating a clicking sound; when many steps are made at once, you hear an all-too-familiar rasping noise. Hard disks that use stepper motors also make this sound, but it is muted by the drive casing.

Voice-coil actuators

Voice-coil actuators work differently. They use a solenoid (a magnet that pulls at a metal rod) to draw the read/write heads toward the center of the disk. The heads are mounted on a hinge with a spring mechanism pulling the other way; when the magnetic field is relaxed, the heads move back toward the outer edge of the disk. Precise adjustments of the magnetic field move the heads to a particular track. The term "voice-coil" is used because the technology employs magnets like those found in loud speakers. The drive shown in Figure 2-7 uses a voice-coil actuator.

UP TO P 18 FORMAT LEVELS
25

Richard Joy Said!

Figure 2-7 **A voice-coil drive**

When a stepper-motor actuator moves the read/write heads a long distance, it pushes the heads a track at a time to their destination. Twice the distance entails roughly twice the time. But voice-coil systems make only a single change in magnetic flux, and the heads fly right to the desired position. This characteristic lets voice-coil drives function at roughly twice the speed of stepper-motor drives.

There is a price to be paid for the higher speed. Voice-coil drives are more complicated, and consequently, more expensive. Stepper-motor drives essentially "feel" their way to the right track by counting positions along the metal band that moves the heads. Although the metal bands are liable to go out of alignment if they overheat, accuracy comes naturally to the stepper mechanism. Voice-coils, however, tend to over- or undershoot their targets, and so constant secondary adjustments must be made. The stepper mechanism is an "open-loop" system; the disk controller commands the motor to move the heads and then proceeds as if the movement has been made accurately. Voice-coil mechanisms, on the other hand, are "closed-loop" systems; the controller repeatedly checks that the heads are locked on to the exact center of a track, and adjustments are made when the heads wander.

Differences between the two technologies

A voice-coil system ensures that the heads are positioned correctly by reading "servo data" that is permanently encoded on the

Servo data

platters. Usually this information is "embedded" between the tracks. Special sensors on the read/write heads monitor these **magnetic bursts**; when they sense a burst too strongly, the controller knows that the head is deviating from the center of the track, and it alters the voice-coil current accordingly. Some high-capacity disk drives use a **dedicated servo surface** (DSS) for which a whole side of one platter is given over to the servo data, instead of embedding the data between data tracks. These drives use higher track densities that don't leave enough room for the servo data between the tracks. Sometimes you may see advertisements for drives that list an odd number of read/write heads; this is because a platter surface is lost to the servo data.

Actuator performance

We'll be talking in detail about relative drive performance in Chapter 3. For now, suffice it to say that, on average, a stepper-motor drive takes from 65 to 100 milliseconds (65 to 100 thousandths of a second) to move from one track to another. Voice-coil drives typically require 30 to 40 milliseconds—about twice the speed of their stepper cousins. But the technology is constantly improving. Manufacturers are turning out 40-millisecond stepper-motor drives, and voice-coil drives working below 20 milliseconds are becoming common. We'll see later that these **average seek times** are only one determinant among many in drive performance.

Settling time

A couple of other terms occasionally crop out in drive performance ratings. One is **settling time**. When the heads move to a cylinder, they vibrate for a moment. They can't be used until they settle down, hence "settling time." Because settling typically requires 5 to 10 milliseconds, it may add significantly to the average seek time. To make their drives look better, manufacturers sometimes exclude the settling time from the average seek time rating; but usually the settling time is included.

Track-to-track seek times

One not-very-useful measure of performance is a drive's **track-to-track seek time**. This tells how long it takes the heads to move between adjacent tracks. The value is usually 2 or 3 milliseconds. Obviously, the value does not include the settling time. A head movement across many tracks is not necessarily the sum of the track-to-track seek times.

Average latency

Another term is **average latency**—a pretty useless concept, which tells how long on average the drive must wait before a specified bit of data rotates under the heads. As *average*, the figure is exactly one-half rotation. Because virtually all microcomputer drives turn at 60 revolutions per second, the value is the same for all: 8.4 milliseconds. It's worth noting that this figure—although a fraction of a typical seek time—is still quite high. When data is read or written sporadically so that the average latency period passes again and again, drive performance plummets. This means that inefficient software can undermine the performance of even a very "fast" drive.

Bump Detection

Bump detection is an error-avoidance feature introduced in recent models of hard disk cards made by Plus Development Corporation; and many manufacturers will likely copy it. When a hard disk drive is jolted, the read/write heads may veer onto an adjacent track. If data is being read, the controller electronics sense that a disruption has occurred and report the failure to the operating system, and the operating system orders a second try. So long as the heads don't touch the disk surface, no damage is done to the data. But when the heads are *writing* data, they continue to operate as they swerve onto the adjacent track, damaging its data. The damaged data may belong to a different file; as a result, repeating the write operation doesn't correct the error.

As we've seen, voice-coil head actuators give constant feedback about the heads' position. Plus Development Corporation has modified the feedback mechanism to include super-fast optical components that instantly sense if heads have wandered off-track. Before the head reaches the adjacent track, a message is sent to the electronics to stop writing data. Because the data is kept in a buffer on the controller while it is written, the controller can try writing the data again after the heads have restabilized. Obviously, this feature is possible only in drives that use closed-loop head positioning—it can't be implemented on stepper-motor drives.

Head Parking

As we've seen, out-of-control read/write heads are the villain behind disk crashes. Clearly, one way to avert crashes is by keeping the heads away from the data when the machine is turned off. This "head parking" has several variants. In most cases, the heads are simply moved to a cylinder set aside for parking (a **landing strip**), usually the innermost cylinder of the disk drive. Although the parking track can absorb any amount of gouging, some manufacturers object to the resulting mistreatment and contamination of the read/write heads, and they have taken additional steps to park the heads. Some have found ways of lifting the heads away from the platter surfaces. Others retract the heads into a "cage" in which the heads can do no harm to the medium or to themselves.

Automatic parking

Though virtually all hard disks can use some form of head parking, only recently has **automatic head parking** become the norm. In automatic parking, the drive senses that the machine has been turned off and quickly moves the heads to their parking place. This action is not so trivial as it seems, particularly with stepper-motor drives, because there is precious little electricity available to drive the mechanics. One clever solution has been to use the drive motor as a generator, siphoning off the rotational energy held in the spinning platters and using it to drive the head actuator. An automatic parking system locks the heads in place so that they cannot skip to other cylinders if the machine is moved around.

Automatic head parking comes more easily to drives that use voice-coil actuators. The magnetic field pulling the heads toward the center of the platters is countered by springs pulling the heads outward. At least in some designs, the heads naturally move to the outer edge of the disk when power is lost. But action still must be taken to stabilize the heads.

Manual parking

Drives that do not have automatic head parking require **manual parking**. For a few odd drives, "manual parking" actually requires you to reach into the machine and pull a lever—an inconvenient and clumsy maneuver. But generally the expression refers to the need to run a small utility program that moves the heads to the parking track. The utility is usually found on the diskette accompanying the drive, although some manufacturers who distribute preformatted drives dispense the utility on the hard disk itself.

IBM's *SHIPDISK* utility is included on the diskette accompanying the *Guide to Operations*. Most other manufacturers have adopted the same name for the program. It is the simplest program in the whole world. You load the program by entering *SHIPDISK* at the DOS prompt, and a message appears on the screen informing you that the heads have been parked. That's it. The IBM AT diskette holds a *SHUTDOWN* program that may be run instead. While it performs exactly as *SHIPDISK*, it entertains you with a graphical presentation of a switch moving from "On" to "Off."

There is no such thing as "unparking" a drive. When the computer is turned on again, the disk-initialization code moves the heads away from their parking zone to the outermost cylinder

where they read the *boot record* and other information DOS needs
to use the drive.

A hard disk can receive a jolt at any time, and its data is safer
when the heads are parked. But it isn't necessary to park the heads
every time you finish using the machine. If your drive doesn't automatically park the heads when you shut off the power, it's probably
not worth doing manually. As its name indicates, *SHIPDISK* is meant
for preparing the machine for rough treatment during moving, including moving between locations in the same office. If you're going to pick up the machine, park the heads. You'll find that virtually
all portables and laptops that have hard disks park the heads automatically.

When is parking
necessary?

Ironically, automatic head parking is becoming standard just as
plated media become more common. Plated media are much more
resistant to head damage, especially when combined with the
lighter Whitney head technology. Nonetheless, manufacturers are
designing automatic head parking into plated drives, perhaps out of
caution, perhaps to keep their marketing departments happy.

The ultimate in head parking is provided by utilities like
SafePark, part of the *Disk Technician* utilities from Prime Solutions
Inc. *SafePark* sequesters a cylinder as a "safe zone" over which the
heads hover when not in use. When the utility creates this zone, it
relocates any data that currently resides there. Thereafter, the program is loaded as a *memory-resident program* every time the machine starts up (through the AUTOEXEC.BAT file). It links into the
DOS disk control routines. When the disk is inactive for seven
seconds, it shunts the heads over to the safety zone so that the effects of electrical surges or mechanical shocks are directed onto a
part of the disk that holds no data. This simple measure greatly
reduces the risk of catastrophic data loss through a head crash because the heads are positioned over data only a small fraction of
the time the machine is running. Figure 2-8 shows how parking
zones are laid out.

Parking during disk
operation

Disk Geometries

Disk drives vary by number of platters, tracks on a platter, and sectors on a track. Because both sides of a platter are recorded upon,
it is clearer to refer to the number of *sides* in a drive, rather than
the number of platters. A particular disk sector may reside at "Side
2, Track 19, Sector 8." Sides are numbered from 0, so that a typical

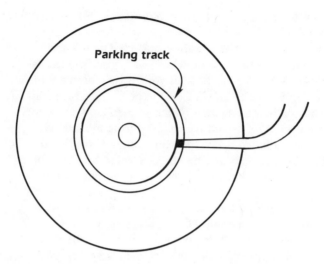

Figure 2-8 **Head parking**

two-platter drive has sides 0 to 3. Tracks are also numbered upward from 0; accordingly, *cylinder 0* consists of the outermost
tracks on all sides. Oddly, sectors are counted from one. A typical
drive counts sectors from one to seventeen.

It's worth understanding this numbering system because usually
drives are delivered with a **bad track table** affixed to the drive
casing. When formatting the disk, you may need to enter the locations of the bad tracks. We'll discuss this point more in Chapter 4.

The BIOS

Although DOS is the "disk operating system," the most fundamental control over the drive is made by the *Basic Input-Output
System* (BIOS), a portion of the operating system residing on read-
only memory chips in the machine. The BIOS isn't sophisticated
enough to operate on files; it can perform only the most primitive
of disk operations: reading and writing individual sectors. Because
the number of sides, tracks, and sectors varies by the drive's capacity and design, the BIOS needs to know the exact characteristics of
the drive it is working with, it needs to know the disk's **geometry**.

The BIOS is held on ROM (read-only memory) chips on the
computer's main circuit board. Part of the BIOS is called the **fixed-
disk BIOS**. It contains a table that lists the geometries for a
number of disk drives. The drives chosen are considered the most
common with sizes ranging from 10 megabytes to well over 100
megabytes. Drive type 2, for example, represents the standard 20-
megabyte AT hard disk.

As BIOS constantly changes, more and more drive geometries have been added with each version. The first AT BIOS, for example, described 14 drive geometries, was then upgraded to 22, and so on. But dozens of new geometries have appeared, most of which are not supported by the IBM BIOS. Lower-capacity drives tend to follow the standard geometries. But high-capacity drives (those with over 100 megabytes) usually require modification of the BIOS. There are a number of ways to do this, as we'll see in Chapter 4.

New drive geometries

Owners of early IBM PCs (those with 16K memory chips) should know that the BIOS in their machines contains no fixed-disk BIOS at all. Because the BIOS resides on removable chips, the old BIOS can be plucked out and replaced with a new one. We'll also discuss this topic in Chapter 4.

Disk Controllers

Hard disks require a controller card just as floppies do. On the IBM AT, floppy and hard disk control are combined on the same adapter taking up only one slot. On the IBM PC or XT, a separate adapter is required for the hard disk. The controller card intermediates the transfer of data between the disk and the computer's random access memory. It is called a "controller" because it contains a specially designed disk-controller chip that sends orders to the drive electronics to position the heads, read and write, and perform a host of other actions.

These tasks aren't trivial—the electronics precisely sequence the disk drive's activities, translate the encoded bit patterns into actual data, and perform elaborate error checking so that it can tell when something has gone wrong. And all of this must be done at extremely high speeds—often faster than the computer itself can process data.

Data Encoding

One way in which controllers differ is in how they *encode* data. **Encoding** refers to the way raw data from the computer's memory is laid down on the disk surface. We may have given you the impression that the pattern of eight "Ons" and "Offs" that make up one character of data is simply written in eight successive magnetic domains along a disk track. This is far from the case. So much data is packed in so little area that the disk controller would lose its way if extra information wasn't inserted within the data.

Consider what a difficult job the controller electronics must perform. Beneath the read/write head spins a track containing perhaps 60,000 flux changes. The track is but a few inches long, and its entire length passes under a head every 17 milliseconds—hardly a thousandth of a second per 512-byte (4,096-bit) sector. How is the controller to know what part of the disk is under the heads? After all, it garbles the data completely if it misjudges the position by a single magnetic domain.

The answer is that the controller orients itself to the beginning of sectors by reading special information written when the disk is formatted. But once the head flies over the sector data, the controller must keep track of thousands of domains before it again encounters the formatting information. If the flux reversals were to fall into a regular pattern, the controller could easily monitor the position of the read/write head. But a sector could be filled with zeros, in which case thousands of magnetic domains would fly by without a single flux change, and the controller would become lost.

FM and MFM encoding

For this reason, data must be *encoded* so that not too many zeros (non-flux changes) occur in a row. In the original **frequency modulation (FM) encoding** scheme, every other magnetic domain was given over as a **clock pulse**. Half the disk space was wasted. Then someone hit on a clever way of encoding flux changes depending on what has preceded. The result is the **modified frequency modulation (MFM)** scheme used for most of today's disks. MFM not only eliminates the clock bit, but also packs twice as much data on a disk as FM encoding.

RLL encoding

Recently, **run length limited (RLL) encoding** has become popular. The technique isn't new, but until now the electronics performing it have been prohibitively expensive. RLL translates data into a series of special codes. These codes are chosen for certain numerical properties, particularly the number of consecutive zeros that occur. The logic is extremely complicated, but the outcome is simple: More data can be packed on to a disk. In **RLL 2,7** the codes are chosen so that sequences of zeros in the codes always range from 2 to 7 (the "run length" of zeros is limited to 7). A fifty percent increase in disk capacity results. RLL 2,7 encoding is most commonly used on microcomputers today; some manufacturers are close to releasing **RLL 3,9** controllers, which nearly double disk capacity.

RLL increases the number of sectors per track, thereby allowing more data to move under the heads in a given time and offering the potential for faster data transfer. In addition, having more data on a track means that files can be squeezed into fewer cylinders, reducing head moves.

RLL is very much the wave of the future, but it does not come free. RLL controllers cost 50% to 100% more than MFM controllers because they call for extremely elaborate and fast circuitry. Moreover, the electronics on the drive itself must be able to handle the more rapid data transfer rates. While existing hard disks can be connected to an RLL controller, most will not work properly. Advertisements sometimes state that a drive is "RLL rated" or "RLL certified."

Drawbacks

Error Correction

The controller also handles error correction. The controller performs a **cyclic redundancy check (CRC)** on the data as it passes through. A block of data is put through a mathematical formula that yields a long number, which is written just after the data in its sector. When the data is read back, the controller recalculates the number and compares it with the value recorded in the sector. If they don't match, the controller knows an error has occurred. This technique is sophisticated enough to catch multiple errors.

Depending on the severity of the errors, the controller may or may not be able to recover. On a typical drive, a **recoverable read error** occurs once in 10-billion bytes. **Nonrecoverable read errors** occur once in 1-trillion bytes. And **seek errors** (where the read/write heads miss their mark) occur once in 1 million tries. Clearly, these levels of accuracy are more than adequate for most applications. Your data faces far greater dangers from mechanical failure and human error.

Interfaces

Data-transfer rates vary by the kind of disk drive **interface**. An "interface," the system by which the drive communicates with the computer, is embodied in the electronics on the disk drive and on its controller card. Generally speaking, there are two kinds of interfaces: **device-level interfaces** and **system-level interfaces**. The more primitive device-level interface supplies the basic electronics with which to access the drive's functions. A system-level interface, on the other hand, links the device interface to the computer. However, the line between the two interfaces is not sharply defined. The system-level interface is said to be "more intelligent" in that it works at a high level.

The ST506 interface

Today, two device-level interfaces are at work in IBM personal computers—the traditional **ST506/412 standard** and the newer and faster **ESDI standard**. The ST506 standard, which usually runs at the 5 megabits per second transfer rate discussed earlier, was developed back in the days when a 5-megabyte disk seemed huge. The 5-megabit rate was plenty fast for the original IBM XT, since the machine could not move data to and from the transfer buffer as quickly as the disk controller—the drive was faster than the computer.

The ESDI interface

The introduction of fast 80286 chips and the 80386 chip changed all this. These microprocessors can shuttle data to and from memory much more quickly, easily keeping pace with the 5-megabit rate. And so drives using the faster ESDI interface have been introduced. ESDI can operate at up to 20 megabits per second, although most introductions have been in the 10-megabit range. From our earlier discussion you'll understand that this rate of data transfer is achieved only on high-capacity drives that squeeze twice the number of 512-byte sectors per track as the standard ST506 drives.

An ESDI interface is more than just a very fast version of the ST506 standard. An ESDI controller is much more "intelligent." Properly designed, it can handle hard drives, floppy drives, and tape backup units, and can itself manage file transfers between these devices, even when they use different sector sizes. The ESDI interface also performs better error checking than the ST506 standard.

Actual data transfer rates

You may be doing a little arithmetic in your head and wondering why a disk drive with a 625,000-byte/second transfer rate may take an appreciable time to load a 100K file. Alas, the electronics can do their speedy work only when the read/write heads are in position. Even with a 40-millisecond average access time, every head move takes up 25,000 bytes worth of transfer time. And, at any given moment, the desired sector must be passing under the read/write heads. At 3,600 rpm, 5,000 bytes of transfer time are taken up waiting for a sector on the opposite side of the disk to swing around. Nor are the transfer electronics constantly active even under the best of conditions. The controller must wait for the CPU to do its half of the job, including redistributing the data in memory. Application software may also be active, processing each data item before requesting the next. This extra processing may create delays exceeding those allowed by the disk interleave, forcing the disk to make extra rotations between reads and writes. All the while, the disk electronics sit idle.

A third standard has become popular: the SCSI interface (pronounced "scuzzy" or "sexy," depending on your world view). A SCSI drive is extremely "intelligent." All functions of the controller card are incorporated directly on the drive itself. It provides a *system-level* interface that can be connected directly to a computer equipped with a SCSI port (which, like an ordinary serial or parallel port, offers a place to plug a cable at the back of the machine). The Apple Macintosh has such a SCSI port, enabling owners to connect hard disks even though most machines lack expansion slots.

The SCSI interface

IBM will promote the SCSI port in the PS/2 machines by offering a SCSI adapter. Using only one slot, the adapter can run up to seven peripherals simultaneously, including hard disks, high-capacity floppy drives, optical disk drives, scanners, and printers. One advantage is obvious: many peripherals can be accommodated without filling up the slots. In fact, IBM may choose to build a SCSI interface into later models. Although SCSI may be the "wave of the future" in some applications, it is not expected to supplant ESDI, which is required for very high-capacity disk drives.

Full-track buffers

For faster data access, an interesting feature has been added to some recent controller cards. Built in is a buffer large enough to hold an entire track. Such **full-track buffers** typically hold nine kilobytes. When a request is made to read any sector on a track, the controller reads the whole track, starting with the sector approaching the read/write head. With all sectors loaded into the controller's memory, requests for succeeding sectors are made at electronic speed, as if from a RAM disk. Figure 2-9 diagrams this scheme.

In a sense, a track buffer gives any disk a 1:1 interleave, because data is mechanically read as quickly as possible. If the actual disk interleave is set to other than 1:1, the sectors are read from the track buffer in a different order than they are inserted. You may wonder what advantage track buffering offers when data cannot be transferred to the machine at a 1:1 interleave. In reality, software

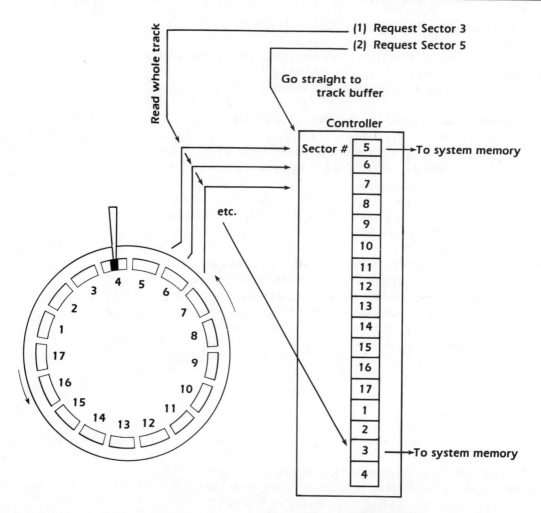

Figure 2-9 **A full-track buffer**

often manages disk input and output very inefficiently. The "optimum interleave" works most efficiently when files are moved to and from memory without processing. Processing breaks up the interleave timing, inserting many extra turns of the platters. A turn of the disk takes 17 milliseconds—half as much time as a head seek on a fast disk. These delays quickly add up. But when the entire track is read during the first rotation, data may be sent to memory the moment the application software calls for it.

Disadvantages

Often only part of a track is accessed, and time is wasted reading unneeded data. Track buffers may actually slow the average access time for random-access files, such as database files, because widely separated positions in the file tend to be accessed in succession. Only one sector's data is required from a track, but the full track buffer fills nonetheless.

So far, we've discussed *reading* data through track buffers. Similar efficiencies are possible when data is written. In principle, nothing should actually be written to the disk until the entire buffer fills, whereupon the whole track is written during one rotation of the disk. But even if the buffer isn't completely filled with new data, its contents are written out when DOS sends a command that the heads access another track. There's a problem in this. The last track "written" into the buffer will never actually be written on the disk. Sooner or later, the machine will be turned off and the data in the buffer lost. To avoid this pitfall, track buffers write out their data after a few seconds of disk inactivity.

Writing data through track buffers

Track buffering can be taken to an extreme by eliminating sectors altogether. For example, the *Tallgrass TG-5525i* controller writes data continuously along tracks, fitting 26 megabytes on a nominally 20-megabyte drive. During a disk read, it copies the whole track into a track buffer, then splits the data into 512-byte chunks. DOS never knows the difference.

Tracks without sectors

Track buffers may be simulated by utility software. In Chapter 7 we'll talk about a genre of software called **disk cachers**. These programs keep copies of frequently accessed disk sectors in memory to minimize the number of times the sectors are mechanically accessed on disk. Some cachers can circumvent DOS and perform track buffering. They may first determine if enough information is on the track to warrant it. They may also perform the reverse of track buffering and write only one changed sector when DOS would have it write several unchanged sectors as well. This approach to track buffering is *less* efficient in that data read unnecessarily is moved all the way to system memory, not just to the controller buffer. But it may be *more* efficient when the caching software is "smarter" than a controller's buffering circuitry, because it can avoid unnecessary reads and writes.

Simulated track buffers

The Disk Format

So far, we've looked at how the disk controller organizes data into sectors, tracks, and cylinders on the disk surface. But our applications programs store data as *files*. Most software is completely insulated from the intricacies of disk management. That is DOS's job.

After all, "DOS" stands for *disk operating system*, and although it does much more than operate disk drives, that's its focus.

There is a hidden side of DOS that only programmers know about. Although most users think of DOS as a collection of commands like COPY and DIR, programmers can call on DOS to perform actions like opening and closing files, or moving the read/write heads to a particular point in a file. Although DOS gives programmers access to particular disk sectors, generally software is oblivious to the precise locations of a files. A program simply asks for data and DOS delivers it, or it supplies data and DOS decides where to place it on disk.

The concept of a "file"

A "file" is the concept DOS uses to insulate programs from the complexities of data layout on the disk surface. It is really nothing more than a chain of sectors filled with data. DOS keeps *lists* of files on the disk, calling them *directories*. These hold the familiar twelve-character filename and extension, some miscellaneous information about the file, and a number that tells the sector at which the file begins. The directory tells no more about the file's layout on disk than its starting point. The rest is left to the **file allocation table**, which we'll discuss in a moment. But first, we need to consider disk **clusters**.

Clusters

When a new file is recorded on disk, DOS doesn't usually allot the *exact* number of bytes required by the file. Because the disk controller cannot read *parts* of a sector, DOS must allocate disk space in whole sectors. If the file is anywhere from 1 to 512 bytes long, a full 512 bytes of space go to it. If it ranges from 513 to 1,024 bytes, the 1,024 bytes held by two sectors are allotted. Disk allocation is *chunky*.

In reality, only single-sided, low-density floppies and high-density 1.2-megabyte and 1.44-megabyte floppies allocate space one sector at a time. Other floppies and all hard disks allot space in two-, four-, or eight-sector chunks. While a ten-byte file takes up 512 bytes of disk space when single sectors are alloted, it takes up 1,024, 2,048, or 4,096 bytes when the minimum allocation is two, four, or eight sectors.

These minimum units of disk-space allocation are called **clusters**. DOS numbers clusters from 0 upward, and uses the cluster number to calculate the locations of the sectors the cluster contains. Standard 360K floppy disks use two-sector clusters; most hard disks run

under four-sector clusters. Cluster size isn't an inherent property of
the disk: It's simply a method by which DOS organizes data.

Obviously, large cluster sizes waste disk space. Whole sectors go
unused in the last cluster given to a file, as shown in Figure 2-10.
The reason DOS groups clusters into sectors will become clear
when we explain how the file allocation table works. First, let's
take a closer look at directories.

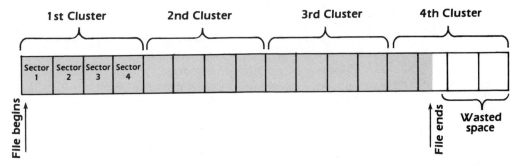

Figure 2-10 **Unused space in final clusters**

Directories

A directory, like a file, is merely a sequence of sectors containing
data. But in this case, the data is made by DOS for its own use.
Thirty-two bytes are given over to each directory entry. Because
sectors hold 512 bytes in DOS, each sector holds 16 directory entries or **slots**. Thirty-two bytes is more than enough space to hold
some crucial information:

bytes	1– 8	the file's name
	9–11	the file's extension (if any)
	12	the file's attribute
	13–22	presently unused "reserved" space
	23–24	the time the file was last accessed
	25–26	the date the file was last accessed
	27–28	the file's starting cluster
	29–32	the file's size (in bytes)

Most of this information appears in DOS's directory listings, including the file's name and extension, its time and date, and its
size. Note that the period between the filename and extension isn't

recorded in the directory; DOS knows that it should be there and prints it when it lists a file. When the filename is less than eight characters long, it is "left-justified" and spaces pad out the positions up to number 8. The same is done for the file extension.

The file's date and time

You may be surprised to see that the file's time and date are allotted only two bytes. After all, when written out, a date like 12-07-1987 ought to take eight bytes (omitting the dashes), and a time reading like 10:57:16 should take at least six bytes. But DOS does not store these readings as written numbers. Rather, it splits up the two bytes into three **fields**, each holding a month, day, or year, or an hour, minute, or second. A whole byte can hold 256 different patterns of "Ons" and "Offs", and so it can represent numbers from 0 to 255. Parts of a byte can hold smaller ranges of numbers. The byte-pairs are subdivided into units just large enough to hold, say, 1 to 12 for month, or 0 to 23 for hours.

The file size

Similarly, the four bytes allotted for the file size can hold a number from 1 to 4,294,967,296—more than adequate for the *Great American Novel*. In reality, DOS cannot create files larger than about 33 million bytes. We'll explain why in a moment.

The starting cluster

As you can see, each directory entry contains some information that is not listed by the DIR command. The **starting cluster** gives the number of the first (and possibly only) cluster allocated to the file. DOS takes this number, converts it to the equivalent sector numbers, and begins to access the file. The file allocation table, which we'll discuss in a moment, points the way to the *next* cluster occupied by the file.

The attribute byte

The other concealed content of a directory entry is its **attribute byte**, which holds a number indicating whether the file possesses certain special characteristics or **attributes**. For normal files, the attribute byte is 0. Adding 1 makes it "read-only," adding 2 makes it "hidden," and so on. Adding 1 *and* 2 makes it "read-only" *and* "hidden." There are six attributes in all.

Read-only, hidden, and system files

Only three of the attributes name special properties for an ordinary file. These are the "read-only," "hidden," and "system" attributes. When the **read-only attribute** is set, DOS knows that it must not write into the file, even if asked to do so by a program. The **hidden attribute** tells DOS not to display the file in directory listings. And the **system attribute** informs DOS that the file is an operating system file. The system attribute, which has not been used very consistently, generally occurs in combination with the hidden attribute. Note that files marked with these attributes are ordinary in all other respects. The attributes merely tell DOS how to handle the file.

The remaining three attributes have special roles and don't categorize files. One is the **volume label attribute**. If you know DOS well, you'll recall that you can attach an electronic 11-character label to any floppy or hard disk. DOS begins directory listings with the volume label, as in **Volume in drive A is SPELLCHK**. The volume label is stored in a disk's root directory as a filename and extension. When DOS scans the directory, it knows from the attribute byte that a directory slot contains the disk's volume label and not a filename.

The volume label

The archive attribute is also special. We'll be talking about it a good deal in our discussion of backups in Chapter 8. DOS *sets* this attribute (changes it to "On") when it writes to a file. When backup utilities make copies of files, they scan directories for files with the archive attribute set, make the copy, then *re*set the attribute (turn it "Off"). The next time backups are performed, the file is copied only if it has been changed in the meantime and the archive attribute has been set once more. This feature makes possible **incremental backups**.

The archive attribute

Finally, the subdirectory attribute marks a file as a subdirectory. To understand the function of this attribute, we need to look at how DOS constructs a directory tree. DOS places the root directory on the outer edge of the disk (on cylinder 0). On hard disks, it allocates 32 sectors for the root directory. Because each sector contains 16 slots, the root directory can hold no more than 512 entries (32 times 16). The root directory is a specially allocated area of the disk. DOS has no trouble accessing it because it is found at the same place and has the same size on any hard disk. The root directory spans the full 32 sectors even when the disk contains but one file.

The subdirectory attribute

Subdirectories, however, are constructed as ordinary files on the disk. Like the root directory, these files consist of a series of 32-byte listings. As with any file, space is allocated to a subdirectory one cluster at a time. When you use MKDIR to add a subdirectory to the disk, DOS makes a file with the subdirectory's name, allocating a cluster to it. As files are added to the subdirectory, the first cluster fills and a second is added. There is no limit to the subdirectory's growth since there is no (realistic) limit to DOS file size. Hence, unlike the root directory, subdirectories can contain any number of files.

Consider the chain of subdirectories that form the path **\MAMMALS\PRIMATES\GIBBONS**. The root directory holds an entry for the subdirectory file **MAMMALS**; **MAMMALS** holds an entry for the file **PRIMATES**; and **PRIMATES** holds an entry for **GIBBONS**.

DOS knows that these files are subdirectory files, not just ordinary data files, because the subdirectory attribute is set in the attribute bytes of each of these entries.

The dot and
double-dot entries

Listings of subdirectories begin with the peculiar "." (dot) and ".." (double dot) entries. The designers of DOS probably ought to have excluded these from the listing, because they cause only confusion. But they represent the contents of the first two slots in the directory. The single dot refers to the file that holds the subdirectory itself. The double dot refers to the file holding the *parent* directory (the directory that lists the subdirectory). The root directory lacks the dot and double-dot listings because it requires neither of these references.

Erased files

Finally, you should know how DOS tells whether a directory slot is occupied or not. When it creates a new directory, DOS sets the first byte of each slot to 0 to show that it is open. When a file is created, the first byte of the filename overwrites this 0 and DOS knows that the slot contains a file listing. To erase the file, DOS merely overwrites the first byte of the directory entry with the value 229. Thereafter, DOS can tell that the slot is available for another file. No other information in the directory slot is destroyed by the "erasure," and the file itself remains on disk until it is overwritten by another. Hence "erased" files are sometimes recoverable.

The File Allocation Table

Directories tell only the starting cluster for a file. Yet most files occupy more than one cluster. How does DOS find the remainder? While formatting the disk, DOS makes a **file allocation table** or **FAT**. The FAT is the most important entity on a disk. When it is destroyed by a head crash or an accidental formatting, it's very hard to recover any data from the disk. When we discuss *unerase* and *unformat* utilities in Chapter 9, you'll see why the FAT is so important. DOS actually keeps two copies of the FAT on disk so that it has a standby when one is damaged.

Structure of the
FAT

The FAT is nothing more than a table of numbers, in which every position in the table correlates with a cluster of disk space. The first position represents cluster 0, the next represents cluster 1, and so on. Each position holds a number telling where a file continues. Consider the file named "LONGFILE." Its directory entry tells that the file begins at cluster 100. DOS reads the sectors in cluster 100 then consults *position 100* in the FAT for the number of the next cluster, say, 105. Then DOS reads the next portion of the file from cluster 105 and checks position 105 in the FAT to find the next cluster in the sequence. When DOS encounters a FAT position containing a particular code number, it knows that it has reached the end of the file.

The size of a FAT varies by the size of a disk *and* by cluster size. Larger disks hold more clusters and, accordingly, require larger FATs. Similarly, when cluster size is reduced, more FAT entries are needed to point to the increased number of clusters. Another consideration is the size of the numbers in the FAT to label the clusters. Floppy disk FATs use numbers a byte and a half long; these can range up to 4,096—more clusters than a floppy can hold. But 20-megabyte hard disks that use four-sector clusters hold roughly 10,000 clusters, so their FATs require two-byte numbers, which range to 65,535. The larger numbers increase the FAT size by a third.

FAT size

We saw earlier that single-sector clusters use disk space most economically. With single sectors, no more than a fraction of a sector is wasted at the end of each file. But small clusters make for many clusters, and that leads to a very large file allocation table. Because DOS must constantly refer to the FAT during disk operations, it keeps a copy in memory. A 20-megabyte disk using single-sector clusters would have an 84K FAT, and DOS would have to set aside 84K of precious RAM to hold it!

When IBM first released the XT, memory chips were still very expensive, and few machines had more than 256K of RAM. To conserve memory, the DOS versions issued for the XT (DOS 2.x) used 8-sector clusters to minimize the size of the FAT. Later DOS versions (3.x) reverted to four-sector clusters as RAM prices fell. Interestingly, the 1.2-megabyte floppy disks introduced with the IBM AT use a single-sector cluster. Because the disks have a relatively small capacity, the FAT is not unacceptably large. And the minimal cluster size helps pack as much data as possible onto a medium primarily intended for backup.

Conserving disk space

You may have heard that DOS cannot handle more than 32 megabytes on one disk and may wonder how manufacturers can advertise drives larger than 32 megabytes. Such a limit doesn't relate to the sizes of clusters or file allocation tables, but rather to the underlying nature of 16-bit architecture.

The 32-megabyte limit

The microprocessor chip (CPU) in PCs and ATs works with 16-bit numbers, which may range from 0 to 65,535. The CPU can handle larger numbers but finds them unwieldly. To keep matters simple, the designers of DOS limited the numbering of disk sectors to the 0 to 65,535 range. DOS refers to the first sector on the first track of the first platter side as "sector 0." The next sector on that track is "sector 1", and so on. The number system extends inward from cylinder to cylinder, all the way to "sector 65,535" if the disk is large enough. Because DOS always uses 512-byte sectors, simple multiplication gives the 32-megabyte limit: 512 by 65,535 = 33,553,920 (programmers like to think in powers of 2, so they call this number "32" megabytes in spite of its being more than 33). DOS cannot access data from sectors numbered 36,656 and beyond, because it cannot count that high!

High-capacity disks

You may be wondering how DOS can work on high-capacity disks that contains many more than 65,536 sectors. In a moment, we'll see how a disk may be *partitioned* to hold more than one operating system. The DOS partition can begin at any point on the disk, even if it is at the 100,000th sector. But starting from that point, DOS can count only 65,536 sectors. That is, the range of 65,536 sector numbers used by DOS is an *offset* from the start of the DOS partition.

The Boot Record

As you no doubt know, when the computer is booted, the main DOS program, COMMAND.COM, is loaded into memory. Once it's in RAM, COMMAND.COM runs the show—it *is* DOS. But there's a paradox in this. "DOS" stands for "disk operating system," and "operating disk drives" is just what COMMAND.COM does. So how can COMMAND.COM be loaded from disk if it isn't already in memory?

The solution to this conundrum lies in the expression "booting," which means that the machine "picks itself up by its bootstraps"—a similarly unlikely feat. A small part of the operating system is built into the machine, kept on read-only memory chips on the main circuit board. When the computer is turned on, it is initially run by this tiny program. The program is just smart enough to find the disk drives, start them turning, and read a single sector on the outer edge of the disk.

The boot record

This sector is called the **boot record**, which resides on side 0, track 0, sector 1; logically, it is the very first sector on the disk. The boot record contains all sorts of information about the disk that is essential for any operating system that will use it. It tells the sector size, the number of sectors per cluster and sectors per cylinder, the number of cylinders, and the FAT and directory sizes. It contains some basic error messages it can throw on the screen if, for example, COMMAND.COM can't be found. And it contains the names of some special files that hold a bit more of the operating system.

With this information in hand, the machine can seek out a file called IBMBIO.COM (in PC DOS, or BIO.SYS in MS DOS). This file immediately follows the root directory, which is located on the outermost cylinder with all sectors contiguous, so that what little there is of a disk operating system does not need to send the read/write heads scurrying around the disk. With IBMBIO.COM loaded, the operating system turns control over to it, and it in turn loads IBMDOS.COM (or MSDOS.SYS), which also begins on the outer cylinder. (Incidentally, in their directory entries, these files are marked with both *hidden* and *system* attributes, so you won't see them in directory listings.) With IBMDOS.COM loaded, the machine is smart enough to load COMMAND.COM, even if the file is dispersed across the disk. The operating system has bootstrapped itself into control.

System files

The files IBMBIO.COM, IBMDOS.COM, and COMMAND.COM are collectively known as the **system files**. They are automatically transferred to a disk during formatting when the FORMAT command is followed by the /S switch. The computer cannot boot from a disk unless these files are present, with IBMBIO.COM and IBMDOS.COM occupying the first two slots of the root directory, and with IBMBIO.COM in contiguous sectors. When the files aren't transferred to a disk during formatting, the sectors they occupy are subsequently filled with data, and it becomes impossible (except for the technically adept) to copy over the files to make the disk bootable.

Sometimes software manufacturers want their distribution diskettes to be bootable. But the system files are under copyright, so they cannot include them. IBM has accommodated this need by providing the /B switch in the FORMAT command, which sets aside room for IBMBIO.COM and IBMDOS.COM in the root directory and on cylinder 0. When software buyers receive the diskette, they apply the DOS **SYS** command, which moves the system files from the DOS diskette to the reserved areas on the software distribution diskette, making it bootable. COMMAND.COM is not copied over by SYS; that must be done by the COPY command.

The SYS command

Partitioning

Our description of the boot record actually applies only to floppy disks. Hard disks have at least *two* boot records, which are required because hard disks can function under multiple operating systems. The disk is *partitioned* into two or more parts, each serving a different operating system. Don't think of partitions as slices of a pie. Because each partition is allotted a series of contiguous cylinders, they're more like donuts.

Earlier, we briefly mentioned **low-level formatting**, which maps out the sectors on the disk surface. A second type of formatting, **high-level formatting**, adds the root directory, file allocation tables, and other critical information to the disk. Partitioning is performed *between* low- and high-level formats. With the sectors in place, the partitioning program decides where each partition begins. It writes this information in the *partition table*, which is contained in the **master boot record**. After the partition is created, the root directory, FATs, and system files are placed at the beginning of the DOS partition, at whatever cylinder it begins.

The master boot record

Like an ordinary boot record on a floppy disk, the master boot record is located on side 0, track 0, sector 1. It contains just enough information to let the BIOS do some elementary disk operations. But unlike ordinary boot records, it contains no information pertaining to a specific operating system, such as the names of system files. Instead, it gives information in the partition table that supplies the starting points on the disk for the various partitions. The computer reads it, learns from it which operating system is used for booting, and moves the read/write heads to the first sector of that operating system's partition. On that sector it finds the ordinary boot record specific to the operating system, which it then reads, booting the machine. Figure 2-11 diagrams this scheme.

The rationale for partitioning

It's easy to see why separate boot records are required for each partition and why a master boot record is used to keep track of them. Each operating system has its own formats for directories, file allocation tables, and whatever. Given these irregularities, it would be impossible to give the operating systems equal access to all files. Generally, all operating systems share the same 512-byte sector size; but special utilities can change the sector size in a partition (as we'll see in Chapter 4).

Most PC users confine themselves to DOS, but they still must partition the disk, simply because the hard disk BIOS expects to initially find a master boot record and not an ordinary one. The partitioning program (called **FDISK** in DOS) gives over the whole disk to DOS and places the DOS boot record on the sector immediately following the master boot record.

Partitioning under DOS 3.3

As we mentioned earlier, DOS limits partitions to 32-megabytes. With the introduction of 40-megabyte drives (and larger) in the PS/2 line, DOS 3.3 was modified to allow DOS to use the entire disk capacity. Unfortunately, this was done by permitting *multiple*

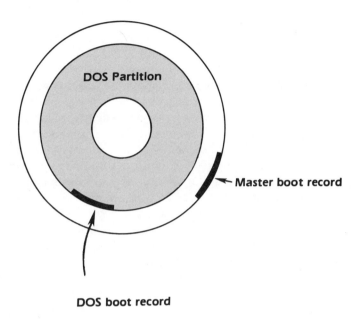

DOS Partition

←— Master boot record

DOS boot record

Figure 2-11 **The boot record layout**

DOS 32-megabyte partitions, not by making a single huge DOS partition possible. Thus, the entire capacity of a large drive may not reside under one drive specifier (such as **C:**). We'll discuss the new system in detail in Chapter 4.

Alternative Storage Technologies

So far, we've described *Winchester* (non-removable) hard disk drives. There are variations on this basic technology, including removable cartridge drives, high-capacity drives, and hard disk cards, which we'll look at in Chapter 3. Besides these variants, alternative forms of data storage technology have appeared, some of which may someday become as prevalent as hard disks. Even the lowly floppy disk has been making an impressive show. Laser disks have entered the market in earnest. And solid-state storage devices (banks of permanently powered RAM chips) are now taken seriously. We'll take a quick tour of these technologies to help you understand them as they unfold.

Floppy Disk Drives

We tend to think of floppy disks as "low-tech." But exciting developments are occurring in floppy disk technology. Floppies are based on the same principles as hard disks, but the design differs slightly. The read/write heads press lightly against the disk surface when you close the drive door. The coating on the disk is made thick to withstand the abrasion of the heads and disk jacket.

Because floppies are *floppy*, they are given to deformation; the dimensions of a disk constantly change with temperature and humidity. And because floppy disks are mounted in the drive by a flimsy hub, they tend to sway off-center. For these reasons, the positions of the tracks are not as precisely defined as on a hard disk. Floppy drives use stepper-motor head actuators which, you will recall, don't monitor a track's position, but simply move the read/write heads to its expected location. To counter these deficiencies, far fewer tracks are placed on the disk, and the tracks are wider. A 360K floppy records tracks at 48 tracks-per-inch (tpi), compared to over 1,000 tpi on some hard disks. The "high-density" 1.2-megabyte drives on the IBM AT double this track density, and the $3\frac{1}{2}$-inch drives double it again.

Why floppies don't crash

You may have wondered why floppy disks don't crash. In fact, floppies would seem to be in a perpetual state of crash, given that the read/write heads always rest against the surface of the disks as they turn. But a "crash" requires the exertion of much energy upon a small point on the disk surface, and a floppy drive is not designed that way. The disk turns slowly, the heads are large, and the disk itself is flexible. When a force is exerted on the floppy drive, the energy imparted to the head is not amplified so much by the disk's own energy; the energy is distributed over a broader surface, and the floppy gives as the head punches it. Very little wear and tear results. Although floppies don't crash, they are gradually worn down by the constant abrasion of the heads and the envelope in which floppies reside. This is why DOS does not keep floppy disks constantly turning.

$3\frac{1}{2}$-inch floppies

As with hard disks, floppies make most capacity gains by packing more tracks on a disk, rather than more data on a track. Paradoxically, the smaller the floppy disk, the higher the track density. A smaller diameter means that disk deformations are smaller too. The hub in the rigid plastic packages can more precisely center the disk. And the package keeps the disk flatter as it turns so that it doesn't bounce away from the heads.

Manufacturers have started releasing floppy drives with extremely high data densities. They may fit up to 20 megabytes on a $3\frac{1}{2}$-inch diskette. This density is achieved in part by writing five times as many tracks as on an ordinary high-density disk. The read/write heads use a closed-loop system (like voice-coil hard drives), and special circuitry compensates for disk-centering misalignment and disk deformation. Embedded servo data is written on the disks during manufacture (the disks are slightly more expensive than ordinary ones). Although they use diskettes, such drives hook up to a standard hard disk interface.

High data densities

High-capacity floppies are not intended to supplant hard disk drives. They run much too slowly. Average seek times are poor, and transfer times are reduced by the slow rotational speed. A cylinder contains only two tracks, doubling the average number of head seeks required to read a file. But super-high-capacity floppies may be the ideal backup or archiving medium because they save the trouble of swapping many diskettes in and out of drives, and they offer immediate random access to any file when data is read back. As larger markets for them develop, they promise to become cheaper than removable hard disks, optical disks, or streaming tape. Another advantage is that even huge programs can fit on a single floppy, reducing software distribution costs.

Applications

Bernoulli Technology

An approach to high-capacity floppy disks that deserves special mention is **Bernoulli technology**, in which floppy disks are enclosed in a special casing to make them semi-rigid when they spin. The disks become as stable as hard disk platters, allowing much higher data densities. The technology sits halfway between that of floppy disks and hard disks.

The technology was introduced as the **Bernoulli Box** in 1982 by Iomega Corporation. It is based on a well-known principle, discovered by the Swiss mathematician Daniel Bernoulli in the eighteenth century, which states that the pressure in a stream of fluid diminishes as the speed of its flow increases. The principle is the same one that accounts for lift on aircraft wings. In fact, it may be said that in Bernoulli technology the *disk* is made to *fly* over the read/write head, rather than vice-versa.

In Iomega's original rendition of the principle, two eight-inch, single-sided disks are enclosed in a thick, hard-plastic cartridge with an opening for a read/write head. The two disks are single-sided,

Cartridge design

with the data-bearing side facing outward. Openings on either side of the cartridge remain closed until the cartridge is inserted into a drive. At the openings, between the read/write heads and the disks, is a "Bernoulli plate," a specially formed metal sheet that makes possible the Bernoulli effect. As the disks spin, pressure drops, the disks draw apart and become rigid, and they are drawn to within a few thousandths of an inch of the plates. The read/write heads project through the plate, and slightly beyond it. Secondary effects draw the rotating disks extremely close to the head.

The first Bernoulli Boxes placed data on only one of the two disks in a cartridge. The second side was devoted to servo data (required by the voice-coil head actuators on these drives). More recent designs apply the Bernoulli principle to 5¼- and 3½-inch disks. For high data capacities in these models, both sides hold data, with the servo data embedded between tracks.

Crash-proof design   A wonderful benefit follows from this design. Because the heads are stationary and the disks are flying, when a disturbance occurs, the magical Bernoulli effect is broken—a disk reverts to its floppy state and pulls **away** from the head. The drives are virtually crash-proof—just the opposite of an ordinary hard disk, in which the heads plunge into the disk surface when the air cushion that supports them is broken. We'll talk more about Bernoulli technology in Chapter 3, where we'll go over some of its advantages and disadvantages.

Laser Disks

These days, the most controversial disk technology isn't magnetic at all. It is the laser disk, best known to the public in its 5¼-inch form as a "compact disk." The same digital techniques that record an hour of music on one side of a compact disk can store 550 megabytes of data. That's the equivalent of 24 20-megabyte hard disks, 1,500 360K floppies, or 150,000 pages of text. Compact disks that store data are called **CD ROMs**, for "compact disk read-only memories." They are rather like ROM memory chips in that they come from the factory with information permanently written on them; they cannot be erased and reused.

Data densities   Laser disks work by creating tiny **pits** on the disk surface. A laser shines on a track, and where a position contains a pit, the surface reflects light, indicating an "On" value (binary 1); the absence of a pit counts as an "Off" (binary 0). The pits are only a third of a micron (millionth of a meter) across, allowing densities of about

15,000 pits per inch. Although this density is on par with that of magnetic recording, laser disks can achieve much higher **track densities** than hard disks. While a hard disk's magnetic domains form long bars in which the edges may interfere with adjacent tracks, the pits in a laser disk are circular and compact. Sixteen thousand tracks per inch are possible—more than ten times as many as on a hard disk. There are signs that doubled, even quadrupled, data densities may evolve, leading to the 1- or 2-billion-byte CD ROM.

The pits are created in several ways. One method has a laser burn them into the surface; another technique forms the pits from opaque bubbles made by focusing the laser under the surface; a third approach uses the laser to alter the medium to and from a crystalline form. The latter technique holds special promise as an erasable technology. A magnet may work in tandem with the laser in a technique known as **magneto-optical recording**. A high-energy laser heats extremely tiny domains on the disk surface to the point that a magnet can make a flux change; the magnetic field may affect a larger area, but the domain is limited to the area struck by the laser beam.

Read/write techniques

The advantages of laser disks are many. There can be no head crashes because only a beam of light touches the disk. Not easily damaged, disks have a lifetime of at least 20 years. The high capacity makes space for elaborate error checking codes. And the disks can be cheaply produced by stamping them out like phonograph records. The drives are also inherently simple and inexpensive to make.

Advantages

An ordinary audio CD player cannot be used with CD ROMs. Although the basic technology is the same, quite different electronics are required. As with any hard disk, a controller card accompanies CD drives, along with device driver software. At the moment, the hardware is expensive. But the electronics can easily be compacted into large-scale integrated circuits, and prices are expected to fall rapidly as the market grows. IBM announced a 200-megabyte drive with the PS/2 line; it carries a hefty $2,950 price tag, though.

Types of drives

Commercial write-once drives are now appearing, often under the acronym **WORM** (write-once, read-many)—that is, each track may be written upon only once, but can be read any number of times.) Write-once technology is simpler than erasable technology. It will have at least a few years of supremacy before true read/write technology supersedes it. Write-once drives are often closely coupled with hard disks. Rather than repeatedly write to the optical disk, consuming its unerasable tracks, software operates with the

Write-once technology

hard disk, and only when work on a file is complete is the file written to the CD.

Write-once drives are an ideal hard-disk backup medium, an application in which their slower access time is less of a drawback. Someday, they may supplant streaming tape backup units. For the moment, write-once drives are expensive; yet even at several thousand dollars, the price is but $10 per megabyte. Unfortunately, blank disks are expensive, sometimes costing $100 or more.

Performance

Beyond the temporary issue of unerasability, the greatest drawback to laser technology is the slow average seek time of the drives. While a hard disk's read/write head may be a tiny magnet, CD drives must move a sizable optical assembly across the disk surface. And since the drives use only one single-sided platter, the *cylinder density* (number of sectors found at one head position) is low. But intense research is rapidly pushing seek times downward; hard-disk performance levels may be in sight. Some experts predict that future CD drives will use a read/write head that is hardly more than a single fiber-optic strand wafting above the disk surface.

If 550 megabytes of storage is not good enough for you, you might want to snap up a *Series 1800 Expandable Jukebox* from Cygnet Systems. With prices ranging up to a modest $155,000, you can have 141 double-sided 12-inch laser ROMs retrieved by a giant jukebox contraption. Now that's archiving!

Market trends

The spread of CD ROM technology is already well underway. A file-format standard has been devised (the "High Sierra" standard), opening the way for anyone to publish a disk that can be read by any drive. The first major CD ROM release was the *Grolier Electronic Encyclopedia*: an entire 20-volume, 9-million word book version transferred to disk and cross-referenced with a mainframe computer for spitfire lookups. Microsoft has issued a collection of standard reference works on a CD ROM. Other important references like the *U.S. Zip Code Directory* and *Books in Print* have appeared. And several business databases have been published (with periodic updates), effectively replacing certain online services. PC special interest groups have released huge public-domain software libraries. A variety of disks containing graphic images and laser fonts are up and coming.

CD-I

The two companies that pioneered audio CDs, Philips and Sony, have developed their own CD data standard called CD-I, for "Compact Disk–Interactive." The standard accommodates computer software, numeric and text data, sound, graphic stills, and primitive motion video. Developed for the consumer electronics market, CD-I incorporates a Motorola 68000 microprocessor, supplying the basis for elaborate interactive entertainments and educational programs. Meanwhile, RCA has developed DV-I, a way of storing 72 minutes of full moving video on a compact disk. Which technologies will ultimately sweep the consumer marketplace is anyone's guess.

Opinions about the future role of compact disks in computing are as numerous as the sands of the Sahara. Some describe CD ROM as "a solution without a problem," believing that its use will be limited until low-priced read/write technology appears. Others claim that read-only CDs can revolutionize information processing. The truth could lie at either extreme or anywhere between. It all depends on your view of computing.

Future trends

Proponents of CD ROM see the technology as handmaiden to more advanced software that could not effectively exist without CD's help. They believe that the near-term application of CD ROM to reference sources and databases will be superseded by elaborate, graphics-based *knowledge bases* upon which software will rely for artificial-intelligence processing. Only compact disks can fulfill this role because only they can act as an inexpensive distribution medium for such vast amounts of data.

Solid State Storage

One way of getting around disk drive performance limitations is to eliminate the drives altogether, replacing them with banks of memory chips. A megabyte of chips becomes a 1-megabyte disk drive. The memory is organized as a **RAM disk**. RAM disks partition the memory into sector-size units (although the concepts of "track" and "cylinder" don't apply). In RAM disks, any sector is instantly accessible, as if a read/write head hovered above every sector at all times. For this reason, file fragmentation doesn't slow down file access in RAM disks. RAM disks come complete with directories and file allocation tables, just like an ordinary disk.

Memory densities

As you surely have noticed, progress toward higher capacity memory chips continues. One-megabit chips began shipping in early 1987, 4-megabit chips are on their way, and 16-megabit chips are on the horizon. (The chips hold mega*bits*, not *bytes*; it takes eight chips to form mega*bytes*.) Although the latest chips tend to be very expensive, if history is any guide, even the very high-capacity chips will ultimately become cheap. Two sets of 16-megabit chips could form a 32-megabyte RAM disk at a price lower than that of a mechanical drive.

Drawbacks

The problem with RAM disks is that they lose their data when power is removed for only an instant. Banks of memory chips can be put into service as permanent RAM disks only by powering the chips separately from the computer; they continue to draw electrical current even when the computer is turned off. These are called **non-volatile RAM disks**. Because power outages sometimes happen, even non-volatile RAM disks require a backup power supply. The chips consume a lot of juice, and it takes quite a substantial (and expensive) backup unit to see the RAM disk through several hours without power. The backup can hardly be optional; without one, it would be only a matter of time until a total loss of data occurs.

Bubble memory

One way to overcome the danger of data loss is with **bubble memory**. While RAM chips store their information in electronic switches, bubble memory uses magnetic "bubbles." Strings of these bubbles rotate in storage loops, typically 4,096 bubbles long. When a bubble is present at a particular string position, it indicates an "On" or if no bubble is present, an "Off."

The microchip circuitry must wait for the bubbles it wants to access to circle into view, and this characteristic makes bubble memory much slower than RAM chips. In fact, banks of bubble chips used for mass storage may actually be given an "average access time," just like a hard disk. This rating was 0.7 milliseconds in mid 1987—not bad compared with the 40-millisecond rating of a "fast" hard disk. But the overall data-transfer rate of the chips is much slower. They can deliver about 1.6 megabits per second, compared with 5 megabits for a standard IBM AT hard disk, or 10 megabits or more with the newer high-capacity drives.

Bubble memory has a special property: the bubble patterns remain when power is removed from the chip. This occurs because the chip is sandwiched between permanent magnets. As a result, bubble memory supplies fast, non-volatile storage without any moving parts and without risk of head crashes. What's more, the chips appear to have a lifetime of 20 or more years.

Bubble memory densities

Bubble memory suits mass storage because very high densities can be achieved. Intel (the maker of many of the most important chips in IBM machines) has been making 4-megabit chips since 1985; by comparison, 1-megabit RAM chips appeared only in 1987. While 16-megabit bubble memories are on the drawing board, their high densities require a different fabrication technique that hasn't yet been perfected. When the bugs are ironed out, experts claim that 64-megabit chips will be easy to produce.

For all of their advantages over disk drives, bubble memories remain obscure. They are too expensive for most applications. To date, they have gone to work mostly in military applications, in which spinning disk drives are far too delicate. But bubble memory boards have been made for personal computers, and there is still hope that higher-density chips will become cost effective.

In the future, perhaps in the mid- to late-1990s, we may be able to look forward to **block-line memory**, a sort of bubble memory in which many bits of information are crammed into a single bubble. Some researchers believe this technology could reach densities of several *billion* bits per square inch of chip surface. For whatever it's worth, someday you may be able to carry around 20 encyclopedia sets on a credit card.

Block-line memory

Where is Hard Disk Technology Going?

Of the various optical and electronic storage options, it's tempting to conclude that the days of hard disks are numbered. But hard disk technology can be pushed far beyond the performance we are accustomed to. Consider, for example, the *Model 2812* drive from Ibis Systems, Inc. designed for supercomputers. It uses 14-inch platters and transfers data at 96 megabits per second. Holding a modest 2,800 megabytes, it sells for an equally modest $77,200 (in mid-1987). Note that the price per megabyte is roughly the same as that of a standard 20-megabyte Winchester drive.

Not too many years ago, mainframe computers ran on 20-megabyte drives, and those drives were fantastically expensive. How much further can hard disk technology go? More advanced encoding technology will at least double recording densities, and it might push them to 50,000 bits per inch. Sophisticated head designs could easily double track densities. Multiplied together, a tenfold capacity increase is in view. Today's standard 20-megabyte disk could be supplanted by a 200-megabyte hard disk in the mid-1990s at, say, $2 per megabyte.

It's conceivable that *erasable* optical drives will be available in the same price range by that time, and they'll likely have several times the capacity of similarly priced hard disks. But whether a particularly *fast* erasable optical disk will be available is another question. Most likely, laser disks will *complement*, rather than *replace*, hard disks well into the 1990s. Acting as *tertiary storage*, CDs will take the pressure off hard-disk capacity requirements. They will become the primary distribution medium for reference materials, databases, and graphic images; and they will be the ideal archive medium for hard disk backups and business records. Meanwhile,

Competition with optical drives

The speed bottle-
neck

the venerable floppy disk will continue to be used for software distribution because no other medium promises to be nearly as cheap.

By 1995, many microcomputers will function at what are now
regarded as mainframe speeds. They will run outlandishly complicated operating systems. Disk drive speed may become the critical
bottleneck in a computer's performance because advanced multitasking operating systems constantly access the disk. If optical
disks don't become much faster, they may be pushed into a back-
seat role, leaving hard disk drives at the center of data storage for
another decade or longer.

Of course, solid-state storage would be fastest. If RAM prices
drop as much as they have in the past, a set of 16-megabit chips
may fall to $25, and a 100-megabyte permanent RAM disk could
cost as little as $200. Even at double that price, permanent RAM
disks would seem to condemn hard disks to extinction. However,
the volatility problem will continue to vex solid-state storage. Completely reliable electrical backup could drive the price out of reach
even after multimegabyte memory chips become cheap.

In summary, we must conclude that hard disks will continue to
be the mainstay of secondary storage until at least the mid-1990s.
They'll run faster and hold more data. And they'll come to possess
more "smarts" that will make for greater reliability and higher performance. Unfortunately, they'll also go right on threatening our
data. Because hard disks won't go away soon, you'll do well to understand them thoroughly.

Chapter 3

What, Where, and How to Buy

In this chapter we'll discuss the bewildering array of options facing the hard disk buyer. Once upon a time, you had merely to decide whether to ask the computer store for a 5-megabyte or a 10-megabyte internal drive. Today, the calculation has become much more complicated. You must anticipate how your own hard disk needs will change as new kinds of software enter the market. A move to desktop publishing, for example, completely changes your disk-capacity requirements. Equally important, you may need to consider how the disk fits into overall procedures. For example, *data security* may become the overriding factor in your hardware selection.

As you'll see, there is a seemingly endless parade of hardware options to choose from in features (types of media, encoding, head actuators) and in types of drives (hard disk cards, removable hard disks, and Bernoulli technology). To make matters worse, manufacturers are defining themselves in a crowded market by advertising special features (such as *track buffers* and *on board caching*) that may or may not be useful to you. You, the potential buyer, face a wide range of prices, often for seemingly identical equipment. How do you judge quality? Should you pay extra for installation and support? What kind of warranty should you expect, and how useful will it really be? How do you protect yourself against unscrupulous dealers? Where do you take complaints? We'll try to answer these questions, and many more, in this chapter.

How Much Disk Capacity Do You Need?

The first question that enters a buyer's mind is "How big?" If you are buying your first hard disk, any disk will seem large beyond all comprehension—even a 10-megabyte unit. If you're buying your second hard disk, any disk will seem like only a stopgap against the rising tide of data that engulfs your life—no number of megabytes seems enough for very long.

But infinity (or what seems like infinity) is beyond the pocketbooks of most consumers, so you must decide just how much hard disk to buy. This calculation is an *easy* one in the sense that it is largely independent of other purchase considerations such as quality and performance. You need at least as much as you need, and to buy any less is to invite trouble and distraction that could undermine the whole point of acquiring a hard disk in the first place. But the decision is complicated, for there are more factors to consider than you might guess.

To accurately forecast how much hard-disk capacity you'll need over the coming years, we'd recommend that first you purchase a crystal ball. It is hard enough to anticipate how many megabytes of data will be churned out per year by the software you now use. If you plan to explore new genres of software, you can be sure that you will never have a very good idea of how much disk space you need to buy.

Perhaps you plan only to move into another kind of traditional application, doing some accounting along with your word processing. In this case, you can consult with someone with experience in accounting packages and get a pretty good idea of how much disk space your accouting files will consume. But if you are moving into emerging, rapidly changing genres of software, such as desktop publishing or computer-aided design, your estimates of needed disk space could easily be off-target by 100% or more. We'll explore the reasons for this quandary in a moment.

First, it is important to ask just how far ahead you need to plan. Although a hard disk may faithfully serve you for many years, like all computer equipment, it is racing towards obsolescence from the moment you buy it. The story is familiar: Programmers create applications that run acceptably only on the fastest, most capable hardware. Equipment prices fall; mass markets develop; so the price of leading-edge software also plummets. Old equipment and software is abandoned in response to the high utility and cost-effectiveness of the new products. Your one-time pride and joy is donated to the kid next door—sometimes before it is completely paid for.

The extent to which you can plan ahead depends on what you do with the machine and on how much of a hacker you are. If you are a programmer and experimenter, avidly examining every bit of software you can get your hands on, you are unlikely to be able to predict the amount of data you'll be generating beyond about eighteen months. On the other hand, if you operate a stable small business in which the computer is strictly used for some undemanding accounting, you can look ahead with some clarity by as much as four or even five years. Typically, however, three years is about the forecasting limit.

Three years spans an entire microcomputer generation. During that time, the industry gestates a whole new level of software engineering, new microprocessors, operating system extensions, new video standards, higher-density RAM chips, new printer technologies, and—as we saw in Chapter 2—whole new disk technologies. Even if you really *loathe* computers, you will be using some of

Forecasting future needs

How far ahead should you plan?

Equipment generations

these introductions, because they will make your life easier, and you won't be able to resist.

So you should probably plan your disk capacity requirements on three years data accumulation, at most. You may be able to keep the disk drive in service somewhat longer by moving older data files to floppies. Or, if you work in an office with a growing computer population, you can look forward someday to consigning your hard disk (and probably the whole computer) to the person at the bottom of the pecking order.

Problems of inade-quate capacity

What matters is that you buy adequate disk space for the two- or three-year planning period in question. If you buy too much, you will have wasted money—perhaps a good deal of money if you are shopping for high-capacity drives. But if you buy too little, you run the risk of undermining your whole computer productivity system (the system we mentioned in Chapter 1, and that we'll be presenting in detail in Chapters 5 through 6). You will be inviting constant disk-management hassles, mistaken file erasures, slower disk performance, a return to the floppy-disk shuffle, user confusion, and general all-purpose calamity.

Still, there is such a thing as *too much* disk capacity, and huge disks carry huge price tags. Indeed, you may have to settle for less capacity than you would like simply out of affordability. If you go this route, plan on putting more effort into managing the disk.

Formatted vs. Unformatted Capacity

Some vendors advertise the "formatted capacity" of a disk; others advertise "unformatted capacity." Formatted capacity is always smaller, usually by about fifteen percent. Formatting lessens capacity because small sections of each track are lost to the spaces between sectors and to the identification codes that begin each sector.

In either case, the specification is not exact. A "20-megabyte drive" might be 21,377,024 bytes in one case, and 21,272,576 in another.

Capacity ratings

You may wonder why a "20-meg" drive is not exactly 20 megabytes. As we saw in Chapter 2, the amount of data that fits on a track and the number of tracks that can be squeezed onto a disk surface depend on the properties of the read/write heads and the magnetic medium spread on the surface of the disk. Manufacturers combine these factors into designs that have capacities in multiples of 10 megabytes more as a marketing decision than an engineering optimization.

WHAT, WHERE, AND HOW TO BUY

Nominal vs. Actual Capacities

A natural impulse is to figure out how many kilobytes of software you'll place on the disk, add the number of kilobytes of data you'll generate with the software over some arbitrary period, add 20% for good measure, and then buy a hard disk at least that large. The general strategy is correct, but the specifics are more complicated than they seem.

In Chapter 2 we learned about *cluster size*—the minimum allocation of disk space DOS makes for any file. Recall that on hard disks a cluster holds eight sectors (4,096 bytes) in DOS 2.x, and only four sectors (2,048 bytes) in DOS versions 3.x. This minimum unit of allocation applies to all files on the disk, including subdirectories. A disk filled with many short business letters can waste a good deal of space. Programmers tend to generate many small files, each holding a small program "module"; they too may require extra disk space to accommodate their special needs.

The impact of cluster size

Say that a small business uses its computer mostly for correspondence. Twenty letters go out 300 days a year, with plans to keep five year's worth on the disk. That's 30,000 letters. Say that they are short ones, averaging 15 lines of 70 characters—about 1,000 bytes each. Now, 1,000 times 30,000 gives 30 million or 30 megabytes. So it's only natural to run out and buy a 40-megabyte hard disk, confident that there's plenty of space to spare for the word-processing software and a video game or two.

An extreme case

In reality, 40 megabytes would be far too little. When a word processor creates a new file, DOS version 3.x allocates a single cluster of disk space, say 2,048 bytes. If the file turns out to be only 1,000 bytes long, the remaining 1,048 bytes of the 2,048 are wasted—they remain allocated to the file even though no information is written on them. If the file extends to exactly 2,048 bytes, every byte of the cluster is used and disk space is used optimally. But if the file is lengthened by one more byte to 2,049 bytes, DOS allocates a second cluster of 2,048 bytes to the file, and 2,047 of them are wasted.

In our example of 30,000 short business letters, each 1,000-byte file would actually require 2,048 bytes of disk space, multiplying to 60 megabytes! Indeed, 60 megabytes would be required even if each letter was but one word long. So the naive estimate of a 30-megabyte disk capacity requirement was wrong by half.

A more typical
case

Generally, minimum disk-space allocation doesn't throw off capacity estimates by nearly so much. Most files are much larger than
1,000 bytes. When the average file is 7,000 bytes, four clusters of
2,048 bytes are allocated, giving 8,192 bytes. The first three of the
four clusters are entirely filled, leaving 1,192 bytes unused in the
last cluster. Thus, a 7,000-byte average file size wastes only about
15% of disk space, whereas a 1,000-byte average size wastes nearly
half. The larger the average file size, the more efficiently disk space
is used.

Many applications produce very large files, making irrelevant the
whole issue of minimum disk-space allocation. Database files can be
immense, running into megabytes. Although they may contain numerous individual records, the records are not allocated disk space
separately. Rather, they are laid out end to end within the single
file; a record may reside half in one cluster and half in the next,
leaving not one byte wasted.

Hidden Requirements

Operating system
requirements

Some additional requirements for disk space are often neglected.
First of all, the operating system will take up some space. The dual
copies of the file allocation table on a 20-megabyte disk take up
30K under DOS 3.0. The root directory consumes over 16K. And
50 subdirectories, each taking up an average of a cluster and a half,
gobble up 154K of disk space. Add COMMAND.COM and some essential DOS files, and we find that the operating system takes up
fully a third of a megabyte. OS/2 needs at least three times as much
disk space.

Multiple software
copies

Another concern is software that may require multiple copies on
the disk. Not all software is able to access files anywhere on disk
without creating confusion. We'll see in Chapter 6 that the DOS
PATH command and special path utilities can help more primitive
software get the job done. Nonetheless, occasions arise when you'll
need to duplicate files in several subdirectories.

Backup files

Backup files can also take up a tremendous amount of space.
Many editors make file duplicates automatically, appending a .BAK
extension to the filename. Proper backups should be kept on media
other than the hard disk itself. But you'll still have to deal with
megabytes of .BAK files. You'll need to allot disk space for them if
you can't trust yourself (or others) to delete them when separate
backups are made.

In some projects you may want to keep a *serial backup* on the
hard disk, making a permanent copy of a file at various stages in its
development so that you can return to an earlier version if things
go awry. Serial backups can easily take up a megabyte in a complicated programming project.

While we're on the subject of backups, you might also consider   File junkyards
keeping a kind of "junkyard" on your disk, a special directory
where old files are put out to pasture—the sort of file that probably ought to be erased but maybe should be kept for just a bit
longer. Special software is evolving to invisibly maintain junkyards.
For example, *SafetyNet* from West Lake Software takes over the
DOS erase command; when files are erased, *SafetyNet* hides them
away instead of deleting them. A file can be reclaimed at any time;
the least recently erased files are actually deleted only when disk
space runs low. Such utilities make further demands on disk capacity.

Finally, you should know that some software creates on the disk   Temporary files
temporary files that you are completely unaware of. The program
uses the files as a work area while it runs; when the program terminates, it erases the file. For this purpose, DOS can give a unique
filename to a program so that the temporary file won't inadvertently overwrite an existing file.

Many word processors create temporary files when they format a
text file for printing. As the document is copied into the temporary
file, the formatting codes are converted into the code sequences
used by the printer; then the data is sent from the temporary file to
the printer. Such temporary files are usually slightly larger than the
data files they serve. Special hardware also may create temporary
files. For example, streaming tape backup units can need 100K of
disk space to do their work.

By definition, temporary files make no demands on your disk
storage capacity, but they can cause problems (a software error
message) when a disk is operated at the edge of capacity. They
constitute one more reason to have more than adequate disk capacity at your disposal.

Emerging Requirements for More Disk Capacity

Creative users will always think of new things to do with their
computers. New genres of software arise. And existing genres that
you think are meant for others find their way into your repertoire.
Let's look at some of the newer disk-hungry applications.

Bit-mapped displays

Generally speaking, on IBM machines there is a move toward *bit-mapped* displays, which write on the screen dot by dot, rather than character by character; the screen is always in a graphics mode, even when only ordinary text appears. This makes possible all manner of fonts and special symbols and icons. Apple's Macintosh showed the world that a graphical, bit-mapped interface makes computers much easier (and more fun) to use. IBM was slow to imitate this approach, partly because IBM doesn't appear to think that computers should *be* easy to use (or, for that matter, fun). But, with the introduction of OS/2, IBM announced its own bit-mapped interface, the *Presentation Manager*.

The point is that bit-mapped displays inevitably produce very large files. All those icons must be mapped out. Font libraries are required. And much more elaborate data files are needed to keep track of font types and other graphical characteristics. In the future, every major application that outputs to the printer will use a page-description language to spin out spiffy visual presentations. The upshot is that disk space requirements are doubled or even tripled.

Desktop publishing

In terms of graphics, desktop publishing is a good example of how a new and "unexpected" application can wreak havoc on the best disk-capacity calculations. For years we contentedly pecked away in *WordStar*, perfectly happy with our daisy-wheel printers. Now, with the introduction of laser printers, nothing short of designer graphics is acceptable. Rather than a small ASCII text file, we now need several huge page-description files. And the new files are created *in addition to* the normal word-processor files they use. Worse, the disk may have to hold backup copies for these files.

Digitized graphics

Higher-resolution bit-mapped screens have also given an impetus to the application of digitized graphics. Digitizers are becoming cheap and commonplace. Run a photo through and the machine sends the image to your computer's memory—and then on to the hard disk for storage. When these images are stored in simple black and white (with no levels of gray), a full-screen digitization takes up 40K. But a gray-scale or full-color digitization may require much more disk space, perhaps a third of a megabyte for just one photo!

It is no wonder that graphics-oriented machines, such as those outfitted for computer-aided design, typically have hard disks in the 100- to 200-megabyte range. In time, the influx of desktop publishing applications will place similar demands on common PCs. Simply put, graphics are the wave of the future, and you had better be ready for them.

Using more programs

Another concern is the proliferation of software. It's easy to count *data* files while neglecting program files. With time, you are bound to use more and more software, even if you don't branch into new kinds of work. Do you just use your computer for a little word processing? Consider the huge spelling checkers and thesauruses that have appeared. What about syntax checkers? Form letter libraries? Text databases? If it seems that there is no end in sight—well, that's right, there will be no end.

You may also find that you'll be using more and more utility programs. Programs like *Metro* from Lotus Development and *SideKick-Plus* from Borland International automatically swap resident utilities in and out of random-access memory, allowing any number to be online. A couple of megabytes of phone dialers, notepads, calculators, and who-knows-whats may soon be the norm. Consider, as well, totally unexpected introductions like *Bookmark* from Intellsoft, which automatically stores a snapshot of all of system RAM (and more) on disk, allowing complete recovery after a power outage. A great idea—but it can consume nearly a megabyte and a half of disk capacity.

There is another consideration. Program files are growing. As applications have become more complex, .EXE files above 100K, even 200K, have become commonplace. In fact, some software houses produce large program files as a matter of policy. Finely crafted programs share bits of code between the many features the program offers. The program module that formats the screen may also format printer output. These interdependencies make programs more complex, more error-prone, and harder to debug. It's often simpler to write two or three similar modules where one could do the job. As with everything else in life, it is easier to be wasteful than economical. The result is larger programs, albeit ones that cost less to develop, contain fewer bugs, and reach market sooner.

IBM's new operating system, OS/2 will impose new demands for disk capacity. For starters, its own files are big. But more important, OS/2 creates large temporary files, especially when multitasking with large amounts of data. OS/2 uses a complicated memory-management technique called *virtual memory*. When system RAM is full, swatches of data not currently in use are moved onto disk to make room in memory. When a program again accesses the data, the operating system shifts it back into memory. For all practical purposes, the machine has as much additional RAM as it has open disk space.

Of course, this technique can severely degrade software performance, and lots of system RAM is still desirable. But it gets the job done and beats an "out of memory" error message. In any case, vir-

Utility programs

Program file size

The impact of OS/2

tual memory imposes yet another burden on hard disk capacity (it also makes hard disk *speed* all the more important).

Fitting More Data Onto a Disk

Often, files can be compressed so that they take up less disk space. We'll talk about data compression in detail in Chapter 5. Some compression software can be loaded as a *memory-resident program* that silently goes about its business as application software is run. It inserts itself between the application and DOS, invisibly compressing and decompressing data as files are written and read. Or, the compression software can be hardwired into the disk controller so that data is automatically compressed and uncompressed during all read and write operations.

In some applications, you may want to take file compression into account in estimating capacity requirements. But it's hard to know how much your files will be reduced; some complicated data files may hardly shrink at all. Text files are usually reduced by about half. Certain kinds of data files, such as some *Lotus 1-2-3* files, may be cut by 90%.

File compression takes time: It's likely to slow disk access. And compression utilities take up precious RAM. So it's not a good idea to acquire *less* disk capacity than you need by planning to store all files in compressed form. An exception to this rule is when you need to *archive* many files on the disk. In general, you should save data compression for the day you discover that your capacity estimates were too low.

Assessing Capacity Requirements

If you're feeling a little overwhelmed by all this, you have a right to be. There really is no way to anticipate your hard disk needs accurately, particularly if you plan to keep abreast of new software developments. Still, a line has to be drawn, because a disk with hundreds of megabytes is clearly too large for most users and prohibitively expensive. Here are some guidelines for making the decision:

- Don't attempt to plan more than three years ahead. If you are a "power user," two years or even eighteen months is more realistic.
- Calculate your data needs for existing and anticipated work loads, taking into account minimal cluster allocation if it's important.

WHAT, WHERE, AND HOW TO BUY

- If you will be moving into desktop publishing, multiply your text-data file calculations by five.
- If you will be using digitized graphic images, carefully research the storage requirements of the resolutions and colors you will be using, consider the need for multiple copies of an image, and figure out how many images will need to be kept on the disk at any one time.
- Add three megabytes for additional software. If you are a heavy-duty power user, add twice this much.
- When all of your needs are calculated, increase the estimate by 50%.
- This total should be regarded as 85% of your disk capacity requirements to leave extra space for temporary files and to avoid performance degradation from overcrowding.

Following these rules, you have a *conservative* estimate of your disk-space needs. You probably won't be able to buy a disk at exactly the right capacity, so buy the increment of ten megabytes above your needs. If you figure you need 13 megabytes, an additional 50%, plus 18% again, comes to roughly 23 megabytes. It would be unwise to buy a 20-megabyte disk; spend a little more for 30 megabytes.

This leads us to one final rule: Never *ever* pass up inexpensive increments in disk space, even if you cannot begin to imagine ever needing the additional capacity. Sometimes an additional 50% costs only 15% more. Think of the extra expenditure as an insurance policy against unexpected requirements—you may never need it, but if you do, you will save much money and trouble by spending a little more now.

Deciding How Many Floppy Disk Drives You Need

Every computer requires at least one floppy disk drive. Floppy drives let you move software and data to and from the machine; floppy diskettes may serve as a backup medium for your hard disk; and a floppy drive is sometimes required to hold a *key disk* in some copy-protection schemes (the software looks for the key disk in the floppy drive and refuses to run if it can't find it).

Once upon a time, all floppy disk drives were full height. Owners of early IBM PCs find that they must abandon one of their floppy drives to make room for a hard disk. Later machines have mostly had half-height drives, but even one of these may be sacrificed when the computer's power supply cannot support two floppies and a hard disk. There's not much of a market for used floppy drives. It's best to hang onto them as a backup drive; sooner or later the installed drive will go out of alignment, and the second drive can take over while the first is in the shop.

Uses for dual floppies

Dual floppy drives are useful in several ways. For starters, they make it easier to use the DOS DISKCOPY command. Second, dual drives complement utilities that break copy-protection schemes to make backups of software distribution diskettes.

Dual drives are also useful when a key disk ties up one of the drives. If you constantly work with software that requires a key disk, it's handy to keep the disk permanently in an extra floppy drive. Similarly, a second drive is useful for software that automatically backs up the hard disk to floppies while you work.

Floppies and backups

Probably the most important application of dual floppy drives is in high-speed backups of your hard disk. Some backup utilities can fill a 360K diskette in fifteen seconds. Because it takes as many as 70 360K diskettes to hold the contents of a 20-megabyte hard disk, you'll be kept plenty busy swapping diskettes (of course, high-capacity floppies impose less work). The time required for a backup can be cut in half by using two floppy drives, swapping diskettes in one as the other records data. Unfortunately, most backup programs require that both drives have the same capacity, so ATs with one 360K drive and one 1.2-megabyte floppy drive won't do the job.

AT incompatibility problems

The two kinds of drives found in IBM ATs also lead to compatibility problems. The 1.2-megabyte drives brought headaches to many owners who did not understand their limitations. These drives use a special-formula diskette for high-density recording, but they can also take ordinary (360K) floppies for low-density recording. Low-density diskettes formatted and written on the drives are not always readable by ordinary 360K floppy drives. And 360K diskettes formatted on a 360K drive and written by a 1.2-megabyte drive may not be readable by any drive at all. Third-party manufacturers have devised 1.2-megabyte drives that are free of these problems.

AT options

Most owners of ATs or AT-compatibles will find that one 1.2-megabyte drive is all they'll ever need. The drives have no trouble reading 360K software distribution diskettes. They're excellent for backups, not just because the larger capacity entails fewer disk changes, but also because they read and write data much more quickly than 360K drives. Although a second 1.2-megabyte drive would ease backups, it wouldn't make nearly as much difference as a second drive does for backups on an XT-class machine.

Owners of PS/2 machines that use 720K disks may want to have two drives if they'll make frequent global backups. On the other hand, machines with a single 1.44-megabyte drive can do the job well. Software houses are gradually dropping copy-protection schemes, including key disks, so that some of the reasons for having a second drive on older machines don't as strongly apply to the PS/2 line.

PS/2 options

Similarly, owners of XT-class machines will need two drives if frequent global backups are planned. Half-height 360K drives have become very cheap, especially when the price is measured against the time saved over months and years. In fact, swapping 65 or 100 diskettes becomes so onerous even *with* two floppy drives that there is a grave danger that you'll make backups too seldom. If a second floppy drive lessens resistance to backups, it's the best investment you can make in your computer.

PC and XT options

One manufacturer, Tall Tree, makes 1.2-megabyte drives (called the JDISKETTE drive) for PC-class machines. These drives come with their own controller cards to replace the IBM floppy disk adapter. (The drives don't work with an ordinary PC diskette adapter card.) Existing 360K floppy drives are run by the new adapter. Special control software (a *device driver*) must be loaded when the machine is booted. This is a relatively expensive solution to backup needs, and a streaming tape unit is usually a wiser choice.

1.2-megabyte drives for PCs

Choosing Among the Options

So far, we've talked about "hard disks" as if the typical 20-megabyte controller-drive combination is the only option. But there are many choices. *Hard disk cards* make installation especially easy. *Removable cartridge drives* extend disk capacity to infinity. And *high-capacity drives* make possible giant files. We'll cover each option in turn.

External Drives

One common distinction among all kinds of disk drives (except hard disk cards) is between *internal* and *external* units. Drawing their power from the computer's power supply, internal drives fit into the **disk drive bays** at the front of the computer. External drives have their own cabinet, a fan, and a separate power supply plugged into a wall socket.

Although external units generally are held in disfavor, they offer a few small advantages. They don't sap the computer's power supply or add to its heat load; and in computers already packed full of floppy drives, an external hard drive saves you from throwing out perfectly good hardware. But external units run at least $150 more than an equivalent internal unit, so these advantages do not come free.

A more serious problem is finding a place to put an external unit. It must be close to the computer because a cable connects them. The drive can't be hidden in a drawer or nearby cabinet because the unit needs cool air for ventilation. So it must sit beside the computer, where it is invariably in the way. This leaves it open to the considerable danger of being pushed, struck, bounced, or knocked off the desktop. The added abuse makes head crashes more likely.

You won't always be able to avoid external units. Most removable cartridge drives are external, as are many high-capacity drives. There's just been no way to make them small enough to fit into the machine (however, the gradual move toward $3\frac{1}{2}$-inch media may make external units extinct in a few years' time). If only an external unit meets your needs, buy it; but avoid them if you can.

Hard Disk Cards

Hard disk cards, sometimes called "card drives," place the hard disk drive right on the controller board. All components are miniaturized, and the drive electronics and controller electronics are integrated. The result is a hard disk unit for which installation is (theoretically) merely a matter of dropping the card in a slot. Because the disk drive is mounted on the controller board, there's no cabling between controller and drive. And, because the card draws its power from the slot, the drive isn't cabled to the computer's power supply. Hard disk cards also have a reputation for being quieter than traditional $5\frac{1}{4}$-inch drives, although some are not.

Hard disk cards were introduced in 1985 by Plus Development Corporation under the trademark "Hardcard"; dozens of imitations quickly followed, made possible by the introduction of $3\frac{1}{2}$-inch disk drive technology. Most hard disk card makers buy the drives from a leading manufacturer and create the controller electronics themselves. Some of the miniaturization in hard disk cards stems from eliminating superfluous electronics so that the drives are customized for IBM machines. Most "bare" disk drives are "universal" in the sense that, equipped with the proper adapter card, they can go to work with any kind of computer, whether a Macintosh or an IBM. Hard disk cards made for an IBM machine are wired up to work only with IBM equipment.

The first hard disk cards held 10 megabytes, with 20-, 30-, and 40-megabyte models quickly followed. Those with higher capacities have with two platters, applying RLL encoding with a 3:1 interleave. Some use stepper-motor technology, with an average access time of about 65 milliseconds. Others, with voice-coil head actuators, may exceed a 40-ms access times. Miniaturization makes it difficult to design *very* fast hard disk cards (in the 20 millisecond range), but they are gradually appearing. Hard disk cards appear to be as reliable as ordinary hard-disk drives, with MTBF (mean time between failure) ratings typically running at about 20,000 hours. Plus Development Corporation is advertising a *50,000-hour* MTBF for some of its drives. In spite of the high MTBF ratings, most hard disk cards come with only a one-year warranty.

Because hard disk cards are sequestered in the inner depths of the machine, no indicator light shows when the disk is active. Though hardly essential, this feature may be useful for spotting disk malfunctions, and an experienced eye can sometimes tell how well a disk is optimized by following the timing and pattern of red flickers. In any case, most hard disk cards are loud enough that you can hear the head movements.

Nonetheless, some hard disk card manufacturers have gone out of their way to supply an indicator for disk activity. Sysdyne! includes an indicator light cabled to the hard disk card and mounted by adhesive to the front of the machine. As a nice touch, besides the usual red light, it has a green light that goes on when the heads park. Plus Development Corporation takes a different tack: Its hard disk cards tap into the computer's video buffer and write a tiny plus sign in the upper righthand corner of the screen when the disk is active; this feature works only in text modes. Or the hard disk card can cause the system speaker to emit a quiet click with every head seek. Both features are user-selectable and may be disabled.

Hard disk cards have been most popular among IBM PC owners who want to upgrade to XT capability. Most manufacturers have included the hard disk BIOS (discussed in Chapter 2) on the hard disk card itself. This is a wonderful feature, because replacing ROM

Capacity

Indicator lights

Hard disk BIOS

chips intimidates many users—and rightfully so—as it is the one part of hard-disk installation that can require a bit of experience and dexterity.

Installation

Some hard disk card manufacturers have gone to great lengths to make hard disk cards easy to install. Often the cards come completely preformatted with the entire disk partitioned for DOS. Recall that high-level formatting places two hidden DOS files on the disk: IBMBIO.COM and IBMDOS.COM. Because these files are under copyright, they cannot be preformatted. But space is set aside for them, and the DOS SYS command copies them over from the DOS diskette. When the hard disk card is first installed, you can't boot from it because these files aren't present. But the drive can hold files, and it is fully functional. Manufacturers may place a batch file on the drive, and it will invoke the SYS command and run other installation utilities as well. Installation may require nothing more from you than naming the drive specifier (such as **C:**).

At least one manufacturer has gone a step further and made the installation program set up an initial directory tree. As we'll see in Chapter 5, this is a highly personal business. You'll probably want to delete the entire structure and start anew with your own plan. Note that utilities for the drive may be included in one of the ready-made subdirectories and these must be preserved.

Compatibility

A single hard disk card won't work in both a PC (or XT) and an AT; you must buy a model for one or the other. Note that an AT won't readily accept a second controller card, which is the case when you insert a hard disk card. Most hard disk card models for the AT are designed so that they can work with the floppy/hard disk controller card. To make matters more complicated, some stripped-down AT clones come with the floppy disk electronics on the main system board, without a hard disk controller card in a slot. Even then, most hard disk cards will work properly, but it's a good idea to check with the manufacturer before purchase.

Power requirements

Most hard disk cards are advertised as drawing no more power than a floppy disk. By disk-drive standards, they indeed *are* parsimonious with electricity, pulling as little as 8 watts; but they nonetheless place an added load on a computer's power supply. The power-insufficiency problem is mostly confined to the IBM PC, with its 63.5-watt rating. On newer PCs equipped with 256K RAM chips, a hard disk card usually finds adequate nourishment in the existing power supply (although an internal modem may push it over the limit). Older PCs may use numerous 16K or 64K RAM chips, which gobble up power and make it less likely that a hard disk card will function without your replacing the power-supply.

Most manufacturer's claim that there is no danger of power insufficiency when their cards *replace* a floppy disk drive, but actual power requirements often slightly exceed those of a floppy drive.

Hard disk cards come in a bewildering array of shapes. Some, like those from Plus Development, form a sleek, inch-thick metal package, of fairly uniform thickness from one end to the other. Most hard disk cards, however, are very thick at the end of the card where the disk drive resides and very thin at the other, with the electronics exposed. Some poorly designed cards are little more than a traditional hard-disk drive turned on its side and mounted on a controller card. True one-slot hard disk cards tend to be more expensive than these imitations.

The assortment of hard disk card shapes would merely be a passing curiosity were it not for its importance in installation. Very few drives are truly one slot wide (about one inch). To avoid taking up two, three, or even four slots, manufacturers have designed the drives for placement in particular positions. When you face the machine, some cards may fit in the leftmost slot, jutting out toward the computer case, as shown in Figure 3-1A. In certain cases, this configuration requires that you detach the system speaker in an IBM PC and move it elsewhere.

Placement

Other hard disk cards are designed for installation in the rightmost slot of a machine, with the drive reaching around the back of the floppy disk compartment (Figure 3-1B). This configuration may leave the drive overhanging the 8088 microprocessor chip. This area around the microprocessor may need to be clear if you add an accelerator card to the machine or perhaps a "slotless" system clock that snaps between the 8088 chip and its socket.

On other cards, the drive is squeezed on the end of the card closest to the front of the machine. Although the drive juts out over some of a second slot that would be used by another full-length card, the socket for the second card remains uncovered, allowing it to receive a half-length card designed for a short slot on an IBM XT. This configuration is shown in Figure 3-1C. You'll also find super-miniaturized, half-length hard disk cards made to fit in an XT's short slot.

Some of these configurations undermine the much vaunted "ease-of-installation" that has drawn so many buyers to hard disk cards. An important rule is that adapter cards should *never* touch even if the point of contact seems non-conducting. There is no predicting what may happen when circuitry between two cards is joined; theoretically, every card in the machine, *plus* the system board, could be damaged. Various piggyback cards (such as the memory

Installation problems

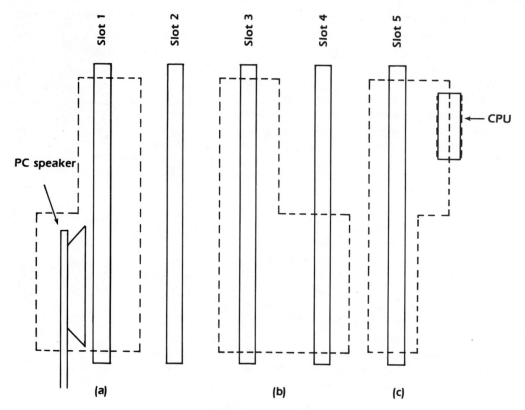

Figure 3-1 **Hard disk card configurations**

expansion module for an IBM EGA) have always been a problem in
this regard, as have transformers and speakers protruding from
modems.

To avoid this danger, you may find yourself shuffling your adapter
cards between the slots, seeking the ideal arrangement. You'll find
that moving the system speaker is a pretty clumsy task; and if you fill
the rightmost slot of the machine, you will have to move the floppy
disk controller cables *over* the newly inserted card, which is safe in
itself, but a nuisance when you remove or replace the computer
cover, because the cables may catch.

Drawbacks   To most buyers, hard disk cards spell "convenience." But some
buyers haven't had it so easy. Installation can take more time than
an ordinary drive-and-controller kit. Extra slots may be lost to card
overhang, the power supply may require replacement after all, and,
as a second hard disk for a machine, there may be serious configur-

ation problems. Still, the best hard disk cards drop right into an
IBM PC, automatically set themselves up, and run beautifully. But if
the card is going into an AT, or the card is to act as a second hard
disk, you should call the manufacturer directly to ask whether the
card will suit your needs.

Finally, do not assume that a hard disk card that works in a standard PC will work in any equivalent machine, such as a Compaq
portable. Often the computer maker has its own hard disk products, certifying only these and not commenting on others. Not surprisingly, prices tend to run higher. If you opt for a cheaper hard
disk card, call the hard disk card maker for a list of certified machines. And, if there is any question that the hard disk card will
work in your system, secure a written money-back agreement.

Removable Hard Disks

Removable hard disks are enclosed in cartridges inserted into specially designed drives. Like floppy disks, any number may be used
in a single drive. At first glance, removable hard disks seem ideal.
They combine the best characteristics of fixed hard disks and floppies, offering both speed and high capacity, plus the ability to
archive endless amounts of data.

The promise of "unlimited storage" can be illusory, however.   Limitations
Five 20-megabyte removable cartridges may not be nearly so useful
as a single 100-megabyte fixed disk. It's not just a matter of the inconvenience of switching cartridges. Every cartridge must be outfitted with the relevant software and utilities. Changes in the
directory tree, in CONFIG.SYS, and in AUTOEXEC.BAT must be
replicated on each cartridge. Software must be installed on each,
and productivity tools like keyboard macro files must be copied
from cartridge to cartridge when changes are made. In short, sharing large amounts of data between cartridges may be difficult or
impossible.

In general, all the problems of managing floppy disks can accompany removable hard disks as well. Often they are best used as an
adjunct to a large nonremovable hard disk. The nonremovable disk
holds the main directory tree, all software, and the entire productivity system of batch files and utility programs. The removable cartridges hold data sets, and little more. If you consider buying a
removable drive, do your best to calculate how large any single
data set will become. Removable cartridges do not presently run to

very large capacities, and you must be sure they'll accommodate future needs.

Until recently, most removable disk drives were housed in external units; the cartridges are just too big to let a drive to fit into a computer's disk drive bay. These units robbed you of desk space, but offered the advantage of not draining the computer's power supply. Today's internal units install much like as ordinary hard disk drives.

Incidentally, the first hard disks were designed along these lines. Even today, a typical hard disk drive for mainframe computers uses giant "data packs" dropped into cabinet-size drives rather like a top-loading washing machine. They may hold a *gigabyte* (1,000 megabytes) or more.

Platter-only cartridges

Cartridge design takes two approaches. One technique places a single platter in the cartridge, with trap doors that open automatically when the cartridge is inserted into the drive and close only after the drive stops turning. The read/write heads are lowered to the drive surface, and they fly over the disk on an air cushion, exactly as in ordinary Winchester drives. Highly filtered air is constantly pumped into the drive to force out invading dust particles. But contamination has been a problem in some drives, and head crashes occur relatively frequently.

Manufacturers claim that cartridge contamination arises primarily from user ignorance. People carelessly label the cartridges, and bits of pencil lead or eraser become lodged beside the cartridge door, entering the cartridge the next time it is used. The cartridges must be immediately returned to their protective sleeves when removed from the machine. When a head crash occurs, the entire drive must be sent in for maintenance; otherwise, contaminants on the heads will enter other cartridges. Cartridges holding 15 or 20 megabytes retail for about $100.

Head-assembly cartridges

A second approach to removable disks places not just the drive platters, but also the entire head assembly inside the cartridge. The cartridge is an entire hard disk drive, minus the electronics. These cartridges are much more expensive, of course. They may cost as much as a discounted bare Winchester drive of like capacity; but dozens of Winchesters cannot be added to your machine, whereas removable cartridges offer infinite expansion.

Tandon has introduced drives based on the all-in-one design. The Tandon Data Pac houses 3½-inch disks and head assemblies in box-shaped cartridges that hold 30 megabytes. The units accommodate two drives to facilitate backups. Tandon prides itself on the shock resistance of the cartridges; salespeople like to toss one on the floor and then show that it still works (they aim for thick carpet, however). To speed access, the drive electronics contains a 128K memory buffer for inbuilt caching (a high-performance technique explained in Chapter 7). In mid-1987, a 30-megabyte cartridge retailed for $349.

Unfortunately, removable drives have not always lived up to expectations, particularly those that enclose just the disk in the cartridge. Because IBM has not created a removable disk drive of its own, there are no standards for the cartridges. Cartridges created on the drive of one manufacturer won't work on drives made by another. Worse, some drives are so finicky that they can't share cartridges made on other drives *of the same manufacturer*.

Drawbacks

Reliability remains a problem in so delicate a technology. The problems are gradually being solved, and many tens of thousands of units have been sold. Still, you should not buy a removable drive without researching it well. Reviews appear periodically in computer journals—some of them extremely uncomplimentary. If you choose to invest in an altogether new design, understand that you are playing guinea pig.

Bernoulli Technology

We described the technical principle behind Bernoulli technology in Chapter 2. Iomega Corporation unveiled the Bernoulli Box in 1982 after the invention was unwisely rejected by several large companies, including IBM. Many tens of thousands of units have since been sold. The drives are popular because they offer an excellent compromise between speed, capacity, reliability, and data security.

The original Bernoulli Boxes used eight-inch disks held in flat cartridges measuring roughly 8½ by 11 inches. The cartridges have a write-protect switch (rather than a notch) to protect data from accidental overwrites. They can be partitioned for multiple operating systems, just like an ordinary hard disk. Gradually, smaller drives have been released that can be installed internally. Iomega now makes 5¼-inch and 3½-inch models, with capacities running to 44 megabytes.

Bernoulli Boxes use a separate controller card, so they claim a slot in the computer. The drives use voice-coil actuators for 40-millisecond access, RLL encoding, and (on recent models) SCSI interfaces. Capacities of up to 44 megabytes are achieved by increasing both the density of data along the tracks and the number of tracks. Although the disks turn more slowly than standard hard disks—

down to 1,835 rpm—higher data density makes for transfer rates of up to a megabyte per second.

Cartridge wear

By the way, the disks turn more slowly to reduce wear. Unlike ordinary floppies, Bernoulli cartridges wear out after about a year because they are constantly turning. To prolong cartridge life, the controller retracts the heads from the disk surfaces when no drive operations occur for a few seconds. In older models, the controller constantly moves the heads about to avoid excessive wear on a few tracks. Special circuitry on the controller card monitors the condition of the disk and informs you when it is time to copy the data over to a fresh cartridge. Cartridges retail for about $80.

Dual-disks

Many users prefer dual-drive units. By having matching drives, you can easily make identical copies of any cartridge. This may be the ideal backup medium, because if the original fails, the backup can be used "as is," without any complicated data-restoration procedure. A tremendous advantage of Bernoulli boxes is that a cartridge used in one machine can go to work in any other Bernoulli Box of equivalent or greater capacity. Most removable disk drives are not nearly so compatible. This feature makes the medium ideal for transporting data.

Iomega has also introduced dual Bernoulli drives combined with a high-capacity hard disk. The hard disk is intended as a network file server, while the cartridge drives serve as an *archive* medium for large quantities of data. This strategy keeps the hard disk clear, prolonging its useful life by seeing to it that disk space remains adequate.

Performance

The fast head access times and rapid data transfer rate seems to point to exceptionally high performance. But remember that a Bernoulli cartridge can offer at most only two platter sides. This means that only two tracks reside at a given head position. While the makers have concentrated on fitting more data onto a track, the cylinder density is still considerably lower than that of an equivalent dual-platter hard disk drive, and thus, more head seeks are required to read a large file.

Installation

Installation is simple. Because the older, eight-inch units cannot be internally mounted, a controller card is inserted into a slot in the computer and cabled to the external unit. The cables are made long to let you place the unit well away from the computer. Because the unit has its own power supply, it makes no demands on the system's. However, the more recent units install just like any internal hard disk. A device driver (control software) must be loaded when the computer is turned on, because the inbuilt BIOS cannot handle the unusual disk format. Dual drives are typically

named C: and D: in machines without a hard drive or else D: and
E:. A special utility is included to format the cartridges. More recent Bernoulli Boxes can boot the machine.

An interesting problem arises when Bernoulli cartridges are
shared between PC and AT-class machines. Because an AT can handle a higher data-transfer rate, the cartridges perform optimally
with a lower interleave factor than is appropriate for a PC. Recall
that too high an interleave keeps the controller waiting a bit longer
than necessary until it can read the next sector; too low an interleave, on the other hand, entails a full rotation of the disk before
the next sector may be accessed. The "acceptable" inefficiency depends on which machine the cartridge is most used in. (Interleave
optimization is discussed in Chapter 7.)

Interleave

Iomega's Bernoulli Boxes come with several utilities, including a
COPY utility, and the IBACKUP and IRESTORE programs. The latter
offer various backup features, including both image backups and incremental backups (explained in Chapter 8). The software supports
backups between two Bernoulli drives, or between combinations of
Bernoulli drive and hard or floppy disk. Recent versions are optimized for copying cartridges by repeatedly swapping cartridges in
and out of one drive; the software makes *incremental backups* possible with only one cartridge change. Backups of high-capacity hard
disks may be spanned across several Bernoulli cartridges.

Data backup

As we'll see in Chapter 8, the quality of backup software varies
greatly among manufacturers. A good program can save much time
for users who have special needs. Be warned that your favorite
backup utility probably won't work with Bernoulli boxes, because
it can't deal with the special disk format. If you're not happy with
IBACKUP, you'll be limited to only a few alternatives. Compatibility
problems may also arise with streaming tape backup units.

High-Capacity Drives

As we've seen, some computer systems require very high-capacity
drives, particularly those serving networks in which the drive is
shared between many users, or in stand-alone graphics-oriented systems for computer-aided design or desktop publishing. Many manufacturers have rushed to supply these drives. Their select clientele
is prepared to pay premium prices for the right mix of capacity and
performance. In mid-1987, capacities to 760 megabytes were available in the usual 5¼-inch *form factor*. The 1-billion byte drive is
near at hand. Comparing these drives to their floppy disk

equivalents—up to 2,000 diskettes—is meaningless; these drives are meant for special jobs.

Cost per megabyte

The cost per megabyte in high-capacity drives typically runs twice that of smaller drives. As with all computer equipment, prices have been dropping steadily. A few drives seem to approach nearly the same cost-per-megabyte as smaller disks. But the cost-per-megabyte for smaller drives has dropped too, and with RLL technology giving small drives higher capacity at little additional cost, it's hard to see how high-capacity drives will ever compete on this level. Generally, the market for high-capacity drives is more feature-competitive than price-competitive.

High-capacity drives are almost never designed to operate on an IBM PC or XT. The 8-bit data bus found in these machines cannot handle the rapid data through put these drives strive for. Some operate from the standard AT controller card, but most come with a specially designed card, often with a fast ESDI interface. Many high-capacity drives follow the standard 5¼-inch full-height form factor, allowing internal installation. They may draw only about 25 to 30 watts. Many of the largest drives, however, come only as external units, complete with their own power supply and fan.

High-capacity drives tend to be very fast. With many platters, and many sectors per track, they have a very high cylinder density. Far fewer head seeks are required to read a file. And the average seek time may be as low at 10 milliseconds. These drives tend to be at the cutting edge of microcomputer disk drive technology. When a tiny box can fetch $8,000, engineers are free to do their very best. These are the sports cars of the hard disk industry. In fact, cutting-edge technology is a *must* if hundreds of megabytes are to fit in the standard full-height, internally mounted form factor.

Platters

We saw in Chapter 2 how drive capacities may be raised by cramming more data on a track, more tracks on a disk, and more platters on a spindle. Large drives take advantage of all these techniques. The most obvious way to increase capacity is to stack more and more platters. However, manufacturers have found that customers don't like external drives; they'll gladly pay $6,000 or $8,000 for a little metal box, but they want it *inside* the machine. Internal drives can accommodate only so many platters. To turn the platters, makers went from using flat "pancake" motors fitted under the platters to tiny motors contained in the spindle upon which the platters are mounted. Eight platters seems to be about the upper limit.

Data densities

Higher data densities on a track also pose limits. Recall that data densities may be raised by using higher quality magnetic media with

special read/write heads or by using the more advanced RLL data encoding methods. RLL technology was first applied to large mainframe
disk drives; naturally enough, RLL first appeared in the microcomputer
world on high-capacity drives, where the expensive electronics were
affordable. Hence, manufacturers of large drives "used up" some of the
capacity gains from RLL years ago. While even more advanced RLL encoding is now appearing, using it to cram data at ever-higher densities
along a track presents severe obstacles. Extremely small heads must
fly even closer to the disk surface, and the magnetic medium must
achieve extremely high "coercivity" so that smaller tidbits of disk surface can act as magnetic domains. This technology is progressing rapidly by engineering standards, but not nearly rapidly enough by
marketing standards, where a doubling of price-performance every
three years has become the norm.

   Higher track densities are also promising. Thin-film technology   Track densities
(plated media) makes possible designs using over 1,200 tracks per
inch. The higher price of large drives allows the use of a dedicated
servo surface. Recall that closed-loop voice-coil technology requires
servo bursts between the tracks to keep the read/write heads on
target. Most high-capacity drives have a **dedicated servo surface**,
in which a whole side of one disk is devoted to servo information,
and the **embedded servo data** is dispensed with. Without the
servo data between the tracks, more can be squeezed on a platter.

   Higher track densities have posed a serious problem: Neither the   The 1,024-track
controller card nor the operating system can handle them. A 1,024-   limit
track limit is built into the system at every level. Track numbers
larger than 1,023 (tracks are counted 0 to 1,023) simply cannot be
processed. Neither DOS, the BIOS, nor the controller card circuitry,
can handle them.

   All three sources of the 1,024-track limit may be overcome. Often, the controller card must be replaced. Although some high-capacity drives use the standard IBM AT controller, most come with
their own. Because many high-capacity drives use an ESDI interface
for faster data transfer, the controller may need replacing in any
case. Manufacturers then supply special software for "patching"
(modifying) the offending BIOS and DOS code.

   At least one drive maker has overcome the 1,024 track limit by
creating a "logical interface" for the drive in which the drive
presents two tracks to the BIOS and DOS as if they were one. A
1,200-track drive appears to be a 600-track drive, albeit with exceptionally many sectors per track.

   No matter how a high-capacity drive is designed, it likely   Unusual drive
presents an unusual geometry to the operating system. Recall that a   geometries

"geometry" is the particular combination of sectors-per-track, tracks-per-side, and sides-per-cylinder described in the fixed disk BIOS. In Chapter 2 we talked about how the BIOS supports only a certain number of disk geometries. These form a list numbered from 0 upward. Initially, the IBM AT supported geometries 0 to 14, and later models supported 0 to 23. The PS/2 models 50, 60, and 80 support nine more geometries. Many high-capacity drives fit none of the geometries. Accordingly, special measures must be taken when the drive is installed, especially in local-area networks. We'll talk about this more in Chapter 4.

Manufacturers' specifications

You should be especially cautious about manufacturers' performance claims for large drives. In mid-1987 drives with *actual* average seek times between 15 and 20 milliseconds were available on the market. But some drive makers advertised seek times below 5 milliseconds! Can this be? Not yet. Some drives have internal electronics that present a "logical" drive geometry to the operating system that doesn't match the drive's "physical" geometry. What from DOS's point of view is a track-to-track seek may require no head movement at all. Traditional measures of drive performance become meaningless—but some manufacturers apply them anyway.

Some drives may have disk-management utilities built into their circuitry, so that file layout is constantly optimized, and sector caching (buffering) proceeds automatically (we'll discuss these techniques in Chapter 7). Any hard disk drive can benefit from these measures by applying readily available, inexpensive software utilities. But manufacturers who have built them into their drives may compare the drive's performance to that of a typical drive that does not use the techniques, and then advertise a relative, "virtual" seek time in the under-5 millisecond range. Caveat emptor.

Planning for Adequate Power and Ventilation

Disk drives and controller cards consume power. The drive is fed by a cable reaching directly from the computer's power supply. The *power supply* is the large black or chrome box at the back-right of the machine; it contains transformers and other circuitry that convert wall-socket power to the dc voltages the computer uses. The controller card is fed power from the slots.

Power requirements vary considerably from disk to disk. As capacity rises, marginally less power is required per megabyte. Most vendors have no idea how much power is consumed by the drives they sell. Nor is a rating necessarily meaningful, because drives

have a higher *start-up* power consumption, and this number is
even harder to come by. Usually this added margin of power consumption will not overwhelm a barely adequate power supply, because the start-up surge takes place while no floppy disk drives are
running.

Power supplies are rated for maximum output. Ratings run at
63.5 watts in a standard IBM PC, 130 in an XT, and 192 to 210
watts on ATs. Among the PS/2 machines, the Model 30, 50, 60, and
80 supply 70, 94, 207, and 225 watts, respectively. These values
are only approximate; the actual power output varies from supply
to supply. Most will output *at least* this much power, perhaps five
or ten percent more. The power supplies found in IBM clones
cover a whole range of ratings from 63.5 watts to 220 watts or so.

The XT was given a larger power supply than the PC mostly to
compensate for the hard disk drive. Users had been filling their PCs
with power-hungry add-on cards, and not enough power was left in
many machines to handle the extra disk drive. Many who installed
a hard disk in their PC found that the machine crashed as soon as
it was turned on.

In response to this problem, many small companies make *replacement* power supplies that offer higher capacity. Except for the
power rating, these power supplies exactly match IBM power supplies, so they are easily substituted and cost as little as $50. We'll
go into the details of choosing and installing a power supply in
Chapter 4, which concerns hard disk installation. It is important to
buy a power supply that affords adequate protection against electrical surges. Be sure to consult the discussion in Chapter 4 before
you buy one.

Whether you need a larger power supply, remember that all
power consumed by the machine is ultimately converted to heat.
You'll find that some disk drives consume considerably more
power than others. Even if your power supply can easily furnish another ten watts, you should consider that the machine will be burdened with that much more heat—the enemy of all computer
components. Everything, including the disk drive, wears out more
quickly because of it. And when temperatures inside the machine
rise too high, the disk drive is likely to go on the blink and refuse
to function until the temperature drops.

Note that merely adding a high-capacity power supply to your
machine doesn't in itself increase the heat load. The wattage rating
tells the maximum power that can be furnished; the increments of
extra power aren't actually supplied until computer components
are added to the machine. So a power supply rating isn't like a

Power supply
ratings

Replacement
power supplies

Heat load

light-bulb rating or an electric heater rating, where a 500-watt rating means that 500 watts of electricity are always consumed. If no new components are added to your machine, you could replace a 100-watt supply with a 200-watt supply with negligible contribution to the heat load.

Cooling
The fan at the back of the computer does its best to circulate cool air, but surrounding air isn't always cool. If you run a heavily loaded machine, perhaps with two floppies, two hard drives, and all slots full, you may need to add a larger cooling fan, particularly if the computer sometimes operates in a hot room. Add-on fans don't cost much. We'll tell you more about them in Chapter 4. For now, keep in mind that these "extras" may cost you more money when you shop for a drive.

Assessing Performance, Quality, and Convenience

We've described a wealth of drive designs and features. Which options are best for you? The decision is a very difficult one because it isn't obvious which features will complement the software you use. For example, compared to database files, text files reap little benefit from fast seek times, but more from full track buffers. We'll look at such issues in this section.

How Important is Disk Speed for You?

Not everyone really needs a high-performance disk. If you work long hours with word processors or spreadsheets that mostly access the disk only when loaded and saved, having a speedy disk is about as useful as keeping a Porsche for driving down to the corner grocery store. Your daily time savings may be counted in milliseconds. Of course, a computer set up for high productivity may employ many utilities well served by a fast hard disk. But many people keep things simple, and, for them, extra dollars spent on a high-performance drive might be better devoted to more powerful software.

At the opposite extreme, if a drive is to serve a network or work in a standalone multitasking system, it can never be fast enough. In networks and multiuser systems, the disk drive jumps back and forth serving the needs of each user. In a single-user, single-tasking system, the read/write heads often hover over one cylinder, reading and writing in sequence. But in a multiuser system, control of the drive is constantly switched from one task to another. Not only is the drive kept especially busy by so many diverse demands, but it also has to do additional work to *return* to the position from which it serves each task.

Further demands are made by **virtual memory**, mentioned earlier in this chapter, a technique by which a multitasking operating system runs more applications than memory can hold by constantly swapping parts of programs and data between memory and disk. Programs designed for virtual memory use **dynamic linking**, in which program **modules** are constantly brought into memory at whatever location is momentarily available. The operating system quickly sets up the module to find other parts of the program; it *links* the module into the program on the fly, that is, *dynamically*. In a sense, the entire program is reduced to a collection of overlays. Data is similarly swapped in and out of RAM. Of course, the hard disk runs helter-skelter to support all of this.

Virtual memory is an integral part of OS/2 (in fact, the Intel 80286 and 80386 microprocessor chips are specially designed to support virtual memory). If you'll be using OS/2, and you expect to be running several applications that are themselves large and need to load much data into memory, you must buy a very fast hard disk. By "fast," we mean a disk with a rapid average seek time. In these applications, the read/write heads constantly scurry from one place to another, reading or writing only a little at each location. Most activity is *random access*, rather than *sequential* access. Hence, the benefits of a high cylinder density are lessened, because whole cylinders are seldom read or written. A fast ESDI interface is also valuable, because a 1:1 interleave is highly desirable under these conditions.

OS/2

If your computing needs fall somewhere between the extremes of simple word processing and high-powered multitasking, you'd do well to buy a voice-coil drive with an average seek time of 40 milliseconds or better. By now, such AT-class drives ought to be the standard. Software is gradually becoming too complicated to be satisfactorily served by the older, slower stepper-motor drives. If you'll be taking the plunge into desktop publishing, disk-based spell checking, or whatever, you should pay the 50% more for a fast drive.

Assessing a Drive's Quality

As hard-disk guru Paul Mace says, "You are the last beta-test site for a hard disk." These words may be a little unkind to hard disk manufacturers, who institute whole departments to test new hard disk designs under various adverse conditions. But manufacturers cannot really know how well their drives will perform over the long run. Drive designs change from year to year, driven by a hotly competitive market and constant technical progress. Last year's experience becomes obsolete along with last year's technology.

Kinds of drive failure

Drive failures fall into two broad categories: mechanical and electronic. A disk drive has few moving parts, but they must be precisely aligned; sometimes the slightest deviation causes the drive to stop working. Other failures are more blatant: the drive motor may simply burn out. The same can happen to a stepper-motor head actuator, or its drive band may go out of alignment. Tiny imprecisions can throw out a voice-coil actuator. There is absolutely no way to judge the quality of a drive on these points; the manufacturer's reputation and a good warranty are your only protection.

Another kind of drive "failure" may reside in the disk's coating or plating. The extreme thinness of the magnetic medium is hard to maintain. If it is too thin, there will be many bad sectors that cannot hold data reliably. On the other hand, the disk invites head crashes if the coating is irregular or mottled. Manufacturers speak of a disk's "flaw density," and a certain percentage of disks must be thrown out. Particularly unacceptable are flaws on the outer track of a disk, which holds critical operating-system information.

Bad tracks

When you buy a disk drive, you will find a **bad track table** written (usually by hand) on a label on the surface of the drive casing, or on an attached sheet of paper. This listing tells which tracks failed the manufacturer's in-house tests. During low-level formatting you will need to enter these numbers into the format program so that it can mark off these tracks. We'll talk about this issue in detail in the next chapter. Sometimes you'll find a disk with no bad tracks at all, but more often there are a few. This is nothing to be upset about; you are losing only a bit of disk space, and the drive ought to be as reliable as one with no flaws at all. Interestingly, as disk-drive electronics become more sophisticated, drive manufacturers will be able to ship *more* flawed disks, letting the circuitry make up for the mechanical imperfections. The result will be cheaper, and just as reliable, drives.

The MTBF

A disk drive's MTBF—"mean time between failure"—purportedly tells how many hours of operation a typical drive sustains before it fails in one way or another. The statistic applies only to the drive and the drive electronics; controller card failures, though rarer, serve to decrease the actual MTBF. Many people regard the MTBF as a sort of "mean-time-to-crash." This conception is incorrect. On any number of occasions, data may be lost as magnetic traces fade or an electrical transient moves through the system. These "failures" may be recovered from (in the worst instance, by reformatting the drive) without physically repairing the drive. From the manufacturer's perspective, the "failure" in MTBF means that the disk must be sent to the shop.

It might seem that you could increase the life of your drive by turning off the computer when it won't be in use for a few hours; but manufacturers unanimously assert that drives will last longer if they are *never* turned off. The temperature changes (**thermal cycling**) that occur during startup and shutdown inflict a lot of wear and tear. You also can prolong the life of a drive by keeping its files *defragmented* (a topic discussed in Chapter 7). More important, see to it that the drive is kept relatively *cool*; heat degrades mechanical *and* electronic components. Of course, as MTBFs rise toward several years, drives can be expected to die from obsolescence rather than mechanical failure. Still, the "M" in MTBF stands for "mean," and any drive can give up the ghost on its first day running.

MTBF ratings

You'll find that MTBFs are always given as a number rounded to thousands of hours, perhaps even to five thousands of hours. Even these suspiciously rounded figures may be grossly inaccurate. For MTBF ratings are not true statistics derived from experience. Technology changes too quickly for that. By the time a manufacturer could leave thousands of drives running for the tens of thousands of hours needed to establish a MTBF, years would pass, the technology would be obsolete, and the company would be bankrupt. Instead, a few drives are subjected to extremes of shock, vibration, and temperature change, and the resulting performance is statistically analyzed as the sum of the probabilities of failure of the drive's individual components. Because they are only estimates, MTBFs for new technologies may even less reliably indicate a drive's performance.

Sometimes a **shock rating** is advertised. This number purports to tell how many "Gs" (multiples of gravitational force) the drive can sustain without permanent damage. The shock rating for an IBM AT runs about 30, and other common drives may measure about 40. Obviously, hard disks in portable computers need more protection, so Compaq has 60 Gs ratings on some of its disks, and Plus Development Corporation is claiming 100 Gs for some of its Hardcards. If manufacturers are honest, these numbers ought to be legitimate, because precise tests are easily performed.

Shock ratings

Noise

A final consideration is *noise*. Many first-time hard disk buyers are unpleasantly surprised to find that the gentle whosh of the computer fan is now accompanied by a high-pitched whine. The noise recedes in a busy office. But in a quiet room at home the constant whirr can be distracting—even oppressive if you sit before the computer for long hours.

You'll never find a noise rating for a hard disk. There really is no way of expressing one meaningfully because the quality of the sound, rather than its magnitude, may be the problem. During read/write head movement the sound output runs from two to eight times louder, making a muffled rasping noise if you have a stepper-motor drive, a thumping sound with older voice-coil drives, or a chirp with some of the newer voice-coil designs, as in the IBM PS/2 machines. Not everybody minds these noises, but the constant background whirr drives some to distraction.

If noise bothers you, listen to a drive before you buy. Keep in mind that a drive will seem at least twice as loud at home as in a busy computer store, particularly if you've acclimatized your ear to street noise on the way to the inspection. What you cannot do with a noisy drive is bury it away in a drawer or other compartment, using long cables. The drive *must* have ventilation.

Drive
manufacturers

You may have heard people say that all hard disk drives are of equal quality, because all vendors assemble their hard disk systems from components made by only a few manufacturers. There is some truth in this assertion—and also some falsity. The number of drive manufacturers has dropped precipitously in recent years. Like other segments of the computer industry, bad market forecasts led to over-production, vicious price wars, and bankruptcies. In the end, there will be only about a half-dozen American makers. But the story is different in Asia, where upstart companies from Seoul to Singapore are making their own drives. One industry maven warns that several small electronics companies in Japan manufacture bare drives to order, without any particular expertise; these drives are "nameless," and their obscure origin is easily hidden behind the vendor's label. Word is out that lower quality drives are entering the market (ironically, just when established manufacturers are turning out ever higher quality drives).

In the final analysis, the various manufacturers' quality ratings aren't very helpful. In one case, drives with excellent MTBF ratings flooded into repair shops like lemmings. Cutthroat competition hasn't helped the ratings game one bit, and it has become more and more difficult to sort out progress in technology from progress in advertising. Yet a loose correlation between ratings and quality does exist. Generally, when the ratings are especially high, the drive is superior. But drives with similar ratings may vary in quality considerably.

Don't assume that buying a drive from a well-known maker guarantees high quality. At one seminar, a band of exasperated computer consultants nearly rioted when a representative of one of the largest manufacturers claimed that drive failures were nearly a thing of the past. The drives incorporated in the first IBM ATs failed in prodigious numbers, probably because of a faulty chip on the controller card. Like automobiles, one drive model may on average be much more reliable than another model from the same maker. If you must have the greatest possible reliability, you might want to shop at a company that competes on quality rather than price, such as Core International. You can expect to pay a good deal more for the added margin of safety, especially because such drives aren't generally sold discounted.

When you shop for a very large disk drive, you take your chances. These drives are designed at the cutting edge of technology. As capacities rise, so does the pressure to use ever more sophisticated technology to cram more data on a track, more tracks on a side, and more platters into the standard full-height package. MTBF ratings may be next to meaningless. Manufacturers devote loving care to producing these drives; they aren't quickly stamped out for mass markets. In a few years we'll know how good they really are.

Where and How to Buy

Once you've decided the type, size, and quality of drive you need, you must deal with a very complicated marketplace. Should you buy from the cheapest mail order house or the ritzy local dealer? How do you negotiate a deal? What should you expect in a warranty? How should you make payment to best protect yourself? And how do you go about returning damaged or unsuitable goods? We'll do our best to answer these question in this section.

First, however, we'll overview absolutely everything that you might need to have your new hard disk up and running. Nothing is more frustrating than waiting days for a drive to arrive through the mail, only to find that you forgot to order a critical component; it happens all the time.

What You Need to Buy

When you buy, be sure to acquire all the little extras. Most hard disk purchases consist of a "kit" containing a drive, a controller card, and various cables and hardware. The vendor customarily includes the two ribbon cables that connect the drive and card, plus a **bezel** if the drive is half-height. (The bezel extends the front plate of a drive to the top of the opening in the front of the machine; you'll find pictures of it, and other equipment mentioned here, in Chapter 4.) When you buy a "bare drive" that will serve as a second hard disk connected to the adapter card already in the machine, the bezel may be omitted (it usually isn't required). On standard IBM ATs shipped with a hard disk, the wider *control* cable accommodates two drives, but the narrow *data* cable is separate for each drive. Be sure to order another data cable when you add a second drive.

Mounting rails

AT owners will also need **mounting rails** for internally installed drives. Widely available, they cost about $5 a pair. PC and XT owners don't require these rails. You may need a couple of screws to fasten the drive in place, however. You'll find them at any hardware store; just borrow a screw from a floppy disk drive and take it along as a sample.

New power supplies

If you own an IBM PC and feel that your machine is loaded lightly enough to handle a hard disk without replacing the power supply, give it a try. No harm is done if the computer refuses to run. But you may have to suffer the frustration of waiting for a replacement power supply.

Power supplies in early IBM PCs send out two leads that supply power to disk drives. Later machines, and many clones, have four. If you'll be running two floppies along with the hard disk, you'll need a Y-connector which splits one power lead into two. Y-connectors, not usually included in hard disk kits, cost about $7.50. If power is insufficient, the replacement power supply you install will definitely have four power leads; so the $7.50 may be wasted.

PS/2 machines

As we'll see in Chapter 4, hard drives install directly into sockets in some PS/2 machines. There's no messy cabling, and the controller card is already supplied. Power should be adequate. So these "extras" are of no concern. However, certain software requirements, which we'll talk about next, may also apply to PS/2 machines.

Many drives come with low-level formatting already in place. Otherwise, a floppy diskette holding a low-level formatting program almost certainly will accompany the drive. When you buy a hard disk "kit," you can be sure that low-level formatting will be supplied in one of these ways, so there's no need to inquire. If you want to avoid the (trivial) task of performing the low-level formatting yourself, see that the drive comes preformatted. But it's probably better to do the job yourself, because the experience will come in handy if a failure of some kind requires you to reformat the drive. Even if the drive comes preformatted, it's wise to ask that a low-level formatting program be included.

When you buy a bare drive to be cabled to an existing controller as a second drive, a low-level formatting utility may not accompany the drive even if it hasn't been preformatted. If your first drive came preformatted and without a utility, you may find yourself without a way to format the second one. Formatting utilities are included in some disk toolkits, including those specialized for installing a second drive, like *SpeedStor*. But these utilities are expensive, and you won't want to buy one just for the formatting program. So be sure to ask about low-level formatting when you buy a bare drive.

Formatting utilities

If you own a relatively fast machine, try to find out what interleave is used when you buy a preformatted drive. For example, for fast ATs, the 3:1 interleave used in most preformatted drives is suboptimal. By knowing the interleave, you'll know whether you need to go to the trouble of reformatting the drive when you receive it. Incidentally, in Chapter 7 we discuss utilities that calculate the optimal interleave for a drive. The best time to apply these programs is when the drive is first installed, so you might want to order such software when you purchase a drive.

A similar problem may arise with head-parking utilities. These utilities accompany most hard disk kits in which the drives don't park the heads automatically. But if you buy a bare drive, you should ask.

Head parking

If you own an early IBM PC, you may need to replace the ROM BIOS chip on the system board, because the BIOS in early PCs doesn't support a hard disk. A new chip is required in PCs that use 16K memory chips to fit a maximum of 64K on the system board. We'll explain how to install the chip in Chapter 4. Replacements are no longer available from IBM product centers. Some small companies are selling them, for about $40. One such company, Diagsoft, is listed in our appendix of manufacturers' addresses and phone numbers.

BIOS replacement

Similarly, if you buy a very-high-capacity drive, you'll need to consider both BIOS and DOS support. Very-high-capacity drives are usually installed by dealers who know exactly how to make the BIOS recognize the drive's geometry. Some drives may come

High-capacity drives

straight to you from the manufacturer with specific installation instructions for your particular machine; this approach is fine so long
as your computer is not souped-up in some nonstandard way. Be
sure to avoid situations in which your hand isn't held the whole
way. It takes considerable technical knowledge, and even advanced
programming skill, to install some high-capacity drives.

Large partitions

On the other hand, 40-megabyte drives are now becoming common so that many users must deal with DOS's 32-megabyte partition limit without outside help. As we explained earlier, starting
from version 3.3, DOS lets you set up multiple DOS partitions on a
drive. If instead you want to create a partition over 32 megabytes,
you'll need to acquire the special software we mentioned. Don't
put off this purchase, because the program is required when you
format the drive. You won't be able to change to a larger partition
later without removing all your files from the drive.

New DOS versions

If you'll need a different DOS version for your drive, order it
early so that it will be on hand when you install the drive. Remember that 2.x versions of DOS use larger clusters that waste disk
space. Buying a recent 3.x version also supplies new commands
that may be useful for organizing your work and navigating the disk
(we'll discuss these features in Chapters 5 and 6). But DOS is not
cheap, and you can save money by staying with your older DOS
version. At today's hard disk prices, a copy of DOS costs half as
much as a (discounted) 20-megabyte drive.

We've put together a list of all these requirements in a sidebar.
Keep it handy when you order. You may drive the order clerk to
distraction if you ask about every relevant item, but it's better to
be safe than sorry. Sometimes it helps to explain the kind of machine the drive will be installed in and whether another hard drive
is already in place. Then let the salesperson list exactly what they
will send you and compare it with the list.

A Shopping Checklist

Hardware

Drive
Controller (IBM PCs, some AT clones)
Cables
Extension bezel (extends front of drive to top of the drive bay)
Mounting screws (often not included in drive/controller kits)

IBM PC Only

Replacement ROM (early PCs only)
Replacement Power Supply
Y-cable (if power supply not replaced in dual-floppy machine)

IBM AT Only

Mounting rails

High-capacity Drives

BIOS extension hardware or software
Special partitioning software for making large partitions or linking
    drives into one logical unit

Software

Low-level formatting software
High-capacity disk installation software
Second drive installation software
Recent DOS version

Documentation

Installation instructions
Controller documentation
Support phone number
Warranty

Choosing a Vendor

You can buy a drive through a local retail store or by mail order.
Mail order has a poor reputation, but, in fact, some of the best vendors sell mostly by mail. Local computer stores often give no dis-
counts but promise free installation and support. That can mean

quite a lot to some users, but the difference in price can run to several hundred dollars, a great deal to pay for a half hour of a technician's time. On the other hand, if the drive will be installed in a network, or if the drive has an unusual geometry, you may save a thousand dollars of your own time by turning over the job to the experts.

Mail order

Most mail order firms make a profit by selling many units at very low margins. They're not likely to have much time to help you or even talk to you about the order. This state of affairs is perfectly acceptable when you're buying an ordinary drive for an ordinary machine. The "kit" they'll sell you should give you everything you need to install the drive in an hour or two. In more complicated purchases, such as for a second drive to connect to an existing controller, you had better know exactly what you're doing, because the mail order company won't concern itself with the particulars of your system.

Systems integrators

Some mail order companies advertise a very different kind of service. These are **systems integrators**, specializing in optimizing disk drives. They constantly test and compare new drives as they appear, matching them with the ideal controller, or building a controller of their own. Sometimes they'll also match a tape backup unit to the drive. Such vendors tend to offer only one drive/controller combination of given capacity for a particular machine. A good systems integrator offers excellent support, including detailed installation instructions. Unfortunately, these days many companies call themselves "systems integrators" without any right. You can spot a true systems integrator by the breadth and quality of the data sent you when you request information. Their ability to provide detailed comparative statistics on drive performance is a measure of their professionalism.

Proximity of the vendor

There's always an advantage in buying from a mail order house within driving distance. On rare occasion, problems can't be straightened out over the phone. When it's not clear whether it's the drive or the computer that's malfunctioning, it's important to be able to take them in together. The vendor won't be terribly happy about your doing this, but usually they'll agree to it rather than have you return the drive. Watch out that you're not charged for the visit. If your machine is at fault, you owe them the $50— but not if the problem stems from poor documentation. If they sell "hard disk kits," by definition the documentation should be adequate. Another advantage of being close to the vendor is that, if the vendor ignores your complaints, you can make a nuisance of yourself until things are set right.

Very poor documentation often accompanies hard disk kits. Less expensive products may be imported from abroad, and the vendor may add a single page of documentation as an afterthought. Generally, the better the price, the more you need to think about how you'll handle problems if they arise. Inexpensive equipment is not necessarily more prone to problems; it's just that you can't count on adequate technical support.

When you phone a vendor to inquire about buying a hard disk, ask if there is a technical support line, its operating hours, and whether there is an 800 number. You might want to go so far as to ask questions more complicated than the usual salesperson can answer ("Do I have to change controller card dip switches to use this as a second drive?"); once you have a "techie" on the line, you'll quickly sense whether they can give good support.

Try to have the drive delivered early in the work week so that support will be available when you install it. If you do have problems, don't waste time trying one thing after another. Follow the instructions to a T. If the drive doesn't work, get on the phone. It should be *their* problem that the instructions fall short, not yours.

Technical support

Payment

Generally, you'll find the best prices on drives approaching obsolescence. When IBM standardized 20-megabyte drives with the release of the AT, warehouses full of 10-megabyte drives suddenly lost their perceived value and prices plummeted. Twenty-megabyte drives are following suit. Conversely, you'll find that high-capacity drives will always be the most expensive, both from the standpoint of performance and cost per megabyte. But occasionally you may spot a high-capacity drive competitive with smaller drives in cost per megabyte and offering much higher performance.

When you order the drive, ask whether there is a surcharge for credit card purchases. Some vendors add about 3%, knowing that the customer is unlikely to balk after shipment has been made. Nonetheless, payment by credit card is always preferable, because you can more easily cancel the order if the vendor fails to ship promptly.

Be very careful about warranties. It's one thing to promise to repair or replace a drive; it's another to promise to do it promptly. Most drives come with a 12-month warranty for parts and labor. The figure is gradually increasing as drives become more reliable.

Warranties

The warranty on the controller may extend to five years. It's important to note that the vendor's warranty may be longer than the manufacturer's warranty. This means that if the vendor goes out of business, some of the warranty may be worthless.

Repairs

Usually, the vendor cannot repair the drive in house; he must send it back to the maker or to a repair service. Because the drive must be shipped twice each way, with all the usual delays, a month can easily pass. Some warranties guarantee replacement of the drive if it isn't repaired within a certain period of time. Be sure the wording in the warranty reflects the actual passage of time from the moment the drive leaves your door and that it clearly states who pays for shipping. It should all be in writing.

Be especially picky about the warranty conditions if you buy a drive to be used with RLL encoding. In the rush to supply drives suitable for the cheap RLL controllers, some unscrupulous vendors have sold drives as "RLL compatible" that weren't intended to be. Find out the exact model of the drive and call the manufacturer to confirm the drive's suitability—it's easy.

Accepting and rejecting goods

There's little danger of damage to the drive during shipment. The heads are parked and the drives are packed very well (you should save the packing materials for the duration of the warranty so you can safely return the equipment). If you have trouble in installing the drive, it's *much* more likely that you've made a minor mistake, such as reversing one of the cables to the controller. Brand new drives carry a manufacturer's seal and logo on the metal shell—be suspicious if one is missing. Unscrupulous vendors have been known to resell repaired drives returned under a replacement warranty. You can call the manufacturer and check to see if the serial number is recent.

When you send equipment back to the vendor for replacement or repair, phone them first and obtain an **RMA number** (returned merchandise authorization). Don't assume that the person receiving the package will know about your earlier conversations with the company. Write a detailed letter explaining the problems and write the RMA number on the letter. Be sure to write the RMA number on the outside of the shipping container.

Mail order houses often impose a **restocking fee** against returned goods, often amounting to 10% of the cost of the goods. They're also unlikely to refund the money they charged for shipping the drive to you. So the refund check may be substantially less than you paid. When the error is entirely their own, they owe you a full refund, and you should demand it when you phone for an

RMA number. Not many vendors will reimburse you for the money you spent returning the drive, even if the fault is entirely theirs.

We don't mean to put you off by pointing out so many hazards. Most buyers receive their drives quickly, install them without a hitch, and run them for years. But it's good to be prepared for the worst, because once you've used a hard disk for awhile, you'll be thoroughly addicted and won't want to work without one for long.

Installation and Setup

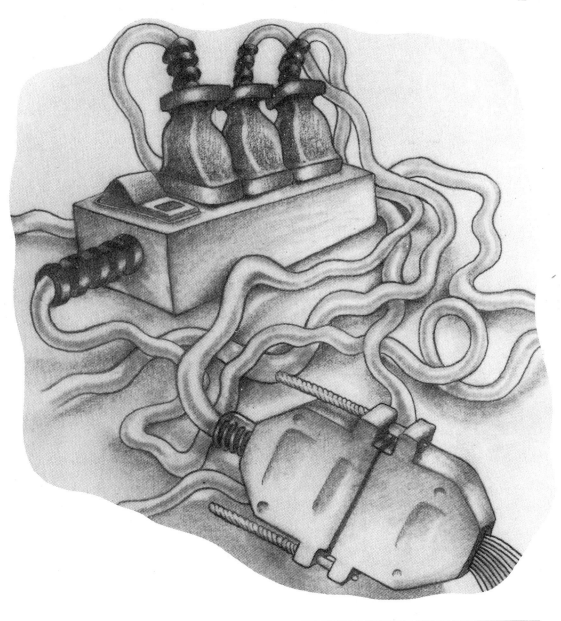

Depending on who you talk to, hard disk installation is either "a snap" or agony akin to death. Having an easy time of it doesn't require any particular technical knowledge or experience; a little reading and a little common sense suffice. Those who have had an awful experience often turn out to have jumped in without doing their homework. Even dealing with a faulty disk drive need not be a terrible experience if you have learned how to recognize that the problem lies in the drive, not in what you're doing. An experienced technician can install and format a new hard disk in under an hour, most of the time just waiting for the formatting programs to finish. A novice ought to be able to get through the process in about two hours, following the step-by-step instructions we give here. The only requirements are common sense and a screwdriver.

Self-reliance

Vendors will often install a hard disk for you. There's no denying the convenience, but you'll only be that much more reliant on the vendor in the future. If your drive crashes and requires reformatting, you'll need to take in your whole computer and wait until the repair department gets around to looking at it. If the drive fails outright, you won't know how to remove it from the machine and send it to the manufacturer. These considerations also apply to floppy disk drives and various adapter cards. You leave yourself terribly vulnerable to the time schedules of others when you are unable (that is, *unwilling*) to connect and disconnect components.

System optimization

Hands-on familiarity with equipment is also useful to users who want to tweak their systems for highest performance. "Power users" need to feel at home with swapping boards, cabling equipment, changing dip switch settings, and configuring DOS. If the very idea leaves you aghast, perhaps you should leave installation to the experts. But most users should take the plunge, particularly those without the deep pockets of corporate business.

Non-IBM equipment

Keep in mind that any installation of non-IBM equipment nullifies the official warranty. Having a dealer install the equipment won't make it an iota more official. But the added equipment can easily be removed if you must take the system unit in for repairs. If you change the power supply, keep the original for the duration of the warranty period (it has little value on the used-equipment market).

Installing an Internal Hard Disk

Generally speaking, installing an internal hard disk entails inserting a drive into a drive bay, inserting a controller card, cabling the controller to the drive, and the drive to the power supply. Unfortu-

nately, IBM has now released machines with so many different designs that there are many differences in detail that we must discuss
here. We'll begin by looking at PCs and ATs, and then we'll move
on to PS/2 models 30, 50, 60, and 80.

Installing a Drive in a PC or AT

Drive installation in PCs and ATs is much the same. The greatest difference is in opening the machines and physically installing the drive.
To begin with, you have to remove the cover. Turn the machine off,
disconnect the monitor, and remove everything from the top of the
machine. Then pull the machine away from the wall or any other obstacle that prevents easy access to both the front and back. If you
own an AT, be sure the key lock is set to the "open" position.

Next, remove the screws in the back of the machine that hold   Removing the
the cover in place. As Figure 4-1 shows, these are located at the   cover
four corners and at the top center (older PCs have fewer screws).
An ordinary screwdriver will do the job (a nutdriver is easiest).
There's no need to unplug the various cables in the back of the machine. However, some ATs have a "vanity plate" mounted on the
back. This decorative plastic plate, which covers the mechanics on
the back of the machine, spruces up a computer that sits on a desk
that doesn't abut a wall. If a vanity plate is installed, you won't be
able to gain access to the five screws without removing it, and that
requires pulling out all the cables in the back of the machine. The
plate is held in place by several swatches of velcro. A few gentle
tugs will remove it.

It's easy enough to reinsert the power and keyboard cables later,   Cables in back
because IBM has designed them differently and made it impossible
to make mistakes. However, the cables that plug into the adapter
cards vary from machine to machine, so you'll want to keep track
of what goes where. An easy way is to attach a piece of masking
tape to each cable, writing on it the position of the card it plugs
into. Even if you don't have a vanity plate to remove, you'll need to
keep track of cables that aren't screwed in tight, because they may
become detached while you're busy installing the drive.

Now you can remove the cover. Pull it straight forward until it   The catch
will go no further, then lift it upward from the front, as shown in
Figure 4-2. The upward motion is required because there's a catch
at the top of the cover that stops the cover from sliding all the way
forward. It's easy to get the cover off, but the catch can make it a
little tricky putting it back on. When you later replace the cover,

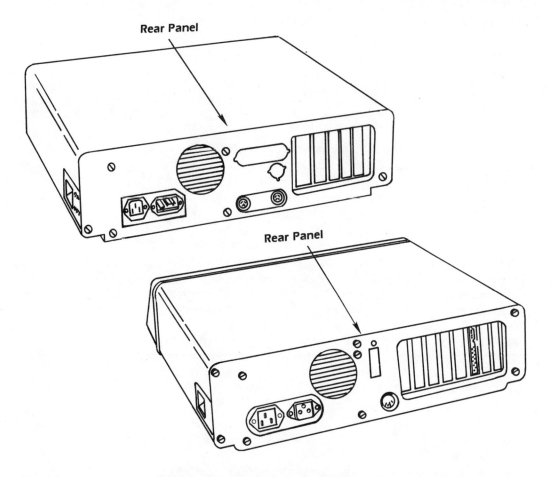

Figure 4-1 **Back panels of PCs and ATs**

you must reverse the motion, approaching the machine with the
cover tilted upward, then tilting it down flat and pushing it forward.

Incidentally, sometimes cables from adapter cards run *over* other
cards, and the catch on the top of the cover may catch on these as
it is pulled forward. So pull forward very slowly and reach back
and loosen the adapter cables if there is a problem.

Inserting the
controller card

If you've never installed an adapter card in a slot, you'll find that
it's very simple. Place the card as close to the disk drive as possible. Many adapters project sockets out the back of the machine, so
there is an opening behind the slot. This opening is covered by an
oblong plate to keep out dust. Take out the screw that holds the
plate in place and remove it. Then place the controller card over

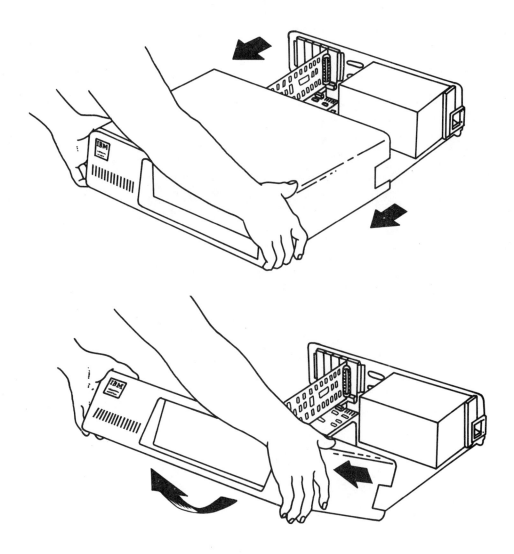

Figure 4-2 **Removing the system cover**

the slot and gently rock it back and forth (toward the front and
back of the machine) until it slips into the socket. Fasten the card
with the screw that held the plate and store the plate someplace
where it can be found if you need to replace it someday. The card
may come with a plastic guide that attaches to the front end of the
computer. It stops the card from swaying when the computer is

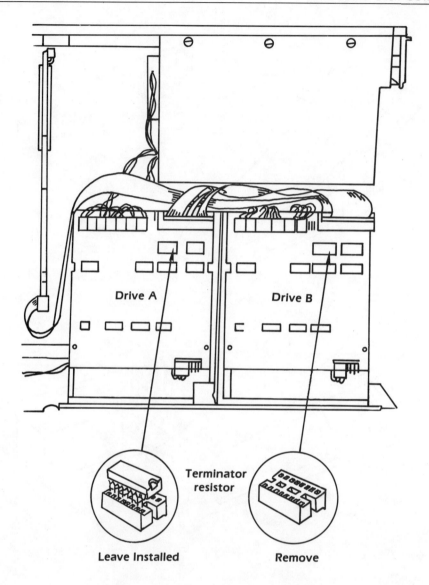

Figure 4-3 **Layout inside PCs and ATs**

bumped. Be sure to snap the guide into place before inserting the adapter. It has a definite top and bottom; so be careful that it's oriented like others in the machine.

Be careful not to drop screws into the computer. If you do, be sure to get them out of the machine before switching on power again. When a screw falls into a hard-to-reach nook, wrap a little masking tape around the end of a screwdriver with the sticky side facing out. Then press it against the screw and carefully lift it out.

Figure 4-3 shows the disk drive bays in PCs and AT machines. In most PCs, one bay is filled with two half-height floppy drives, and the other is empty but for a face plate that blocks the opening in the front of the machine. Face plates install in different ways, usually by a clip that slides on and off with the help of a screwdriver or another pointed tool. Because the designs vary, you'll have to check the instructions or just play around with it until you figure out how it is held in place.

The disk drive bays

Older PCs may have full-height drives installed. One of these must be removed if the hard drive will be mounted internally. In PCs, both floppy disk drives and hard disk drives simply slide into the bay, where they are affixed by a screw on each side. These screws are the same size as those that bolt down adapter cards. A floppy drive is removed simply by undoing these screws and pulling out the cables that connect it to the floppy disk adapter card and to the computer's power supply. These cables are designed so that they can't be plugged in the wrong way.

Removing a floppy drive

When two floppy disk drives are installed, they are not identical. One is equipped with a **terminator resistor** that is mounted on the top of the drive. The resistor usually looks like an ordinary integrated circuit chip. Its location varies from drive to drive; if the drives are the same model, you can usually identify the resistor by looking for a socket that is filled on one and empty on the other.

Terminator resistor

You'll find that the cable from the floppy disk controller has two plugs in it, one in the middle of the cable. It is the plug at the end of the cable that is connected to the drive with the terminator resistor. You should remove the drive connected to the *middle* of the controller cable and keep the one with terminator resistor. If, for some reason, you want to keep the other drive instead, you must move the terminator resistor to that drive and connect the drive to the end of the controller cable. When the drive with the terminator resistor is not in the desired position, you'll find it easier to move the drive between bays than to change the chip.

The location of the terminator resistor varies from drive to drive, so you will need a diagram. When changing chips, you must be sure that you and your clothing are free of static electricity. Don't wear

Removing the terminator resistor

artificial fabrics that "cling," and always touch the power supply casing before touching a chip (this siphons off electricity from your body). It's best to pull chips with a special tong-shaped tool sold for a couple of dollars in any store offering electronic components. Place the tool around the ends of the chip and gently toggle it back and forth, lightly pulling upward. You can pry a chip up with a small knife, but it must be done very carefully. If the chip suddenly comes loose at one end, pins will be bent or broken. Then you'll have to replace the chip, and that can be a king-sized headache. Avoid changing the terminator resistor unless you really have to.

AT floppy disk drives

You'll have none of these complications if you own an AT because the machine has room for a second hard disk drive beneath the two floppies. Although you wouldn't guess it from the front of the cabinet, when the cover is removed a face plate is exposed that projects to the bottom of the machine. Two screws hold the plate, and when it is removed, an empty cavity is exposed. This cavity is just large enough to hold a half-height drive. As in a PC, the floppy drives in an AT connect to the controller card by a single cable that has connectors in its middle and end (this cable attaches to the controller at the point marked "J1").

Guide rails

While PC disk drives are held in place by screws, IBM responded to the proliferation of half-height drives by introducing **guide rails** in ATs—strips of plastic screwed into the sides of disk drives so that rails run along both sides of the drives, from front to back. The sides of the drive bays are notched to receive these rails, so the drives slide in like drawers, as shown in Figure 4-4. Recall that in Chapter 3 we warned you to be sure that guide rails are included when you purchase a drive. To stop the drives from sliding out the front of the machine, small metal retainers are screwed in at the front of notches, blocking the rails. These in turn are hidden by the computer cover. No doubt this all sounds quite complicated, but you'll understand the system the minute you set eyes upon it. Note that the rails have a front and back and that the tapered ends of the rails point to the back of the drive.

Inserting a drive in a PC

In a PC or XT, the drives slide into place, and the mounting screws are attached through the metal siding. This would be simple enough were it not that it can be a terrible bother to reach all the screw holes. Only the outside hole for the rightmost drive bay is easily accessed. The screw holes between the two drive bays are accessible by removing a drive in the opposite bay and reaching through with a short screwdriver. The holes closest to the slots can be reached only by removing most of the cards. This is a very large bother and probably not worth the trouble.

REAR VIEW

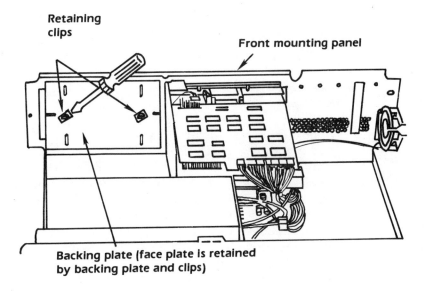

Retaining clips

Front mounting panel

Backing plate (face plate is retained by backing plate and clips)

FRONT VIEW

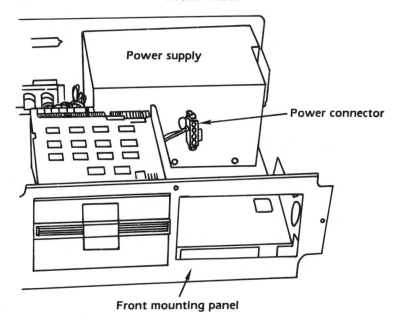

Power supply

Power connector

Front mounting panel

Figure 4-4 **Installing the drive**

Inserting a drive in an AT

In an AT, it's easy to install either a first or second drive. The full-height drive bay (entirely enclosed by the cabinet) is easily accessed. When installing a second, half-height hard drive, just remove the plate covering the compartment beneath the floppy drives and insert the drive. You may need to screw the guide rails onto the drive first. Then replace the plate to hold the drive firmly in place.

Cabling the drive

Cabling is equally simple. On both PCs and ATs, two kinds of **ribbon cable** (flat, multiwire cable) stretch from the controller card to the drive, a **data cable** and a **control cable**. The control cable may be shared by two hard disks, like the cable that serves floppy disk drives. One drive connects to a socket at the middle of the cable and one at the end. The control cable is wider than the data cable. When two drives are installed, each has its own data cable. Sometimes hard disk kits are shipped with a control cable that accommodates only one drive. When you add a second drive, you'll need to replace the control cable with one that has two sockets. You *always* need to obtain a second data cable when you add a second drive.

The cables connect to the drives in a way that you can't put them on backward. But they meet the controller card through an array of pins that jut from the card surface, and it's easy to reverse the connection. One edge of the cable will be color-coded, usually with red or blue. The colored edge goes to "pin 1," which may or may not be labeled. Generally, the cables plug into the controller so that the specially colored edge of the cable is directed downward in PCs or XTs or toward the back of the machine in ATs. Because there aren't hard and fast standards, read the instructions carefully.

Power cables

You'll also need to connect cables from the power supply. These are easily spotted protruding from the silver or black box at the right-rear of the computer. They also are made in a way that they can't be inserted upside down. The power cables tend to be a little harder to connect to a drive because of the angle of their connection. So attach them first. Incidentally, you'll find all sorts of harrowing warnings about imminent electrocution plastered all over the power supply. These refer to the inside of the metal box that you see. You can touch the box to your heart's delight without danger. But never, *ever* try to enter the box, even when the machine is unplugged.

Cabling is much easier while the drive protrudes from the front of the machine. Push the drive all the way back and screw it in place only after the cabling is finished. Also take care to channel the cables behind the drives while you still have room to do so. When many

drives are installed, there's barely enough room for all the wires. If
you're installing a second hard disk on an AT, you'll find that IBM
has positioned the middle connector of the control cable at the back
of the empty chamber beneath the floppy disk drives.

An AT uses two extra cables. One is the cable that attaches the   MIscellaneous
controller to the hard disk indicator light on the front on the ma-   cables
chine. This cable extends from the controller card to a little box
that sits behind the light. IBM ATs also have a **grounding cable**
that runs from drive to drive. You'll see thin black cables reaching
to special connection points on the IBM drives. Note that these
cables may be absent from an AT clone. If the drive you're installing isn't accompanied by instructions for this cabling, forget about
it. Figure 4-5 summarizes the cabling in an AT.

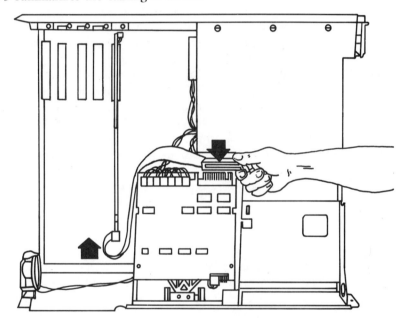

Figure 4-5 **Cabling the drive**

Installing a Drive in PS/2 Machines

You're unlikely ever to need to install a drive in a PS/2 machine,
because most will ship with a hard disk, and most have no room
for a second internal hard drive. Still, let's take a quick look at how
their drives are connected.

The Model 30

The PS/2 machines adopt markedly different approaches to hard disk installation. Of the four models discussed here, only the Model 30 keeps the drive at the front of the machine. The Model 30, not intended to be a high-powered computer, was designed to hold only one hard disk. The drive must be specially made for this computer because it holds the controller card on board. A cable stretches a short distance from the back of the drive to a special socket nearby on the mother board (next to the socket for the optional 8087 mathematics coprocessor chip).

The Model 50

The Model 50 relies on a very unusual installation scheme. The innermost slot receives the hard disk controller card, and the drive is positioned immediately next to it, so that it plugs directly into the card. Two plastic tabs at the other end of the drive hold it in place. The drive can be removed in seconds. It rests on an intermediary board that is in turn supported by the mother board. The controller accepts only one drive; a second drive would have to be installed externally.

The Model 60 and Model 80

Ironically, of the PS/2 line the most advanced machines resemble the earlier PCs. Hard disk drives connect to a controller card through separate control and data cables, and the controller can handle two drives. The drives, positioned toward the back of the machine, are held in place by a mechanism that tightens against rails running along the sides of the drive. Incidentally, the Model 80 comes with a very fast ESDI controller as standard equipment; the same controller is an option on the Model 60.

Installing External Drives

Installing an external drive is much easier than installing an internal one. You won't have to deal with mounting the drive, which may entail pulling out floppies to reach screw holes, installing rails (in ATs), and affixing bezels. Nor will you need to contemplate installing a new power supply, because the drive has its own. But you *do* have to think about where you will place the drive, and in the long run that consideration may cause you more grief than the momentary trouble of mounting one internally.

Cabling problems

Although the drive can be placed some distance from the machine using long ribbon cables (if you can find some) it must not be hidden away in a drawer or other sealed environment. It requires room-temperature air for cooling, and the air in any closed space will become quite hot. Even if the drive performs properly in confinement, high temperatures could lower its reliability.

Because external drives are small, they are more likely targets for mistreatment. If the drive sits beside the computer, ensure that it isn't shoved around and that objects aren't placed on it, or vice versa. *Don't* place the drive on top of the video monitor; by doing so, you'll block the monitor's cooling vents and increase the drive's own heat load.

Positioning the drive

Replacing the Power Supply

Generally, only IBM PC owners may need to replace the power supply when they add a hard disk. The 130-watt supply on an IBM XT (and many PC clones) should be more than adequate to support even two hard disks. Any power supply has a sticker giving its rating.

Ironically, the machines that need power most have the smallest supplies. The earliest PCs used 16K memory chips. By today's standards, memory was fantastically expensive then. A machine loaded to the 640K limit required 360 chips! Power consumption was tremendous, and nearly every other component in the computer required more power than similar components do today. Still, some PCs can run a hard disk drive without changing the power supply, particularly if the slots are not filled. (Memory and modems draw the most current.)

If power is insufficient, you'll probably know it right away. Once the hard disk is installed, you'll be booting up from a floppy in drive A. Even if the new drive is defective, it shouldn't interfere with this normal booting procedure. So if the machine freezes when you turn it on, it's time to shop for another power supply.

Anticipating insufficient power

Sometimes the power supply seems adequate, but the machine crashes periodically. If the machine has worked flawlessly before you installed the hard disk, and the disk has worked well since, repeated crashes indicate either that you are operating at the edge of the power supply's capacity or that overheating is interfering with the drive. After a crash, quickly go into the computer and see if the drive is hot (it won't burn your fingers if overheated, but it will be decidedly hot, not just warm). If cooling seems adequate, your best bet is to install a new supply and see what happens. When crashes continue, it's time to seek outside help.

You may wonder why a power supply is adequate some of the time, but not always. For starters, floppy disk drives add to the power burden, and when they start up, they pull extra power. DOS uses only one floppy at a time, but it leaves a floppy spinning for a

Sporadic power failures

short time after it is finished to avoid repeated starts and stops in close succession. Sometimes one floppy drive starts up while a second still turns, pulling an exceptional amount of power. Because two floppies are seldom used simultaneously on a machine equipped with a hard disk, this situation may be avoided for a long while until one day it occurs and crashes the machine. In addition, higher temperatures raise the resistance of electronic components, making them require more power. On a hot day, your whole computer may need a little extra power; if you're operating near its limit, the machine can lock up for no apparent reason.

Noise

You might want to save yourself some inconvenience and delay by just replacing the power supply whether it's actually needed or not. Discount houses offer upgrades for as little as $75. But keep in mind that your new power supply may be as noisy as a vacuum cleaner, particularly if it's a cheap one. One reviewer found that the typical replacement power supply is five to ten times louder than the original and actually two to four times louder once installed. There is good reason to try to keep the original supply if you can (the early PC power supplies were especially quiet).

Quiet power supplies

At least one company makes super-quiet power supplies. *The Silencer* from PC Cooling Systems (Figure 4-6), tested by an independent party, was found to be 84% quieter than a standard PC supply, in spite of its 155-watt rating. Paradoxically, this blissful quietude is achieved by using two fans instead of one. Because there are two, the fans can run more slowly, and this feature combined with a special blade design makes for much quieter operation. Unfortunately, a quiet power supply costs at least 50% more than an ordinary one.

Power supply quality

When a short circuit occurs in the machine, the power supply ought to shut itself off. All IBM power supplies are of this "total-shutdown" variety. But many models on the market are of the "current-limiting" type, which refuse to supply power beyond a certain level; others offer no protection at all. The only real danger of a short circuit arises when someone pulls or inserts a card in a slot without first shutting off the power. This is a pretty dumb move, but an amazing number of computer aficionados admit to having done it absentmindedly at one time or another. You should know that many, perhaps most, of the inexpensive power supplies on the market don't offer adequate short circuit protection. If the worst happens, you could "fry" the electronics of your system board and every board in the slots; that is, you could pretty much lose the whole computer.

Figure 4-6 **A quiet power supply**

IBM sells an XT power supply, but at a hefty $325 price. You can buy a good power supply much more reasonably. The problem is in knowing which ones perform "total-shutdown." Even those having this feature aren't ordinarily marked as such. Many vendors will assure you that the supply is "exactly like" an IBM supply, but most won't know for sure. A good supply may come in a plain brown box, a bad one in fancy packaging. And, because most cheap replacement supplies are made in East Asia, you may require an act of Congress to gain reimbursement for damage done by an inferior unit. Still, there haven't been many reports of damage from poor power supplies; if you're on a tight budget, an inexpensive unit may be all right. If you want to play it safe, buy the unit from a domestic company with written specifications guaranteeing the supply's quality.

Installing a power supply is easy—if you bought the right one. The power supply has two connectors that plug into the system board, and many clones use plugs different from those in IBM machines. The IBM system board uses rectangular pins 0.095 by 0.036 inches. Some compatibles use 0.045-inch square pins. Because one variety of pin is square and one not, it's easy to tell them apart. Be sure to check the shape of the pins before you go shopping.

First, of course, you must remove the older supply. Its label will adamantly warn you to keep out, that you can kill yourself. Again,

Choosing a replacement power supply

Power supply installation

this message refers to the consequences of going *inside* the power supply. The supply is contained in a metal box, which you can handle all you like without danger. Inside the box, high-voltage capacitors hold power for a long time after power is shut off or the machine is unplugged. If you have an insatiable curiosity to find out what's inside—**don't!**

Cabling the supply

Four screws on the back of the computer hold the power supply in place. Before removing the screws, disconnect the cables joining the supply from disk drives and from the computer's system board. Two cables plug into the system board just beside the supply. The connectors snap into place; to remove them, push the end of a screwdriver between the snap and the plug to pull back the snap. The connector closest to the back panel is "P8," the other is "P9." The replacement supply may have its two connectors labeled with these letters. If you can, check that they are labeled when you buy the unit. Be *very* careful not to mix them up when you insert the new supply. If labels are missing, observe the color coding of the wires on the original drive before you disconnect it.

Adding extra cooling

If overheating is crashing your system, you can increase ventilation by adding an auxiliary fan, such as *Turbo-Cool*, also made by PC Cooling Systems. It hangs on the back of the machine (Figure 4-7), quietly forcing in extra air. One test showed the fan lowering the computer's internal rise in temperature from 30 degrees to 15. Even without a specific equipment failure, you may want to add extra cooling if you find that components become noticeably hot to the touch. Overheating can shorten the lifespan of all parts of a drive and contributes to the degeneration of electronic components—the leading cause of drive failure.

Sealing the case

Be sure to keep the back of your computer sealed. When the machine is new, a metal plate is installed beside each slot on the back panel. These plates are removed, one by one, as adapter cards are added to the machine. Often, when a card is later removed, the plate is nowhere to be found. Gradually, more and more holes are left open in the back of the machine. At first glance, these holes seem to promote ventilation. Actually, the holes interfere with the internal ventilation scheme. Air that would otherwise be forced to circulate across the hard disk and other components instead escapes out the back. You should keep the plates in place when no card is installed.

Improving ventilation

You can improve the ventilation on an IBM PC (not necessarily on clones). When you remove the cover, you'll see a strip of slots along the *bottom* of the front panel. Take one-inch wide plastic tape and block this strip across the entire width of the machine.

Figure 4-7 **Add-on cooling**

Paradoxical though it may seem, this measure *increases* ventilation across the slots. Later IBM PCs were shipped with this modification already made. And at least one expansion card manufacturer includes a piece of tape with its shipments.

Replacing the ROM BIOS

The **BIOS** in early PCs lacked an important routine that causes the operating system to search for hard disks and link them into operations. When hard disks were first sold for these machines, special code had to be loaded from diskette every time the computer was booted. But this approach didn't allow booting from the hard disk.

Following the introduction of the XT, IBM made available a replacement BIOS chip that contained the special routine. This chip is only one of several read-only chips in the machine. Alas, IBM discontinued shipments in mid-1987. We explained in Chapter 3 how to get one now. Clear installation instructions should accompany the replacement chip, so we won't go into the specifics here.

Finding the BIOS
date

To find out if your early PC needs a replacement chip, follow these instructions exactly. Place the main DOS diskette in drive A and type **DEBUG** to load the DOS debugging program. The cursor will be set beside a dash, and you should enter:

```
D  FØØØ:FF7F
```

Then strike the Enter key. Several lines of symbols will appear, some of them random, some intelligible. At the bottom right you'll see a date. If the date is earlier than October 28, 1982, you'll need the replacement BIOS.

Reconfiguring the System

On a PC-class machine, once the drive is installed, it's installed. There's nothing more to do. In particular, the dip switches shouldn't be changed. They reflect the number of *floppy* disk drives in the machine; there is no setting for hard drives. DOS names the first drive **C:** even when only one floppy drive is installed.

The SETUP pro-
gram

AT-class machines require a tad more work. Usually, all you need to do is boot the machine from drive A and run the *SETUP* program. This program comes with the *Guide To Operations*. Just type **SETUP** and the program will ask you a few simple questions about the equipment installed. It will ask for the "drive type"—that is, the code number that corresponds to the drive's geometry. The number may be written in the drive's documentation; if not, call the vendor. The information you enter is stored in a special chip (the **"CMOS chip"**) that also keeps the date and time. Thus, while you're at it, you can reset the system clock. This chip is powered by a small battery that is easily visible on the system board. Be aware that this battery runs out after roughly two years. Keep a replacement handy when the time nears.

Nonstandard
drives

If you're installing a drive with a non-standard geometry, it will be accompanied with special instructions and software. The CMOS chip can record the specifications of a non-standard drive geometry. The software holds these specifications, and installs them on the chip. Or, you may want to use *SpeedStor* from Storage Dimensions. This program, which we'll discuss later, performs all aspects of hard disk setup and formatting and is well equipped to deal with unusual drive geometries.

In special cases, the geometry of an unusual drive cannot be kept   Add-on ROM
on the CMOS chip. This often is the case when a high-capacity
drive is installed as a network server. The system software will demand that the drive geometry be described by the BIOS. The only
solution is to replace or extend the BIOS to include the geometry
used by the drive. Storage Dimensions offers a chip set for this purpose. If the idea of pulling chips off the system board doesn't ap-
peal to you, consider the *DUB-14* add-on board from Golden Bow
Systems; the chips are mounted on a board that slips into a spare
slot. If you're shopping for a large drive for a local-area network
(LAN), ask the manufacturer whether you'll need to change the
BIOS chips.

Mopping Up

After your new pride and joy is merrily whirling along, do a
good job of mopping up. Place the drive documentation in your
system library. What? You don't keep a system library? A *library*
simply means one place for all of your computer documentation.
It may be only a file folder or clearly marked manilla envelope.
Nothing compounds your exasperation more when you have
trouble with the drive than not being able to find the documentation. Write on the documentation the vendor's address, the duration of the warranty, its starting date, and the technical
support phone number.

If a utility diskette accompanies the drive, you may want to make
a copy—just in case. File the diskette away, and, if your diskette library is as messy as most people's, record the diskette's location in
the documentation. Finally, set aside the original packaging in case
you need to send the drive through the mail for repairs. If someone
else might throw out the box, label it with a message. You may
want to record the location of the packaging in the documentation.
Although few of us often rise to these sublime heights of organization, the effort is bound to pay off sooner or later.

Formatting

Once the disk is successfully installed, the machine will boot normally from a floppy in drive A. Although drive C now exists as a
physical entity, DOS cannot recognize it, so you must resist the

temptation to make the hard disk the current drive by entering **C:**.
First, the drive must be formatted at low level, partitioned, then
formatted at high level, and during these three steps the current
drive remains drive A (or another already existing drive).

Recall from Chapter 2 that low-level formatting defines the sectors on the drive, that partitioning creates the master boot record
and sets aside some or all of the cylinders for use by DOS (as op-
posed to other operating systems), and that high-level formatting
writes the DOS boot record, root directory, file allocation tables,
and system files (IBMBIO.COM, IBMDOS.COM, and COM-
MAND.COM).

Formatting utilities

Many drives are delivered with low-level formatting in place.
Some manufacturers (or vendors) even partition the drive and
perform high-level formatting at the factory. In the latter case,
the entire disk is partitioned for DOS. While you may not have
to bother with any formatting at all, it's worth understanding the
process, because sometimes it's necessary to *re*format hard disks.
Particularly as hard disks age, the original formatting markings
gradually deteriorate (Chapter 9 discusses utilities that find and
restore failing magnetic traces). Reformatting may also be required after a serious head crash. Or, if you add accelerator
hardware to the machine, you may want to reformat the disk to
optimize the interleave.

As a general rule, you should use the low-level formatting program supplied with a disk rather than a separate utility because
some disks have special information encoded on them that an ordinary format program will wipe out. Some, for example, have bad-
track information written on the disk, which is used by the accompanying format program. Another example is found in some hard
disk cards, which keep an 18th sector on each track; these may be
substituted for a defective sector so that a whole track doesn't
need to be marked as unusable.

Low-level Formatting

Low-level formatting programs are very easy to run. The instructions that accompany the drive tell which program on the utility
diskette is the one to use. If you need to reformat a disk and
lack a low-level formatting program, try phoning the vendor for
one. Otherwise, you'll need to buy one, usually as part of a
larger disk utility package. IBM supplies one in its Advanced Diagnostics, which cost roughly twice as much as others. The

HFORMAT program provided by the Kolod Research Inc. is shipped with the *HOPTIMUM* interleave-optimization program, which we'll discuss in Chapter 7.

ROM code

A few drives adopt an unusual, and slightly intimidating, approach to low-level formatting. They place the formatting program on ROM on the controller card. There's nothing wrong with a program sitting in hardware instead of a diskette, but how do you get it going? It's done by loading the DOS *DEBUG* program, which resides on a DOS diskette as **DEBUG.COM.** Instructions that accompany the drive explain a short sequence of keystrokes that make the computer start executing the format program. This all seems like gobbledygook, so don't even *try* to understand it. Just type in *exactly* what the instructions say. This approach scares the gee-willikers out of computer novices, and fewer and fewer makers resort to it.

The drive specifier

Once loaded, low-level format programs prompt you for various information. Sometimes the information is input on the command line. The first issue is the drive specifier that will be used, such as **C** or **D**. When a first hard disk is installed, this parameter may often be omitted, and the software defaults to naming the drive **C**. But when you are installing a second disk or *reformatting* a disk, this information may be essential to direct the program to the proper drive. Some programs request a drive *number*. The numbering refers to hard drives only; so a first hard disk is number **1**.

Bad tracks

Most drives are shipped with a **bad track table** affixed to the drive. This table lists the numbers of tracks that failed in the manufacturer's tests of the drive. By entering the track numbers, the formatting program can mark these tracks off bounds. You'll be asked for a **side number** and **track number**. The side number, of course, refers to the platter side that the bad track resides on.

At this technical level, numbers are sometimes given in **hexadecimal** form. These funny numbers use the letters A through F as well as the usual numerals 0 through 9. For example, the bad track table might list **Side 0, Track 3E** as a bad track. You don't have to understand the numbers to type them in. But be sure that you're entering numbers in the right form when you use a low-level format program not supplied with the drive. For example, *HFORMAT* takes *decimal* numbers. A drive could list bad tracks as hexadecimal numbers without your realizing it, because many hexadecimal numbers contain only numerals. If you entered a hexadecimal value into a program expecting decimal values, the wrong track would be sequestered. If you're unsure, call the drive manufacturer.

Setting the inter-leave

All low-level format programs ask for an **interleave factor**. We've expressed interleave values as **6:1** or **3:1**, but formatting programs usually take a single numeral, such as **6** or **3**. We'll talk about finding the optimal interleave in a moment. As a rule of thumb, ordinary XT-class machines should use an interleave of **5**, and AT-class machines should use **2**.

Fancy format programs like *HFORMAT* offer various extra features of interest only to the technically sophisticated. For example, you can set the starting and ending cylinders for the format. This lets you reformat a single partition without altering data elsewhere on the disk.

Testing

Low-level format programs test the disk after writing upon it, checking the integrity of the sectors created. As we'll see in Chapter 9, testing can be very elaborate, and most format programs fall far short of the state of the art. Still, a good low-level format program tests and retests (*HFORMAT* does it 32 times). This testing adds to the time that the format takes. Generally, a low-level format takes about one to one and a half minutes per megabyte. So a 20-megabyte drive takes 20 to 30 minutes. However, a formatting program that performs extensive testing could take an hour or longer. Most programs give some feedback on the screen, telling which cylinder is being processed. Others make no changes on the display until the format is complete. These may leave you wondering whether the machine has crashed. Be patient—low-level formatting takes time. But if the format on a 20- or 30-megabyte disk isn't complete after two hours, and there are no changes on the display, it's time to seek help (unless the instructions tell you otherwise).

Optimizing the Interleave

Once a disk has been formatted at low level, a utility may be run that analyzes whether the current interleave is optimal or not. If, as a result of its tests, the program suggests a better interleave, you must repeat the low-level format using a different interleave factor. As you know from our discussion in Chapter 2, there is really no such thing as an "optimal interleave," because every application program accesses the disk in its own pattern. The "optimal interleave" prescribed for disks usually refers to disk behavior in simple reads and writes of sequential files through DOS, in which the file moves between disk and memory without any intermediate processing.

The *HOPTIMUM* program from Kolod Research Inc. performs this test. The program goes to work, reformatting a group of cylinders in every possible interleave for the drive, clocking the read and write speeds at each setting. When it's finished, it reports the optimal setting. Recent versions can reformat the disk to the optimum interleave without distrubing data. We'll discuss this further in Chapter 7.

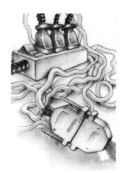

Partitioning

The DOS partitioning program *FDISK* is found on one of the DOS diskettes as **FDISK.EXE**. Prior to DOS version 3.3, partitioning was uncomplicated. *FDISK* simply created the master boot record, telling where the partitions begin, and it set up the boot record in the DOS partition (these concepts are explained in Chapter 2). Recently, matters have become more complicated.

Let's look at the simpler, pre-version 3.3 case first. You load FDISK from the DOS diskette in drive A by typing **FDISK**. The screen displays:

The FDISK menu

```
FDISK Options

Current Fixed Disk Drive: 1
Choose one of the following

1. Create DOS Partition
2. Change Active Partition
3. Delete DOS Partition
4. Display Partition Data
5. Select Next Fixed Disk Drive

Enter choice: [1]
```

The usual choice, number 1, is offered by the program, so you need only strike the Enter key to select it. Other choices are made by striking 2 through 5, then Enter. By choosing option 1, you'll receive the message:

```
DOS partition already exists
```

if the DOS partition has already been set up or else:

```
Create DOS Partition
```

```
Current Fixed Disk Drive: 1
```

```
Do you wish to use the entire fixed

disk for DOS [Y/N]..............? [Y]
```

Again, the program offers the most common choice, in which the entire drive is devoted to DOS. Just strike Enter to select it. Finally, after the drive starts up briefly, the message appears:

```
System will now restart
```

```
Insert DOS diskette in drive A:

Press any key when ready. . .
```

Alternative
commands

When you strike any key, DOS reboots from drive A, presenting the usual date and time queries. The process takes only a minute, because only a few sectors on the disk are affected.

The other FDISK options are seldom used. In the first option, if you type **N** when asked if the entire disk should be used for DOS, FDISK tells how many cylinders are available, and asks how many should be devoted to DOS. The second option lets you change the partition used for booting. The third selection deletes the DOS partition from the disk, destroying any data it contains (in fact the data remains, but access to it is lost; it can sometimes be regained by recreating the partition on exactly the same cylinders). The fourth choice displays information about the disk partitions. It displays information like this:

```
Display Partition Information


Current Fixed Disk Drive: 1


Partition Status    Type    Start End Size
    1        A      DOS      000  149  150
    2        N    non-DOS    150  249  100
```

The Status reads **A** when the partition is active, **N** when not. The "Start" and "End" columns give cylinder numbers (partition A extends from cylinder 0 to cylinder 149), and the "Size" is reported as the number of cylinders allocated to the partition. Finally, the last selection in the FDISK menu lets you select a second hard disk as the one for FDISK to work on. Incidentally, the DOS documentation for these commands is uncharacteristically clear.

Starting from version 3.3, DOS can overcome the 32-megabyte limit. With the introduction of 40-megabyte drives (and larger) in the PS/2 line, DOS *had* to be modified to allow it to use the entire disk. Unfortunately, this was done by permitting *multiple* DOS partitions, not by making a single huge DOS partition possible.

Partitioning under DOS 3.3

In the new system, only two partitions may belong to DOS: a **primary partition** and an **extended partition**. The primary partition is exactly like DOS partitions in earlier DOS versions, and it is used for booting. An extended DOS partition can be as large as the drive itself, but it may be subdivided, with each subdivision, or **volume**, acting as a **logical drive**. This means that each volume is given a drive specifier from **D:** to **Z:**, and, from the user's point of view, it acts as an independent drive, with its own directory tree. A volume may be as small as a single cylinder and as large as 32 megabytes but no larger. Hence, the 32-megabyte limit on file size remains in force.

Primary and extended partitions

Figure 4-8 diagrams this system. In the diagram, logical drives **C:** through **F:** are contained on a single hard disk. Note the introduction of **logical drive tables**. Analogous to the partition table in the master boot record, they reside in the **extended boot record** that begins each volume of the extended DOS partition (calling these "boot records" is a misnomer, because they're not for booting). The logical drive table for the first volume tells the location of the next and so on.

124 THE HARD DISK COMPANION

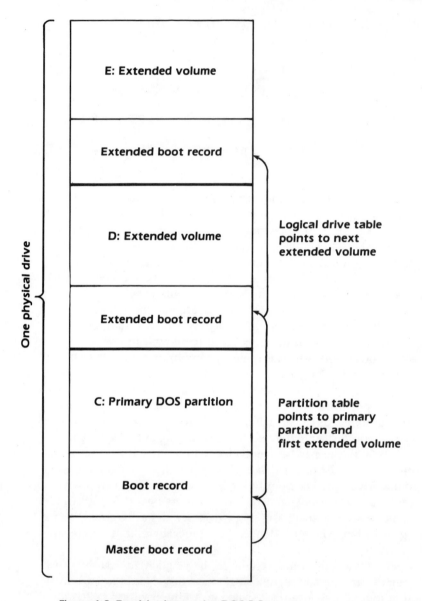

Figure 4-8 **Partitioning under DOS 3.3**

Cluster size

Oddly, DOS creates eight-sector clusters when a volume is under 16 megabytes and four-sector clusters when volumes are larger. To conserve disk space, avoid small volumes. Thus, on a 40-megabyte disk, you shouldn't give 32 megabytes to the primary partition.

Make it small enough that the extended partition can hold 16 megabytes or more.

FDISK's opening menu in DOS 3.3 is identical to earlier versions. **FDISK in DOS 3.3** When you select the "Create DOS Partition" option, the screen displays:

```
Create DOS Partition

Current Fixed Disk Drive: 1


    1. Create Primary DOS partition
    2. Create Extended DOS partition


Enter choice: [1]

Press ESC to return to FDISK Options
```

The program continues with easy-to-follow prompts.

High-level Formatting

High-level formatting takes longer than seems necessary. Strictly, all this formatting must do is write a boot sector, the root directory, two copies of the file allocation table, and the DOS files IBMBIO.COM, IBMDOS.COM, and COMMAND.COM. But FORMAT.COM takes about a minute for every megabyte of disk space. During this time, it takes a last look for bad sectors, and when it finds them, it marks them off-bounds in the file allocation table.

Start the program by placing the DOS diskette (or, better, a copy) in drive A and enter:

```
FORMAT C: /S
```

The /S switch makes the program move the three DOS system files to the disk. Then, in DOS versions 3.0 and later, the message appears:

```
WARNING, ALL DATA ON NON-REMOVABLE DISK

DRIVE C: WILL BE LOST!

Proceed with Format [Y/N]?
```

This message protects the disk from accidental reformatting (we'll talk about this danger at length in Chapter 9). Earlier DOS versions gave no such warning. If you use a pre-3.x DOS version and you find yourself about to accidentally reformat the hard disk, *get away from the keyboard*. While Ctrl-Break or Ctrl-Alt-Del ought to get you out of trouble, the precise timing of the keystrokes is important. If you hit Del before Ctrl and Alt, formatting may begin and continue for a fraction of a second—long enough to damage crucial DOS structures on the disk. The safest thing to do is to reach around the side of the machine and turn it off.

Once formatting is underway, the screen displays only the message:

```
FORMATTING...
```

It won't give you any idea how far along the process has gone. Finally, you'll see the message:

```
Format complete

System transferred
```

When finished, the *FORMAT* program tells you how many bytes are available on the disk, and how many are taken by the system files, the root directory, and the two copies of the file allocation table.

The volume label

Using the /V switch in the FORMAT command causes DOS to prompt you for a *volume label* after formatting is complete. A volume label is a tag up to 11 characters long that identifies the disk. These labels are useful with floppies because they let you identify a diskette without pulling it from the drive. For hard disks, however, it's difficult to think of any reason to have one. Because the label takes up a slot in the root directory, some users find this wasteful. However, the root directory will never approach being full in a well-thought-out file system.

If you do place a volume label on the disk, it will be displayed by the **DIR, CHKDSK**, and **TREE** commands. DOS versions 3.0 and later supply the **LABEL** command to change the volume label. The label ordinarily cannot have spaces in the eleven-character string. You can tricksome versions of DOS into accepting a space by using the /V switch and striking <Enter> when DOS asks for the label. DOS then issues another prompt asking for the label, and at that point you can enter a string with spaces in it.

Occasionally, a disk has many bad sectors on the outermost tracks that hold the root directory, FATs, and DOS files. Some of these *must* be placed on contiguous sectors. When the *FORMAT* program is barred from doing this, it issues an error message and quits. Try reformatting the disk at low-level. This will change the placement of the sectors, and bad spots on the disk surface may move outside sector boundaries. If you don't succeed after several low-level reformattings (and much exasperation), the disk is a dud, and it must be returned to the vendor for another.

The cylinder 0 problem

If you've been using a pre-3.0 version of DOS, installing a new hard disk is just the occasion for an upgrade. DOS is expensive, but more and more valuable commands have been added, as we'll see in coming chapters. While 2.x versions of DOS use an eight-sector cluster size, 3.x versions use only four sectors. We saw in Chapter 3 that a smaller cluster size can make quite a difference in a disk's effective capacity. Also, in DOS 2.x, FORMAT.COM cannot reliably check a 20-megabyte (or larger) disk for errors (the program was designed for the old IBM XT 10-megabyte drives).

Which DOS version?

You may already have a hard disk and want to upgrade to a recent DOS version. If you have been running DOS 2.x, you'll need to reformat the disk, because the file allocation tables are quite different. But moving between like-numbered versions, say, from 3.1 to 3.3, is trivial. Just put the new DOS diskette in drive A and type **SYS C:**. The IBMBIO.COM and IBMDOS.COM files are transferred over. Then use COPY to move over COMMAND.COM. Be sure to purge all old DOS files from disk, because most won't work with the new DOS version. Only then should you introduce the other files from the DOS diskettes.

Switching DOS versions

Some drives are advertised as being "completely preformatted." These receive both low- and high-level formatting before shipment, and they typically are partitioned so that the whole disk is devoted to DOS. But the three copyrighted operating system files cannot be included unless the vendor is selling you DOS as part of the bargain. So these drives are actually *almost* completely formatted. If you buy one, you'll still need to use SYS to install the system files and COPY to install COMMAND.COM.

Preformatted drives

Adding a Second Drive

Adding a second hard disk drive is easy on an AT-class machine, but often problematic on PCs and XTs. In either case, cabling is the same as for dual floppy drives. The drive with the higher specifier (D:) is plugged into the connector at the *center* of the control cable. A terminating resistor will be present on the top of the drive, and it must be removed. In addition, somewhere on the drive will be a jumper or DIP switch that sets the drive specifier to C or D. This jumper is ordinarily set to C at the factory, so it is ignored when only one drive is installed in a machine. The positions of the jumper and terminating resistor must be found in the drive documentation.

On an AT, once the resistor is removed and the drive specifier is set, there's nothing more to do beyond the usual cabling. Afterwards, run the SETUP program and then format the drive as usual. That's all there is to it.

On a PC or XT, however, matters are more complicated. Many controller cards have a jumper that must be changed when a second drive is connected, and some will demand that the second drive be identical to the first. If you lack documentation for the controller card, you may have quite a headache on your hands. Worse, DOS will refuse to partition and format the drive when drive C already exists. The solution is to make the former drive C into drive D and format the new drive as drive C. Hence, the drive must be recabled, and jumpers and terminating resistors must be set accordingly (remember, the terminating resistor goes on the drive connected to the *end* of the control cable). The new drive will readily be installed by FDISK and FORMAT, and DOS will accept the old drive as D. Mistakes occur easily in this process, so be sure to make a double backup of the original hard drive before installing the second.

Creating Oversized Partitions

It's a sign of how far microcomputers have come in a few years that many users find DOS's 32-megabyte partition an obstacle. Although version 3.3 can bring any amount of disk capacity under DOS, it does so by creating a series of partitions, none of which can exceed the 32-megabyte limit. This means that if you have more than 32 megabytes of files, you can't organize them in one directory tree. Worse, if you have a huge database, you may have to cut it in two.

Fortunately, various software houses have responded to this limitation, by offering system software that loads into memory and sits between DOS and the drive. The two best-known such programs are *Vfeature Deluxe* from Golden Bow Systems and *SpeedStor* from Storage Dimensions. Recall that the 32-megabyte limit arises because DOS cannot number sectors beyond the range 0 to 65,535. These programs stay with this scheme but increase the sector size to whatever is required for the desired partition. Partitions as large as 1,000 megabytes are possible.

Of course, larger sectors make for larger clusters, and a good deal of disk space can be wasted. If a 250-megabyte drive is set up as a single DOS partition, the sector size must be 4,096 bytes—eight times the standard 512-byte sector size. A four-sector cluster holds 16,384 bytes. And that will be the minimal unit of allocation. A three-line batch file will take up 16K. And *every file* will, on average, waste eight kilobytes of disk space in its last cluster.

This special formatting software can pull off an even more amazing trick. It can *span* a partition across two hard drives. That is, two *physical* drives become one *logical* drive, accessed through one drive specifier, and one directory tree. This setup does not hinder disk performance, and in some cases actually helps it, because the single logical drive has two sets of read/write heads.

To work this magic, these programs must take the disk through every step of formatting, both low- and high-level. Because they are often applied to super-high-capacity drives, they are specially designed to deal with the problems of unusual drive geometries. They can, however, go to work with drives of any size. Your involvement in disk formatting is limited to entering bad track numbers and installing the DOS files through the SYS command. The rest is a breeze.

Hard disks formatted by this special software cannot be accessed by programs that bypass DOS and go straight to the disk controller. Very few applications do this, but much utility software does. Most high-speed backup programs circumvent DOS. So do many disk-maintenance utilities, including those that boost disk performance, such as disk caching programs and file defragmenters (discussed in Chapter 7), and various disk repair programs (Chapter 9). The makers of partition extension programs have issued their own equivalents to some of these utilities—some of them quite good. Still, you're limiting your options when you use partition-expansion software.

Sector size

Spanning drives

Limitations

An Inside Look: Installing a Second Hard Disk with SpeedStor

SpeedStor from Storage Dimensions is especially suited to installing high-capacity drives on AT-class machines, but it can make hard disk installation easier in most cases, because it handles every step of formatting and partitioning. When you start the program, it asks whether you want to install drive one only, drive two only, or drives one and two. You then specify the partitioning, either as "no DOS partitions," "equal sized partitions," "32-megabyte partitions (as many as will fit)," or "one large partition" greater than 32 megabytes. *SpeedStor* then displays a list of drive manufacturers, as shown in Screen A.

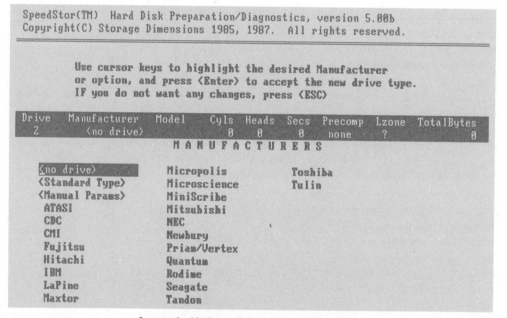

Screen A. **Listing of Drive Manufacturers.**

The program contains information for each model from each manufacturer. For this reason, the program is constantly updated, and if you own a recently released drive, or a very unusual drive, you should check with Storage Dimensions about the necessary version number. Screen B shows a listing of Seagate drives.

```
SpeedStor(TM)  Hard Disk Preparation/Diagnostics, version 5.00b
Copyright(C) Storage Dimensions 1985, 1987.  All rights reserved.


            Please pick the drive model for Drive 2

        Use arrow keys to point, then press ENTER to select.

 Drive   Manufacturer  Model    Cyls  Heads  Secs  Precomp  Lzone  TotalBytes
   2        <no drive>           0     0     0     none     ?          0
                    S e a g a t e   D r i v e   M o d e l s
   ModelName   Cylinders  Heads  Sectors  PreComp  LandingZone  TotalBytes

   ST213        615        2      17       300       615        10,705,920
   ST225        615        4      17       300       615        21,411,840
   ST412        306        4      17       128       305        10,653,696
   ST251        820        6      17       none      820        42,823,680
   ST4026       615        4      17       300       615        21,411,840
   ST4038       733        5      17       300       733        31,900,160
   ST4038M      733        5      17       none      977        31,900,160
   ST4051       977        5      17       none      977        42,519,040
   ST4053       1024       5      17       none      1023       44,564,480
   ST4096       1024       9      17       none      1023       80,216,064
                      Home   PgDn  ↑   ↓   PgUp   End
```

Screen B. **Choosing the Specific Drive.**

SpeedStor cannot locate bad tracks on its own. It prompts you for this information, and you must read it from the label on the drive (or the accompanying documentation) and carefully enter each head and cylinder number. Beyond that, there's nothing more to do but sit back and wait. The program performs low-level formatting and error checking, partitions the disk as you have specified, and then performs high-level formatting. In AT-class machines, it automatically carries out the "setup" procedure that can be so confusing. Because an AT supports a limited number of geometries, **SpeedStor** must maintain a device driver in memory to manage the drive and its non-standard partitions. The driver does not slow down drive operations, but it takes up about 12K of RAM.

Configuring the System

Once high-level formatting is complete, the disk is ready for use. A couple of final chores remain, however. The machine now boots up from the hard disk. (You must leave the door to drive A open because the machine will always look for the DOS diskette there first.) As you probably know, when the machine boots, it looks for the files CONFIG.SYS and AUTOEXEC.BAT in the root directory. Strictly speaking, these files are optional. You can run the machine without them. But they can do much work for you.

Many people learn to use AUTOEXEC on their floppy disk systems, usually to load utility programs, such as *SideKick* or *SuperKey*, and to execute short programs that configure the system, such as a utility that sets the time in DOS from a real-time clock. "AUTOEXEC" means "automatic execution." You're unlikely, though, to have used CONFIG.SYS until you install a hard disk. It configures the operating system in certain ways, particularly for working with a hard disk. Its functions are more technical and harder to understand than those of AUTOEXEC.BAT.

Creating CONFIG.SYS and AUTOEXEC.BAT

Both CONFIG.SYS and AUTOEXEC.BAT are simply ASCII text files. This means that they are made of ordinary characters with no special formatting codes, and the file ends with a Control-Z character (^Z). There are any number of ways of creating a file. Most word processors can do the job (some, like *WordStar*, normally produce non-ASCII files, but they have a special command that strips out formatting information and saves a file in ASCII form). The DOS diskette contains EDLIN, a simple line editor (non-word wrapping text processor) that would be ideal for creating these files were it not deadly hard to use and inflexible as well. Perhaps the easiest way to create the files is by a notepad utility, as in Borland's *Side-Kick*.

Last, but not least, the DOS COPY command can do the job. It is best for short, simple files. To create CONFIG.SYS, you would simply enter:

```
COPY CON: CONFIG.SYS   <Enter>
```

or, if drive C is not the current drive, type:

```
COPY CON: C:CONFIG.SYS   <Enter>
```

Then write each line of the file in succession, followed by a carriage return. For example:

```
BUFFERS=20   <Enter>
FILES=8      <Enter>
```

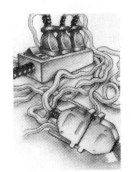

Finally, enter the terminating Control-Z character. Either press the F6 key, which causes DOS to output the character, or hold down the Ctrl key and strike Z. You'll see the symbol ^Z on the screen. When you strike Enter once more, DOS writes the file to disk, displaying:

```
1 File(s) copied
```

Note that word processors automatically insert the Control-Z character. Merely creating an AUTOEXEC.BAT or CONFIG.SYS file doesn't put its commands into action. You must reboot the machine (via Ctrl-Alt-Del), and the commands in the files will be executed as DOS is reloaded.

Configuration Commands

In the preceding example, we showed two lines that you must put in any CONFIG.SYS file. The **BUFFERS** command tells DOS how many buffers to set aside in memory to receive data from the hard disk. Each buffer holds one sector. Because programs tend to access the same sectors again and again, multiple accesses to the same sector can be avoided by *buffering* a number of recently used sectors in memory. In Chapter 7 we'll discuss the logic behind this. For now, you should know that the default value in all DOS versions before 3.3 is only two or three buffers—far too low for efficient hard disk performance. Hence the command:

The BUFFERS command

```
BUFFERS=20
```

which creates 20 buffers. Roughly 10K of memory is consumed by these buffers, but it's well worth it. DOS 3.3 automatically sets a reasonable number of buffers based on the amount of RAM present.

The FILES
command

The **FILES** command causes DOS to set aside small blocks of memory, each of which is devoted to tracking a file when it has been opened. No more files can be opened at any one time than there are blocks allocated. The default value of 8 would seem plenty. But DOS uses three internally. A higher value is required if you start using your computer in complex ways. Many memory-resident programs (such as print spoolers) may keep files open while your application programs are at work. Programs may open *temporary files* that you never know about (they're erased when the program terminates). And some genres of software, particularly relational databases, are gluttons for file access. If you use your system intensively, you'll want to put into CONFIG.SYS the line:

```
FILES=12
```

Older software may use a different method of file access that entails **file control blocks** (FCBs). These are staging areas for data transfers; they generally go unused. The number of staging areas is selectable by the **FCBS** command. There's no need to concern yourself with it, but note that the command exists. If a program ever issues an error message stating that it cannot open a file control block, check the DOS manual under FCBS and place a line in CONFIG.SYS increasing the number available.

Device drivers

CONFIG.SYS may also contain **DEVICE** statements. These load into memory **device drivers**—programs that intermediate between DOS and a mechanical device that DOS isn't equipped to deal with, such as a mouse, a plotter, or an expanded memory board. When DOS asks for data from a device, the "driver" translates the command into instructions the device can understand. Conversely, when the device sends data to the computer, the driver converts it to a form that DOS can accept. To illustrate, a device driver for a mouse named **MOUSE.SYS** is loaded by the statement:

```
DEVICE=MOUSE.SYS
```

As you add more and more hardware to your system, you'll develop a small library of device drivers that must be loaded whenever the device is used.

In summary, these commands are the most common. A few others are listed in the DOS manual in the section titled "Configuring Your System." But most CONFIG.SYS files hold only a BUFFERS statement, a FILES statement, and DEVICE statements. At the bare minimum, be sure to set up a CONFIG.SYS file holding the **BUFF-ERS = 20** statement.

Limitations

Unfortunately, there's no way of making CONFIG.SYS and AUTOEXEC.BAT intelligently interactive, so that they can configure the system differently for the task at hand. Because some device drivers are quite large, you may want only the ones that will be used in memory. The only solution is to make a series of CON-FIG.SYS and AUTOEXEC files under different names. Then create batch files that will copy the versions you want over the files actually named CONFIG.SYS and AUTOEXEC.BAT.

For example, say that you've created one file named **CAD.SYS** that contains the line **DEVICE = VIDEO.SYS**, an 80K device driver that runs a super-duper graphics card. Another file, named **FRAMEWK.SYS**, holds the line **DEVICE = EMS**, which controls the expanded memory card that you only use when you run *Framework*. Each file should be the CONFIG.SYS file for a particular application. You can make batch files named, say, **CAD.BAT** and **FRAMEWK.BAT**, that contain the lines **COPY CAD.BAT CON-FIG.SYS** and **COPY FRAMEWK.BAT CONFIG.SYS**. By executing one of the batch files and rebooting, the machine is instantly reconfigured for the job before you.

And that's it! Your hard disk is ready to serve you. But don't just start off using it like a giant floppy. Devote a little extra time after installation to organizing a directory tree that will keep your work orderly for months and years ahead. That's the topic of our next chapter.

Chapter 5

Organizing Your Files

As file after file is added to a hard disk, a sort of data sprawl engulfs the directory tree. Long forgotten subdirectories lie like ghost towns on the outskirts of the disk. Directory listings scroll on and on, filled with cryptic filenames that made perfect sense when they were made, but not six months later. The root directory—home to oddball files that fit nowhere else—fills with hundreds of listings.

Amid this chaos, trying to find a long lost file is a nightmare. You must move from directory branch to branchlet to twig to twiglet, trying to keep track of which subdirectories you have covered. Within each directory you may have to look into scores of files. Multiple versions of files can deepen the confusion. And even after the file has been found, six months from now it will be just as lost again.

This sort of confusion is *the norm*. Very few people take the time to set up the directory tree properly and to periodically "clean house" and catalog files. When the disk fills, half of its bulk may be deadwood. But the more disorderly the disk, the harder the task of deleting superfluous files. When many people share the machine, this level of disorganization verily *begs* for disaster.

Managing files takes time. Like backups, no one likes to do it because it bestows no direct rewards. But you'll find that it takes much less time to manage files than to recover from the consequences of not managing them. Equipped with the proper software utilities, it takes very little effort to keep a disk in order. And you'll enjoy some hidden benefits: DOS is easier to use on a properly organized disk, and software may run more quickly.

An orderly disk grows out of a well-conceived directory tree structure, good habits in file placement, and periodic house-cleanings. When many people use a machine, the system can be maintained only through constant surveillance and thorough training.

Some tried-and-true rules apply to disk organization, but there is no "best" way. The ideal scheme varies by many factors, including work habits, the number of people using the machine, the sophistication of the users (particularly their skill with DOS), the peculiarities of the software in use, the availability of disk space, and the system that backs up the disk. It's important to look ahead to the time when the disk fills and to have concrete plans to expand to a second disk.

If you already work with a hard disk, you'll probably find that hardly any of the rules have been followed. Indeed, your disk may be so chaotic that the only way to re-order it is by backing up all files, reformatting it, and starting all over. If you do go to this extreme, be sure to make a thorough, *double* backup. You won't regret investing time to renovate the disk.

Designing the Directory Tree

After a year of use, the typical hard disk is a sorry sight. Most users christen a newly formatted disk by dumping the entire contents of the two DOS diskettes into the root directory. Then subdirectories are created for the major programs that will be used—a *WordPerfect* subdirectory, a *Lotus 1-2-3* subdirectory, and so on. All files on all diskettes that accompany these programs are poured into the respective subdirectories. Perhaps subdirectories for data files are created at the level below—perhaps not. Batch files and keyboard macro files are scattered all over the disk. Utilities end up in odd places, often in the root directory, sometimes in whatever directory was current when the utility was first required and transferred to the hard disk.

What's wrong with this? Just about everything. Several megabytes of disk space are wasted; DOS is slowed; work is disorganized; individual files are hard to find; batch files won't work. Finally, cataloging and maintaining the disk is made much more difficult.

We don't claim to know the ultimate system for hard disk organization. But there are some rules that you should follow until you know your computer so well that you can think of a better way of doing things. These are the rules that most consultants would impose on your hard disk. Religiously followed, they ward off confusion that costs minutes every day, and hours every month. More important, they help avert the kinds of disasters that can cost you *weeks* of time. We'll step through them one by one.

Reserve the root directory for subdirectory listings. The root directory should serve as the master index to the directory tree. It is not a place to run programs from, to keep utilities, or to store data files. The only files that belong there are COMMAND.COM, AUTOEXEC.BAT, and CONFIG.SYS—the files required to boot the machine. Ideally, the entire contents of the root directory can be displayed on a single screen.

Many people place device drivers (say, to run a Hercules card) in the root directory because they are called for when the machine boots. It's also tempting to include little programs called upon by AUTOEXEC.BAT, such as those that fix the DOS time setting from a real-time clock. And you may load any number of resident pro-

RULE 1

grams (TSRs) through AUTOEXEC.BAT, including keyboard macro
programs, background spelling checkers, or whatever. Any of these
programs can be placed in other subdirectories and listed in
AUTOEXEC.BAT or CONFIG.SYS with a DOS path.

When these device drivers and utility programs are placed in the
root directory, three problems arise. First, your root directory can
no longer act as a single-screen "table of contents" for the disk. Second, all file searches are made longer because DOS must scan the
entries for these seldom-used files during every file request. And
third, the utilities themselves are parted from their related files that
are kept in subdirectories devoted to DOS files and UTILITY files. If
you're using Borland's *SideKick*, you're far better off keeping the
SideKick program, **SK.COM**, in a file with *all* SideKick files, and loading it by placing **\UTILITY\SIDEKICK\SK** in AUTOEXEC.BAT.
When you upgrade to a a new *SideKick* version, you can easily erase
all old files and just as easily transfer all new ones to the hard disk.
This principle applies to all kinds of files, including DOS files.

Make the tree broad and shallow. It's tempting to create a
grandiose logical design for the directory tree, subdividing files into
categories, subcategories, sub-subcategories, and so on. (We'll refer
to the first level of subdirectories below the root directory as *level-
1 subdirectories*. They, in turn, are parent to *level-2 subdirectories*.) The result is a tree that reaches down five levels or more.
There's a certain pleasure in the logical elegance, but it's far out-
weighed by two drawbacks. First, you'll be forced to constantly
enter long path names for nearly any DOS command. Not only is
the extra typing tiresome, but you're much more likely to make
mistakes, and DOS won't let you edit the command line.

The second drawback in many-leveled directory trees is that DOS
takes longer to find files in them. To find a file five levels down,
DOS must consult every subdirectory between, which means that
the hard disk's read/write heads must shuttle back and forth across
the disk surface to the various subdirectory files. In addition, time
is spent scanning the subdirectory entries until the listing for the
subdirectory is found. For many kinds of applications, this may not
be a major drawback. But programs that constantly load overlay
files may be slowed when the overlays are located deep in the directory tree. The problem is especially important to programmers
because compilers and linkers may open dozens of files every time
they run.

Recall that our first rule is that the root directory should hold
hardly anything but subdirectory entries so that it acts as a *Table*

of Contents for the disk. Many computer sophisticates recommend that level-1 subdirectories should also contain mostly reference to other subdirectories, and only a few files. The files they *do* contain should be limited to program files (and certain auxiliary files). Data should be kept in level-2 subdirectories, as should utility programs for the software. Figure 5-1 shows this scheme.

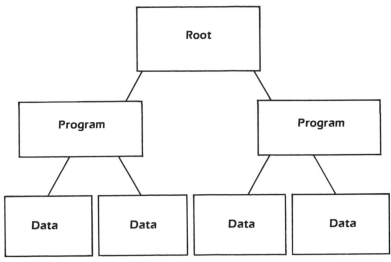

Figure 5-1 **A conventional directory tree**

Drawbacks

This approach has two drawbacks. First, it means that you'll constantly need to type paths containing at least two subdirectories. More important, your work becomes classified by the kind of software that works on it. Spreadsheets and database reports related to the same project end up in separate subdirectories belonging to the spreadsheet and database programs. This makes no sense. Most software can access any file in any subdirectory, so there's no technical necessity.

As you gain experience with more and more software, your projects are likely to use files produced by various programs. For example, if you're busy writing a business report, you may have word-processing files, outliner files, spreadsheet files, image files, and desktop publishing files, all of which will be combined in the final product. It makes no sense to have these files distributed in separate subdirectories residing under those holding the software that creates them, as shown in Figure 5-2.

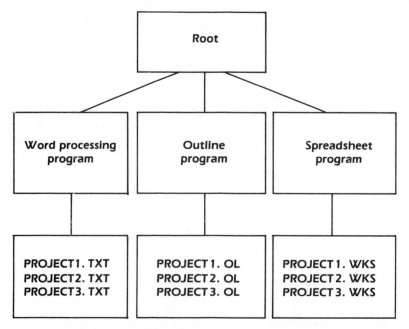

Figure 5-2 **The wrong way to organize files**

Our recommenda-
tion

Instead, subdirectories should be organized by project and should be placed immediately below the root directory. Files subsidiary to the project belong in subdirectories below. Each software package ought to have its own subdirectory, also just below the root directory, as shown in Figure 5-3.

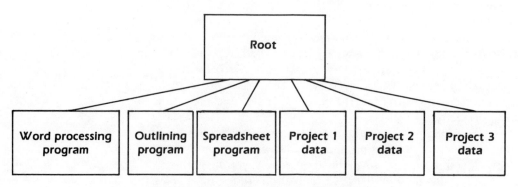

Figure 5-3 **A better way to organize files**

In fact, you may want to push software entirely out of the way. After all, your work centers around your data. The software that operates on it should be thought of as a plumbing system that ought to be kept as inconspicuous as possible. In this case, the tree diagram would look like that shown in Figure 5-4.

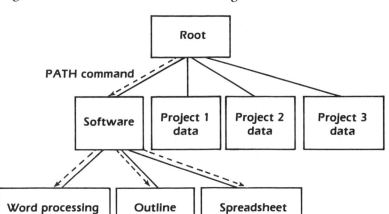

Figure 5-4 **The best file organization of all**

In this design, the root directory lists nothing but projects— except for the **SOFTWARE** subdirectory, which leads you into the basement where all the pipes and wires reside. You may complain that, in this scheme, the user is forced to type in a long path every time a program is loaded. That would indeed be the case, but as we'll see later in this chapter, DOS can be set up to find a program file on its own (using the PATH command), no matter the current directory. By following this directory plan, you can keep all related files together, you can gain access to any program from any place, any program can reach any file in any place, and you seldom need to enter a DOS path that contains more than one subdirectory.

Build as much of the tree as you can before transferring files. DOS doesn't let you make changes easily in the directory tree. For reasons of efficiency and flexibility, it's a good idea to build as much of the tree as you can when the disk is freshly formatted. By doing so, you ensure that the subdirectories are compressed in a few cylinders near the outside of the disk; this makes for faster access. It also ensures that child directories will be the topmost entries in a directory listing; this also lets DOS find files more quickly, because less time is spent scanning directories.

RULE 3

Once the tree is built, it's hard to make changes. DOS makes no provision for renaming a subdirectory or for moving it (and its child directories) to another spot on the tree. Some utilities, such as *PC Tools*, have a "prune and graft" feature that can perform these tasks. Otherwise, to rename a directory, you must create another with the desired name, copy over all files, and remove the original. Without the aid of a utility, moving a whole branch of the tree is much more troublesome, and mistakes can be disastrous.

RULE 4

Create many small subdirectories. This rule is the same as saying, "keep directory listings short." Subdirectories containing 100 files or more take a long time to search. On average, DOS must pass over 50 files before it finds the one it wants. It's also hard to visually scan a long subdirectory and grasp its contents. This is true even when you have a DOS shell at your disposal (discussed in Chapter 6) which will let you scroll directory listings up and down.

Short directories are especially valuable when it comes time to clean house. You can quickly see what is new and what is old, and you're less likely to make deletions you'll later regret. You're also more likely to delete files at the time they become obsolete because you can more easily spot them and more readily be sure that it's all right to delete them.

RULE 5

Use short directory names. Short subdirectory names are best. Drop as many syllables from the end of the word as you can while still being able to decipher the meaning. For example, a **UTILITY** subdirectory is shortened to **UTIL** with little danger of confusion because the word "utility" naturally comes to mind when you see "util." But substituting **CONT** for **CONTRACT** is riskier because many words begin with "cont."

Avoid reducing long phrases to complex mnemonics. It's fun to decide that **NWOMRMC** should stand for "New Wave Outer Mongolian Ragtime Music Criticism," but you won't remember it easily, and the fastest touch typist will slow to a snail's pace. It's better to create mnemonics that capture the essence of a subdirectory's contents: **MONGRAG**. Incidentally, you'll find it easier to remember names, and to type them, if you leave in the vowels.

Subdirectory name extensions

Many people are unaware that subdirectory names may be given three-character extensions, just like filenames. For example, if you're working on the Great American Novel, you could create a subdirectory **NOVELS**, it could hold subdirectories called **AMERNOVL.CH1, AMERNOVL.CH2, AMERNOVL.CH3**, and so on—one subdirectory for each chapter. It's easy to think up grandiose schemes for classifying subdirectories in this way, but generally it's not a good idea. File paths are hard enough to type and read without inserting periods: **NOVELS\AMERNOVL.CH2\ NOTES.OLD\GARBAGE.OUT\BADIDEAS.TXT**.

There is one situation in which extensions for subdirectory names come in handy. Say that you name all subdirectories that contain *Lotus 1-2-3* spreadsheets with the extension **.123**, such as **PROJECT1.123, PROJECT2.123**, and so on. You can quickly get a listing of all 1-2-3 subdirectories through a normal wildcard search: **DIR *.123**—an awfully small benefit for the extra typing you must do each time you enter a path to one of the subdirectories.

Don't give files the same names as subdirectories. Take care not to give matching names to files and to the subdirectories that hold them. DOS does a good job of keeping them straight, but you may become confused about whether a particular DOS command will operate on the subdirectory or the file. For example, if the current directory contains both a file named **WP** and a subdirectory named **WP**, the command **DIR WP** results in a listing of all files in the subdirectory **WP**; it doesn't search for a file named WP in the current directory. DOS would have no trouble opening the file **WP** if required, so there is no danger in crossing file and subdirectory names. For your own clarity, however, the practice is best avoided.

RULE 6

Keep utility software in one place. A common subdirectory is the *utility* subdirectory, often named **UTIL** or **UTILITY**. As your system grows, you'll acquire many software utilities. Besides the utility libraries you may acquire, you'll find that many add-on boards are accompanied by a diskette that holds software required for their use. Most everyone has a RAM disk utility, a print spooler, a file uneraser, and a head-parking utility (*SHIPDISK*). You may also have device drivers for a mouse or other input device, an expanded memory board, and so on. Another class of utilities are disk maintenance tools like disk cachers or defragmenters, which we'll discuss in Chapter 7. All these should be kept in a common toolshed where you'll be able to quickly find them.

RULE 7

If you own an extensive toolkit, like the *Norton Utilities* or *Mace Utilities*, make a subdirectory for it below the UTILITY subdirectory. Don't mix utility packages in one subdirectory; software houses sometimes use the same filenames, so confusion may result. There's much to be said for keeping the dozen most commonly used utilities in the UTIL subdirectory and stashing the others away in subdirectories a level below. For example, even if you've made a subdirectory called **UTIL****NORTON** to hold the *Norton Utilities,* you might want to place a second copy of *File Find* (a file search utility) in **UTIL**.

Unless you've gobs of open disk space, you probably shouldn't blindly copy over all files on utility diskettes to subdirectories on the hard disk. You'll find that most utility software is tailored for special needs you'll never confront. You don't need drivers for a Hercules card if you don't own one. Move what you need to the hard disk and no more.

RULE 8
Create a subdirectory exclusively for DOS files. List a DOS subdirectory in the root directory and keep DOS files there. Then be sure to include the subdirectory in a PATH command (PATH \DOS;...) placed in AUTOEXEC.BAT (we'll talk about PATH a bit later). This approach has two advantages. First, you can use any DOS command no matter what subdirectory is current. Second, you can easily replace all DOS files when upgrading to a more recent DOS version. Some users who don't know about the PATH command keep copies of certain DOS files in many subdirectories so that commands like XCOPY and CHKDSK will be on hand without typing a long DOS path. Not only does this approach waste disk space, it makes it very difficult to track down all old DOS files when replacing them with new ones.

The first mistake (of many) made by new owners of hard disks is to dump the entire contents of the DOS diskettes into the root directory. As we explained above, the root directory should have almost no files at all. Unfortunately, the DOS manual actually instructs the reader to copy all files to the root directory. That's incorrect; don't do it.

Many of the dozens of files on the two DOS diskettes have no business being on your hard disk at all. Of these, some are without value for many users, such as the enhanced graphics adapter driver. Some rightfully belong in the UTILITY subdirectory, such as the RAM disk program, **VDISK**. And some are useful only to programmers, such as **LINK** and **EXE2BIN**. There's something to be said for having all of the files on the hard disk to have them on hand as you learn to use new commands. But, once you understand what the individual programs do, you can save a few hundred kilobytes of disk space by deleting the useless ones.

RULE 9
Keep batch files in one subdirectory. Just as the files for external DOS commands need to be online from any directory on the disk, many batch files need universal access. For example, you may

create a file called **NOTES.BAT** that changes the current directory to the NOTES directory and starts up a card file program. If **NOTES.BAT** is located in the **BATCH** subdirectory, and AUTOEXEC.BAT contains the statement **PATH \BATCH**, then from any position on the disk you can type **NOTES** and be instantly conveyed to note taking. A system of batch files lets you change tasks at whim without typing a single DOS path.

Some batch files process files *within* a single subdirectory, and it might seem more natural to place them there. Sometimes this is a good idea, but there's much to be said for keeping all in one subdirectory. By doing so, you can easily survey the entire system. If changes are made in the tree structure, it's much easier to perform surgery on the files. Seldom-used batch files won't be overlooked.

Transfer to disk only the program files you need. When you acquire new software, you're often confronted with many disks full of unidentified files. These days, it's not uncommon for five or six diskettes to accompany the program manual. That's *two megabytes*, $\frac{1}{10}$ of a 20-megabyte disk. Usually about half of this amount can safely remain on the floppies. Tutorials don't need to be on the hard disk; if moved to the disk, they should be removed once you're finished with them. Also, you'll need only one or two of the dozens of printer drivers commonly supplied with software. Don't fill your disk with them. No matter how small, each file will take up at least two kilobytes because of the minimum cluster allocation.

The problem, of course, is that when you first install software, you don't know which ones you'll need. The best course of action may be to move everything to the hard disk, *keeping it in separate, related subdirectories*. Then remove files as you can. For example, once you've isolated the printer driver you need, copy it to the program directory and eliminate the printer driver subdirectory.

RULE 10

Make dangerous files hard to access. On most machines, the most dangerous file is FORMAT.COM. As you'll learn in Chapter 9, utilities that "unformat" an accidentally reformatted disk may achieve only partial results. If you own a low-level formatting program, keep it off the disk. The same applies to FDISK, the DOS partitioning program. However, FORMAT.COM is required for formatting floppies. As you know, you must always be careful to use this program correctly. But if a machine is used by many people, including beginners, words of caution are not enough.

One way of keeping FORMAT.COM out of harm's way is by making it hard to find. *Don't* keep it with other **DOS** files in the **DOS**

RULE 11

subdirectory, where it can be easily called through the PATH command. Instead, place it in its own subdirectory below the DOS directory—that is, at **\DOS\FORMAT**. Other dangerous files should receive similar treatment. This includes certain file erasure utilities that can destroy a whole branch of the directory tree with a few keystrokes.

An even better way of hiding the FORMAT program is to rename it and call it from within a batch file. Say that you rename it as **F.COM**. Then you can make a batch file named **FORMAT.BAT** that contains the single line **F A:**. When the batch file is called, it runs the FORMAT program, always directing it to drive A.

If you're *really* worried about accidental formatting, the safest procedure of all is to keep the program off the hard disk. Simply format all new diskettes when purchased (or buy them preformatted—it's only about ten cents more per diskette). In a business office, the original DOS diskettes, like all originals, can then be locked up by the system manager.

Linking Files across Subdirectories

Directory trees are a boon to file organization, but they create problems of their own. On disks containing only a root directory, all files are listed in the same place so that software can find any file by scanning that directory alone. In a directory tree, software must have a way of accessing files in subdirectories other than the one in which it resides. Although DOS could have been designed to scan every directory in the tree automatically when a file isn't found in the current directory, the process would be inefficient and would not cope with instances where several files of the same name are distributed in several subdirectories.

The issues

There are two issues: First, software needs to be able to find files in other directories; second, you need to be able to run a program when working from a directory other than the one holding the program file. Neither requirement is an obstacle if you are adept at writing DOS paths. If a program named *TRASHER* is in the subdirectory **UTIL**, and it is to work on the file **BADIDEAS.TXT** contained in the subdirectory **NOTES**, you can load the file from any directory by entering **\UTIL\TRASHER**, and once in the program, you can specify the file as **\NOTES\BADIDEAS.TXT**. The software may even allow you to name the program on the command line, so that you could load the software and file by the command **\UTIL\TRASHER \NOTES\BADIDEAS.TXT**. In this way, work-

ing from one directory, you can run a program in a second and
have it load a data file in a third.

Unfortunately, three difficulties interfere with this elegant
scheme. First, you don't always remember where a particular file is
located. Second, repeatedly typing DOS paths becomes very tiresome. And third, some software can't access certain files in other
subdirectories. In any case, many inexperienced PC users have a
poor understanding of tree directories, making it desirable to avoid
DOS paths as much as possible. Next we'll discuss the various techniques for overcoming these obstacles and avoiding DOS paths.
These complex techniques can lead to more confusion than they
avoid. But one measure, the PATH command, should be part of every user's bag of tricks.

Obstacles

The DOS PATH Command

DOS supplies the PATH command to help load program files from
subdirectories other than the current one. You give DOS a list of
subdirectories to search if it cannot find a program in the current
directory. For example, say that you are working in the subdirectory **WORD** and want to load Lotus 1-2-3 from the subdirectory
\STATS\123. If you enter **123**, DOS will look in the **WORD** directory and inform you that the file has not been found. But if earlier
you had executed the PATH command **PATH\STATS\123**, DOS
would proceed to search the subdirectory **\STATS\123** for the
1-2-3 program file, where it would find it and load it.

Many file paths can be listed in a PATH statement, and they must
be separated by a semicolon. **PATH \NOTES\TANK; \STATS\123**
would cause DOS to first search the **TANK** subdirectory (containing the *ThinkTank* outliner and then the 1-2-3 subdirectory. This
statement lets you run both *ThinkTank* and 1-2-3 from anywhere
on the disk. You can name drive specifiers in the PATH command,
so a statement like **PATH C:\NOVEL; D:\NOTES** causes DOS to
search on two separate disks. Avoid naming floppy disk drives in
PATH commands because you'll constantly turn up "not ready" errors when the drive is empty.

PATH, an *internal* DOS command contained in COM-
MAND.COM, doesn't require a separate file from the DOS diskette.
This command isn't very flexible; you can't ask it to search all subdirectories in a branch of the tree or the entire tree. Every time
you enter a PATH command, it replaces the previous one so that
no more paths may be entered than will fit on the DOS command

Path order

line. You can find out the current path by entering only the word
PATH (this action does not affect the current setting of the PATH
command). To cancel the path settings, enter **PATH;**.

Limitations

Unfortunately, the PATH command functions only from the DOS
prompt and works only for program files and batch files. Once a
program is loaded, PATH won't help it find data files in other subdirectories. And even from the DOS prompt, PATH cannot help
DOS commands find data files. For example, if you enter **TYPE
MYFILE.TXT**, DOS will look *only* for MYFILE.TXT in the current
directory, even if a PATH statement lists other subdirectories. DOS
consults the other directories only for files with an **.EXE, .COM**, or
.BAT extension. Even when you name the data file along with the
program file on the command line, as in **WORD DOCUMENT.TXT**,
the PATH command is of no help.

Applications

Still, the PATH command can be very useful, particularly in its
ability to locate and run batch files. Many users insert a PATH
command in AUTOEXEC.BAT that (minimally) reads **PATH
\BATCH;\UTIL;\DOS**. This simple command means that any
batch file, utility, and external DOS file can be run from any directory on the disk. Including the batch file subdirectory in the PATH
command is essential if you want to use batch files to change to
one subdirectory from any other.

Because DOS proceeds through the subdirectories named in a
PATH command in the order that they are listed, you can speed up
its operation by naming the most frequently accessed subdirectories first. It's important to not make PATH commands too long.
Time is wasted searching through many subdirectories to find a
program residing in the last subdirectory specified. It's better to
make multiple PATH commands, placing them in batch files that
reconfigure the machine for the task at hand (as we'll discuss a bit
later).

Path Programs

Programmers have created *path utilities* that make up for some,
but not all, of the deficiencies inherent in the DOS PATH command. In part, these programs help make computing easier by saving the user the trouble of entering long DOS paths, and by finding
files the user can't locate. But path programs were primarily devised to meet two common deficiencies in software design.

Why path
programs exist

One shortcoming is that some outdated software cannot handle
file paths at all. Recall that tree directories were introduced with

DOS version 2.0. Earlier versions didn't support hard disks. Thus, early PC software didn't support file paths, and some programs were not updated for this feature for a long time. The best known instance is *WordStar*, which was late in adopting DOS paths. The program was at its apogee just when hard disks became popular on PCs, imposing a tremendous need for file-path capability. Today, only the most amateurish programs are released without file path capability.

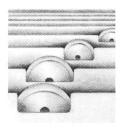

Overlay files

The second, more devious, deficiency is that the DOS PATH command can't load *verlay files* from a subdirectory other than the current one. *Overlay files* are parts of the program that are loaded into memory as the main program requires them. This technique, which conserves memory, has become less popular as RAM has become cheaper. But some popular programs still use overlays or other auxiliary files that they must be able to find while they run. When you load such a program from a different subdirectory than it resides in, the program will probably look for overlays in the *current* directory. Of course, the program won't find the overlays, so it will come to a stop and may even crash the machine.

Surprisingly few programs are completely flexible in regard to file placement in the directory tree. Some strictly require that overlay files or auxiliary files be positioned in the home directory (the same directory as the main program file). Some can find data only in subdirectories that are a child of the home directory. This rigidity may be imposed to make initial program configuration easier. But in some instances it forces you to keep multiple copies of a program on a disk, along with all auxiliary files; tremendous amounts of disk space may be wasted.

Software limitations

Path programs overcome these problems in a clever way. When programs open a file, they issue a request to DOS. The requests are made through a device called an **interrupt**, which uses an address, stored at a fixed position in memory, that tells the location of the DOS routine that opens a file. Path programs *chain* themselves into the interrupt, substituting their address in memory for that of the DOS routine. When the software calls on DOS to open a particular file, it actually activates the path program, which looks at the file-name, then searches the entire directory tree until it finds the file. Once the file is found, the path program sets up a full file path and calls the DOS routine. In a sense, the path program *inserts itself* between the program and DOS.

Path programs work well when software opens existing files but not when a new file is created. Say that the current directory is 1-2-3 and that you want to use the word processor in WORDSTAR.

Problems using path programs

You enter the command to load *WordStar*, the path program searches the directory tree for the program file, finds it in WORD-STAR, and runs the program. If you then create a new file, it is written in the *current directory*—that is, in the 1-2-3 subdirectory, not the WORDSTAR subdirectory. The path program has no way of knowing where the file should be placed. Because of this limitation, it's easy to create files and later have no idea where they are.

Special features in path programs

Quite a few path programs are on the market, and the competition has driven authors to fill their programs with features. Some, like *SmartPath*, use a syntax very similar to that of the DOS PATH command. Others provide more powerful features. For example, *FilePath* from SDA Associates lets you extend the file search to all child directories of a named directory; optionally, you can have the entire directory tree searched. *DPATH + Plus* can direct all files created with a particular filename extension to a particular subdirectory. Several path programs can use wildcard characters in various ways.

The DOS APPEND Command

Starting with version 3.3, DOS offers the **APPEND** command to provide automatic tree searches for *any* kind of file, whether a program file opened from the command line or a data file loaded from within a program. This means that DOS has finally come to offer many of the features of a path program. APPEND is an *external DOS command*, but when it is called, it permanently loads itself into memory and is active in many DOS commands, such as DIR—but not without serious problems.

Syntax

The syntax of APPEND is just like that of the PATH command. The expression

```
APPEND \NOTES\TANK; \STATS\123
```

extends searches to two subdirectories. In this form, the APPEND command searches only for non-program files. To have it take on the role of the PATH command, so that it searches for files with .COM, .EXE, and .BAT extensions, you must add the /**X** switch.

```
APPEND \NOTES\TANK; \STATS\123 /X
```

Unfortunately, many problems result. For example, if you execute this APPEND command and then ask for **DIR ORANGUTAN** while in the root directory, DOS will report that the file ORANGUTAN is in the current directory even when it finds it in another. Another problem is that when software opens a file through APPEND and then tries to rename it or delete it, DOS returns error messages. APPEND is also incompatible with BACKUP, RESTORE, and XCOPY.

Path programs, whether the DOS PATH and APPEND facilities, or full-blown path software, aren't a way of avoiding typing in DOS paths. Because software may rewrite files found through these commands in different directories, they are an endless source of disruption to a carefully planned directory system. Employ them, if you must, with older software that cannot deal with DOS paths, but don't use them as a crutch.

Limitations of path programs

DOS Commands that Temporarily Modify the Directory Tree

The designers of DOS understand the occasional liabilities of tree-structured directories and have gradually added commands that make DOS think that one drive is another, that a subdirectory is a drive unto itself, or that one drive is a subdirectory in another drive. This magic is accomplished by the **ASSIGN, SUBST,** and **JOIN** commands. All three are *external commands*, so you must copy their associated files to your hard disk from the DOS diskettes. Let's look at each in turn.

The ASSIGN Command

The ASSIGN command was developed to help old programs that *must* access drives A and B. Many of the first IBM PC programs were written before hard disks were available at all—a "fully equipped" machine had just two floppy drives. Often these programs required that the program diskette reside in drive A and a data diskette in drive B. Such programs were very easy to use because you didn't have to specify so much as a drive, let alone a long path (this was before the days of tree-structured directories, in any case). Today, if one of these programs is kept on a hard disk, it won't work. It will look on drive A for auxiliary files and try to write its data to a (possibly) non-existent drive B.

ASSIGN comes to the rescue in these cases because it lets you treat drives A and B as if they were drive C. The statement:

```
ASSIGN A=C
```

makes any operations on drive A be directed to the current directory in drive C. As a result, if you ask for a directory listing of drive A, you'll get the directory for C. To assign both drives A and B to drive C, enter:

```
ASSIGN A=C B=C
```

That's all there is to it. To cancel the assignments and return all to normal, just enter:

```
ASSIGN
```

The ASSIGN command should only be used when absolutely necessary. It's a dangerous command, in that things can go mysteriously wrong. *Never* use ASSIGN with the BACKUP, RESTORE, LABEL, and PRINT commands or with the other tree-modifying commands SUBST and JOIN. FORMAT, DISKCOPY, and DISKCOMP ignore the new drive assignments made by ASSIGN.

The SUBST Command

The SUBST command, introduced with DOS version 3.1, does all that the ASSIGN command does and more. It can cause any subdirectory to be represented as a drive. For example, the subdirectory **C:WATER/SNOW/POWDER** can be renamed **D:**. This feature was added to DOS to overcome some of the deficiencies that path utilities were developed to counter. Some old software cannot use directory paths, yet can interact with subdirectories other than the current directory by pretending the subdirectory is a drive in itself. For example, you might keep the program in **C:OLDPROG** and want to direct its output to the subdirectory **C:DATAFILE\FILE5**. To make the subdirectory addressable as drive D, enter:

```
SUBST D: C:\DATAFILE\FILE5
```

If you use a DOS version that has SUBST, it's favored over ASSIGN, because it's less likely to run into troubles. If you're using software that always directs data files to drive B, you can direct them to **C:\NOTES** by entering:

```
SUBST B: C:\NOTES
```

SUBST can also be handy during disk housecleaning. When you copy files from all over the tree to a particular subdirectory, you can set up the subdirectory as a drive to save yourself the trouble of copying its path over and over again. To undo a substitution, follow **SUBST** with the fake drive specifier, and then **/D**. For example, if you've renamed a subdirectory on drive C as **D:**, then enter:

```
SUBST D: /D
```

To see the current list of substitutions, enter:

```
SUBST
```

For the case given above, it would return:

```
D: => C:\DATAFILE\FILE5
```

By default, DOS allows drive specifiers only up to **E:**. It can extend the range to **Z:** if you execute the **LASTDRIVE** command, either manually or through AUTOEXEC.BAT. The statement:

```
LASTDRIVE = F
```

extends the range to **F:**. Don't forget this requirement if you use the SUBST command several times over. Like ASSIGN, SUBST has trouble with commands such as BACKUP, RESTORE, FORMAT, DISKCOPY, and CHKDSK.

The JOIN Command

The JOIN command is in some respects the opposite of the SUBST command. Rather than split off a subdirectory as a separate (logical) drive, it incorporates an actual drive as a subdirectory in the tree of another drive. It lets you link floppy disk drives into your hard disk directory tree. The statement:

```
JOIN A: C:\NEWDATA
```

makes the floppy disk in drive A appear as a subdirectory called **NEWDATA**, a child directory of the root directory (that is, at the first level under the root directory). No other position in the directory tree is allowed. **NEWDATA** is actually the *root directory* of the disk in drive A. If the disk holds a directory tree, the entire tree is appended to the tree in drive C. This is true even when the current directory on drive A is not the root directory.

If **NEWDATA** were already to exist as a level-1 subdirectory on drive C, JOIN would link in drive A only if **NEWDATA** is not empty. If **NEWDATA** doesn't already exist, JOIN creates the subdirectory. To unlink drive A, enter:

```
JOIN A: /D
```

The subdirectory **NEWDATA** will be removed from the drive C directory tree.

You can join several directory trees together through multiple JOIN commands. To see a listing of the current linkages, simply enter:

```
JOIN
```

JOIN must not be used in combination with ASSIGN or SUBST; nor should you use BACKUP, RESTORE, FORMAT, DISKCOPY, or DISKCOMP.

Dangers in ASSIGN, SUBST, and JOIN

Be very careful with ASSIGN, SUBST, and JOIN. In many instances they will become confused and lock up the machine. Here are some special cases:

- DOS shells, menuing programs, and operating environments are likely to become completely confused.
- The commands may tangle up your system of batch files.
- You may overwrite files of the same name in different directories that have been linked together.
- The commands won't help you with the *key disk* problem, in which a program won't run unless its distribution disk is in drive A.
- You may temporarily lose access to data when the specifier for one drive is handed over to the subdirectory of another.

Finding, Sorting, Viewing, Printing, and Cataloging Files

When a hard disk has been in use for a year or more, keeping track of an ever growing number of files becomes a serious problem. If you've organized the directory tree well, half the battle is won. The rest is done through ordinary DOS commands and utility software. Besides the solutions we discuss here, see the discussion of DOS shells in Chapter 7.

Viewing the Directory Tree

DOS provides the TREE command for viewing the directory tree structure. Unfortunately, the command gives a linear listing of sub-directories that is next to useless. The record for each subdirectory looks like this:

```
Path: \CREEPY\CRAWLIES

Sub-directories: \ANTS
                 \EARWIGS
                 \SPIDERS
```

This output results from the command:

```
TREE C:
```

You can make DOS insert the names of every file in the subdirectories by adding the /F switch:

```
TREE C: /F
```

To show the listing one screen at a time:

```
TREE C: |MORE
```

Pressing any key takes you to the next screenful of data. Unfortunately, breaks are not made between subdirectory listings so that they may be hard to read. Incidentally, the MORE command creates a small temporary file on disk; so occasionally you may have trouble using it with floppies. To print out the listing, add **>LPT1** (or **>COM1** if you have a serial printer) to the command:

```
TREE C: >LPT1
```

or

```
TREE C: /F >LPT1
```

Most DOS shells present a graphic image of the directory tree, as do utilities found in disk tool packages. Figure 5-5 shows a tree diagram made by the *NCD* ("Norton Change Directory") program in the *Norton Utilities*. Like many tree diagrams, you may move a cursor around the tree to change directories, or to create, rename, or remove subdirectories.

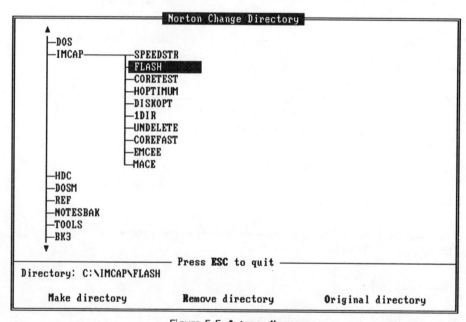

Figure 5-5 **A tree diagram**

Searching for Files

There are two ways in which you may want to search for files. In one case, you remember the filename, but not its subdirectory. In the other, you remember the file's content, perhaps even its subdirectory, but not its name. DOS won't help you in either situation.

When you remember the filename, the best you can do in DOS is move from directory to directory, asking for the file by the command **DIR FILENAME.EXT**. To search directories for a filename you can *almost* remember, add the /W switch with the DIR command. It displays directories in five columns, showing only the filenames. To make DOS stop after it has displayed a screenful, use the /P switch. Thus, to comfortably view an overstuffed directory, enter **DIR /W /P**. The next screen is shown by striking any key.

Directory searches

Many disk toolkits include a program that searches all or part of the directory tree for one or more files. This program is called *FF* (for "File Find") in the *Norton Utilities*. By simply entering **FF KINGKONG**, the program searches the entire directory tree and lists every instance of the file **KINGKONG**. A switch lets you extend the search to every drive in the machine. It also accepts the /W and /P switches, exactly as in the DIR command. You may use wildcard characters in the filenames. Thus, the request **FF *.BAT** returns a listing of every batch file on the hard disk.

File search utilities

Searching inside files is much trickier than scanning directories. Some very elaborate programs can poke into files to see if they contain particular strings of data. Yet, with little trouble, a program can scan thousands of files and report which contain a particular expression. This technique is very helpful in locating certain kinds of text files; for example, you could look for **"Dear Mr. Rosen-crantz"** and locate all your correspondence with Mr. Rosencrantz. You may even be able to find spreadsheets that contain the heading **"Bonus Payments."**

Searching into files

DOS can look inside files using the FIND command. The expression

DOS searches

```
FIND "To be or not to be" HAMLET.TXT
```

searches the file **HAMLET.TXT** for the line "To be or not to be." The FIND command is *case-sensitive*; it searches for strings with the same capitalization given in the command. Had Shakespeare been repetitious, every instance of the string would be reported. The /N switch causes FIND to list the *line number* of each occurrence. (Text files are divided into lines that usually correspond to a row on the screen; these are numbered from 1 upward, with empty rows counted as a line.) To search more than one file, enter:

```
FIND "To be or not to be" HAMLET.TXT,
LEAR.TXT
```

Text search
programs

Unfortunately, the FIND command doesn't allow wildcard characters in the file names. So a general search is impossible.

Once again, disk toolkits come to the rescue. Many contain
a text search program that can scan some or all files in some or
all directories, giving a complete listing of the files that hold a
match. In the *Norton Utilities*, the *Text Search* program seeks a
string without regard to capitalization. It can be made to stop
and display the string every time it finds it, or it can channel the
output to a file or printer. Besides searching files, it can scan disk
sectors for the target string, covering either the entire disk, or
all sectors that fall outside files (a useful feature for finding lost
data).

Advanced features

Far more complicated searches are possible with specialized utilities. For example, *Electra-Find*, which can use wildcard characters
in the search string, can even perform a phonetic search for similar
sounding words. It can find strings split between two lines, even
when hyphenated. It can search for more than one string simultaneously, using the logic of AND, OR, and NOT; hence, you could
ask for all sentences that contain "apples" or "oranges" but not
"pears." You can even ask for occurrences of particular kinds of
sentence structure. You could have it make a file of all section
headings in a document by describing the particular formatting
codes your word processor uses to define them. Options are available for searching through non-standard text file, like *WordStar* files
and complex data files.

Perhaps most important, advanced search utilities can specify
how much text is displayed when a match is found. While simple
programs merely return a "line" in the file (often corresponding to
a line on the screen when the file is displayed), advanced utilities
let you specify that the entire sentence or paragraph be reported,
or all text up to specified border characters.

Search tools for
programmers

Even more complicated search programs have been designed for
programmers. These often mimic *GREP*, the granddaddy of such
utilities, which descends from AT&T's UNIX operating system. In
their purest form, these are *pattern matching* programs, which use
metacharacters—an extended set of wildcards—that can denote
particular constructions. For example, a metacharacter could indicate an end-of-line position, and the utility would return a match
only if the search string occurred at the end of a line. Programmers
especially value these utilities because they give complete control
over the interpretation of *control codes* embedded in a file. Such
tools aren't for everyone, but they can be invaluable in large programming projects.

A simple search program can move through 100 kilobytes of files   Performance
in about 30 seconds on a standard IBM PC; an AT will be about
twice as fast. At these rates, it would take an hour or two to search
20 megabytes of data. But most searches are limited to files specified by wildcard characters, and the job is completed amazingly
quickly. Of course, the more capable the program and the more
complicated the search, the longer it takes.

Sorting File Listings

Sometimes it's useful to sort directory listings to help you find files.
DOS does this with the SORT filter—a short program on the main
DOS diskette. Keep SORT.EXE in the DOS subdirectory and access
it through a PATH command; this approach makes it available for
any directory. To sort the file names alphabetically:

```
DIR ISORT
```

Any other field in the directory listing may be sorted by telling the
command the starting character, using the format /+. Because filename extensions begin at position 10, you can make an alphabeti-
cal sort by extensions using the expression:

```
DIR ISORT /+10
```

All subdirectories are listed first. Here are some other values:

```
File size:     DIR ISORT /+13
Date:          DIR ISORT /+24
Time:          DIR ISORT /+34
```

The month-day-year format used for dates makes a sort useless. In
DOS 3.0 and later, you can arrange the date in year-month-day by
adding the line **COUNTRY = 046** to CONFIG.SYS. This makes DOS
use the Swedish format. Sorting the time is also a problem because
there is no way to sort by *am* and *pm*. You can display the listing
screen by screen by appending I**MORE**, as in:

```
DIR ISORT /+10 IMORE
```

It's hard to remember the offsets of the various directory fields.
You can quickly create batch files that will do the job for you. For

example, name a file **SORTSIZE.BAT** and place **DIR | SORT /+13**
in it. With **SORT.EXE** in the DOS subdirectory, **SORTSIZE.BAT** in
a batch file subdirectory, and the PATH command set to (minimally) **PATH \DOS;\BATCH**, you can enter **SORTSIZE** from any
subdirectory, and a listing for that directory is given, sorted by file
size.

Permanent sorts

All of the sort techniques mentioned so far only sort the *display*
of directory information. The actual ordering of directory entries
goes unchanged. Many disk toolkits, including *PC Tools*, the *Mace
Utilities*, and the *Norton Utilities*, include programs that can physically reorder directories by various criteria. These usually place all
subdirectories at the top of the directory to hasten file searches
along DOS paths. Searches are also speeded by compressing the
entries so that empty slots move to the bottom of the directory.
Once one of these utilities is run, you probably won't be able to
recover files that have been erased (a technique we discuss in
Chapter 9).

Viewing Files

The cryptic filenames used by DOS mean that you'll often need to
look into old files to see what they contain. The best way to examine a file's contents is to load it into the software that created it.
But this approach may be inefficient when you're searching
through dozens of files. The software will probably load the entire
file into memory and process it before showing it to you. It's much
quicker to use a DOS command or utility to display the file. This is
easily done with most text files, which are readily displayed and
understood. But data files for software like spreadsheets, databases,
and outliners are filled with gobbledygook that only programmers
can understand (and then only with great effort). Amid this gibberish you'll find nice, reassuring words—the data for spreadsheet labels, outline headings, or whatever. These swatches of data can tell
you what the file contains.

The TYPE
command

Thanks to the cryptic filenames used by DOS, often a particular
file can be found only by examining all likely candidates in a directory. The DOS **TYPE** command is a quick way of looking into files.
You merely enter **TYPE DATAFILE**, and DATAFILE is displayed,
scrolling upward when the screen fills. The TYPE command reads
straight through from the beginning to the end of the file. It reads
only a bit of the file, displays it, and goes on reading more as
scrolling continues; this means you can't scroll backward.

The data is written as fast as DOS can manage, so when many short lines or empty lines occur in a row, the screen suddenly scrolls very quickly—too quickly to view. You can make TYPE pause after displaying each screen by appending │**MORE** to the command:

```
TYPE DATAFILE │MORE
```

Striking any key moves you onto the next screen. Instead, if you're quick, you can temporarily stop the scrolling by typing Ctrl-NumLock (or Ctrl-S); again, display continues when you strike any key. Ctrl-Break interrupts the TYPE command and returns you to the DOS prompt.

Many kinds of data files resist inspection by the TYPE command. You need to understand a little about how files are constructed to understand why. All files are made up of a string of bytes, where each byte holds a value from 0 to 255. When the sequence of bytes is displayed on the screen, each value from 0 to 255 is represented as its corresponding **ASCII character**, an arbitrarily assigned symbol from the ASCII standard. For example, the value **65** is represented as **A**, the value **97**, **a**.

The upper- and lowercase letters, plus numerals and punctuation marks, take up less than a third of the character set. Many of the remaining values are assigned to special European language characters or to the box-graphic characters that frame information on the screen. But some values have a special status. The lowest 32 characters, numbers 0 to 31, are treated by DOS as **control codes**. When DOS encounters some of these characters as it writes data on the screen, it *interprets* them as a command. For example, character 9 causes DOS to tab the cursor, and character 13 brings about a "carriage return." Actually, there *are* symbols associated with these values, but DOS chooses not to display them.

If you use the DOS TYPE command to examine an ordinary text file, the document scrolls before your eyes much as if it were viewed in the word processor that created it. These files contain control codes but only those for tabs, carriage returns, and line feeds (in combination, the latter two end a paragraph and send the cursor to the beginning of the line below). But many programs insert other codes into files, whether command codes or special graphics characters. For example, a word processor might insert values before and after words to be italicized. When the word processor displays the information, it strips out the special characters so that only written text is seen. But when the DOS TYPE

Limitations of the TYPE command

Impact of control codes

command displays the file, it isn't privy to the special coding scheme for italics; as a result, it displays the special characters as if they were text.

Problem codes

Certain codes cause funny things to happen on the display. The cursor jumps around, writing the file here and there. The screen may suddenly clear, making it impossible to read the file. Another oddity is that DOS "beeps" the system speaker when it encounters character 7. This value represents the "normal" white-on-black color that displays characters, and some files hold this value repeatedly; if you use TYPE to look into the file, the speaker beeps endlessly. Finally, when the TYPE command finds character 26 in a text file, it interprets it as an "end-of-file" marker, and it stops writing data on the screen. Often you'll find that if you use TYPE to display a very large file, it displays only a few lines and then abruptly halts—it has encountered character 26.

File types

We've explained this phenomenon because it may interfere with your attempts to look into files to find the data you're searching for. Most word processor files are easily examined, but not all. Some, like *WordStar*, modify every character in the file, making it appear as nothing but gobbledygook. *Most* non-text files, such as spreadsheet files or outliner files, are filled with graphic characters and control codes that make it very difficult to view the file. The extreme case is *program files*, which present total nonsense when viewed by the TYPE command. Because there's no need to look into program files, this should be no problem. Still, you should know that when you look into an unidentified file that displays only gibberish, then the file probably contains code (program files always end with **.COM** or **.EXE**, but extra code may be stashed away in files that do not have these filename extensions). Incidentally, just because program files may be displayed as a series of random characters, you shouldn't think that program files are a kind of text file. They're made of a series of numbers, many of which are two or more bytes long, but DOS *displays* the numbers as sequences of ASCII characters.

Alternatives to TYPE

The TYPE command has been the source of much complaint. People need an easy and quick way of looking into *any* file. A number of developers have released modified TYPE programs that load the whole file into memory and let you scroll back and forth. Some would like to part you from $30 for this utility—far too much. You'll find perfectly good offerings in the public domain or in disk toolkits. Note that the DOS diskettes hold the DEBUG program, which can display any file but in a way that only the technically sophisticated can understand.

In the next chapter, we'll look at *DOS shells*, which add many features to DOS. Many shells have an inbuilt editor that can look into most files. Not all editors are created equal, and some are better than others for examining complex data files. For example, the editor in *QDOS II* has a "full-ASCII option" that interprets all control codes as symbols. Any file can be viewed completely and without interference. The editor also offers an option in which it modifies data from *WordStar* files to make it appear as ordinary text. DOS shells are particularly useful for viewing many files because most let you move the cursor down a directory listing and show any file at the press of a key.

Printing Files

You may sometimes want to print a file or part of a file perhaps for a rough-and-ready copy of some data. For text files, you can do this with the TYPE command by appending **>LPT1** to the command (or **>COM1** if you have a serial printer). The **>** sign tells DOS to *redirect* output from the screen to the printer. For example, **TYPE MYFILE>LPT1** prints the document **MYFILE**. Or **COPY MYFILE LPT1** does the job. Don't expect the fancy formatting your software supplies when it prints out the same file. There will be no page breaks, and text may fall right atop the folds in your printer paper. Formatting codes you've written into a document are printed out exactly as they appear on the screen.

Non-text files, or modified text files, can't be printed this way. You must use the software that created the file. The printer interprets tabs and carriage returns, but other control characters may only confuse it. Most printers treat box-graphic characters as italicized forms of alphabetic characters. Sometimes control codes in files cause the printer to switch into special print modes; suddenly *everything* is written as subscripts.

Non-text files

A good DOS shell may let you make quick-and-dirty printouts of files. Or you can use a printer utility, such as the *LP* ("Line Print") program in the *Norton Utilities*. Among other features, it makes page breaks, sets margins on the page, sets line spacing, and adds headers, footers, and page numbers. It also can send a setup string to the printer, and it can deal with non-standard text files, such as *WordStar* files. A utility like *LP* won't give you the pretty formatting you expect from your word processor, but it produces output that's far superior to DOS's.

The Ctrl-PrtSc trap   Incidentally, you can also copy files to the printer by striking
Ctrl-PrtSc. This activates the "printer echo" feature that sends everything appearing on the screen to the printer. When you then
enter **TYPE MYFILE**, the file displayed by TYPE is also directed to
the printer. Striking **Ctrl-PrtSc** a second time toggles off the feature. Unfortunately, computer novices often inadvertently strike
this key combination. If the printer is turned off, the machine
freezes up and issues a printer error message—one that Ctrl-Break
can't get you out of. In despair, many people reboot the machine
and lose the work that was in progress. It's good to know about
this little gremlin and a good idea to inform coworkers of its existence.

Printing directories   It's very easy to print out directories using the > sign. Just append **>LPT1** (or **>COM1**) to the DIR command. To print any directory:

```
DIR >LPT1
```

To print a listing of all files with a **.TXT** extension, sorted by file
size:

```
DIR *.TXT ISORT /+13 >LPT1
```

Some of the *DOS shells* we discuss in the next chapter can scan the
directory tree and print combined directory listings. Wildcard characters may be used in the search, so you can get a sorted listing of,
say, every *1-2-3* worksheet on the disk.

Cataloging Files

A filename is a tiny thing. Although over a quintillion filenames are
possible (count them and see!), it's very hard to find eleven characters that describe the content of a file. Finding *another* name for a
related file is even more difficult. Unfortunately, future versions of
DOS don't seem destined to allow descriptive tags for files. Even
OS/2 doesn't appear to be headed in this direction.

Descriptive files   One way of cataloging files is to keep a descriptive text file. If
you use a desktop utility package like *SideKick*, you can keep a
notepad file in every directory for this purpose. When you create
or delete a file, quickly call up the resident editor and enter the
filename and a note about its content. Another desktop utility,
Dayflo, supplies a ready-made template (a "DOS file" record).

Some utilities set up their own files in each directory to hold information about other files. The *FI* ("File Info") program in the
Norton Utilities accepts comments of up to 65 characters for each
file. It places the comments in a file, and you can call upon this file
for an annotated directory listing (using wildcard characters, if you
like). The comments are created at the DOS command line. For example, if you've just created a file named **GODZILLA.DOC**, you
might enter:

```
FI GODZILLA.DOC  Field report from July herpetology expedition
```

A more elaborate file-tracking facility is offered by Polaris Software in its aptly named *Zoo Keeper* program. It restricts a file's descriptive tag to 40 characters. But it also allows three 20-character
key words to be attached to each file. You can perform keyword
searches across all or part of the directory tree, and *Zoo Keeper*
gives a combined directory listing of the results. The program is
memory resident, and when DOS opens a new file, a *Zoo Keeper*
window opens on the display and prompts you for the file's descriptive tag and key words.

Utilities

Managing Disk Space

The secret to hard disk management is *discipline*. It makes much
more sense to put files where they belong when they are first created and to erase them the moment they become obsolete, rather
than run a periodic housecleaning. You might argue the virtues of
procrastination in the name of "economies of scale." But eight-char-
acter file names give flimsy descriptions of a file's contents. If you
put off dealing with files when they are created or modified, you'll
later face the huge *dis*economy of having to look into each file to
find out what in heaven's blazes it is—if you can figure it out! And
when you misjudge an old file's value and delete it, the "disecono-
mies" loom larger.

Installing New Software

When you install new software on the hard disk, be wary of automatic installation. Programs that install themselves often create
their own subdirectories and transfer absolutely everything on the
distribution diskettes to these subdirectories. Usually you can make

other directories that fit your scheme and then copy the files over and remove the unwanted subdirectories. But some badly crafted programs *demand* that certain files be placed in subdirectories of particular names and that the subdirectories be children of the root directory. A letter of complaint is in order.

Interference with
DOS files

Installation programs may also insert lines into AUTOEXEC.BAT or CONFIG.SYS. Some may even *replace* these files, believe it or not. The documentation glowingly informs you that you don't even need to know what a CONFIG.SYS file is; the software will make it for you. It's hard to trust software that does such a stupid thing. As a precaution, make copies of AUTOEXEC.BAT and CONFIG.SYS before running installation programs (keeping files named AUTOEXEC.BAK and CONFIG.BAK is a good idea in any case— these files are amazingly difficult to reconstruct).

Copy protection

When you buy copy protected software, you should closely examine the documentation to find out how many hard disk installations are allowed. In the chapters ahead we discuss techniques for optimizing the disk and backing it up. Several of these can interfere with the copy protection scheme copied over to the hard disk. If application software stops you from using utility software, consider whether it shouldn't be returned to the vendor.

Sometimes programs that break copy protection schemes are the answer. *COPYII PC* is the most famous. One problem with such programs is that they are limited by the capabilities of the disk controller chip. If the distribution disks are created with a more sophisticated controller, no amount of software magic can mimic the copy protection scheme in your more primitive floppy disk drives. For this reason, the makers of *COPYII PC* now offer an add-in board carrying more advanced electronics.

Key disks

Key disks, which present another problem, work in a copy protection scheme in which one of the distribution diskettes must be in a floppy drive (usually A:) for the program installed on drive C to work. In this approach, utility software cannot interfere with the copy protection scheme. But often you'll want that floppy drive available, especially for making backups. The *COPYII PC* package includes a utility called *NOKEY* that can often trick DOS into thinking that the key disk is in place when it isn't.

Mass File Deletions

Paradoxically, people often delete files accidentally because they don't use the DOS **ERASE** command *enough*. Users should get into the habit of removing files when they're no longer needed, either by archiving them on floppy diskettes or by erasing them once and for all. When directories become clogged with obsolescent files, confusion blooms, and mistakes occur.

DOS protects you from certain kinds of catastrophic mass erasures. The RMDIR command can't delete a subdirectory unless it is emptied of all files and references to child subdirectories. Without this safeguard, in a few keystrokes you might wipe out most of the directory tree. DOS also won't let you simultaneously erase every file in a subdirectory (**DEL *.***) without first answering "yes" to a query that asks whether you really want to do that.

DOS safeguards

You may still inflict gross damage through the use of wildcards, however. **ERASE *.TXT**, for instance, could wipe out a whole novel in one blow. Many users don't properly understand the use of the asterisk as a wildcard. The statement:

```
DEL ZZZ*.WKS
```

erases all worksheets (.WKS) for which the first three letters of the filename are ZZZ. Files named **ZZZ.WKS** and **ZZZABC.WKS** are deleted, but not **ZZ.WKS**. Now, imagine a case in which you have two files named **AZZZ.WKS** and **BZZZ.WKS**, and you want to delete both with one command. If you enter

```
DEL *ZZZ.WKS
```

the DEL command will erase *all* files with a **.WKS** extension in the directory, not just the two you desire. It interprets every character following the asterisk as a wildcard. This mistake could cost you scores of files. To avoid it, *never use an asterisk at the beginning of a filename*. To delete just the two files, use the question mark instead:

```
DEL ?ZZZ.WKS
```

Another common error arises from careless typing. Many programs generate duplicate files with a **.BAK** extension. These should be deleted as soon as work on the file is complete. Otherwise they clog directories and may be unnecessarily copied during backups. They are eliminated from a directory by typing:

Typing errors

```
DEL *.BAK
```

but you may inadvertently enter:

```
DEL *.BAT
```

or

```
DEL *.BAS
```

in which case you'll lose all batch files or all *BASIC* program files in
the directory. To avoid this error, make a one-line batch file containing **DEL*.BAK**, place it in the batch file subdirectory with the
PATH command pointing to it, and name the file something like
KILLBAK. Then you can routinely eliminate the BAK files from any
subdirectory without raising your blood pressure.

To protect yourself against all sorts of wildcard erasures, make a
batch file named **DELETE.BAT** that contains these lines:

```
CLS
DIR %1
PAUSE --- STRIKE ANY KEY TO ERASE %1, or CTRL-
ERASE %1
```

If you were to enter **DELETE *.WKS**, this batch file would list all
files about to be erased, then it would ask your consent, offering
the option of using Ctrl-Break to abandon the erasure. When Ctrl-
Break is used, the message **Terminate batch job (Y/N)?** appears,
and you must enter **Y**.

In addition to the ***.*** wildcard combination, you can erase all
files in a subdirectory by naming the subdirectory alone. For example, to erase all files in the subdirectory **PAJAMAS** along the
path **\CATS\PAJAMAS**, just enter:

```
ERASE \CATS\PAJAMAS
```

Before making the erasure, DOS will prompt you with the usual
Are you sure (Y/N)? message. Now, say that you really want only
to erase the file **MEOW.COM**, but you make a little mistake and
leave out the backslash between it and **PAJAMAS**:

```
ERASE \CATS\PAJAMAS MEOW.COM
```

Because of the error, DOS doesn't know how to interpret the end
of the line. In versions 3.0 and later, rather than issue an error message, DOS just goes along as if the expression **MEOW.COM** weren't

there. And so it tries to erase all files in the subdirectory, asking
Are you sure (Y/N). Of course, to the inexperienced user it appears as if DOS is checking whether **MEOW.COM** should be erased,
and so he or she may answer "Yes." Be aware that DOS asks **Are
you sure? (Y/N)** *only* when it's about to erase everything in sight.

Incidentally, sometimes you'll want to use RMDIR to remove a
subdirectory and will dutifully delete all files in it beforehand by
DEL*.*. But RMDIR won't work. This happens because there is a
hidden file in the directory (a file in which the attribute for "hidden" status is turned on). The DOS ERASE and DEL commands
don't operate on hidden files, and the DIR command won't list
them. You'll need to change the file to "normal" status before DOS
can get rid of it. We'll explain how to do this in a moment.

Problems with RMDIR

If you're tempted to erase a file but want to keep it a bit longer,
consider squirreling it away in a "junkyard" subdirectory. This
batch file would do the job, provided that there's no danger of a
"full-disk" error:

Junkyards

```
REM Moving these files to the Junk Yard
DIR %1
COPY %1 \JUNKYARD
ERASE %1
```

If the batch file were named **DISPOSE**, you'd need only to enter
DISPOSE OLDFILE.TXT to move OLDFILE to the junkyard directory. Some utilities, such as *SafetyNet* from WestLake, perform this
service automatically by completely replacing the DOS file erasure
routines. The files may be completely hidden from directory listings, but they can be listed and retrieved at any time. There are
various schemes for deleting older erasures as the disk fills. You
may be able to set a limit on how many files or how many
megabytes fit in the erasure queue.

Some special erasure utilities are far more capable than DOS. The
SDADEL program in *FilePaq* from SDA Associates can erase hidden
and read-only files, traverse the directory tree during wildcard erasures, and be made to query the user before completing erasures.
The tree-traversal feature, though extremely dangerous in the hands
of inexperienced users, nonetheless can be very useful for general
housecleaning tasks like removing all **.BAK** files. Be wary of public
domain file-erasure utilities. If you can't find a qualified recommendation, don't use them. These programs must be extremely well
crafted, lest they run amuck and wipe out scores of files.

Advanced erasure utilities

Setting File Attributes

In Chapter 2 we learned about the *attribute byte* residing in the directory entry of every file. Ordinarily, the attribute byte is set by software. But there are occasions when you may want to intervene. By changing the *archive bit*, you can determine whether backup utilities or the DOS XCOPY command will include the file when they transfer data. Second, you can change the file's *read-only* status to protect it from changes and accidental erasure.

DOS supplies the **ATTRIB** command to change file attributes. It can change only the archive and read-only attributes. It uses the expression **+A** to *set* the archive bit (turn it "On") so that a file will be readied for backup. The expression **–A** *resets* the archive bit (turns it "Off") so that backup software passes over the file. Similarly, **+R** makes a file read-only, and **–R** returns it to normal status. To reset the archive bit in the file **2NDCOPY.BAK**:

```
ATTRIB -A 2NDCOPY.BAK
```

To make the file read-only:

```
ATTRIB +R 2NDCOPY.BAK
```

Starting with version 3.3 of DOS, the ATTRIB command uses the **/S** switch to change all files in the current directory and all subdirectories below it. To set the archive bit of every file on the disk in preparation for a global backup:

```
ATTRIB +A \*.* /S
```

As you can see, ATTRIB can take wildcard characters. In this example, the expression ***.*** **/S** means "all files in the root directory, and all files in all subdirectories below."

If you have an earlier DOS version, you'll need to turn to a disk toolkit, most of which have a routine that sets attribute bytes. In the *Norton Utilities*, the program is called *FA*, for "File Attributes." In addition to performing all functions of the DOS 3.3 version of ATTRIB, this utility can search the disk and *display* files with a particular attribute. Besides the archive and read-only attributes, it can handle the *hidden* and *system* attributes, which, you'll recall, mark files relating to the operating system and hide files from directory listings. These files cannot be copied or erased.

Such utilities have a surprising number of applications. By turning off the archive bit in files with a **.BAK** extension, you can avoid copying the files during backups (who needs backups of backups?). You can hide files that you want to stop others from interfering with or can unclutter directory listings. Conversely, you can use a program like *FA* to look for hidden files in subdirectories that refuse deletion when you apply the RMDIR command (they are sometimes created by copy-protection schemes).

Finally, you can *protect* files by giving them read-only status. Such files can be opened and read but not written to or erased. Read-only status is ideal for configuration files and batch files, which seldom change and are difficult to re-create after they've accidentally been destroyed. Be aware that when COPY duplicates a read-only file, the copy isn't given read-only status. Also, be wary of how software may respond when it tries to write to a read-only file. You could do hours of work to a file and then find that DOS won't grant a program's request to write it back to disk. Many programs cannot recover from this situation.

Applications

Data Compression

Data compression, often the simplest solution to dwindling disk space, is certainly the least expensive solution because compression utilities usually cost only $50 to $75. Often a file's size may be cut in half. In some cases, half of disk space can be reclaimed by compressing all applicable files as if a 20-megabyte disk suddenly became a 40-megabyte disk! Data compression can also be very useful in data transmission across phone lines. A file reduced to half its former size takes only half as long to send. Of course, the parties at each end must own copies of the compression/decompression utility. But these are quickly paid for by the savings in long-distance charges.

The best file compressors may be used in a **RAM-resident mode**. The program is loaded by AUTOEXEC.BAT when the machine is booted, and it links itself into the operating system's disk-access routines, just like the path programs discussed earlier in this chapter (if they're well designed, the two kinds of programs should be able to coexist peacefully). When a file is loaded, the compression utility automatically decompresses it as it is fed to DOS; when the file is saved, it is recompressed. Any utility also lets you com-

RAM-residency

press and decompress files by command so that a file can be permanently returned to normal, decompressed form.

It's important to be able to turn off the RAM-resident automatic compression feature. There are instances when it isn't required, such as with the DOS COPY command. It makes no sense to decompress a file and then immediately recompress it as it is copied elsewhere.

Compression utilities take advantage of several techniques to squeeze the air out of files. It may surprise you that files can be compressed at all. Upon inspection, a 10,000-byte text file contains fully 10,000 characters (spaces are characters, too). But most files contain *patterns and redundancies*, and it is the compressor's job to find them and represent them more economically. Here are some important techniques:

Compression techniques

ASCII compression A byte of memory holds a pattern of eight bits ("Ons" and "Offs"). Not all bits are always used, and some patterns occur much more often than others. The standard ASCII system for representing characters may be rearranged so that frequently used characters are encoded in only a few bits, while seldom occurring characters are encoded in longer bit strings.

Dictionary lookups Some utilities are optimized for English-language text-file compression. They use a small dictionary of the most common words to substitute codes for these words.

String compression Words not found in dictionary lookups may occur repeatedly in a file. Once the first occurrence has been identified, subsequent instances may be replaced by a *pointer* to the first; that is, a code tells the compression program to go find the first instance and insert it in place of the second. This technique is particularly effective in very long files.

Digraph encoding Certain vowel-consonant pairs occur very frequently in English; these are encoded as single bytes.

Run-length The utility seeks out sequences of the same character or pattern and encodes them as a repetition count. Many database and spreadsheet files contain long sequences of zeros or other "filler" characters that may be eliminated in this way.

Software-specific analysis Some software may encode data in special ways. *WordStar*, for example, slightly changes the standard

ASCII character set for its own purposes. For popular software, a compression utility may offer a special mode that deals with just those special files.

If you look into a compressed file, you'll see mostly gobbledy-gook. Text files may hold a few remaining English words that couldn't be compressed by any of the techniques at hand. This means that your files are even less browsable than before, and that file organization and cataloging is more important than ever. The files are nonetheless perfectly ordinary DOS files so that they may be copied, compared, and checked by any standard DOS utilities.

Some compression utilities are dedicated to only one kind of file. *SQZ*, from Turner Hall Publishing, operates *only* on Lotus 1-2-3 worksheet files. Like database files, spreadsheet files often contain much unused space. Data fields are sized for the largest data item that will occur, and most fields are only partially filled. Such files are packed full of zeros that may be quickly eliminated. Some 1-2-3 files may be compressed to as little as 5% of their original size, and most can be reduced by more than half. *SQZ* comes with a built-in communication option that reformats spreadsheets for modem transmission. It also includes a password provision that keeps snoops out of your files.

Specialized utilities

Most file compressors are general-purpose. Two examples of RAM-resident utilities are *Squish* from Sundog Software Corporation and *Cubit* from SoftLogic Solutions. The *Arc* program is a favorite public domain program found on electronic bulletin boards. These programs can deal with any kind of file, although they are much more effective with some than others. You choose which files will be compressed by first going through the disk with a utility that makes an initial compression. *Cubit* lets you choose groups of files by wildcards, whole directories, or even the entire disk.

General-purpose compressors

Typically, general-purpose utilities can reduce text files by 50% (40% to 70%), database files by 75% (70% to 90%), and spread-sheet files by 30% (much less than the results achieved by a special-purpose utility like *SQZ*). Files containing graphic images vary widely in their compressibility; most commercial utilities are poorly equipped to deal with them. Many utilities report how much they've compressed a file. Of course, no matter how much a file is reduced, disk space is still allocated in clusters. As a result, compressing a file smaller than one cluster (2,048 bytes in DOS 3.x, 4,096 bytes in DOS 2.x) makes no sense.

Effectiveness

Program files are nearly random in content; because they lack patterns, they are hard to compress. Sometimes they may be reduced by as much as 15%, but some may actually be made *larger* by compression utilities. A good utility will recognize this situation and leave the file in its original state.

Performance

At first sight, file compression seems the ideal solution to dwindling disk space. But all the processing required in compressing and decompressing files can exact a heavy toll on performance. The time required by compressors varies greatly by the kind of file, and by the compressor's own strengths and weaknesses. A 100K text file might require 15 seconds to compress. This time penalty isn't very great when one loads a few business letters every hour. But if you are a programmer whose compiler must work with dozens of program files, the delay is completely unacceptable. Database sorts can take five times as long when the data files are compressed. On the whole, decompression takes less time than compression because the search for patterns has already been performed.

Amazingly, file compression can sometimes actually *speed up* disk access. When a compression utility does little more than strip zeros from a spreadsheet, it takes very little time to reinsert the zeros when the file is read. Because the file is held on far fewer disk sectors, less time goes into the actual disk read operation. This gain may outweigh the time lost to decompression. As CPUs become faster, this advantage is beginning to accrue even to general-purpose utilities. The makers of *Squish* report that file compression *speeds up* disk operations on 16-MHz 80386 machines.

Memory requirements

Another disadvantage of RAM-resident compressors is that they take up precious memory to use as a work area. Although a program like *Squish* consumes only 40K, you still suffer the loss of that much more RAM. Here is one more example of trade-offs between two kinds of efficiency (disk-space preservation vs. memory preservation).

Hardware-based compressors

Soon data compression may be built into many disk controller cards. Some of the souped-up RLL adapters, such as the *Awesome I/O Card* from CSL, already contain onboard compression that is performed on all files as they pass through. Similarly, Megamedia International Inc. of Clearwater, Florida is releasing ROM chips that replace the ROMs found on standard IBM XT controller cards and automatically compress and decompress data as it passes through (the chips are priced competitively with compressor software). These compressors are much faster than software utilities, but because they cannot look at an entire file at once, they are less effective. Still, they may on average reduce files by a quarter.

Data compression is a valuable tool to help you through a period of insufficient disk capacity. If you're strapped for disk capacity and you own a particularly fast machine, it may be worth compressing all your files. But, if you own an 8086, 8088, or 80286 machine, and your applications are disk-intensive, you should avoid data compression if you can. You're far better off spending more for a larger disk than clocking in tens of hours of extra disk-access time.

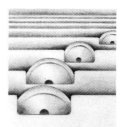

Chapter 6

Navigating the Disk

Managing files in a directory tree ought not to be intellectually challenging. We all grew up around actual botanical trees so that it should come naturally to us to think about the consequences of loading programs and data files in remote directories. But a directory tree exists only in our less-than-perfect imaginations. When we use a hard disk, our minds are always burdened with keeping track of where files are and how to get to them. Easing that burden is the subject of this chapter.

The goal is to find ways to keep track of where you're working in the tree, ways to copy, rename, and delete files easily, and ways to cut down on the keystrokes required to perform these tasks. Not only will you save time and energy, but you'll make fewer mistakes, lose less data, and generally work with less tension. First, we'll look at how to do things through DOS, and then we'll move on to sophisticated software that will make you wonder why you ever bothered with DOS commands.

Moving Around the Disk

DOS offers a multitude of features to help you move about the tree and transfer files from one subdirectory to another. Some of these can reward a few minutes study with hours of saved labor.

Tracking Your Location in the Tree

It's important to always know where you are in the tree. When DOS displays only the austere **C>** prompt, it's easy to become confused. You can use the PROMPT command to make the DOS prompt display the name of the current directory. Simply enter:

```
PROMPT $p
```

If the current directory is **\ACCOUNTS**, the DOS prompt is transformed to:

```
C:\ACCOUNTS
```

As you can see, the symbol **C:** begins the command. The command changes the DOS prompt for all drives, so when you switch over to drive A, it becomes:

```
A:\
```

In this expression, the backslash indicates the root directory (though floppy disks aren't ordinarily given tree directories, they can be, and what we think of as a floppy's "directory" may be regarded as a root directory).

Displaying just the subdirectory name in the prompt leads to confusion because the words you write on the command line become hard to read. For example, if you run CHKDSK:

```
C:ACCOUNTSCHKDSK
```

It's better to place a > symbol after the prompt. This is done with the expression **$g**. Thus:

```
PROMPT $p$g
```

results in:

```
C:ACCOUNTS>
```

Better still, add a few dashes to make an arrow:

```
PROMPT $p---$g
```

Giving:

```
C:ACCOUNTS--->
```

PROMPT takes other special symbols. The most useful are **$t** and **$d**, which print the time and date. **$_** inserts a carriage return. To make DOS show the time on one line, and the current directory below, enter:

```
PROMPT $t$_$p---$g
```

The result:

```
12:06:28.78
C:ACCOUNTS--->
```

If you feel that you can get along without knowing the time to the hundredth of a second, you can insert *backspaces* into the command using **$h**:

```
PROMPT $t$h$h$h$h$h$h$_$p---$g
```

Of course, you won't want to write this out each time you boot up the computer. So include your prompt in AUTOEXEC.BAT.

Changing Directories

When you perform complicated tasks that touch on files in several directories, you may find yourself changing directories constantly. The designers of DOS must have anticipated this because they were kind enough to give a short form (CD) of CHDIR. But the real problem is in retyping long DOS paths. There are several ways of sidestepping this labor.

Batch files

One solution entails making batch files for your most active directories. Each file holds the single line:

```
CHDIR \LEVEL1\LEVEL2\LEVEL3
```

or whatever the DOS path is to the subdirectory. Place all of these batch files in the BATCH subdirectory and set the PATH command so that DOS will always search for them:

```
PATH C:\BATCH
```

Then you can change to the directory with only a few keystrokes: **ACCOUNTS, EDITOR, NEWDATA.**

The "." and ".." symbols

Let's digress a moment to talk about the "." and ".." symbols. Everyone has seen these at the top of subdirectory entries, but not many users know what they stand for. The first, '.', refers to the directory itself. It's most useful for referring to a child subdirectory without typing the entire directory path. For example, say that the current directory is the subdirectory **COUNTY** along the DOS path **\REGION\STATE\COUNTY**. If you want a directory listing from the child directory, **CITY**, you could enter:

```
DIR \REGION\STATE\COUNTY\CITY
```

But the "." symbol can save you some keystrokes by representing all subdirectories up to the current directory:

```
DIR .\CITY
```

The symbol ".." represents the *parent directory* of the current directory. Using the prior example, when the current directory is **CITY**, the statement **CHDIR ..** makes **\REGION\STATE\COUNTY** the current directory. If the current directory is **\CHICKEN\EGG**, then the statement:

```
COPY \CHICKEN\EGG\YOKE.DAT ..
```

copies the file **YOKE.DAT** from **EGG** to **CHICKEN**. Or you could enter:

```
COPY .\YOKE.DAT ..
```

Later in this chapter we'll talk about DOS shells, which often present a diagram of the tree with a cursor that can be moved to the subdirectory you wish to make current. This feature is also available in small utilities. The *Norton Utilities* include the *NCD* (Norton Change Directory) program. It keeps a file that maps the tree and must be updated whenever you change the tree structure. The diagram it shows can be scrolled up and down, and you can position the cursor to add or remove subdirectories.

Tree diagrams

The *NCD* program also lets you move to a subdirectory by typing just its name, without the DOS path leading to it. You can even use only the first part of the subdirectory's name as long as it distinguishes it from all other subdirectories. For example, the command **NCD ELE** would take you straight to **\MAMMALS\PACHYDRM \ELEPHANT**. In this case, no tree diagram is shown.

Moving About through Simple Menus

We've seen how you can easily change subdirectories through batch files placed in a BATCH subdirectory accessed by the PATH command. Of course, you could add more commands to these batch files to make them load software once the subdirectory change is made. The entire system may be streamlined by creating a master menu of batch file choices. A bit later we'll talk about

complicated menuing software. But, for now, let's say that we want
to create just a simple menu offering three selections:

1. Word Processing
2. Outlining
3. DOS

First, you need to create the menu screen by creating a standard
ASCII text file with any word processor. None of the word processor's formatting commands can be used to make underlinings,
center the text, or whatever. Rather, you must create a what-you-
see-is-what-you-get image of the menu. Let's say that the file is
named **MENU.TXT**.

Next, create batch files named **1.bat, 2.bat**, and **3.bat**. The first
of these files corresponds to the first menu selection. It moves to
the word processing subdirectory, clears the screen, and loads the
editor (say, *WordPerfect*). When the program terminates, the next
line in the batch file is executed, a TYPE command that redisplays
the menu screen:

```
CHDIR \EDITOR
CLS
WP
TYPE MENU.TXT
```

Once the menu is displayed, the batch file is finished, and control
returns to DOS. When a selection is made from the menu screen,
and the Enter key is struck, DOS interprets the numeral as a program name, searches for the program, finds a batch file by that
name in the BATCH subdirectory, and starts executing the commands in the file. In this way, the menuing system keeps moving
from application to application.

After the menu is redisplayed, the DOS prompt appears. You can
refine the menu by using a PROMPT command that asks for a
menu selection. For example:

```
PROMPT Select a number and strike ENTER--$g
```

Returning to DOS

The third selection in the menu exits the menu system and returns control to the DOS prompts. To achieve this, place nothing
more than a **CLS** statement in the file **3.BAT**. That's all there is to
it.

Building Interactive Batch Files

If the simple menu scheme seems contrived, be assured, it *is*. DOS doesn't allow *conditional branching* in batch files. That is, a batch file cannot receive a keystroke and execute particular lines of code on the basis of it. If it could, the command sequences of the separate files (1.BAT, 2.BAT, and so on) could be combined into one file.

Happily, it's possible to write a utility that can make batch files interactive, albeit in a roundabout way. The *Ask* program in the *Norton Utilities* can display a prompt such as:

```
Run the (E)ditor, (D)atabase, or (Q)uit?
```

To make this prompt, the ASK program is called from within a batch file in the format:

```
ASK ""Run the (E)ditor, (D)atabase, or (Q)uit?'', edq
```

The characters at the end of the line (edq) tell the ASK program the characters that represent the menu selections and the order in which they appear. Ask waits for a key to be pressed. And then it does a funny thing—it creates an *error condition*.

When programs are forced to terminate because they can't access part of the computer's hardware, they return an error code to DOS. Batch files may intercept these codes in the form of an *errorlevel*. Once a menu selection is made, the ASK program terminates and returns an errorlevel code that corresponds to the position of the menu selection within the menu listing. It does this even though technically no error has occurred. If **Q** has been struck, "errorlevel 3" is returned. **D** returns "errorlevel 1".

Batch files can make conditional branches for errorlevel codes. Look what happens in this batch file:

```
ASK ""Run the (E)ditor, (D)atabase, or (Q)uit?'', edq
   if errorlevel 3 goto quit
   if errorlevel 2 goto database
REM Not 3 or 2, so must be (E)ditor
REM Editor instructions begin here
:editor
   CLS
```

```
    CD\EDITOR
    WP
    GOTO QUIT
 :database
    CLS
    CD\DATABASE
    DB
 :quit
```

When **Q** is selected, errorlevel 3 occurs, and control jumps straight to the end of the batch file. When **D** is selected, errorlevel 2 occurs, and control jumps to the tag **:database**. From there a series of commands clears the screen, moves to the database subdirectory, and loads the database program. Finally, when **E** was chosen, errorlevel 1 occurs. There's no need to write a "goto" statement because control will run on to the editor's commands by default. After the editor has been run, another jump is made to quit the batch file (otherwise control would flow into the database instructions).

If you want more flexibility than this in your menuing system, you need to acquire a full-blown menuing program, which we'll discuss later in this chapter.

Moving About with Keyboard Macros

Till now, we haven't mentioned *keyboard macros*. You may have some experience with one of the many keyboard macro programs, such as *Prokey, SuperKey,* or *SmartKey*—memory-resident utilities that watch keystrokes as they arrive from the keyboard. You can associate a string of characters with any particular key, and when you strike that key, the macro program replaces the keystroke with the sequence of characters. For example, you could link "antidisestablishmentarianism" with **Alt-A**. Then, as you're typing along in your word processor and feel an overwhelming need to impress, you can strike Alt-A, and "antidisestablishmentarianism" is inserted into the document.

Keyboard macros can just as easily hold elaborate sequences of DOS commands and other instructions. In essence, certain keystrokes become menu selections—but no menu is displayed. The absence of a menu listing is, in fact, one of the disadvantages of keyboard macros. Over time, it's easy to forget what key does what. Another problem is that complicated commands can become difficult to modify. Still another problem is that a typographical error can suddenly send you off to the Twilight Zone. But keyboard macros offer one advantage over menuing: they don't insulate you from DOS. You're always working at the DOS prompt—in full control.

A feature to watch for when purchasing a keyboard macro program is the ability of one keyboard macro to load a set of different macros. Any keyboard macro program can save the keyboard assignments you make in a file. You can load one file for word processing macros, another for spreadsheet macros. A first-rate program can have a macro load one of these files and pass control to a different set of macros—an impressive trick. The software essentially pulls the rug out from under itself—without crashing. When a macro program offers this feature, you can *toggle* between tasks with one keystroke.

DOS Shells

The inadequacies of DOS have spawned a genre of software called *DOS shells*, which add new capabilities to DOS and make existing capabilities easier to use. A good DOS shell makes DOS what you always wanted it to be. Loaded like any other program, a shell takes you into a world of menus, tree diagrams, and fancy directory listings.

Although DOS appears to have grown in many ways, a shell does not actually modify DOS. In a sense, it *surrounds* DOS, which is why it is called a "shell." Beneath, COMMAND.COM continues to manage memory and operate the disk drives. But the shell performs most DOS commands like COPY and ERASE, adding many powerful features to them. Further, you can run programs from within a shell, exactly as if the program were loaded from the **C>** prompt.

These days, you cannot open a computer magazine without finding yet another DOS shell on the market. At least 100 exist, from well-established firms (*XTREE, 1DIR*, and the *Norton Commander,* for instance), seat-of-the-pants software houses, and freeware or shareware. From all this activity, you might think that DOS shells are enormously popular. Although some have sold in large numbers, most PC users still go without. Yet this is one kind of software that virtually everyone can profitably use. The makers enthuse wildly about the utility of their products while users yawn, shrug their shoulders, and demur, "it's nice, but I already know DOS."

The proliferation of shells

Perhaps it is the manufacturers' own fault that DOS shells are seen as an aid for beginners. Their advertisements harp on the *ease-of-use* theme: "a rank beginner can master DOS in 30 minutes!." Although these claims may sometimes be true, beginners tend to miss the opportunity of using a shell because they know too little about computers to realize what they're missing. Meanwhile, more experienced users, who pride themselves on their fluency in DOS, regard DOS shells as *sissy stuff.*

Capabilities

Too few people understand that a good DOS shell can automate complicated DOS chores that otherwise require lots of mental and digital energy no matter how well-versed the user. Many shells let you edit the directory tree; you can rename subdirectories and even move them around the tree. They'll make fancy searches across the whole tree for files of particular characteristics. And they'll let you *tag* selected files in subdirectories for copying and backups, saving endless typing. Even those of a Puritanical bent who would rather just do it the hard way will find that a good shell helps avert errors, such as faulty file erasures or the copying of bad files over good ones. For system managers who must constantly mop up after others on a large hard disk, a DOS shell is indispensable.

The frenetic competition among DOS shell makers has lead to the most extreme *feature creep* of any software genre. You name it, and somebody has incorporated it into a DOS shell: data encryption, printer spooling, file recovery utilities, floppy disk cataloging. Some shells make the video display as complicated as a space shuttle control panel. In fact, for truly timid computer novices, a DOS shell may cause more confusion than it alleviates (a *menu generator*, which we'll discuss later, is a better choice). But, in the hands of advanced users, a good DOS shell is always a powerhouse.

Trees and Directories

DOS shells center around the directory tree and directory listings. They may display the tree and directories differently, but all serve the same goal: to let you operate on files by moving a cursor to their listings on the screen rather than by remembering their names and laboriously typing them in.

Tree display

Many shells are based on a diagram of the directory tree. Unlike the very primitive DOS TREE command, these diagrams give an instant overview of the shape and organization of your directory tree. A tree diagram may be scrolled up and down. Usually, a bar cursor

moves through the tree, and you can change directories simply by
shifting it to the desired tree position and striking one key. Another
keystroke opens a directory listing for the subdirectory. Some shells
create combined tree-directory displays, with directory listings
nested in a tree diagram.

All DOS shells let you easily create and remove subdirectories
from the tree, often by moving the cursor to the desired position
in the tree diagram. Some shells can rename subdirectories, and a
few offer a tree-grafting function that can move single subdirectories or whole branches from one part of the tree to another.

It takes several seconds for a shell to search an entire disk to assemble a tree diagram. Rather than perform this action every time
the diagram is displayed, most DOS shells keep a file that holds the
tree structure. The file is modified whenever changes are made to
the tree through the shell but not if DOS commands alter the tree
when the shell isn't loaded. The shell offers a special command to
update the tree file. A well-crafted shell recovers gracefully from
errors that occur when the tree diagram doesn't correspond to the
actual subdirectory structure.

Like tree diagrams, directory displays may be scrolled up and
down. This feature alone is worth the price of a DOS shell because
you're freed forever from the frustrations of executing the DIR
command repeatedly to scan back and forth in a directory. Many
shells offer special "wide" directory listings that fit many files on a
screen. Some let you look at two separately scrollable directories
side by side, or you can toggle between multiple directory listings.

Directory display

Many shells give more information about files than DOS does.
They may show each file's attribute, or they may tell how many
clusters a file takes, as well as its size. Besides the usual wildcard
searches, many shells let you list files chosen by attribute, date, or
time. Combining these features makes for very powerful searches.
For example, you might be able to ask to see a listing of all read-
only files with the extension **.TXT** dated between January and
March. It's also useful to be able to see hidden files, because DOS
won't show them, and they may be present in subdirectories that
you want to erase.

An especially valuable feature is the ability to combine many directory listings into one. Some DOS shells can create an amalga-
mated listing (a **global directory**) of a whole branch of a tree or
even the whole disk. These listings may also be made by wildcards
and other search criteria so that you could request, for example, a
listing of every batch file on the disk. Of course, different subdirectories may hold files of the same name, so confusion can arise.

*Combined
directories*

Many shells overcome this problem by having you move a bar cursor to a file in question; its DOS path is then displayed.

Sorting directories

The directory sorts that take great effort in DOS are easily performed in DOS shells. Most shells have a special sorting menu that lists the options. You need merely tick off the sort criteria you desire: filename or extension, date, time, file size, attribute. Like DOS sorts, most shells don't actually change the physical order of the directory listings. The sort features may be applied to combined directories, letting you assemble, for example, an alphabetized listing of all *Lotus 1-2-3* files created in 1987.

Printouts

A good DOS shell lets you print out any listing it makes on the screen. As a result, it can be an invaluable tool for cataloging the disk. You can print out the tree diagram (usually with rather crude graphics) and any of the various directory listings. And, if you like, in many shells you can sit back and have a complete catalog of every file on the disk printed out. Such a catalog may be very useful for recovering data when a serious disk failure occurs and your backups aren't up to date.

Managing Files

Copying files

Copying files is easy in DOS shells. In most shells you move the cursor to the file in a directory listing, strike a key, and then move the cursor to a position on the tree diagram and strike *Enter*. In some shells, all this moving about may actually be slower than typing an ordinary COPY command on the DOS command line. But in mass file transfers, DOS shells offer a decided advantage. They can select files not just by wildcards, but also by *tagging*.

Tagging

In tagging, you move the cursor up and down a directory listing and "tag" a file by striking the space bar or some other key. A symbol appears beside each tagged file. Some shells let you set the tags by wildcards. For example, you might have the shell tag all files with the extension **.DOC** by tagging for ***.DOC**. Then you could use the cursor to *untag* those few files that you don't want affected. You also may be able to reverse the tags, so that untagged files become tagged and vice-versa. This feature is useful when you want to copy all but a few files in a subdirectory. You need only tag the few, then reverse the taggings.

Backups

The COPY facilities in some DOS shells are so powerful that they may be used for a simple backup scheme. Some shells can span diskettes as they copy groups of files. When the first disk fills, the shell prompts the user for a disk change, then goes on copying files from the group. Some shells will copy files by any combination of wildcards, dates, and attributes, searching the whole directory for matches. So you could easily have the shell backup all files changed in the last week.

The **MOVE** command in most DOS shells should really have been included in DOS itself. MOVE shifts a file from one directory to another (or one disk to another). Little more than a combination of **COPY** and **ERASE**, it saves keystrokes and confusion. The command sees to it that the file is erased only if it has been successfully copied. MOVE commands have all the flexibility of COPY commands, including tagging.

Moving files

Properly designed, a MOVE command is extremely fast. Because there's no need to duplicate the file, all the shell must do is move the file's directory entry from one subdirectory to another. Using wildcards, dozens of files may be moved in the blink of an eye. Incidentally, you'll occasionally encounter "move" utilities in disk toolboxes, or on public domain bulletin boards. Use only versions from trustworthy sources because files are easily lost if the software malfunctions or handles errors badly.

Tagging may also apply to the shell's ERASE command. Some shells offer special facilities for avoiding accidental file erasures. Often, they'll display all files about to be erased and ask your permission before going on. This feature is invaluable when wildcard characters are used in erasures; a mistake could cause dozens of files to be erased when only a few were intended. A good shell can extend an erasure to the entire disk so that you can eliminate, say, all .BAK files in a single blow. In this situation the shell may display the name of each .BAK file it finds, asking whether it should be deleted.

Erasing files

Finally, nearly all DOS shells let you view files easily. Unlike the DOS TYPE command, which reads and displays a file line by line, shells load the whole file in memory and let you scroll back and forth in it. Consequently, most cannot handle files larger than available memory. Some have special facilities for handling unusual text files, such as *WordStar* files or encoded data files, which often cannot be looked into at all by the TYPE command. Often the shell provides a full-screen editor that lets you change the file. Such editors are not to be mistaken for word processors; they can edit text and make block moves, but they don't perform fancy printer formatting. They are best suited for writing batch files or for jotting down notes.

Viewing and editing files

Running Programs

When a DOS shell is in charge, it can run any program. It employs a special feature in DOS (the "EXEC" function) that allows one program to run another. Most shells load the program by moving the bar cursor to its directory listing and typing a command code. Of course, many programs take information on the DOS command line when they are loaded; often, one lists the name of the work file immediately after the program name, as in **WP CHAP-TER7.TXT**. Some shells let you add command line information, although with difficulty.

Automatic loading

The *Norton Commander* uses a special "point-and-shoot" approach to loading programs. It requires that you assign a particular filename extension to any data files that work with a particular program. Then you can move the cursor (using a mouse, if you like) to any data file in a directory listing and "shoot"—the *Commander* uses the filename extension to figure out the program the file runs with and loads the program and the data file. To work this magic, you need to set up a simple file telling the extensions that match the programs. The data file may be anywhere on the disk; the *Commander* supplies the DOS path for the file when it loads the program.

No DOS shell accommodates all DOS commands. To execute unusual commands (like SUBST or SET) from within a shell, the shell must give *DOS access*. The shell loads a second copy of the main DOS program, COMMAND.COM, giving you access to any command. It's a sort of Rube Goldberg way of doing things: DOS loads a DOS shell that loads DOS.

Memory requirements

One common complaint about DOS shells is well deserved. To put it indelicately, many DOS shells are *fat*. All that "featuritis" takes its toll on program size. Shells approaching 200K are not unheard of. It's no wonder Microsoft did not give COMMAND.COM so many capabilities. If the shell is kept in memory and programs run from within it, memory available to program data is greatly diminished. On the other hand, if the shell is used only for managing the disk, returning to DOS before running a program from the command line, the shell doesn't cost you a byte of RAM.

Reloaders

Many DOS shells give you the best of both worlds—keeping the shell in memory yet not taking up any memory—by writing the program with a *reloader*. When a program is run from within the shell, most of the shell's bulk is abandoned, and only a small part stays in memory to execute the program. When the application terminates and control returns to the shell, the *reload module* reloads the rest of the shell from disk, returning it to its full splendor. The module that stays in memory may take up only a few thousand bytes of memory. Although you must wait momentarily for the shell to reload, you're saved the trouble of constantly exiting to DOS when you want to free memory to run a program and then manually reloading the shell after returning from the program.

Some DOS shells always remain in memory, either by being unable to reload or because they are constructed as true *RAM-resident* utilities. In the latter case, the shell is available at all times, even from within a program. *WindowDOS* from WindowDOS Associates is one example. A *hot key* stops your application and starts up the shell, allowing you to check directories, search for files or whatever. It's handy having these capabilities online, but the loss of precious RAM may be too high a price.

Miscellaneous Features

There are endless variations on the basic DOS shell design. You'll find "disk toolkits" like *PC Tools*, which offer many DOS shell-like features in separate utilities. Some of the new memory-resident utility managers like *Lotus Metro* and *SideKick Plus* provide some DOS shell capabilities. For users who like the DOS command line the way it is, there is *Command Plus*, which replaces COMMAND.COM with a version offering many more services, all exploited in the usual command-line format. This approach is the opposite of simplification: it gives extra switches for the normal DOS commands, expanding their power. This solution may be preferred by technically adept users who dislike menus, icons, and other gimmicks that promote "ease-of-use." In fact, *Command Plus* includes **SCRIPT**, a Pascal-like language for writing elaborate interactive batch files.

Every implementation has its own special features. You'll find data encryption, rudimentary menuing systems, password protection, printer control, screen blanking, keyboard macros, file unerasure—just about anything you can think of. Many offer varying degrees of online help, sometimes "context-sensitive help" that senses what your problems may be and advises you accordingly. Some help systems are practically tutorials; The *QuickDOS* shell keeps 10,000 words of help online.

A particularly interesting feature is offered in *1DIR Plus*, which lets you set "directory personalities" in which you may preset characteristics for individual subdirectory listings. Whenever the direc-

(continued page 196)

An Inside Look: File management with 1DIR+

1DIR PLUS ("Wonder plus") from Bourbaki Inc. is an exceptionally detailed DOS shell—perhaps too complex for some users. Besides file management facilities, it offers a simple menuing system and rudimentary password security. At startup, it displays a listing for the current directory, as shown in screen A. There are options for displaying a "wide" directory (as in DOS), showing multiple directories, or creating a combined directory listing. You may specify a default "personality" for directory listings so that they are always displayed in the way you prefer.

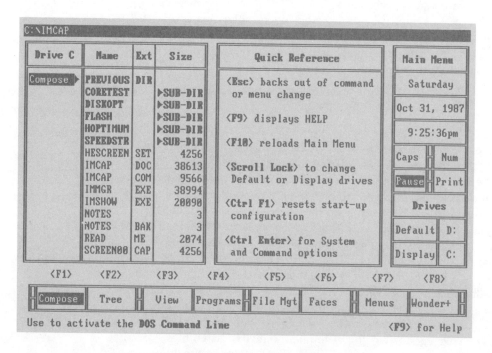

Screen A. **The Main Menu and Directory Listing.**

The main menu choices are given along the bottom of the screen. Striking the **F1** key enables a "point and shoot" feature for loading programs from a directory listing. **F2** displays a directory tree diagram (Screen B). You can quickly change directories by moving the bar cursor across the diagram, and you can modify the tree, adding and removing subdirectories.

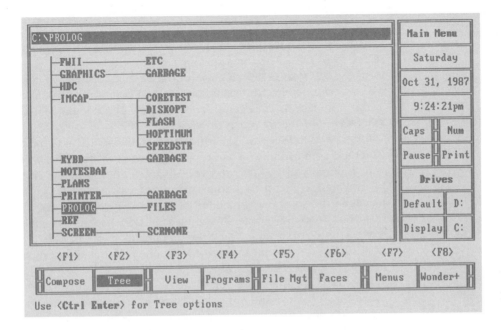

Screen B. **Displaying a Tree Diagram.**

The "view" option lets you look into a file. Screen C gives an example. You may scroll up and down in the file, edit it, search for strings in it, make block moves, and print it out. A special "Batch Builder" helps construct batch files.

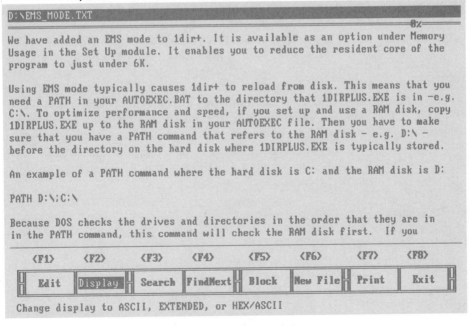

Screen C. **Viewing a file.**

tory is displayed, it's shown exactly as you want, with a particular selection of files sorted in a specified way, using a selected screen format. *1DIR Plus* is programmable to a degree, letting you customize powerful commands (using looping and conditional testing). You pay a price for this versatility, however. The documentation is extensive, and there's much to learn.

Command stacks

Another useful feature is a **command stack**—a list of all recently executed commands. You can review the stack to track the work you've done. And you may re-execute any command in the stack by moving the cursor to it and striking the appropriate key. Commands in the stack may be edited before being executed again so that you can avoid repeatedly typing long DOS paths by changing only parts of commands. You'll find command stacks in only a few DOS shells (the *Norton Commander* is one) or in some keyboard macro programs, like *SuperKey*.

Installation

Most DOS shells require very little by way of installation. Because they tend to send only plain "vanilla" output to the printer, there's no printer driver to deal with. Some need to reside in the root directory; some use auxiliary files and overlays that they expect to find in a subdirectory of a particular name; and some use standard DOS external commands like CHKDSK and require that the associated files reside in a particular subdirectory.

Choosing a DOS shell

For most users, the question is not "which DOS shell should I buy?," but rather "do I need a DOS shell at all?" Some shells aren't very easy to use, and some have confusing documentation; it's natural to avoid extra work when the benefits don't answer pressing needs. Even if you think that you wouldn't gain much by having a DOS shell online, keep in mind that a shell can be invaluable during periodic disk housecleanings. A shell is the best way to monitor the state of a hard disk, because it gives comprehensive statistics, shows the tree structure, gives full file listings, and lets you quickly look into individual files. The ability to apply wildcard operations across subdirectories can save you much time that would otherwise go to moving from directory to directory and repeating commands. Even when used only a few times a month, a shell may quickly repay its price.

Menu Programs

Earlier in this chapter, we showed how batch files can form a primitive system of menus for running applications and DOS functions. Menus make computers very easy to use, and many businesses use them to insulate employees from the rigors of DOS. Menus take the user to the proper directory without any need to type a CHDIR command. No comprehension of the directory tree is required, and a menu system can help enforce a scheme for distributing files. It also may help avert disasters by channeling DOS commands like ERASE and FORMAT. It doesn't make much sense to set up a menu program on a machine that you alone use. If you can set up the menu system, you can certainly handle a DOS shell, which will give you much more power.

Disadvantages

Three disadvantages accompany menu systems. First, the user cannot do any more than the menu system allows (short of leaving the menu system and returning to DOS). Second, the menuing system assures that computer users will remain computer-illiterate. And third, *setting up* the menu system usually requires a level of sophistication far exceeding that required for the tasks the system will perform. Still, work must get done, and the world cannot stop while people learn to use computers.

Like many genres of software covered in this book, menu systems do not always fall into a neat and tidy category. Some DOS shells have menuing features (*1DIR Plus*, for example). And nearly all **security systems** (which we'll discuss in a moment) are based on menus. Some systems completely take over the machine, cramming the menus into only a few files. Other systems, mere extensions of DOS batch files, leave scores of files scattered across the disk.

Advanced Features

Menuing systems are as much a victim of *feature creep* as any other software genre. Some programs include editors, notepads, and calendars. Some can scan directories to find a file or supply a more sophisticated equivalent of the DOS PATH command. Some have an inbuilt command language in lieu of DOS batch files. Some offer an elaborate scheme for creating help screens as menu selections. Some mimic operating environments by offering overlapping windows and a cut-and-paste facility. Some are optimized for networks.

Such features are nice, but it's more important to find a program that gets the basics right. On the surface, most menuing systems look the same. But not all can achieve a high level of interactivity with the user. More important, there is a tremendous range in the ease with which menus may be created and maintained.

Most menuing systems are loaded by AUTOEXEC.BAT. Like DOS shells, some act as memory-resident programs. When a menu selection is made, the menuing program loads the program and runs it. Also like a DOS shell, only a small part of the program may remain in memory as the program runs, and the rest reloads when control returns to the menus. Many menu programs don't adopt this approach; instead, they work through a series of DOS batch files, in which the final command in each file returns control to the main menu. One program, *Hot!*, lets you add additional special-purpose menus to function keys.

Prompts

When a menu selection is made, a good menu program can be made to prompt the user for a filename or other command line information. For example, the main menu might read:

```
1. Word Processing
2. Spreadsheet
3. Outlining
4. DOS utilities
```

When the user types **1**, a message would appear saying:

```
What is the name of the file you want to edit?_____
```

A first-rate menu system will be able to perform error checking on some kinds of user response—checking, for example, that the input is a valid DOS filename. The ease by which a menu program can pass command-line information to a program is a measure of its quality.

DOS access

Most menu programs make special provision for DOS commands. Some have a ready-made DOS command menu that you can alter very little. Others let you set up complicated DOS commands as a menu selection. But even when DOS access is flexible, no menu system will contain every possible DOS command. For this reason, some menu programs let the user exit to DOS; the return to the menu system may be automatic or may require reloading. In these programs, you should be able to disable direct access to DOS if you want to keep programs like FORMAT.COM out of the hands of inexperienced users.

Menu programs vary greatly in flexibility. Most limit the number of listings in one menu because it isn't very practical to scroll menus up and down. Some limit the number of submenu levels, and some restrict a submenu to one subdirectory. This means that the menuing system must exactly coincide with the directory tree structure. You can't set up a menu titled "Programming" that would branch to applications in several subdirectories. Some menu programs impose arbitrary constraints, such as the form of the main menu. Only a few give you complete control over the appearance and formatting of the menu screens.

Creating Menus

The hidden half of any menuing program is the part that creates the menus. These facilities are usually off-bounds to the person ultimately using the menus. They may be in a separate program or hidden behind a sequence of keystrokes. Because this part of the program isn't used very often, it's doubly important that it be clear and easy to use. Otherwise, you'll have to study the documentation every time you want to change the menu system.

The best menuing software is itself menu-driven. It may present a series of prompts for information about filenames, paths, and command-line parameters. A few programs can display directory listings or a map of the tree while making menus. Another valuable feature is the ability to check that input information is correct—that DOS commands are valid, program files are present in the directories you say they are, and so on. Some of the most capable programs are the easiest to use; some of the least capable are insanely difficult. Be sure that any menuing program you select has a good reporting facility that can lucidly display and print the existing menu system.

Usage Tracking

Usage tracking, a particularly valuable feature of menuing systems, creates a file that records how long particular users worked with particular applications. The program knows who is using the machine by asking for a name (or a password) before a menu selection may be made. At first sight, this may seem like spying. But such a record has many positive uses. It may be used as a record for billing clients or for tracking computer use for tax write-offs. It shows how heavily the equipment is used, and who needs it most. And it tells which programs and data are accessed most, or not at all to better manage disk space.

A good menu program can sort the information about usage in various ways: by the user's name, project number, date and time, and application name. Often these programs cannot report which data files were accessed, because the menu system is dormant while the files are loaded and an application is run.

It's hard to choose a menu program. From the outside, they tend to look much alike. But internally, some are a breeze to use and others a never-ending headache. Keep an eye out for reviews, which appear frequently. And if you *do* decide to set up a menu system, be sure that it doesn't become an impediment to those who want to learn more about computers.

Security Systems

Security systems are menu programs that limit a user's access to particular subdirectories or files. They remain in memory (and in control) the entire time the computer is turned on. Most work through a system of passwords that offer a tremendous range of capabilities and protection. Some do little more than stop people from accidentally erasing each other's files, but the most sophisticated programs protect data so well that, if the key password is lost, the data can never be recovered, not even by the software's manufacturer.

Passwords

Depending on the system design, passwords may be required to enter particular subdirectories, to use particular types of files, or to apply particular DOS commands. Conversely, a user can lock his or her password to a particular file to keep others out. When a file is protected in this way, no one can open it, erase it, or copy it to a floppy diskette. In some systems, a special password is required to apply the COPY command to a program file; this makes software piracy impossible. Passwords are also required for access to the facilities that create the menus.

Passwords are also often required to use particular peripherals, such as printers or floppy drives. This prevents someone from walking off with data that they have permission to work on. Passwords may also limit a user to accessing the computer at certain times of the day.

Intelligent
passwords

In some systems, users can create their own passwords; in others, the system manager assigns them. First-rate security systems use a system of *intelligent passwords*. In *TheEMCEE*, passwords age and must be replaced periodically; this measure stops password violations from extending *ad infinitum*. A change in the access rights assigned to a particular password automatically extends to all menus. And a global lockout of passwords allows a system manager to temporarily disengage everyone from the system. The system watches illegal passwords carefully. If it finds someone trying passwords at random in an attempt to break in, it shuts them out.

You don't necessarily need to install a security system to reap the benefits of passwords. Some DOS shells (including *1DIR Plus*), have an inbuilt password system. Passwords are also sometimes built into particular applications. Many database programs have some sort of access-denial scheme. These approaches are necessarily limited, however. Unless the entire system is protected, a technically sophisticated individual can always start up a debugger and peer into the files "through the back door."

Alternatives

Boot Security

The Achilles' heel of many security systems is that they can be penetrated simply by booting the machine from drive A. Because the system is brought into action by the AUTOEXEC.BAT file on the hard disk, all that's required is to stop AUTOEXEC from executing. It's astounding how many security systems share this vulnerability.

Many systems are free of this problem. Some use special hardware that occupies a slot in the machine. It holds passwords on read-only memory chips, and the machine is simply not allowed to boot from any drive without the proper password. Other systems work by making subtle changes to the hard disk surface. DOS cannot access the disk because of these changes. But when the security system is booted, it gives the help DOS needs.

Often, a security system disables the DOS Ctrl-Break key combination so that users cannot leave programs and return to DOS. Various other provisions stop people from starting up software other than approved programs. Without these restrictions, a clever hacker could find ways of moving a Trojan horse into the system.

Ctrl-Break

Earlier, we discussed "usage tracking" in menuing software. The same feature exists in security systems, but the process is called an *audit trail*. An audit trail keeps track of the names, programs accessed, the date and time of access, the time spent in each program, and so on. Reports may be generated that are sorted by the various criteria. These reports help manage work. But they are also designed to sniff out interlopers who are testing the system to see how it can be broken into.

Audit trails

Encryption

Sometimes restricted access to subdirectories and even to individual files is inadequate. The next step is *data encryption*; using a password as the basis, the file is scrambled in utter gobbledygook. Most encryption is based on the DES (data encryption standard) developed for the government by IBM. It uses a seven-byte *key* that combines with eight-byte chunks of data to produce the encrypted file. The standard is gradually becoming dated as powerful supercomputers evolve that can simply try all possible combinations of the seven-byte key.

Encryption is regarded as a second line of defense. It protects data when the machine is stolen and guards data that has been backed up from the hard disk. In less sophisticated security systems, it stops people from accessing certain files in subdirectories they have access to.

Applications

Virtually all security systems offer encryption, and some automatically encrypt all files when written to disk. Encryption utilities also appear in just about any software. You'll find encryption in the keyboard macro program *SuperKey*, the DOS Shell *Path Minder*, and the file defragmentation utility *Disk Optimizer*.

Security systems offer nearly complete control over a sprawling multi-user system (or a stand-alone system used by many), but there are problems. It takes lots of work and time to build up a system. Some systems require that you reformat your disk. And the system can harass users. In particular, experienced computer users may feel shackled by the system. Many of the DOS commands and software utilities they use to great advantage aren't allowed within a security system. Exceptionally heavy demands may be made on the system manager, who must struggle to find a balance between security and productivity.

Security systems are an elaborate topic. To learn more, take a look at *Microcomputer Data Security*, written by Daniel Cronin and published by Brady.

It's ironic that we've ended this chapter with a discussion of software that generally makes hard disks *more difficult* to use. That's not how we started out, and in our next chapter we will turn to another source of heightened productivity: speed.

An Inside Look: Menuing and Security
with TheEMCEE

TheEMCEE is a straightforward, easy-to-use menuing and security system. When installed, it provides a ready-made system of menus (screen A), which can then be modified to the exact menu system you desire. This on-screen approach makes it easy to get started and frees you from writing specially formatted files that are then converted into menus.

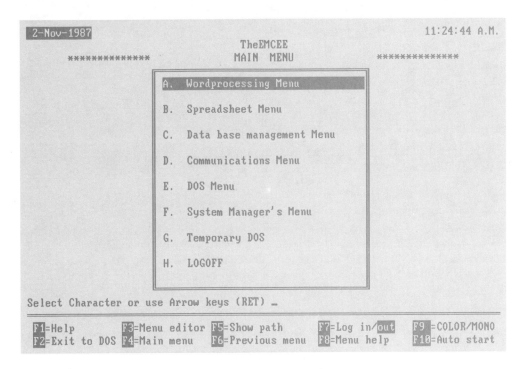

Screen A. **The Main Menu.**

From the menus, it would seem that any user could change the menuing system. But passwords control access to menu choices (such as the **Menu Editor** via F3). The multilevel system of passwords can be made to "age" so that they require periodic renewal. The **System Manager's Menu** is the gateway to the program's inner workings (screen B). Through it you can set up passwords and user IDs, monitor a system log to see who has been working with particular files, and create, delete, or edit menus. Data encryption is also supported.

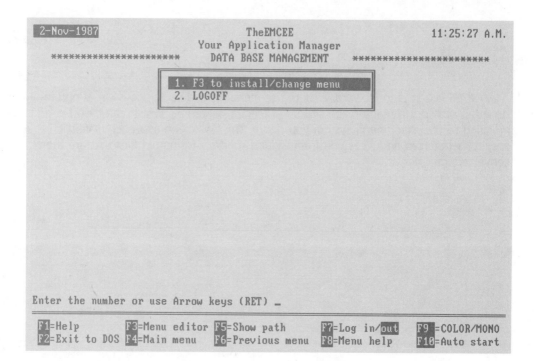

Chapter 7

Optimizing Speed and Productivity

People who use computers all day become *speed junkies*. Somehow, having a tool that performs tasks in milliseconds makes people *more* impatient. And that impatience grows as ever more complicated software configurations bring the hard disk to its knees. Advanced users expect more from microcomputers than they were designed to deliver. An IBM PC wasn't intended to support real-time spelling checking within a multitasked, multifile word processor running under Microsoft *Windows*. The higher users push their productivity, the heavier the hard disk's burden.

A 6-MHz IBM AT runs at about five times the speed of a standard XT. Depending on the application, a third to half the increase in performance may be attributed to the faster hard disk. No wonder speed junkies drool over rapid seek times, track buffers, and other technical goodies.

Developing speed

There's no denying that money can buy speed. But you also can *develop* speed by thoughtfully optimizing your system. The world's fastest hard disk will slowly degrade in performance if steps aren't taken to keep it optimized. Conversely, a relatively slow stepper-motor drive can be made to zip along faster than a poorly maintained voice-coil unit.

As heavier and heavier demands are placed on disk performance, just buying the fastest hardware isn't good enough. You need to work at optimizing the disk drive's throughput. Some of the optimization is done when the disk is first formatted. Some is done by periodic maintenance. And some is done on an ad hoc basis, adopting techniques appropriate for some tasks but not others.

Technical skill

Once upon a time, disk optimization was the domain of the techno-nerd. Less technically oriented souls could undertake some of the available optimization measures, but they couldn't precisely determine the results of their actions, making it impossible to fine-tune the system. A disk access takes a fraction of a second—far too short to measure with a stop watch. It took considerable programming skill to tweak a disk into high performance. Today, matters have changed. A broad offering of disk analysis and optimization utilities are available, most at low cost.

Relative gains

Some disk optimization measures give large gains, and the improvement is immediately apparent. Other optimizations are subtler, leading to only a 10% gain. But the benefits are cumulative, with a half-dozen 10% gains resulting in doubled performance. Sometimes what should be a small gain becomes a large one because a bottleneck in the system has been opened and other performance factors are given free rein. Conversely, one bottleneck can severely hamper a disk that should be quite fast.

You need to understand disk drives pretty well to use all the optimization strategies open to you. If you haven't read Chapter 2, read it before going on. We begin with an overview of the path data travels from its origin in magnetic domains on the disk surface to its final destination in system memory. Then we'll tackle the optimization solution for each step along that path. Finally, we'll try to sort through the conflicting claims about the relative value of the various optimizations.

Fifteen Factors in Hard Disk Performance

Let's begin by examining 15 determinants of hard disk performance, starting from the disk surface.

Cylinder density. The greater the number of sectors per cylinder, the fewer head moves required to read or write a file.

File defragmentation. Files compacted onto as few cylinders as possible are read more quickly than those scattered across the disk.

Average seek time. A fast average seek time maximizes the percentage of disk-access time spent reading or writing data.

Interleave. An optimum interleave minimizes the number of turns of the disk required to read all sectors on a track.

Data transfer rate. Disk access on very fast computers may be speeded by faster data transfer.

CPU speed. A faster microprocessor speeds up DOS, influences the data transfer rate, and lets software process files more rapidly.

Track buffering. Whole tracks may be read in one rotation of the disk, even when the CPU cannot handle a 1:1 interleave.

RAM disk support. A hard disk may be unburdened by placing certain repeatedly read files on a RAM disk.

DOS buffers setting. Selecting the right number of DOS buffers helps DOS avoid reading the same data again and again.

Sector caching. Disk accesses may be greatly reduced by a sector-buffering system that is more extensive than that provided by the DOS buffers.

Directory tree design. The directory tree can be designed to minimize the disk activity required to search for a file.

Subdirectory layout. Subdirectories can be compacted into only a few cylinders to minimize the time DOS needs to trace through a directory path.

File layout. Placing certain files near the outer edge of the disk gives modest performance gains.

PATH command. The DOS PATH command can be tailored to quicken directory searches.

FASTOPEN command. Starting with version 3.3, DOS can be made to remember the location of recently accessed files so that it can reopen the file without searching directories and the file allocation table.

Of the 15 factors, four are limited by hardware. Average seek time depends on the drive itself; neither a new controller nor special software can change it. The cylinder density and data transfer rate can sometimes be altered by switching to a different controller card, and the CPU speed may be changed by an accelerator card. Many of the remaining factors rely on software, but some, such as track buffers and disk caching, may be hard-wired into the drive controller. A few performance gains are made entirely by managing the disk well.

Disk-level Optimization

Optimization at disk-level is directed toward minimizing time spent in *mechanical motion*. A high cylinder density means that a file can fit into fewer cylinders, reducing the number of head seeks required to read it. File defragmentation compacts files into as few cylinders as possible. Fast seek times lessen the time the controller is kept waiting while the read/write heads shuttle between cylinders. And an optimal interleave reduces the time spent waiting for sectors to rotate beneath the read/write heads.

Cylinder Density

Cylinder density is increased by adding more sectors per track or more tracks per cylinder. Of course, the number of tracks per cylinder depends on the number of platters in the drive. There's nothing to do to increase this factor except to buy a larger drive.

Many people don't sufficiently appreciate the benefits of higher cylinder density. Two drives, one with two platters and one with four, may have the same average seek time. But the drive with four platters may be said to have an effective seek time only half that of the former because only half as many seeks may be required to read a file (less benefit results with *random-access files*, such as database files, because the heads usually must move between cylinders after reading only a snippet of the file). This advantage argues for buying a large drive up front, rather than adding capacity later.

The number of sectors per track can be changed on some drives by substituting an RLL controller card, as explained in Chapter 2. Depending on the encoding system, the sector density per track may increase by 50% or 100%. A 100% gain means that head seeks may be cut in half—in effect doubling the number of platters.

Keep in mind that gains from a higher cylinder density are completely defeated by allowing your files to become very fragmented (we'll talk about defragmentation in a moment). A file spread across many cylinders requires numerous head seeks, no matter what the cylinder density.

You may be able to achieve a pseudo-increase in cylinder density by compressing files. Compressed files take up fewer sectors; as a result less head movement is required to read them. File compression results in performance gains only in special cases where a simple utility can collapse a simple file structure. For example, some spreadsheet compressors simply strip out thousands of zeros from the file and insert codes telling how many have been removed from a particular location. (We're oversimplifying a bit.) Files compressed in this way can be uncompressed extremely quickly, and the job can be done automatically when the file is read or written

File compression

(see Chapter 5). Elaborate file compression takes more time to perform than it saves in disk access time.

Reducing File Fragmentation

When you distribute files to a freshly formatted hard disk, each file is laid out in contiguous clusters, filling each track on each side at any given head position (note that clusters are *physically* contiguous only with an interleave of 1:1). Ideally, DOS would do its best to confine a file to as few cylinders as possible. For example, a 35K file can fit in one cylinder on many two-platter disks (four tracks of seventeen 512-byte sectors). But DOS doesn't optimize the file's layout; it simply uses the next available sectors so that the 35K file likely resides on two adjacent cylinders, thus requiring a head seek when it is read or written. Still, the file is said to be "contiguous" even if it isn't optimally located.

Loss of contiguity   But files don't stay contiguous for long. Because no space is left between them, when files grow, the additional sectors required must be found elsewhere on the disk. On a newly installed hard disk, these sectors will be found on inner tracks, because DOS allocates disk space starting from the outer edge (cylinder 0). But when files are erased, sectors become available at all locations on the disk. When DOS needs an additional cluster for a file, it doesn't look for one in the same cylinder as the last occupied by the file. Rather, it takes whatever cluster is available closest to the outer edge of the disk. (DOS versions 3.0 and later allocate fresh clusters until the whole disk is filled and thereafter opt for the outermost cluster).

The result is chaos, pure and simple. A "mature" hard disk with many erasures and reorganizations becomes very fragmented. Consider how this might happen with only a few files if each is constantly growing. Additions to each file take up successive positions in the same cylinders. Files that might fit in only a few cylinders spread across a dozen or more. Moreover, if an erasure opens up a cluster far from the rest of the file, that cluster may be used even if a cluster is open in the same cylinder occupied by the end of the file. Consequently, when a large file is loaded onto a much-used hard disk, it will be fragmented into many pieces.

Inefficiency   The result is endless, needless head movement, wasting all the advantages of a fast CPU, fast controller, and an optimized interleave because, the disk doesn't read data quickly enough to push these features to their limits. The degree of performance degradation depends on the kind of file in use. Large random-access files naturally require much head movement, but program files, text files, or spreadsheet files are loaded in sequence, and severe fragmentation greatly reduces the speed at which they are read or written.

Fragmented *subdirectory* files are an underappreciated hindrance to disk performance. Recall that subdirectories are files like any other, except that they are marked as subdirectories in the attribute byte of their directory listing. When you search for a file in a third-level subdirectory, such as **MAMMALS/PRIMATES/OLD-WORLD/GIBBONS.APE**, DOS looks for the subdirectory called **MAMMALS** in the root directory, reads that file, searches for the entry **PRIMATES**, reads that file in turn, and so on. A four-sector cluster holds 64 directory entries. Subdirectories with more than 64 files require a second cluster, which may be discontinuous. When many subdirectories are fragmented and accessed by the PATH command, just *finding* one file can call for much head movement.

Fragmented
subdirectories

The obvious remedy for this chaos is to *defragment* the files, packing each into as few cylinders as possible and using adjacent cylinders to minimize the distance a head must move. True optimization is an impossible ideal because it requires grouping files in a way that minimizes the "wrap-around" of files from one cylinder to the next. Defragmenting a disk is one of those inherently futile undertakings in life, like raking leaves or washing the car. Chaos begins creeping in again only moments after you've finished because DOS takes no pains to avoid fragmentation.

Defragmentation

Defragmented files extend some hidden benefits. Utilities that unerase accidentally deleted files work flawlessly when used with a perfectly contiguous file. Even massive erasures can be reliably restored without requiring you to piece the files together. Defragmentation also makes file-by-file backups proceed more quickly and helps tape backup units achieve *streaming* for longer periods (we'll touch on this in Chapter 8). A third advantage is that defragmented disk drives live longer. Fewer head seeks means less overall wear and tear on the drive. A defragmentation utility may well pay for itself in this way.

Hidden benefits

There are two strategies for defragmenting a disk. You may acquire a defragmenting utility (some hackers call them "defraggers") or back up the whole disk, reformat it, and restore the files. Admittedly, the latter approach doesn't sound very practical, but it has a certain logic. We'll discuss the backup approach first and then move on to defragmentation utilities.

Defragmenting by backups

As noted, defragmentation isn't a problem with freshly formatted disks, because nothing but contiguous sectors are available for DOS to allocate to each successive file. The same benefit accrues if you backup all your files on diskettes or tape, reformat the disk, and then restore the files. DOS lays them out one after another. For this reason, you can speed up floppy disk access just by making a direct file-by-file copy to a second diskette: **COPY A:*.* B:**. Note that the DOS *DISKCOPY* program doesn't defragment a diskette, since it creates a sector-by-sector image of the original.

Reformatting

But why *reformat* the disk? Isn't erasing all the files good enough? In Chapter 8 you'll learn that a good backup utility can preserve an entire directory structure, re-creating every subdirectory when it restores to a reformatted disk. It is simply easier to exploit this capability than to go from subdirectory to subdirectory, erasing files. And because subdirectories are themselves files, they also require defragmentation, which means tearing down the subdirectory tree and then re-creating it. It's really a *lot* easier just to reformat the disk and have a backup utility do the work for you. This entails only a high-level format, as explained in Chapter 4.

Problems

Of course, this technique doesn't work if you use a streaming tape drive to make an **image backup** of a disk (as explained in Chapter 8). If you use tape, make a **file-by-file backup**. These days the distinction between image and file-by-file backups on tape are blurring, and some tape units can restore file-by-file from an image backup. Even if your tape drive can do this, it would be very inefficient and it isn't advised.

To really do the job right, you should make *two* global backups. It's a pain, to be sure. If you make only one backup, however, you will have only one copy of your data when the disk is reformatted. Backups sometimes go awry, and you'll be sorry not to have a *backup to your backup* if you have trouble restoring data to the reformatted disk. Be sure you know your backup software well before defragmenting your disk this way.

Defragmenters

You're probably thinking that it must be much easier to spend a few dollars on a defragmentation utility. You're right—the backup method is a very inconvenient way of doing the job. Let's take a look at defragmenters. They analyze file layout and copy clusters back and forth until every file is contiguous. They require some open disk space to do this because they tend to produce large temporary files. Some operate more quickly than others; the time required depends on the capacity of the disk and the degree of fragmentation. On a 20-megabyte disk, the process typically takes between fifteen minutes and an hour. Some general disk utility packages, such as the *Norton Utilities (Advanced Version)* or the *Mace Utilities*, include defragmenters. Others are sold as stand-alone programs, such as *Disk Optimizer* from SoftLogic Solutions.

You may be a trifle alarmed at the prospect of a program cutting up and reassembling your precious files. And well you should be—defragmenters perform major surgery. One point you needn't worry about is a power failure. Most defraggers write a second copy of a sector before erasing the original. But it *is* a little messy recovering from a system crash during defragmentation because you'll have to weed out temporary files left by the defragmenter.

Dangers

There are ways that defraggers can scramble your data, however. For greater speed, some defraggers directly access the disk controller hardware, going around DOS. This is a risky undertaking, and mishaps have occurred, particularly in computers using accelerator hardware. Software houses have avoided drawing attention to such dangers. You won't see ads touting a defragger's safety. But accidents have happened—many times. It is only prudent to back up the disk before defragging and to look over the disk thoroughly after the defragger is finished. Don't reuse the backup diskettes or tape cartridge until enough time has passed to alert you to any damage.

"Featuritis" has attacked defragmenters as much as any kind of software; you'll find all sorts of options. Some defraggers can perform a quick cleanup of the disk, operating only on clusters that are easily defragmented. Some can optimize the placement of files in as few cylinders as possible. Some can optionally arrange the files in the same order as they are listed in their directories. And some can accept a command file that lists files that should be concentrated on the outer cylinders (this brings them closer to the directory and file allocation table so that access times are slightly improved). Another handy feature is the ability to halt the defragmentation process if you need to return to work. Most defraggers check for bad sectors and make the necessary corrections when they find one.

Features

How are you to know when defragmentation has gone too far? CHKDSK can give a clue. Just include a filename on the command line with CHKDSK, as in CHKDSK \NOVEL\CHAPTER1.DOC. When CHKDSK returns its usual information, it tells how many blocks the file is broken into. You won't want to test many files this way, however, because you have to wait for CHKDSK to analyze the whole disk each time. Many defragmenters include a utility that indicates how badly fragmented the disk has become. But they can't tell whether the files you use most are badly fragmented.

When to defragment

An Inside Look: File Defragmentation with *Disk Optimizer*

Besides file defragmentation, version 3.0 of *Disk Optimizer* from SoftLogic Solutions offers several optimization features. It automatically sorts all directories so that sub-directories are listed first. Moreover, it lets you specify any number of "priority direc-tories" to be placed on the outer edge of the disk. You may also specify a list of "static files" (those that never change size) and have them placed on outer cylinders; this measure makes subsequent optimizations run faster. Static files may be specified by a filename extension, so that you can group all program files using ***.EXE** and ***.COM**.

Before starting up the *OPTIMIZE* program, you may want to run *ANALYZE* to see how badly the disk is fragmented. The program rates each file on the disk, reporting **100%** when all clusters are contiguous, **0%** when the clusters are completely scat-tered. *ANALYZE* concludes with a "total drive percentage," which typically runs about 75% on a poorly maintained drive. Screen A is taken from this program.

```
List of files larger than 1 cluster in STORAGE
EXEMOD.EXE     19 %  COUNT.ASM      49 %  README.DOC    65 %  TURBO.COM     56 %
ASM.EXE        79 %

List of files larger than 1 cluster in FAKEFILE
MAKEFILE.BAK 100 %  MAKEFILE.PAS 100 %  MAKEFILE.COM 100 %  FAKEFILE.     100 %
TURBO.COM     93 %  ASM.KEY      100 %  INLINE.COM   100 %  FILEINFO.PAS 100 %
ASM.EXE      100 %  FILEINFO.BAK 100 %  FILEINFO.LST   0 %  FILEINFO.ASM 100 %
WRITEKEY.BAK 100 %  WRITEKEY.PAS 100 %  WRTSTATS.ASM  49 %  WRTSTATS.PAS  84 %
TURBOBUG.BAK  52 %  TURBOBUG.ASM  80 %  LINK.EXE      88 %  KEEPX.ASM    100 %
SPEEDWRT.BAK 100 %  SPEEDWRT.PAS 100 %  SPEEDWRT.LST 100 %  SPEEDWRT.ASM   0 %
TRIAL.COM    100 %  WRITELBL.LST 100 %  WRITELBL.PAS 100 %  PUTLABEL.LST 100 %
WRITEKEY.ASM 100 %  WRITEKEY.LST 100 %  DRWBOX.BAK   100 %  DRWBOX.ASM   100 %
DRWBOX.LST   100 %  DRWBOX.PAS   100 %  DRWBIX.LST    60 %  GETLABEL.LST 100 %
MKDIVIDR.LST   0 %

List of files larger than 1 cluster in INCLUDES
CHARBOX.PAS   49 %  ROWCOLOR.PAS 100 %  KEYPAUSE.PAS 100 %  PADENDS.PAS    0 %
WRITEKEY.PAS 100 %  WRTSTATS.PAS  84 %  WRITELBL.PAS 100 %  FILEINFO.PAS 100 %
SPEEDWRT.PAS 100 %  DRWBOX.PAS    74 %
        TOTAL DRIVE PERCENTAGE -  75 %


Press any key to continue._
```

Screen A. **Output from the ANALYZE Program.**

To run the **OPTIMIZE** program, you need enter no more than **OPTIMIZE C:**. It immediately goes to work resorting directories and marking the changes in the file allocation table. Then it displays a status screen (shown in Screen B) that constantly cycles through a series of four steps for every file: reading clusters into memory, writing clusters for re-allocation, updating FAT chains in memory, and writing to the FATs and directories. A line of characters is written and overwritten to display graphically each step of the process.

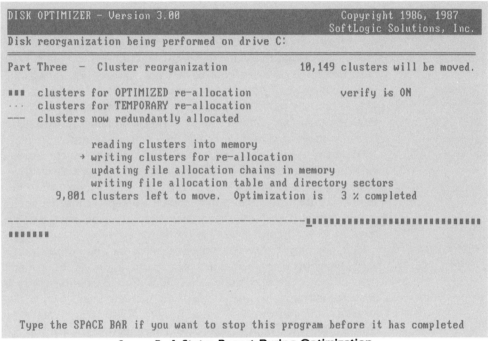

Screen B. **A Status Report During Optimization.**

It takes Disk Optimizer roughly 30 minutes to defragment a 20-megabyte disk on a 6-MHz AT. Frequent optimizations don't lessen the time required very much, because most files must be relocated when only a single cluster opens on an outer cylinder. The optimization can be stopped at any time if you need to get back to work.

Defragmentation is especially valuable when you install new software or after you make many deletions. Large program files tend to be scattered widely on a heavily used disk, making them load slowly. Erasures create numerous "holes" on the disk, and new files become fragmented filling these holes. The defragmenter eliminates the holes by compacting all files on to the outermost cylinders.

Avoiding fragmentation

You can't do much to prevent file fragmentation from happening in the first place. Loading program files *first* on a freshly formatted disk helps postpone the day of over fragmentation. But the phenomenon is inherent in the way DOS manages disk space. If you've run a hard disk for a long time without defragmentation, you're probably thinking that your files must be chopped to bits. Actually, most untended disks turn out to be from 50% to 75% contiguous; that is, 50 to 75 of *possible* cluster contiguities are achieved. Users who constantly move and erase files have the most fragmented disks. Programmers tend to create severe fragmentation and hence have the most to gain from acquiring a defragmenter.

Frequency

Generally speaking, a very heavily used disk can benefit from defragmentation about once a month. This is also just about the right time to back up the disk globally, so there's much sense in scheduling them together. (Incremental backups—those entailing only files that have been changed—should be made more frequently, as we'll explain in Chapter 8.)

Copy protection

Defragmenters can create serious trouble for copy-protected software. Many protection schemes place parts of a program at specific disk locations, often as hidden files (files *hidden* from directory listings by their attribute markings). If the defragmenter changes these locations, the software won't run. Backup utilities have similar difficulties with some copy-protected software; hence, the backup approach to defragmentation may not work either.

Many defragmenters won't touch hidden files; a few can be told to leave particular files alone. These precautions may or may not overcome the copy-protection problem. Even when a manufacturer claims that its defragmenter can deal with copy-protection schemes, you must consider that new schemes constantly arise and that trouble may ensue.

As a result, you may be forced to *deinstall* copy-protected software before using the defragger, reinstalling it afterward. Because the software may limit you to only so many installations, you've clearly got problems. Although it may not solve your problem, we recommend that you telephone the manufacturer and complain loudly and long about the whole protection scheme.

In the future, defragmentation facilities will be hard-wired into every hard disk drive or its controller. This new generation of "high intelligence" drives will invisibly optimize the sector layout. This feature has already appeared on commercially available controller cards, such as the *Awesome I/O card* from CSSL.

Seek Times

We discussed average seek times in Chapter 2. There is not much more to say about this factor in connection with optimization. We'd like to warn you again about misleading manufacturers' claims for very fast seek times that actually represent a "virtual" seek time achieved by hardwiring into the controller some of the optimization techniques presented here—particularly defragmentation and sector caching. Having these facilities built into the disk electronics is handy, saves labor, and conserves precious RAM. But you won't have the flexibility offered by utility software offering the same services, and you may pay much more for them.

Benefits

How much does a fast seek time matter? Or to put it differently, how much will performance suffer if you opt for a slower stepper-motor drive? Naturally enough, the answer depends on how much head movement the drive must make to serve your needs. You can judge this simply by watching the red indicator light on a disk (for an accurate reading, you should first defragment the disk). Running the software from a floppy disk even more dramatically shows the importance of seek time.

Tasks that use many small files benefit greatly from fast seek times. Programmers have the greatest need because they repeatedly run compilations of dozens of files. The files are likely to be spread all over the disk, and each requires a search from subdirectory to subdirectory to find it. A huge number of head seeks go into a typical program compilation.

Another role in which fast seek times make a big difference is in disk-based data sorts. Lacking enough memory, software dumps the data into large temporary files. These files span many cylinders, particularly if recent erasures have left the disk badly fragmented. The result is a non-stop churning of the read/write heads. Database users know well the seemingly endless grinding of the drive and flicker of its indicator light.

OS/2

With OS/2 or another multitasking operating system, fast seek times are extremely important. When multiple large tasks run at once, available RAM quickly fills, and the operating system starts to swap data and program modules in and out of memory. All of this occurs *in addition to* normal file reads and writes. This activity may defeat other performance-optimization measures. For example, even if a series of records are packed into one cylinder and accessed in sequence, the read/write heads may have to constantly leave the cylinder to take care of various operating system demands. Also, the heads may need to scamper back and forth to serve the input-output needs of several programs at once.

Remember that drives with very high cylinder densities make average seek time less important because they fit a file into fewer cylinders. Ironically, the highest cylinder densities are in high capacity drives, and these tend to have the fastest head seeks of all. But these drives are often intended to serve networks, in which *no* drive can ever be fast enough.

Measuring performance

One way to determine a drive's performance is by running a disk performance test. CORE International publishes such a test. It takes only a few seconds to run, and it displays the information shown in Figure 7-1. Because it measures more than average seek times, it is a valuable tool for comparing drives. It is available from CORE for a nominal fee, or it can be found on many electronic bulletin boards free of charge.

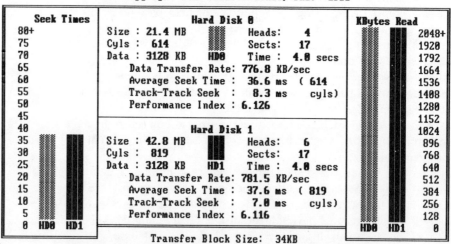

Figure 7-1 **The CORE disk performance test**

Optimizing the Interleave

In Chapter 2 we explained how the disk sectors on a track are numbered discontinuously, allowing time for the electronics to "digest" the data from one sector before accessing the data at the next. Because *logically* adjacent sectors are not usually *physically* adjacent, they are said to be *interleaved*. An interleave factor of 3:1 means that sectors #100 and #101 are three sectors apart on the disk surface (that is, there are two sectors between them). As a result, it takes three complete rotations of the disk to read all sectors in a track.

Recall that the interleave is set during low-level formatting, which creates and labels tracks and sectors. The formatting program prompts you for an interleave factor. The number you enter is quite an important decision. If the interleave is too high, the electronics end up waiting an unnecessarily long time until the next (logical) sector spins under the read/write head. And if the interleave is too low, the electronics won't be ready, and an *entire turn of the disk* is inserted between each sector access. Clearly, a too-low interleave factor is a far more serious problem because it creates delays much larger than a too-high interleave.

An improper interleave setting can greatly degrade overall disk performance. When a too-low interleave forces an unnecessary spin of the disk after each sector is read, the time required for 17 revolutions adds to the time required to read or write a full 17-sector track. At 60 revolutions per second this amounts to over a quarter of a second, or more than a full second when all sectors are read from a two-platter cylinder. Fast head seeks ($\frac{1}{25}$ of a second) are lost amid this inefficiency. An overlarge interleave, though not as inefficient, still may add appreciable fractions of a second to every cylinder read or write operation.

Finding a proper interleave setting has become more of an issue as hardware has differentiated. IBM PC clones run at many different speeds, depending on their version of the 8088 chip. ATs run at literally *thousands* of different speeds because continuously variable add-on clock crystals allow users to push the speed as high as other components in the machine allow.

Some users change a disk's interleave to accommodate a faster clock rate, believing that IBM's original interleave settings are too conservative and that the interleave of disks on ordinary machines also require adjusting. The interleave factor is 6:1 in a standard IBM

A too low interleave

The proper setting

An Inside Look: Interleave Optimization
with *HOPTIMUM*

HOPTIMUM from Paul Mace Software analyzes the interleave of a hard disk and reformats the disk to that interleave. It preserves any data on the disk by reading it into memory as it reformats each cylinder; it then writes back the data. It can handle disks of up to eight platters and 1,024 cylinders.

The program issues a report comparing performance at various interleave factors. The example shown in screen A was made on a 6-MHz IBM AT using a Seagate ST251 40-megabyte drive. According to the test, an interleave of 2:1 is optimal. Note how slowly the disk operates when the interleave is set too low. At a 1:1 interleave, read/write operations require six times as long! A 1:1 interleave usually requires a 386 machine; even 10-MHz ATs do best at 2:1. Most XT-class machines are fastest at 4:1, but some may run even faster with an 8- or 10-MHz **turbo speed** option.

Pre-2.0 versions of *HOPTIMUM* destroyed the data on the cylinders they tested (by default, ten cylinders are affected). This posed no problem on a newly installed disk, but made it hard to test a disk filled with files. The trick is first to defragment the disk so that all data is compacted into the outermost cylinders. So long as the disk is not nearly full, ten innermost cylinders will be emptied, and these can be selected as the site of the test when *HOPTIMUM* is started up. No matter the version of *HOPTIMUM*, make a global backup before starting. This program performs major surgery, and a power outage or other glitch could cost you dearly.

```
Now read testing...
At interleave    7 the elapsed time for reading was     8 seconds

Formatting specified area at interleave      8 ...
Now read testing...
At interleave    8 the elapsed time for reading was     9 seconds

Summary is as follows...

    Interleave          Total access time            Total clock ticks
                      (rounded to nearest sec.)     (normally 18.2 / sec)
    ----------      ---------------------------     ---------------------
      CURRENT                   4                            65
         1                     20                           362
         2                      3                            48
         3                      4                            65
         4                      5                            85
         5                      6                           105
         6                      7                           125
         7                      8                           145
         8                      9                           165

Program has terminated normally
A:\---_
```

Screen A. **A Status Report from** *HOPTIMUM.*

XT, and 3:1 in the faster AT. Various studies have been made of the performance of these disks under varying interleaves, with mixed results. The measurements are sensitive to the test methods and the kinds of files and software used. Some conclude that IBM set the interleave just about right. Most, however, claim that IBM's interleave factors are too high. One study found a 15% to 20% performance increase when the interleave is set to 2:1 in a 6-MHz AT. Standard XT hard disks may do better with an interleave of 5:1 or 4:1, possibly even 3:1 on clones with an 8-MHz alternative clock speed.

Finding the optimum

Because you have no way of monitoring the disk's activities from microsecond to microsecond, how are you to know which interleave factor is optimal? Indeed, how do you find out the interleave factor your drive currently uses? It's a lot of work to reformat a disk and reinstall files, and it's hard to time disk operations.

Fortunately, *HOPTIMUM* will do the job for you. It comes with the *HTEST/HFORMAT* programs from Kolod Research (distributed by Paul Mace Software). Starting with version 2.0, *HOPTIMUM* saves the data in several cylinders and reformats the cylinders again and again using different interleaves. Once it determines the optimum interleave, it reformats the entire disk in that interleave without disturbing the data. Earlier versions of the program didn't save data, making it inconvenient to optimize a disk already full of files. See the box, "*An Inside Look: Interleave Optimization with HOPTIMUM.*"

Controller-level Optimization

Once the data is read from the disk surface, it is buffered on the controller. Controller-level optimization speeds the transfer of the data to DOS. In some cases this can be done by replacing the controller card with a faster one. More often the controller is already capable of transfer speeds that the computer cannot handle, and the computer's own electronics must be speeded up to improve transfer rates.

Two other ploys hasten data transfer. Track buffers ensure that all data on a track is buffered by the controller so that all subsequent accesses to the track are made at electronic speed. RAM disks take this process a step further by eliminating the mechanical disk and storing files as if they were entirely buffered on the controller.

Increasing the Data Transfer Rate

As we learned in Chapter 2, data moves between the controller's holding buffer and the disk surface faster than most machines can move data from the buffer to RAM. But microprocessors have come a long way since the lowly 8088 chip was incorporated into the first IBM PC. These days, 12- and16-MHz clock rates go to work with the much more powerful 80286 and 80386 microprocessors, and these may overtake a controller using a 5-megabit transfer rate.

In Chapter 2 we talked about how the ESDI interface will gradually replace the current standard, the ST506/412 interface. You can't just buy an ESDI controller and hook it up to an ST506 drive. The drive electronics are an integral part of the interface, so you must buy an ESDI drive to go along with the ESDI controller. Current ESDI interfaces run at about 10 megabits per second, but the technology can be pushed to twice this rate.

ESDI controllers

Some disks *can* be made faster by adding an RLL controller. As we explained in Chapter 2, RLL 2,7 encoding places 50% more sectors on a track. To handle the greater work load, the controller typically runs at 7.5 megabits per second. RLL encoding promises to become the norm, increasing the potential speed of hard disks in computers that are fast enough to make use of it. The electronics in most existing disks cannot reliably handle RLL; as a result, this optimization measure isn't available to everyone.

RLL controllers

Increasing CPU Speed

The speed of the computer's system clock sets the rate at which the microprocessor and various support chips function. A faster clock hastens disk transfers in two ways. First, it increases the rate of data transfer between the controller card and main memory. Second, it speeds disk access by making software, including DOS, run more quickly. Once directories and file allocation tables are read into memory, DOS can scan them more rapidly. And DOS can transfer data from its buffers to programs more quickly. Application software also must process incoming data. For example, text editors break up text files into one-line units and place each unit at a separate memory location. A faster CPU cuts the time required.

Two strategies can increase system speed. You may increase the clock speed of your machine, possibly replacing memory chips and support chips with faster versions. Or you may replace the CPU with a faster model. As we'll see, the first solution is much more effective in speeding disk operations.

The system clock

A **clock crystal** sets the pace at which microprocessors work. The 8088 microprocessor in a standard IBM PC runs at 4.77 million **clocks** (pulses) per second and accordingly is rated at 4.77 MHz; "MHz" stands for megahertz (millions of cycles per second). The original IBM ATs ran at 6-MHz; though not much faster than a PC's clock, the AT's microprocessor works three times as fast. It processes data so much more quickly because the 80286 microprocessor uses better designed circuitry to perform the same tasks using fewer clocks.

Speed is gained by running microprocessors at ever higher clock rates. This is possible in AT-class machines that use versions of the 80286 microprocessor that can handle the higher rate. In fact, changing the computer's clock crystal makes every part of the machine run more quickly.

Circuitry speed

Not all circuits are created equal, and some can run faster than others. If the clock speed is gradually raised, a point is reached where some component can no longer cope—it is fed data faster than it can handle it, data is lost, and the machine crashes. Manufacturers give their chips a speed rating theoretically not to be exceeded. But the ratings tend to be set for the lowest quality chips in a batch. Most chips can be pushed faster—the trick is to find out how far.

The AT "speed trap"

When IBM released the AT, users quickly discovered that the 6-MHz clock crystal could successfully be replaced with an 8-MHz chip in all machines. Some machines even accepted a 10-MHz chip, much to the glee of their owners. Alas, IBM was less gleeful; the company planned to bring out an 8-MHz machine at a considerably higher price and didn't want users making their own with a $10 chip. So the Grinch stole Christmas. IBM added code to the BIOS of subsequent ATs that stopped them from working if a faster clock crystal was installed. This bit of devilry is popularly known as the "speed trap."

In the end, the free market triumphed. Small companies have released *variable speed* clock crystals that plug into the normal clock crystal socket but connect to a dial that mounts outside the machine. The dial is initially set to 6 MHz; after the speed trap has made its inspection and allowed the computer to proceed, you can turn up the clock speed to as high as the system can withstand. Not only can you overcome the speed trap, but you can tweak the clock crystal until you find the computer's maximum speed.

It is very difficult to know which computer component is the first to fail. Any of the boards in the computer's slots may be the culprit. Often memory chips set the limit on clock speed. Memory speed is measured in **nanoseconds** or billionths of a second. Standard ATs use 150-ns (nanosecond) RAM chips; but once the machine exceeds 8 MHz, 120-ns chips may be required. Of course, replacing all your memory is an expensive proposition.

Another way of speeding up the machine is by installing an **accelerator board**, which fits into one of the computer's slots. Accelerator boards have a faster, more powerful microprocessor that supersedes the computer's. If used at all, the original microprocessor chip works as an auxiliary processor to handle input-output. These days, most accelerators for IBM PCs or XTs replace the 8088 chip with an AT's 80286, and most accelerators for ATs replace the 80286 chip with an 80386.

Accelerator boards

An accelerator board has its own clock crystal on board, and this chip doesn't affect the clock rate in other parts of the computer. If a PC receives an accelerator card that runs an 80286 chip at 8 MHz, *only* the circuitry on the card runs at 8 MHz. Data transfer across the system bus (across the slots) continues at the 4.77-MHz clock rate, as does access to system memory. This means that the DMA chips that perform data transfer between the disk controller and memory work no more quickly when an accelerator is installed. The CPU-based data transfer in ATs is similarly limited because the data passes across the system bus, which runs no faster.

Although accelerator cards cannot help with disk transfer rates, they can make a difference in how quickly DOS can scan directories and file allocation tables once these are loaded into memory. And, of course, software can process incoming and outgoing data much more quickly. Some boards achieve much faster memory access by keeping a memory *cache* on the card. Special, super-fast memory chips keep copies of the most recently accessed memory locations. Because the same memory addresses tend to be read repeatedly, the boards save time by going to the onboard cache, rather than constantly rereading data from slower RAM chips.

Hidden benefits

For example, the *Breakthru 286* from the Personal Computer Support Group (Figure 7-2) places 16K of fast cache memory on an 80286 accelerator board. The cache fills with the most frequently accessed data. When the microprocessor requests data, the cache is checked first. The search is made by extremely fast circuitry so that if the data is not found, not much time is added to the task of finding it in system RAM. But usually the data is present in the cache, and memory access time is reduced considerably. Special circuitry lets the 80286 CPU go on working at a high speed while data is sent to memory at a slower speed.

Figure 7-2 **The Breakthru 286 accelerator board**

Price vs. perfor-
mance

Accelerator boards typically offer a threefold increase in process-ing speed. If you buy a 286-based accelerator for your PC, remem-ber that it won't give true AT performance because disk operations will continue at PC speeds. Nor do these boards come cheap. If you are upgrading from PC to AT speed, it may cost no more to sell your PC and buy an inexpensive AT clone.

Track Buffering

Recall from Chapter 2 that track buffers are built into some hard disk controller cards. When a request is made for a single sector, the controller reads the entire track where the sector is located, starting with the sector closest to the read/write head. It reads the sectors in their physical sequence, as if the disk had a 1:1 in-terleave. Then it takes the requested sector from the buffer and sends it to DOS. The next request for a sector from the track can then be delivered instantly, at *electronic speed*, because there is no need to wait for the sector to swing under the read/write head.

Track buffering increases performance only when files are thoroughly defragmented. Otherwise time is spent reading in data that isn't called for. Similarly, track buffering can be wasteful with random-access files, because the next sector required is likely to reside on another track.

Track buffering can also be performed by certain disk caching utilities, such as *Flash* from Software Masters. Instead of buffering the track on the controller card, it is kept in system memory. This approach slightly increases inefficiencies when some sectors on the track aren't used, because *all* sectors are transferred to system memory. (A controller-based track buffer takes time to transfer a sector to memory only when the sector is requested by DOS.) Because track buffers may slow some applications, it is useful to be able to switch it on and off—something that can't be done with controller-based track buffering. A utility like *Flash* makes this possible with only a few keystrokes.

Software-based buffering

Of course, track buffering may be used for writing data as well as reading it. In this case, when DOS "writes" a sector, it is inserted into the track buffer. Under ideal conditions, every sector on the track is given new data, and the data is physically written on the disk only when the track buffer is full. However, to avoid data loss through power outages and other glitches, the track is actually written after a specified delay or when a request is made to move the read/write heads to another cylinder. The delay is typically a few seconds. Performance doesn't suffer even when more sectors on the track are subsequently written, because the delay period is quite long compared with data transfer times, and it's unlikely that another sector will be sent to the buffer just as the track is written out. Long delays (say, 10 seconds) may be risky when track buffering is used with floppy disks because diskettes can be swapped during the delay. Track buffering may be made *more* efficient during write operations by sorting out which sectors have changed and writing less than a full track.

Writing data

There is one more potential problem. When the last sectors of a file are sent to the track buffer, the data may remain in the buffer for several seconds. From the point of view of the application software, the file has been completely and successfully written to disk. The program might immediately terminate, perhaps through some sort of "save and terminate" command. A moment later the track buffer begins to spill its contents onto the disk surface and—bang!—it runs into an unrecoverable disk error of some kind—perhaps a full diskette. But the program is gone so that its inbuilt error-recovery facilities cannot come into play. The file is lost.

RAM Disks

One way to circumvent slow head seeks is to eliminate them altogether by using a RAM disk. We discussed RAM disks in Chapter 2 as one of the data storage alternatives and described *non-volatile* disks that maintain their data even when the computer is turned off. Because non-volatile RAM boards are still quite expensive and are unreliable when faced with prolonged power outages, few users opt to add megabytes of RAM storage to their systems. But smaller, transient RAM disks can play an important role in improving disk performance.

How they work

A RAM disk sets aside part of memory and divides it into sections corresponding to disk sectors. A device driver (control program) sits in low memory, performing the same functions as a disk drive's electronics. From DOS's point of view, it is just another disk drive. But it is the fastest possible disk drive because there is no waiting for read/write heads to move across the disk surface, and no waiting for platters to turn. Completely fragmented files are read and written as quickly as perfectly contiguous ones.

RAM disk speed

The CPU makes data transfers in most RAM disks; the data moves from the RAM disk part of memory to the microprocessor chip and then to a DOS buffer. Special-purpose RAM disk boards may be equipped for DMA (direct memory access) transfers, which move the data directly from one memory location to another, roughly doubling the RAM disk's performance. Reviews of hard disk performance sometimes compare disk access speeds as multiples of RAM disk performance, in which the RAM disk is taken as the measure of optimal speed. In fact, DMA-based RAM disk hardware sets the standard for the fastest possible disk drive.

Several manufacturers make *dedicated* RAM disk boards, some of which use DMA. Two-megabyte capacities are available by using 256K chips. These boards have their own power supply and line to a wall socket. When the computer is turned off, they continue to pull current, making them *non-volatile*. Among the manufacturers are Kapak Designs (*Novo Drive 1000*) and ABM Computer Systems (the X2C shown in Figure 7-3). Non-volatile boards come equipped with a small backup power supply. Because dynamic RAM chips take a lot of power, the backup units help the board through only a short power outage, perhaps as little as ten minutes. A daily backup to a hard disk is only prudent.

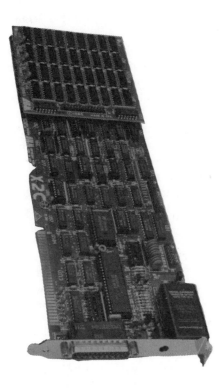

Figure 7-3 **The X2C non-volatile RAM disk**

Dangers

Software-based RAM disks are notoriously risky because they are destroyed by the slightest power disruption. A small program creates the RAM disk, and files are moved to it from a hard disk or floppy; when work is finished, the altered files must be copied back. Although power outages are rare, instances in which software malfunctions force you to reboot the computer are not. When important data is kept on the RAM disk, it must be constantly backed up. This is very easy to do by stopping work periodically and executing a simple batch file that copies the endangered files over to your hard disk.

Read-only files

RAM disks, however, aren't best suited to holding data files. They are best reserved for *read-only* files under more or less constant access—*program overlays*, for example. Overlays are parts of a program that remain on disk while the main program is loaded. As various program functions are called upon, the corresponding overlay is loaded from disk onto an area in memory reserved by the program for this purpose. By *overlaying* the same section of memory with different modules of code, a program occupies less room. Newer programs tend not to use overlays now that 640K of memory is the norm. But some older programs are impeded by the constant disk accesses that overlays impose. Overlay files are normally marked by an **.OVL** extension.

Reference files

RAM disks are also good for holding the electronic dictionaries for spelling checkers and thesauruses. When spelling checkers constantly watch for errors during text entry, the hard disk holding the dictionary never stops working. Performance may degrade to the point that the screen doesn't echo characters as quickly as they are typed in. And the incessant flicker of the hard drive's indicator light tells of excessive wear and tear. Both problems are completely eliminated by placing the dictionary on a (large) RAM disk.

Temporary files

Temporary files also benefit from RAM disks. Word processors often create temporary output files containing special formatting codes for the printer. Much disk access may be required to fill in cross references between pages. Directing the temporary file to a RAM disk can greatly speed the process. Similarly, the compilers and linkers used by computer programmers may create elaborate temporary files that are under constant random access. The entire cycle from source text to finished code can often be cut in half just by moving the process over to a RAM disk.

Program files

Finally, RAM disks may make a big difference in system performance when you move back and forth between programs. It is easy enough to create batch files or keyboard macros that will shut down one program and begin another, but waiting for the programs to load can be onerous. By placing the program files on a RAM disk, the load time is made as fast as possible.

An important point to note about all of these applications is that none place critical files on the RAM disk. If power is interrupted, the only losses are unchanging program files or data files that can be easily reloaded from the hard disk. There's no need to back up the RAM disk at all.

Drawbacks

The problem with RAM disks is that they gobble up the one resource that few have enough of: random access memory. It's usually practical to devote only a small part of system RAM to a RAM disk. But even a 64K RAM disk can hold many program overlays, a large printer output file, or the temporary files from a compiler.

Fortunately, there are two ways to set up a large RAM disk using almost none of your precious 640K. The RAM disk may go in **extended memory** or may reside in **expanded memory**. Extended memory exists only in 80286 (AT-class) and 80386 machines. It is made up of RAM residing at memory addresses 1 million through 16 million. The IBM PC/XT microprocessor cannot access memory in this range, and even the more advanced chips require Microsoft's OS/2 operating system to use it with programs. But a RAM disk can be installed in extended memory and run with DOS. In fact, we'll see in a moment that DOS actually includes software that creates a RAM disk in extended memory.

Extended memory

Expanded memory, which is easily confused with extended memory, is actually quite different. It works in both PC- and AT-class machines. These machines are limited by DOS to 640K of memory, but the CPU can in fact reach a full 1000K of memory addresses under DOS. Some of the unused memory range is reserved for special needs, but most is left open. Expanded memory takes over a 64K stretch of addresses in the high end of memory and uses it as a "window" for passing data back and forth to programs. Although up to 32 megabytes of expanded memory may be installed in the machine, at any moment only 64K is accessible to the microprocessor through this 64K window. When a program requires a particular piece of data, the section of expanded memory holding the data shifts into the 64K window so that the CPU can access it. (Actually, the window is divided into four 16K sections so that a program can reach four sections of expanded memory at once.) This process is called **bank switching**, which is diagrammed in Figure 7-4. Programs must be specially written to keep data in expanded memory.

Expanded memory

Today, many memory expansion boards can be set to work as system memory (640K), extended memory, or expanded memory. Some of these boards let you use part of the installed memory in one way and the remainder in another. Part might be devoted to programs like *Framework* and *Symphony* that can keep huge data sets in expanded memory, and part might go to a giant RAM disk. Many people who own expanded memory boards never use them as RAM disks, wasting a valuable productivity resource.

RAM disk programs are available from many sources. DOS versions 3.0 and later include a RAM disk program. Many add-on memory cards supply a RAM disk on their utility diskettes (owners of the ubiquitous AST SixPakPlus memory card will find *SUPERDRV.COM*). And myriad commercial and public domain offerings are available. If you use a public domain program, be sure to choose a tried-and-true one, such as *MEMBRAIN.SYS*.

RAM disk software

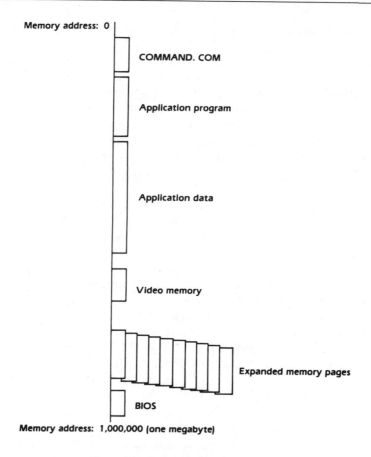

Figure 7-4 **Expanded memory**

Each program is tailored differently. Although most allow you to size the RAM disk in 1,000-byte increments, some also give control over sector size, the number of directory entries accommodated, and other specifications. Some let you avoid these complications by demanding the simple equivalent of a single-sided or double-sided floppy diskette.

Some RAM disk programs come as device drivers that must be installed via CONFIG.SYS when the computer is booted. Others can be loaded at any time. Several RAM disks may be created if you prefer smaller disks under multiple drive specifiers. No matter how the RAM disk is created, or what kind of memory it resides in, a small amount of system RAM (1 to 3K) is devoted to the device driver. You must reboot to get rid of RAM disks.

Most RAM disk programs create the disk under the next highest drive specifier. For example, if you have a floppy drive as **A:** and a hard disk as **C:**, the RAM disk will be created as **D:**. Some programs let you specify the name for the disk; you could make it **B:**. Or you may *insert* the drive between others. In a machine with two floppy disk drives, inserting a RAM disk as **B:** makes the second drive **C:**. (Be warned that doing this invites confusion.) You may even be able to "replace" a disk drive with the RAM disk so that a RAM disk named **B:** completely hides from view the floppy disk drive normally at **B:**. This feature can be useful when a drive goes out of whack and your batch files and software are configured to rely on it; the RAM disk can stand in for the drive until it is repaired.

Positioning the RAM disk

The DOS RAM disk program called *VDISK* is complicated, and we won't describe it in detail here. As a device driver, it is explained in the DOS manuals under the **DEVICE** command. *VDISK* takes several optional parameters that set the disk size, sector size, and number of directory entries. As you know from our discussion of high-capacity disks, large sectors waste disk space when many small files are used. Similarly, the option of setting the number of directory entries saves a little space. If the parameters are omitted, *VDISK* defaults to a 64K drive with 128-byte sectors and 64 directory slots. *VDISK* uses an /**E** switch to place the RAM disk in extended memory (it doesn't support expanded memory).

VDISK

RAM disks are useful, but they are not infinitely fast. Because they rely upon the CPU to transfer data between memory locations, their performance very much depends on how fast a machine you own. Tests show that a RAM disk on an ordinary 4.77-MHz IBM PC functions only marginally faster than a fast hard disk on an AT (provided that the hard disk's files are unfragmented). Perhaps your work doesn't entail the sorts of constant disk access that can easily move to a RAM disk. But if your work *can* benefit from a RAM disk, it is an easy, cheap way to improve performance.

DOS-level Optimization

A disk is optimized at DOS level by minimizing the work DOS must do to find its way to a file or to extract data from a file. We saw in Chapter 2 that DOS reads disk sectors into an adjustable number of buffers. Setting the number of buffers correctly is the easiest and most important of all optimization measures. Buffering can be taken much further through disk caching utilities, which may keep hundreds of sectors in system memory.

DOS finds files much more quickly when the directory tree is designed to complement the process. Files, including subdirectory files, may be laid out on the disk in particular patterns that minimize head movement. Also, the DOS PATH command, or path utilities, can be set up in a way that helps DOS find a file in the shortest time. Finally, starting with DOS version 3.3, the FASTOPEN command can greatly reduce the time it takes DOS to find and open a file.

Optimizing the Number of DOS Buffers

With buffers, DOS minimizes physical disk accesses. When an application program requires only a few bytes of information from a sector and then a few more, it would be senseless to read the same sector repeatedly from the disk surface. DOS keeps the most recently accessed sectors in memory, and before going to disk for information, it first checks to see if it is already on hand in one of the buffers. Similarly, when a program sends data items to disk, DOS may wait until a sector is filled with data fragments before actually writing the sector on the disk surface.

An example

Say that in a random-access data file every record is 128 bytes long. Data is entered for a record and "saved." Only a quarter of a 512-byte sector is changed, and if DOS writes the sector to disk, three-quarters of the data will be an exact copy of what is already written. The disk drive must work in sector units; as a result, there is no way to write just the data that has been changed.

Now, if you were to continue entering new data into the next three 128-byte records in the database, the same sector would be written to disk four times in a row, each time changing a different part of the sector's contents. Obviously, if all four records were entered before any disk access, three of the four disk accesses would be eliminated.

This is the rationale for sector buffering. When data is entered into one of the buffers, DOS waits to see if more is coming. It writes out the data only if the buffer is required for another sector or if a delay period has elapsed without disk access.

Writing data

Application programs have a way of ensuring that all buffers holding new data are recorded on disk before the program terminates. You may have lost power while working in a database, only to find that when you restarted the program, data that you thought had been saved was nowhere to be found. The data was lost because the software didn't have the opportunity to "flush" the buffers on to disk during a normal program termination. That's why you should always quit a program through the proper exit command, never by rebooting.

DOS lets you choose how many buffers it sets up when the system is booted by including the line **BUFFERS = number** in CONFIG.SYS. DOS allows from 1 to 99 buffers; as we'll see in a moment, **BUFFERS = 20** is about right. You'll need to reboot to bring the new command into action. When no BUFFERS setting is made, DOS defaults to two buffers on a PC or XT, or three on an AT. Starting with version 3.3, DOS checks the amount of system memory installed and sets an appropriate number of buffers. Like many DOS default settings, these numbers were chosen to conserve memory and are extremely conservative, even from the standpoint of a floppy-disk-only machine.

The BUFFERS
setting

It's easy to see the advantage in having many buffers. With only a few, DOS must empty buffers before the sectors they hold have been completely processed, because other sectors are momentarily required. The discarded sectors must be written to, or read from, the hard disk a second time, and perhaps *many* times. Much time is wasted on unnecessary disk accesses.

However, as useful as buffers are, it's possible to have DOS create *too many*. It takes time to search for a particular sector among the buffers and if not found, a disk access must be made anyway. When many buffers are searched, the time required may exceed that taken by simply going to disk without any buffering scheme at all.

No single "optimal" value exists for the DOS BUFFERS setting. It varies by the way particular applications process files and depends somewhat on a computer's speed, because a faster CPU can search the buffers more quickly. Those who have run tests on buffer settings recommend values between 15 and 20 for both XT- and AT-class machines. Each buffer takes up 528 bytes—512 for the sector and 16 for DOS's bookkeeping—so 20 buffers take up about 10K of RAM. If you have a hard disk and you've relied on the DOS default settings of two or three buffers, when you increase the number to 20, you'll notice an immediate improvement in performance with most applications.

The optimal value

DOS versions 3.0 and later search the buffers more quickly; if you use an earlier DOS version, 15 buffers may be optimal. Here's is yet another reason to upgrade to the latest DOS version, if you haven't already.

Having more DOS buffers doesn't help all software. In fact, some applications are slightly slowed by a larger buffer setting. When sequential files (such as text files) are read or written, no sector is

Relative
performance

repeatedly accessed and hence the whole buffering system serves no purpose. But the CPU overhead for the buffer searches remains. Conversely, *completely random* file accesses aren't helped by having many buffers because nearly all accesses require a sector not currently held in the buffer pool. Fortunately, most "random" accesses aren't all that random—the software tends to work on only a few file locations at once—and having more buffers generally speeds data throughput.

Some application software opens many files at once. It may be tempting to increase the number of DOS buffers to accommodate them all, but if you think about it, you'll see that this makes no sense. The BUFFERS setting is a kind of gambling. You are setting *odds* that, on the average, a specific unit of data is more likely to be in memory than not. In essence, you are agreeing to risk wasting time looking for data that may not be in memory, rather than undergo the certitude of losing many milliseconds to a disk access. The balance is set by a contest between CPU speed and disk speed—the number of sectors or files involved has nothing to do with it. Similarly, it's erroneous to think that the larger the disk, the more DOS buffers it needs.

Applying Disk Cachers

Disk caching (pronounced "cashing") combines the best features of RAM disks and DOS buffers. A section of memory is set aside to hold frequently accessed disk sectors, and when DOS issues a command to look for a sector on disk, disk-caching software first searches through the cached sectors; if it finds its target, it supplies the sector to DOS from the cache, saving the time it takes to read data from the disk surface. The logic is the same as for DOS buffers. But disk caching programs can keep *megabytes* of sectors in memory when extended or expanded memory is used. And in this way it is more like a RAM disk—whole files may be kept in memory.

In our discussion of the DOS BUFFERS command, we warned you against creating too many buffers because DOS could spend more time searching them than it is worth. You may wonder how a disk caching program could possibly be efficient when it keeps many times as many sectors in memory as would be prudent for the DOS buffers. Disk cachers are much smarter than DOS in this regard; they maintain logic that ensures that only minimal processing time goes into the search. And because the cacher can keep so

much of a file in memory, a more protracted search is less risky
than with DOS buffers because a program is much more likely to
find the sector it needs.

The cache sits between the physical disk and the DOS buffers, as
shown in Figure 7-5; it doesn't replace the DOS buffers. Its role is
more like that of a RAM disk, in that it acts as a sort of pseudo-disk
that can supply sectors to the DOS buffers more quickly than a
physical disk access can. When a cache is operating, it is redundant
for DOS to keep many buffers of its own and search through them.
Accordingly, the number of DOS buffers is usually set to 1 or 2
when cache software is used.

*The role of DOS
buffers*

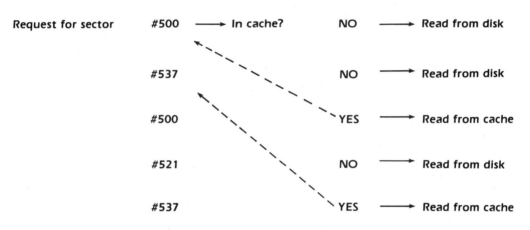

Figure 7-5 **Disk caching**

When DOS reads a new sector, it is forced to give up a sector
held in one of the buffers. It allots the buffer on a "least-recently-
used" (LRU) scheme. Discarding the least-recently-used sector
makes sense, but it isn't the optimal logic. Disk cachers use a combination of least-recently-used logic and least-frequently-used logic;
a cacher may hang onto a sector that has been "hit" many times,
even if it is the least recently used.

Sector selection

Why isn't DOS so smart? It's certainly not for lack of ability on
Microsoft's part. Disk cachers take up 20 to 30K of memory—extra
code that would bloat DOS. DOS needs to run in systems with too
little memory to devote to a disk cache and too little to hold a
larger rendition of DOS. Even in systems equipped with 640K,
memory shortage is a persistent problem, and it's much better to
allot a portion of memory to disk caching for some applications
and not for others.

Performance

The benefits of disk cachers are not apparent when a program starts up. Many sector reads are required to fill the cache. But gradually the cache fills with the disk information in greatest demand. The makers of caching software tend to make outrageous claims about the performance gains cachers achieve, often citing a doubling or tripling of speed. Such gains occur only rarely. In most applications, a disk cacher increases the speed of disk-intensive operations (such as a database sorts) by 30% to 60%. The greatest gains are made using random-access files in which the software constantly accesses physically distant points in the file. As with DOS buffers, in some circumstances disk cachers can actually slow software.

FATs and
directories

Because disk cachers may use large amounts of memory, they usually end up holding the whole file allocation table, the root directory, and recently used subdirectories. This lets DOS search for files more quickly, particularly when the directory tree is complicated and subdirectories are fragmented. This performance gain is particularly noticeable to programmers when they compile or link many small files.

Reading vs writing
data

Theoretically, a disk caching program should achieve performance gains when writing data as well as reading it. For example, when a database program changes one record held in a sector, the sector can remain in the cache for a few seconds before being physically written to the disk; this allows time for further changes to the sector, saving the trouble of multiple disk accesses. Most caching programs write data directly to the disk, however. It's considered too dangerous to leave data loitering in memory, especially because FAT sectors or other crucial information could be destroyed if the machine is turned off or rebooted. Instead, cachers write sectors directly to disk, but they keep a copy in the cache on the presumption that it may be called upon again. These programs are called **write-through cachers** because in a sense they write data *through* the cache.

The *IBMCACHE*
program

IBM included the program *IBMCACHE* with most members of the PS/2 line. It's distributed as a hidden file on the DOS Reference Diskette. By running an installation program, a DEVICE statement is automatically inserted in CONFIG.SYS, and thereafter the cacher is loaded when the machine boots. You may specify a cache size from 16 kilobytes to 512 kilobytes for system memory, or 16 kilobytes to 15 megabytes for extended memory. *IBMCACHE* won't run on expanded memory. The program isn't very flexible and to change the amount of memory it consumes you must edit CONFIG.SYS and reboot.

Quite advanced features are available in some disk cachers, especially *Flash* from Software Masters. In its "high priority" mode you can allocate portions of the cache to particular files, whether or not they are currently in use. This allows you to switch back and forth between tasks without constantly reloading the cache with the files used by each. The "high priority" configuration can be saved in a file for use at another time, and the entire system can be reconfigured on the fly, without rebooting. *Flash* can also be made to read whole tracks at a time in anticipation of requiring other sectors from a track; it creates a sort of *full track buffer*.

Advanced disk cachers

Most caching programs issue reports that help you assess their effectiveness. They tell how many disk accesses were made by DOS, how many were handled by the cache, and how many required physical reads or writes. Using these data, you can determine whether the cache is worth the memory devoted. Caching software isn't very expensive, especially when you consider that often it can impart voice-coil speeds to stepper-motor drives. However, using a cacher is inexpensive only if you already have spare memory on hand.

Optimizing Directory Tree Organization

File searches are a particularly time-consuming aspect of disk access. When a file is listed in a subdirectory several levels below the root directory, the read/write heads must jump from subdirectory to subdirectory as DOS traces its way to the file. Little time is lost when only a file or two are opened. But some applications repeatedly access scores of files. Programmers keep their code in many separate files and link them to produce the complete program. Half of the *link time* may go to DOS file searches.

There are three ways to minimize file search times. First, keep the size of subdirectories to one cluster. Recall that a directory entry takes 32 bytes. A 512-byte sector holds 16 such entries, so a four-sector cluster holds 64. Because two slots are given to the *dot* and *double dot* entries, a single-cluster directory can hold 62 files. This amounts to nearly three screens in a directory listing. It's more files than most subdirectories should hold.

Subdirectory size

When subdirectories are restricted to one cluster, the entry for the next subdirectory along the path can always be found without moving the read/write heads to another track. Subdirectories tend to be fragmented, because clusters are usually allocated gradually as more and more files are listed in it. The one-cluster restriction also

(continued page 242)

An Inside Look: Disk Caching with *Flash*

Flash from Software Masters is an exceptionally versatile disk caching program. Once it has been installed, the program is called into action merely by entering a command such as:

```
FLASH 100
```

which sets aside 100 kilobytes of RAM for caching. Typically this command would be placed in AUTOEXEC.BAT to load the program at startup. Many features may be activated at any time by calling the program from the DOS command line. For example, to measure caching's effect on disk operations, you can call for a status report by entering:

```
FLASH /S
```

and the status screen shown in screen A appears:

```
 F L A S H   S T A T U S    VER:5.33

Memory:100 K-C  Priority:L  Active:Y
Hi-Pri Used :00009 Mem Unused:00000
Hi-Pri Other:00000 Hi-Pri MAX:00100
Buffer FLASH:Y        DOS Flush:N
Smart Write :Y       Track Read:N
/W Active   :N       Track Write:N:3

Control ON:ABcde
Turned OFF:
Write-Pro :
Format OFF:
Media Call:

              Reads         Writes
Real        0000755        0000460
Saved       0000573        0000089
            --------       --------

Total       0001328        0000549
Saved         043%           016%

D:\FLASH---_
```

Screen A. **A Status Report.**

By entering the word **FLASH** alone, a full listing of the features is displayed
(screen B). The **/A** and **/O** switches turn caching on and off, and **/U** removes **FLASH**
from memory. The **/M** switch lets you select which kind of memory (system RAM, expanded, extended) the cache will occupy. Various other switches let you activate
and control the **high priority mode** ("HI-PRI"), where part of the cache is reserved
for particular files, potentially allowing it to act as a RAM disk.

Two features are particularly interesting. First, the **/J** and **/K** switches let you turn
track buffering on and off. You can set the delay time for writing sectors to the
disk; if you don't mind living dangerously, you can make the delay long to obtain
true full-track write operations. Second, features let you protect a disk from accidental damage. The **/T** switch **write-protects** a drive—a useful feature for floppy disk
drives. And the /- switch makes it impossible to accidentally format a drive. Both of
these features may be toggled on and off.

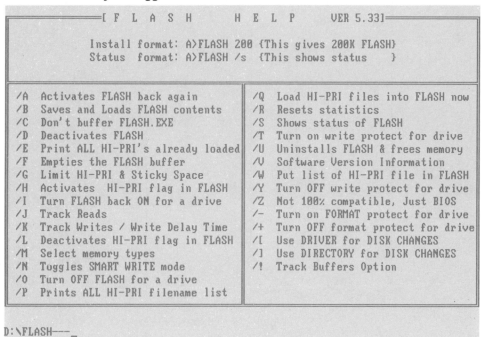

```
=[ F  L  A  S  H       H  E  L  P      VER 5.33]=

         Install format: A>FLASH 200 {This gives 200K FLASH}
         Status  format: A>FLASH /s  {This shows status     }


/A  Activates FLASH back again        /Q  Load HI-PRI files into FLASH now
/B  Saves and Loads FLASH contents    /R  Resets statistics
/C  Don't buffer FLASH.EXE            /S  Shows status of FLASH
/D  Deactivates FLASH                 /T  Turn on write protect for drive
/E  Print ALL HI-PRI's already loaded /U  Uninstalls FLASH & frees memory
/F  Empties the FLASH buffer          /V  Software Version Information
/G  Limit HI-PRI & Sticky Space       /W  Put list of HI-PRI file in FLASH
/H  Activates  HI-PRI flag in FLASH   /Y  Turn OFF write protect for drive
/I  Turn FLASH back ON for a drive    /Z  Not 100% compatible, Just BIOS
/J  Track Reads                       /-  Turn on FORMAT protect for drive
/K  Track Writes / Write Delay Time   /+  Turn OFF format protect for drive
/L  Deactivates HI-PRI flag in FLASH  /[  Use DRIVER for DISK CHANGES
/M  Select memory types               /]  Use DIRECTORY for DISK CHANGES
/N  Toggles SMART WRITE mode          /!  Track Buffers Option
/O  Turn OFF FLASH for a drive
/P  Prints ALL HI-PRI filename list


D:\FLASH---_
```

Screen B. **Menu Selections within** *Flash*.

means that DOS never has to search further than 62 entries to find the subdirectory's listing. (DOS searches directories top down, quitting the search once it finds its target.)

Reordering listings   In Chapter 5 we mentioned utilities that sort a directory by physically reordering it on disk. Properly designed, one of these utilities can help speed disk searches by placing all entries for child subdirectories at the top of the directory, as shown in Figure 7-6. Although seldom-accessed subdirectories might not deserve a priority position, on the whole this is the optimal way to order directories.

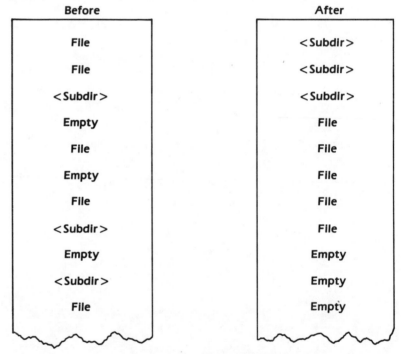

Before	After
File	<Subdir>
File	<Subdir>
<Subdir>	<Subdir>
Empty	File
File	File
Empty	File
File	File
<Subdir>	File
Empty	Empty
<Subdir>	Empty
File	Empty

Figure 7-6 **Subdirectory sorting**

The second benefit of utilities that permanently sort directories is that a good one moves all unused directory slots to the end of the directory sectors. DOS scans each sector before reading the next. If sectors early in the directory are mostly filled with empty slots made by file erasures, the search takes that much longer. One of DOS's minor inadequacies is that it doesn't discard sectors once it allocates them to a subdirectory file. If three clusters are allocated to hold many files and all files are then erased, the subdirectory file continues to take up three clusters. Although DOS always assigns a new file to the topmost available slot, a lot of empty space may separate actual file entries, putting your disk drive through unnecessary head seeks.

Finally, subdirectory access is quickened by creating a tree with as few levels as possible. If a programmer places 40 code modules in the subdirectory **PROJECTS\PASCAL\DATABASE \REPORTS\MODULES**, DOS will have to perform (in the worst case) seven head seeks to get to the start of each file, or 280 seeks to link all modules. Even at a 40-millisecond average access time, that's over 11 seconds wasted in head movements—not to mention the time spent scanning each subdirectory. (In a moment we'll see how the FASTOPEN command makes an end-run around this inefficiency.)

Tree leveling

Optimizing Subdirectory Layout

By grouping all subdirectory files in only a few cylinders at the outer edge of the disk, you can greatly reduce head movements when DOS looks up a file nested several levels down the directory tree.

An ordinary 17-sector-per-track, two-platter disk drive has 68 sectors in a cylinder. RLL encoding increases that number to 100 or even 136 sectors. Sixty-eight sectors equals 17 clusters, or 17 subdirectories. Hence a well-developed directory tree made up of 68 subdirectories can fit on only four cylinders or only three cylinders using RLL 2,7 encoding.

When subdirectories are compacted this way, subdirectory-to-subdirectory searches proceed much more quickly. DOS is much more likely to find the next subdirectory in the chain in the same cylinder, averting the need for a head move. Even greater speed is attained by positioning the subdirectory cylinders as close to the outer edge of the disk as possible. This measure limits the *distance* of head movements to and from the root directory and file allocation table.

If you can plan out your entire directory tree when the disk is first formatted, you can easily build up this system of compacted subdirectories. You need merely create the entire directory tree before placing any files on the disk. Not only are the subdirectories compacted onto a few cylinders, but the entries for each child directory are positioned at the very beginning of the parent so that they are immediately found during the directory search. If COM-

Planning the tree

MAND.COM has been automatically installed during formatting, temporarily erase it, because it occupies one or two cylinders on the outer edge of the disk. Then create the tree, working *vertically* rather than *horizontally*. By "vertically" we mean that subdirectory chains should be created in sequence, instead of making all level-one subdirectories first, then level-two subdirectories, and so on.

An example

Consider, for example, a simple three-level tree with only two subdirectories at level one, three subdirectories under each of these, and eleven subdirectories distributed under both of these groupings of three. Now, there are 30 subdirectories in total, and they can fit into exactly two cylinders on an ordinary 20-megabyte disk. The level-1 subdirectory **ANIMALS** has fourteen subdirectories below it, and all fifteen could fit into one cylinder. Similarly, the subdirectory **ANIMALS** and all child directories below it could fit into a second cylinder.

If all subdirectories below ANIMALS were placed in one cylinder, the search for **ANIMALS\MAMMALS\PRIMATES** would require only one head seek (from the root directory to the single cylinder). On the other hand, if all level-1 subdirectories were created, then level-2 subdirectories, and so on, then no three-level path would be found in one cylinder, and a second head seek would be required.

Actual performance

Of course, real-world directory trees won't fit into cylinders so perfectly, and it isn't feasible to start a level-1 subdirectory at the first logical cluster in a cylinder. But the basic principle applies. If your work entails many frequent directory searches, taking the trouble to lay out your directories in this way is well worthwhile. This is particularly true if you use the PATH command to search many directories for a file.

Optimizing File Layout

You can reap very modest performance gains by positioning crucial files as close to the outer edge of the platters as possible. The point is to minimize the *distance* the read/write heads must travel to reach the file. Of course, DOS accesses the file's directory immediately before moving to the first cluster of the file, so the presumption is that the directory will also be near the outer edge. This is necessarily true for files listed in the root directory; otherwise, you must follow the prescriptions in the preceding discussion of subdirectory compaction.

This measure is useful for files that are frequently and repeatedly accessed, such as overlay files. You'll see more difference on stepper-motor drives, in which the seek time is proportional to the distance the heads are moved. Many people do not have such high-priority files in their system, and for them this optimization measure is a waste of time.

Of course, you have real control over file layout only when a disk is empty. You can set up as much of the directory tree as possible and then copy over high-priority files. But there's no way you can *maintain* an ideal file layout without help from utility software. Some defragmenters (such as the shareware program, *DOG*) let you specify which files should be positioned on the outer reaches of the disk.

Limitations

Optimizing the PATH and APPEND Commands

In Chapter 5 we examined the DOS PATH command. Recall that this command automatically searches a list of DOS paths for a file you wish to load. Starting with version 3.3, PC DOS added the AP-PEND command, which extends the search to data files opened by programs. In both commands, you list a series of paths, and DOS searches them in that order.

You can optimize path searches by listing paths in the PATH and APPEND commands in their order of relative importance. If the first path listed is **/IDEAS/NOTIONS/INKLINGS/INSIGHTS**, and the second path is **/BATCH**, DOS must search through five subdirectories every time a batch file is used. If batch files are used often, the path sequence should be the reverse. The same logic applies when you list paths in an APPEND command.

Path order

This optimization varies from day to day, depending on the work you do. As a general rule, you should placc short searches before long ones in the path sequence.

Using the FASTOPEN Command

Starting with version 3.3, DOS provides the **FASTOPEN** command to speed repeated accesses to files. Typically, every time DOS opens a file, it must work its way through the directories that make up the file's path. When FASTOPEN is activated, it stores in memory the locations of recently accessed files, including subdirectory files. For example, when **/PLANTS/FLOWERS/ROSES.DAT** is loaded,

FASTOPEN saves the cluster number of the data file **ROSES.DAT**, and of the subdirectory files **PLANTS** and **FLOWERS**. Next time you open the file, DOS can send the read/write heads directly to **ROSES.DAT** without shuttling through the subdirectories. Similarly, if you then ask to load **PLANTS/FLOWERS/BUTTRCUP.DAT**, DOS can find its way straight to the **FLOWERS** subdirectory to look for the file.

To activate FASTOPEN for drive C, you must enter:

```
FASTOPEN C:
```

By default, up to 34 files and subdirectories may be recorded. This number may be changed from any value from 10 to 999. To set it to 100, enter:

```
FASTOPEN C:=100
```

Every file takes 35 bytes of memory. The number must be at least one greater than the most levels of subdirectory you'll be using. FASTOPEN must never be used with the JOIN, SUBST, and AS-SIGN commands discussed in Chapter 5.

FASTOPEN, a welcome addition to DOS, can make a significant difference in certain applications, especially when overlay files are repeatedly called; the cost in memory is negligible.

Choosing Optimization Measures

We've looked at 15 factors in disk performance, and only a few can't be changed once you've bought your disk and controller. So which measures make the most difference? And how does a measure's cost compare to its gains? If you've been reading closely, you can probably guess that the answers to these questions vary not only from machine to machine but also from application to application. For example, if you work with large databases that are accessed fairly randomly, file defragmentation will be of less benefit to you than to those who access many sequential files.

Trade offs

You'll find that some optimizations nullify the benefits of others. Conversely, some optimizations are undermined when other optimizations aren't performed in tandem. Let's take a look at these trade offs:

Cylinder density. A doubled cylinder density cuts in half the number of head seeks required by most applications, making fast seek times less important. However, the benefits of a high cylinder density are defeated by file fragmentation.

Average seek time. Faster seek times make less difference on drives with a higher cylinder density, on drives kept defragmented, on drives in which the subdirectories have been compacted, and on drives used with substantial disk caching.

Interleave. Track buffering makes the interleave irrelevant. Adding an accelerator card may undermine a previously optimized interleave. Slow software can undermine an effective interleave by inserting additional delays between sector reads and writes.

File defragmentation. File defragmentation is less important when disk caching is used; it is entirely irrelevant when files are kept on RAM disks.

Interface type. A fast interface is useless if the CPU cannot handle the higher data rate. Its benefits are largely squandered when the disk hasn't been optimized to minimize head movements.

CPU speed. A faster clock speed hastens data transfer from the controller to memory, allowing a faster interleave. It also speeds up the processing of data in DOS buffers, caching software, and so on. The benefits of accelerator boards are more limited. Their greatest impact is made when inefficient software creates delays that interfere with the disk's interleave optimization. An accelerator board may also hasten searches of DOS buffers and disk caches.

Track buffering. Track buffers may significantly increase performance accessing sequential files, and slightly slow performance using random-access files. Disk caching largely duplicates the benefits of track buffering. Track buffering is undermined when files have not been defragmented.

RAM disk support. In applications that read many small files, transferring them to a RAM disk can cut disk access time greatly. An intelligent disk cacher can do the job just as well, using about the same amount of RAM.

DOS buffers setting. Failure to change the default BUFFERS setting to a value from 15 to 20 undermines most optimizations because the disk is forced to do unnecessary work. With disk caching software, however, the BUFFERS setting must be very low to avoid redundant searches.

Disk caching. By keeping much data in memory, disk caching reduces the benefits of all measures that optimize mechanical access to files, including fast seek times, high cylinder densities, track buffering, and file defragmentation. Conversely, a disk cacher would slow a RAM disk because it already operates at electronic speed.

Directory tree design. An optimized tree design makes most difference when your software accesses many files or a few files repeatedly. Disk cachers, subdirectory compaction, and the FASTOPEN command reduce the value of this optimization.

Subdirectory layout. The benefits of compacting subdirectories into a few cylinders are duplicated by a shallow directory tree design, the FASTOPEN command, and disk caching.

File layout. File layout makes a very minor contribution to disk speed. It is most useful for frequently read overlay files. There is no gain when RAM disks or large disk caches are used.

PATH and APPEND optimization. Optimization of the PATH and APPEND commands is less important when FASTOPEN is used or when a large disk cache keeps the relevant subdirectories in memory.

The FASTOPEN command. The FASTOPEN command matters only when files are repeatedly opened. It makes less difference when tree organization, subdirectory compaction, and disk caching increase the speed of directory searches.

Cost Effectiveness

Now let's look at the relative costs of the various optimization measures, using mid-1987 retail prices where actual dollar values are given. Most products are available at discounted prices.

Cylinder density. Very expensive when it results from the purchase of a very high-capacity disk because these disks tend to cost more per megabyte. But inexpensive when acquired through RLL encoding because RLL controllers cost only about $50 more than ordinary MFM controllers. However, a disk drive that can use RLL encoding may be more expensive.

Average seek time. Still relatively expensive. Voice-coil technology adds about 50% to the price of a slower stepper-motor drive. But keep an eye out for new stepper-motor drives in the 30 to 40 millisecond range. High-capacity drives always use voice coils, so you'll have no say in the matter.

Interleave. The IBM Advanced Diagnostics cost $150, and include a basic low-level formatting program. But you're much better off with the *HFORMAT/HTEST* program from Paul Mace Software, which includes the *HOPTIMUM* program for optimizing the interleave ($90).

File defragmentation. Many defraggers are available at a reasonable price. You can buy a stand-alone utility, such as *Disk Optimizer* from SoftLogic, for $50. Or you can go for economies of scale and buy a general disk toolkit that includes a defragger, such as the *Norton Utilities Advanced Edition* ($150) or the *Mace Utilities* ($99).

Interface type. To date, ESDI interfaces have been used only with large, expensive drives. Currently, a switch to RLL encoding is the cheapest way to have a higher data rate. If your drive can handle one, an RLL controller retails for about $250.

CPU speed. Higher CPU speed may come very cheap or very dear. The fastest accelerator cards cost $500 or more. Simpler accelerators that fit into the microprocessor socket may cost only about $150. On the other hand, a replacement clock crystal for 6-MHz

ATs runs about $15 at electronics stores. Variable-speed clock crystals cost roughly $100.

Track buffering. Track buffers tend to be a luxury feature to promote more expensive controllers (and their accompanying drives). *Flash*, which offers software-based track buffering, retails for $70.

RAM disk support. DOS supplies *VDISK* for free, and you'll find that RAM disk software is included with many add-on memory boards. Commercial programs are sold for $30 to $50.

DOS buffers setting. The DOS buffers setting is free except for the effort required to type two words into your CONFIG.SYS file.

Disk caching. Disk cachers, like defragmenters, come as standalone packages, or as part of a general disk toolkit. They run $50 to $75 alone or less when included in a utility package.

Directory tree design. The tree design costs nothing. But it takes a lot of careful thought. Utilities that reorder subdirectory listings are usually found within disk toolkits, including *PC Tools*, the *Mace Utilities*, and *The Norton Utilities*.

Subdirectory layout. Again, the optimization is free, but it requires time for planning.

File layout. There's no cost, unless you use a defragmenter that can rearrange files by a specified plan.

PATH and APPEND optimization. PATH is standard to all DOS versions from 2.0 onward. The APPEND command appears only with DOS 3.3 ($129).

The FASTOPEN command. Available starting with DOS version 3.3 ($129).

Recommendations

All in all, too much attention is given to hardware solutions to optimization and too little to software solutions. In particular, fast seek times have taken on mythical proportions. There's no point in owning a 28-millisecond drive if it runs in an unoptimized system.

A file defragmenter is the most important optimization measure open to you. It costs little and likely will give you at least a 50% boost in performance on a drive that has long been filled with data. *Everyone* should have one of these programs and use it regularly. Disk caching is second in line, especially if you have expanded or extended memory that often sits idle. The software also is inexpensive. In some applications, disk speed may triple or quadruple with just these two optimization measures. With a little smart shopping, you can acquire both for under $100. Adding $100 to your hardware purchase won't buy nearly so much speed.

The importance of other optimization measures depends on your applications. If you often find yourself waiting for the disk to stop churning, stop and think about what's happening. How many files are accessed? If only a few, perhaps a RAM disk is the solution. In what way are the files accessed—sequentially or randomly? Perhaps a larger cache is what you need. Do the files remain open, or are they repeatedly opened and closed? Maybe FASTOPEN will do the job. Now that you understand the principles behind disk optimization, you should be able to experiment effectively and push your hardware to the limit.

Priorities

Backups without Pain

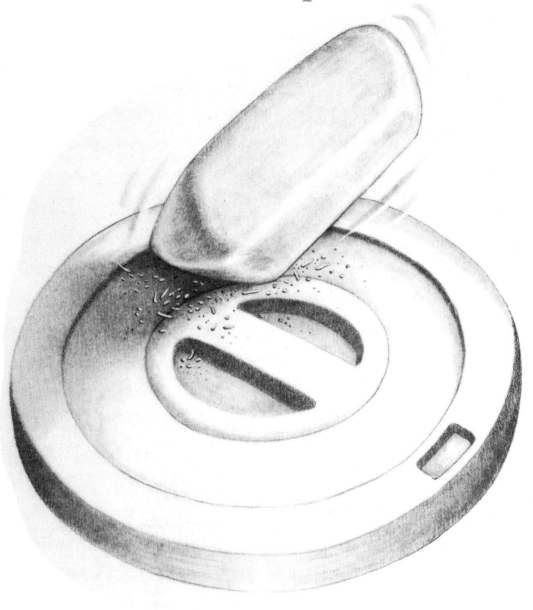

Hard disk backups may be the most boring topic in all computerdom. It's not that backup techniques are inherently dull—
quite the contrary, there are many interesting tricks and strategies.
But it's hard to sustain interest in something so unproductive. Like
military expenditures or health insurance, the most desirable outcome is when the effort is a waste.

Unfortunately, backups have a way of being useful all too often.
In a moment we'll survey the dozen-odd ways that people lose data
day in and day out. So many data-munching monsters inhabit the
world, it's very hard to work with computers and not suffer occasional losses, either by your own hand or through various hardware
or software calamities. And no real respite is in sight. Even as these
words are written, a prominent software company begins a massive
recall of a popular program that "in certain instances" erases hard
disks at random. Your data is never *completely* safe from attack.

Risks to Your Data

It would be nice to begin this chapter without the usual lecture
about the importance of backups, but forgive us if we indulge a little. Six years after the appearance of the first IBM PCs, most data
goes unbacked up as if every newcomer must learn the hard way.
Studies show that only a third of hard disks in offices are backed
up. Yet 3.6 workers use the average office PC, making it all the
more difficult to reconstruct lost data.

One way of looking at the expense and effort devoted to backups
is to regard them as an insurance premium. A good backup utility
program and 100 360K diskettes cost about $150. A tape backup
unit with a few cartridges might run $900. For a 20-megabyte hard
disk, a monthly global backup plus two incremental backups per
week take up roughly 25 hours per year using floppies or 15 hours
using tape (assuming unattended operation during the global backups). At $20 per hour and amortizing the software and equipment
costs over three years, we arrive at $550 per year for disk backup
and $600 per year for tape.

Putting a price on
data

Now what is the value of your data? If you write only letters and
you keep paper copies of each, your disk files are hardly worth anything. If your accounts receivables are entrusted to your hard disk,
however, a data loss could easily cost you tens of thousands of dollars directly, and thousands more scurrying about trying to reconstruct your business. It's harder to put a price on the damage to
your reputation among customers and colleagues. Most priceless of

all is the inspiration lost when you obliterate several chapters of the *Great American Novel*. An already-precarious project may never recover from such a disaster; it's just too dispiriting to go on.

For data worth $10,000, a year's backup costs $5\frac{1}{2}$% to 6% of value. This figure is higher than common full-replacement insurance premiums. But for $20,000 worth of data (or $20,000 worth of chaos-avoidance), backups start to seem cheap. In fact, in a typical business, backups are by far the cheapest insurance premium. The time required to make backups increases only slightly as disks (and their holdings) grow.

Most users think of backups as a precaution against a *crash*. True, most haven't a clue about what exactly constitutes a crash. But we all know about auto crashes and plane crashes, and we certainly don't want something like that to befall our data. The fear is not unjustified: Sooner or later, all hard disks fail. Yet for every out-and-out hard disk holocaust, hundreds of individual files are maimed or erased by well-meaning users. Backups are every bit as valuable for protection against user-failure as against hardware-failure.

Many users seem to acquire a false sense of security from owning file-recovery tools. We'll look at these tools in depth in Chapter 9. They certainly can be valuable at times. But all file-recovery tools have limitations. In many situations they can make only a partial data recovery, and what they recover may be so garbled that, well, all the king's horses and all the king's men won't be able to put it back together again. Having a backup is nearly always preferable to trying to reverse the damage.

File-recovery tools

Still, for all their utility and cost-effectiveness, backups are avoided. They may be an endless source of apprehension, guilt, and angst, but somehow the resistance to sitting down and making the backups survives. Why such perversity? Is the cybernetic flesh really so weak? Do we need an Eleventh Commandment?

Aversion to backups

The answer, we fervently believe, is no. Making backups can be trivial, but organizing a system in which backups are trivial *isn't* so trivial. People avoid backups because they aren't organized. A small but ample investment of time is required to set up the backup procedures. And that investment needs to be approached as a distinct project. Otherwise, you'll be too disorganized to make proper backups when they are needed. You won't want to stop for backups because they'll take much longer than the five or ten minutes they ought to. And so there will be no backups at all.

If you're already making regular backups, you may think that this chapter should be left for the sinners. Perhaps your backups are ad-

Dangers to your data

equate for your needs. But before taking your leave, consider all that can happen to your data.

- A disk sector can go bad, wiping out part of a file. You can use a repair utility to mark the sector off bounds, but the data is gone for good.
- You may erase one or more files accidentally. If the files are badly fragmented, and the disk has many scattered unallocated sectors, an unerase utility may not work, particularly for non-text files.
- You may modify a file in a regrettable way and not be able to reverse the damage.
- You may accidentally reformat a disk. As we'll see in Chapter 9, utilities that undo the damage of a reformatting may be only partially successful (they won't work at all on floppies, incidentally).
- The hard disk may suffer an unrecoverable head crash, mechanical failure, or electronic blowout. A power outage occurring at the moment a file is being saved may cause loss of the file in memory and on disk.
- You may copy a file to another subdirectory, overwriting a different file with the same name.
- You may purposely erase files you would want to keep but have misidentified. This happens often during disk housecleaning, particularly when you're hurriedly trying to make space on a full disk.
- You may inadvertently destroy a file while working on it, say by deleting most of it accidentally and then saving it.
- Malfunctioning software may mangle its own files or unrelated files. Or it may write into DOS buffers in main memory; when the buffers contain file allocation table sectors, both copies of the FAT are rendered useless and everything on the disk is lost.
- As part of your education as a computer programmer, you may murder a disk directory or file allocation table.
- You may give the wrong command to a disk-management utility program and wipe out whole branches of the directory tree. A disgruntled employee may erase scores of files or simply reformat the disk (perhaps at low level).
- A destructive *worm* may enter your system through public domain software and wipe the disk clean.
- Thieves, fire, or another calamity may claim your whole machine (*and* your backups, if you're not careful).
- Your meticulously crafted system of batch files and software configuration files may be wiped out in a general crash, and you must re-create the whole system by going back to the manuals.

Regular backups can save you from all these situations. But the backups must be made intelligently. Otherwise the backups themselves can turn on you:

- You may repeatedly back up a file but not be able to find the most recent version.
- You may make backups that are useful for restoring all data to the disk but not for restoring only a few files.
- You may make a global backup that cannot be restored following damage to the disk surface.
- You may back up files with the same name kept in different directories, and not be able to tell which is which.
- You may back up all data files, but not the tree structure, system files, and batch files.
- You may corrupt important files without realizing it and then record them over your good backups.

There's a lot to learn to put together a good backup system. For starters, you need to read this chapter. Then you must sit down, think through the options, and decide just how detailed your backups should be, and what hardware you'll use for them. Once decided, you'll have to begin research on the latest offerings in the marketplace—what's best changes from month to month, so we can't make specific recommendations here. After the shopping is done, there's software study and practice, followed by some busy-work setting up record keeping for the system. Finally, you must fight a titanic struggle of self conquest and bring yourself to obey your own system.

What it takes

We'll lead you through all of this in the following pages. The whole process should take about 15 to 20 hours, perhaps more if you invest in a tape unit. That's a lot of time—as much as you can expect to invest in backups yearly once the system is established. After that, backups will be a tiny afterthought in your work schedule. And they'll be out of mind not because you can't face up to the precariousness of your data, but because you'll know that, no matter what happens, you're safe.

Some General Concerns

Before we launch a discussion of various hardware and software options, we want to lay out the basic issues and methods of backup. You'd think that copying some files wouldn't require a lengthy dissertation. We certainly don't want to make matters more complicated than necessary. But, alas, they *are* complicated. Seeing only part of the problem may lead you to backup procedures that won't do the job you actually require.

Hardware vs. Software

The first point to understand is that backups are a software phenomenon. You may want to buy special hardware to help with backups, such as a tape unit or removable cartridge drive. But the flexibility and reliability of your backups is largely entrusted to software. No matter how slick and powerful the hardware may appear, the accompanying software determines whether it can meet your needs.

Tape backup software

For this reason, you'll find that most of what we have to say about floppy disk-based backups applies to tape-based backup; each is run by very similar utility software. The only real difference is that with one medium you must diligently swap diskettes into your computer, whereas the other allows you to walk away while the backup proceeds. If tape cartridges had much smaller capacities, there would be little distinction between the two media. The same logic applies to high-capacity removable disks.

We'll look long and hard at software in this chapter. "Ease of use" is a nicety for most software, but it becomes a life-and-death issue of "likelihood of use" with backup software. When backup software is user-unfriendly, backups tend to not be made at all. Software also varies in its flexibility and error-correction capabilities. Inflexible software may require lots more work to achieve the same backup plan. Flexible software can accomplish much with a few keystrokes, and it can remember your backup scheme and repeat it automatically. Software with good error-correction can help avoid the double-whammy of damaged backups for damaged originals.

Dilemmas

Choosing a backup utility confronts you with all the usual dilemmas of software selection. Having lots of features is nice, but it makes the software harder to use. If it's hard to use, it may not be used at all. If it can be customized, it can be made easier to use. But such software is even harder to use for the person who must customize it. With many features and customization, the software becomes complicated so that it's more likely to have bugs, which can lose your data even as you try to guard it. But if the software is simple, it may not do what you need, and so you'll lose data for lack of proper backups. Got it?

Choosing software

Today, some hard disk vendors throw in a backup utility as a promotional ploy. Of the many good backup utilities on the market, you might end up with a good one, but perhaps you won't. You may be using your backup software several hundred times before it's supplanted by something else. The street price for a typical utility is roughly $70, so it will cost you under twenty-five cents each time you use it. That's not much compared to the time (and grief) a good utility can save you. So *you* choose the utility; don't let it choose you.

Unfortunately, most tape drives operate only with the software that accompanies them. The tape unit may look great, but the software can be awful (or vice versa). This danger makes it much riskier buying a $1,000 tape unit than a $50 floppy-backup utility. If the software is no good, you're stuck.

Speed vs. Flexibility

One issue we haven't touched on yet is *speed*. People so thoroughly detest backups that they're suckers for speed—the sooner it's over, the better. There's no denying that backup speed is important, particularly for backups made on floppy disks, in which the time between changing disks may be too short to divert one's attention but too long to keep one occupied. But speed is only one feature of many, and flexibility, reliability, and ease-of-use should not be neglected just because one program runs a little faster than another. You'll find that most of the good software falls in roughly the same performance range, and a 10% to 20% advantage is hardly noticeable.

In Chapter 2 we discussed DMA, *direct memory access*. DMA is the key to high performance in backup utilities. Recall that in PCs and XTs, DMA moves data between the disk controller's holding buffer and system memory. Rather than route each byte of data from the controller to the CPU, then from the CPU to system memory, DMA shunts the data directly between the two locations. In ATs, the CPU transfers data between the controller and memory, but floppy disks still use DMA.

DMA

When a not-very-clever backup utility like the DOS BACKUP command copies data from hard disk to floppy, it first transfers a block of the data from hard disk to memory, and then it shifts the data from memory to floppy disk. But high-performance backup utilities can keep both processes going simultaneously through clever DMA programming. As data streams into memory, a DMA channel constantly siphons it off to diskette.

Software that works in this way doesn't use DOS, which isn't highly regarded for its speed, and the trick of running two pro-

Going around
DOS

cesses simultaneously can't be performed by DOS in any case. Instead, the backup program takes over the disk (or tape) controller cards and tweaks the hardware for the very last drop of performance. Rather than read files one at a time (which entails lots of time-consuming head movements), these programs use all available RAM as a buffer. They may read whole cylinders at a time, bringing many files into memory simultaneously. It takes some pretty complicated logic to pull this off efficiently.

Incompatabilities

Like all computer electronics, the circuitry that handles DMA has gradually improved. The first IBM PCs used relatively slow DMA chips. Later versions were faster. AT-class machines are faster still. Backup software is designed to run on all of these machines. But if it demands too much performance from a machine, DMA *overruns* occur, and data is lost. Accordingly, some software comes with a DMA test utility that checks the speed of data transfers that the DMA circuitry can handle. The software then adjusts its timing to suit. Early PCs may require a replacement DMA chip. Incompatibility problems with PC clones are common.

Because most backup utilities go around DOS, you should be especially wary of unknown software for which you have no positive recommendation or review. The software can malfunction without giving any signs. If it errs in making the backup, you'll be wasting time diligently making useless copies. If it errs during data restoration all your data is at risk.

Ease of use

As we'll see in a moment, most backup sessions are quite short because only a small portion of the hard disk is copied. In these quick sessions, the time it takes to get the software moving is significant. A terrible user-interface can send you scurrying back to the manuals again and again. Inflexible design may force you to manually specify individual files for backup. And software that can't remember your backup plan may require you to type in long code sequences each time you repeat the backup. What good is a five-minute backup when it takes a half hour to start it?

Manufacturers' claims

Be wary of manufacturers' claims of backup speed. These benchmarks are sometimes made with hard disks organized in a way that optimizes the program's performance. Data verification (which can double backup time) is turned off. Head movements are reduced by using only one level of subdirectories. Large files avoid the added overhead of looking after many small files. And the disk is completely defragmented before the backup begins. Often the advertised speed will be for a whole-disk *image* backup, rather than a more time-consuming *file-by-file* backup (we'll get to this topic in a moment).

Conversely, software reviewers may sometimes test a backup utility with an artificially complex tree structure, perhaps using 1,000 subdirectories to see if the utility can manage extreme cases in which their memory management facilities are pushed to their limit. Software that performs admirably under ordinary circumstances may fail when confronted with very large files or many small files.

To some extent, backup speed is set by hardware rather than software. If you own a fast hard disk, backups proceed more quickly. You can accelerate backups by optimizing your hard disk's performance, as described in Chapter 7. Having lots of RAM available helps too, because it provides more work area for the software. If you have a 1.2-megabyte floppy drive, backups to diskettes work more quickly both because the drive is faster and fewer disks need to be swapped. Finally, as we'll see later in this chapter, some kinds of tape drives operate more quickly than others because of the way they format data.

Performance

Image vs. File-by-File Backups

In Chapter 2 we explained how DOS allocates disk space in a way that causes files to be spread across many cylinders. When files become fragmented, DOS takes longer to read or write them because more head movements are required. Similarly, when backup utilities copy files, the backup takes longer when the files are badly fragmented. For rapid backups, files need to be compacted into as few cylinders as possible (most fit into one cylinder).

The fastest possible backup moves the read/write heads to each cylinder only once, starting from the outer edge of the disk and moving inward cylinder by cylinder. Backups made in this way are called *image backups* because they make an exact copy of the surface of the disk without regard to the distribution of files. Image backups are necessarily *total* or *global* backups, because there's no simple way of ensuring that any given file will be completely backed up unless every disk sector is copied.

Image backups

Image backups usually require an *image restore*. Every sector is taken from the disk and rewritten to exactly the same location it was originally recorded from. This approach doesn't work well when only one file has been damaged. Other files on the disk will have changed since the last backup, and the image restore will return them to their previous state. Hence *file-by-file* backups are generally preferred. In these backups, whole files are recorded one

File-by-file backups

after the other. You can reclaim any one file, or group of files, without altering other data on the disk.

Relative performance

Owing to the increased head movement, file-by-file backups may take much longer than image backups. But more advanced software can close the performance gap. Intelligent backup programs may analyze the directory listings and file allocation table and then read whole cylinders of data at once, filling memory with bits and pieces of various files. The software will process groups of files this way, greatly reducing head activity.

Another advance in software design lets you make a file-by-file *restoration* from an image backup. The software examines the file allocation table, which always resides at the start of an image backup. It learns the location of the parts of a file and then moves through the image in sequence, copying the parts of the file into memory, where it reassembles it and then rewrites it to the hard disk.

DOS vs. Proprietary Formats

Backup programs save data on diskette or tape in a variety of formats. In the simplest (and usually slowest) case, individual copies of each file are made in standard DOS format. If you like, you can insert the backup diskette in a drive, scan its directory, and copy a file back to the hard disk. Many programs use **proprietary formats**, however. Often, all files are linked into one giant file to make best use of disk space. Sometimes the data is compressed into a sort of gibberish that only the restoration program can understand.

Directory paths

All backup formats require some way of storing the directory paths of the files they contain. Even DOS-like backups may have special files on the diskettes to hold this information. Or they may re-create part of the tree on the backup media. By knowing the directory paths, the restoration program can return the file to its rightful place. If the file's subdirectory no longer exists on the hard disk, the restoration program will re-create it.

Data compaction

You'll find that proprietary formats don't usually create significantly more compact backups. The great advantage in proprietary formats is that they may contain advanced error-correction facilities. When diskettes are damaged, the restoration program can re-create corrupted data, if not too much has been harmed.

It's a little scary having your data encoded in a proprietary format. If serious problems arise during data restoration, there's no way to fish your data off the diskettes using a word processor or a recovery utility. This is not an unreasonable fear. As noted, backup software often doesn't perform as well in restoring data as in backing it up. Early versions of the DOS BACKUP command sometimes refused to restore data. Because BACKUP uses a special format, total data loss resulted; it's happened many thousands of times.

Backup vs. Restore

Backup programs are actually backup-and-restore programs. But we tend to neglect the restoration part because 99% of our experience with the program is making backups. This emphasis influences our thinking when we choose backup hardware and software, with priority given to features that make backups quick and flexible. But it's important to give adequate attention to the problems of *restoring* data after some kind of calamity has passed.

You can work out the world's most reliable and easy-to-use backup system only to find that you can't easily recover your data in the way you need it. As we've learned, total data loss is the least likely event in which you'll call upon your backups. More often you'll want only one file. Or you may use backups to archive data and may want to restore a complicated branch to the directory tree. Perhaps you'll need to restore only files of a certain extension that have dates falling in a particular range. And, in mass-restore operations, you'll need some way of stopping older files on the backups from overwriting more recent versions on the hard disk. Often you'll want to restore files to a different directory from which it was originally taken. Some restoration software can manage these requests; some cannot. Feature-mania has not carried over to restore functions to the extent that it has permeated backup functions.

Besides the flexibility that abundant restoration features make possible, several broader issues must always be kept in mind. It's hard to make a file-by-file restoration from an image backup. Image backups are ideal for restoring the entire disk following a major calamity because every sector in the backup is in the order it will be rewritten to disk. When files are fragmented on the disk, though, they are scattered around the backup. One cluster may be at the beginning of track three of a tape, the next cluster at the end of track five. More and more tape backup units come with software that can make file-by-file restorations from an image backup, but the process is time consuming. Fancy feature-filled restorations of groups of files may be impossible.

Major issues

Media flaws
Some backup software, whether for floppy disk- or tape-based backup systems, doesn't cope well with errors in the backup media itself. Poorly designed software may refuse to continue when it encounters an error (some early versions of the DOS BACKUP command have this fault). You may only lose one file in a file-by-file disk restoration. But if the software balks during an image restoration, you can lose everything. Backup utilities that store data in a proprietary format are all the more dangerous because ordinary recovery utilities can't help repair your backup diskettes, which may not use ordinary 512-byte DOS sectors.

Most backup software has trouble making an image-restoration to a disk that has more bad sectors than when the backup was made—the situation that often follows a disk crash and reformatting. Although a different layout for the data would be all right, the software is confronted with more sectors on the backup than it can fit on the hard disk. Good software keeps track of which backed-up sectors are unallocated so that it can safely discard some.

Practice backups
You should check out the restoration features *before* you actually need them. This is not a simple matter for some kinds of backups. Try making an image backup with your brand new tape unit and then immediately make a practice restoration; watching the tape slowly overwrite every disk sector is enough to make anyone's blood pressure rise. It's scary because if something goes wrong, you'll lose everything. Yet, if you're unwilling to undergo a trial run, how can you possibly trust the backups over the long term?

Attended vs. Unattended Backups

To many, the ideal backup system is invisible. Backups are automatically made without human intervention. Manufacturers have introduced an array of special hardware for this purpose, including tape drives, high-capacity cartridge disks, and special hard disk cards. Perhaps the ultimate solution is a special controller card that automatically maintains an identical copy (a *mirror image*) of a hard disk on a second, identical disk; a backup is made following every disk write operation. Floppy disks can sometimes serve for automatic backups when only a few files are changing.

Effective automatic backups may require special hardware; nonetheless, again *software* is most important (except for mirror-image systems, which require no software). The software sits in memory, watching the system clock for its cue to begin. There are two strategies. The backup may be set to begin when the machine isn't in use, perhaps in the middle of the night. Or backups may run constantly *in the background* as you use the machine.

Setting backups for off-hours is the easier approach, but it may require some attention. The backup can only be initiated by the software, not the hardware. So the software must be active at the time the backup is to occur. If it sits in memory as a *resident program*, precious RAM is wasted. But if it must be loaded at the end of the working day, someone has to attend to it. Of course, the machine must be left on, and the system clock must be set properly.

Off-hours backups

Background backups operate as memory-resident programs that periodically kick in, scanning the disk for changed files, and making backups. The software may postpone its actions if the machine is especially busy. When backups begin, they are *multitasked* with whatever else is going on in the machine. Work can continue, but it is slowed.

Background backups

The software used by background backups can tell only when a file has been changed; it cannot know if the changes have been substantial. As a result, it may repeatedly back up the same file. Some background backup software overcomes this problem by making backups only at preset times.

Note that most "automatic" backup schemes still require some aid from human hands to set up the system. Software may need loading; blank disks or tape cartridges need inserting; and power must be switched on for external units. Only the completely internal systems using a second disk drive are truly automatic. And they suffer from the disadvantage that the backups themselves are not safe from dangers like theft or fire.

Error Checking

You'll often hear that backup software has "excellent error checking." There are many kinds of error checking, and not all programs perform them all. They test:

- that data has been correctly read from the hard disk during backups.
- that the backup media has no faults.
- that data has been correctly written to backup media while the backup is going on.
- that data has not been corrupted while it resided on the backup media.
- that data is not restored to bad sectors on the hard disk.

• that the data has been correctly written to the hard disk when it is restored.

Proprietary formats give the best error correction because the embedded error codes can tell if the backups have been corrupted, and often they can help reconstruct it. Many backup programs offer a "verify mode" in which data is read or written twice for safety's sake. These modes nearly double the time a backup takes, so you may not want to use them very much.

Be aware that the ability to recognize a particular kind of error doesn't necessarily mean that a program can recover from it. Some backup utilities will promptly quit when they encounter a bad sector during data restoration. If the data is in a proprietary format, it's as good as gone.

Obstacles to Backups

Some assorted problems interfere with backups, no matter the medium. One problem is backing up hard disks that have been partitioned for multiple operating systems. Backup programs are designed for a specific operating system. They expect sectors of a particular size and files organized in a particular way. Most tape backup systems, and a few floppy-based utilities, can make an image backup in which all partitions are recorded. But restoration of single files from an image backup (if possible) will serve only the DOS partition. Generally you must buy a separate backup utility for each operating system. You may have trouble finding a tape unit that can serve all operating systems on the disk.

Large partitions

We saw in Chapter 3 that one way of surpassing the 32-megabyte limit on a DOS partition is by using larger sectors. The utility software that performs this magic hides what it is doing from DOS. But backup software that circumvents DOS encounters the larger sectors directly, and it probably won't be able to deal with them. Manufacturers of the special partitioning software usually offer their own backup utility to overcome this problem. But the software may not be particularly good. There aren't many choices in this matter, and you may be forced to adopt an inferior backup package.

Flexibility

Another difficulty is that many backup utilities cannot support all hard disk-like devices. While many can service the ubiquitous Bernoulli Box, many have trouble with unusual removable disk drives, very high-capacity floppies, or whatever. If you're considering buying unusual equipment, think about how you'll back it up. Some-

times the only way is to buy an identical second unit so that you
can make a direct copy from one to the next.

Local-area networks (LANs) present more non-standard hardware. **LANs**
Many backup utilities can function on a LAN, but only when the
entire network is off duty. All LAN makers offer a solution to the
backup problem, but whether it will be flexible, speedy, and reliable is another question. Make backups an integral part of your research when considering a LAN purchase.

Copy protection is another common backup problem. There are **Copy protection**
many schemes for "installing" copy-protected software on hard
disk. Most place certain parts of a program at particular locations
on the disk surface. When data is restored to the disk, the copy
protection scheme is not reinstituted, and the program becomes
unusable. It's easy to exhaust the limited number of hard disk installations allowed by some copy-protected software.

Finally, be careful of variable CPU speeds around backup soft- **CPU speed**
ware and hardware. The intricate machinations of high-speed backups may depend heavily on precise timing. Many PC clones have a
variable clock speed selectable from the keyboard; sometimes
backup utilities will only run at the slower speed, particularly when
they format diskettes on the fly.

Varieties of Backup

Back in the days when a dual-floppy disk system was the norm,
"backups" usually meant copying everything from the source diskette to the backup diskette, either by DISKCOPY or *.*. Today, 30-
megabyte hard disks are becoming the norm, and disks ten times
that size are not uncommon. It's just not practical to regularly copy
that much information to backup media. Diskettes used for backups
may hold less than 1% of the volume of the hard disk. And moving
so much data is time-consuming. Data-transfer speeds haven't increased in proportion to hard disk capacity.

While a complete, *global* backup of everything on a hard disk is
sometimes desirable, most backups must be partial. And even partial backups vary—some need to be more complete than others.
We don't mean to make matters complicated, but we count fully
six kinds of backups, and each has a unique application. They are
as follows.

Global backups. A backup of all data on the hard disk, including
the tree structure and system files.

Partial backups. Backups of a related group of files that make a "snapshot" of the data at a given time.

Incremental backups. Copies of all files that have changed since the previous backup.

Simultaneous backups. Backups in which special mirror-image systems write data twice to two identical hard disks.

Temporary backups. Creation of second copies of files which are kept on the hard disk along with the originals.

Serial backups. A series of backups of the same file(s), capturing each stage in the file's evolution.

Let's look at each kind of backup in turn.

Global Backups

Global backups copy everything on the disk. This may sound straightforward, but the word "everything" is open to definition. Sometimes backups are considered "global" when confined to all *data* files on a disk. Often, files with .COM or .EXE extensions are omitted from the backup, because copies are held by the diskettes on which the software was distributed.

The point of copying *everything* on the disk is that it is easy to get back to work after a total data loss. Much work goes into setting up a directory tree, distributing the files among subdirectories, configuring software, and working out batch files and other utilities. This work is performed over many months and years, and the many hours invested in it tend to be undervalued. When data files alone are copied, restoration of a crashed disk may take days. Reconfiguring software can be the most time-consuming part of the process because you'll have to work your way through all those incomprehensible manuals once more.

Partial Backups

Partial backups are a sort of mini-global backup. All files related to a particular project or theme are backed up together. You capture the state of a project at any one time. When data is lost, you can restore all files together, safe in the knowledge that the file versions complement one another. This approach is superior to saving only changed files by *incremental* backups because you may have trouble restoring the proper versions.

Partial backups are especially useful for complicated programming projects, where many files are intricately interrelated. If code files are restored to the disk and an out-of-date file is mixed in, endless confusion may ensue.

Of course, a global backup does all that a partial backup does, but partial backups take much less time. Often they fit on one diskette and can be performed simply by entering **COPY *.PRJ A:**, where **PRJ** is an extension used for all files in a project. Many backup utilities support partial backups, either by a tagging feature, filename extensions, or a command file that lists particular files (*COREfast* is one utility with this feature). Partial backups are an ideal way of moving work between machines.

Incremental Backups

An *incremental backup* copies all files that have changed since the last backup. As a minimal backup it has certain limitations, and should not be the only kind of backup you do. If a hard disk has not been backed up at all, it first requires a global backup and then incremental ones. Without the global backup, program files and special data files (such as spelling-checker files) may never be backed up. Of course, you'll have copies of these files on their distribution diskettes. But much time will be wasted restoring them to disk if you suffer a total data loss.

Backup software may approach incremental backups in two ways. It may *append* new backups of changed files to old backups, or it can *overwrite* the old backups. In the first case, you have a kind of *serial* backup, in that you can go back and recapture the state of the file at several points in time. Overwriting old backups uses media more economically, however, because you keep only the most recent version of every file since the last global backup.

Overwritten incremental backups are easier to use when all data must be restored to the disk. In this process, the prior global backup is first restored, followed by the incremental backup(s). When incremental backups are appended, you may have to restore each backup to the disk in its entirety, even though more recent versions of some files will be held in the next incremental backup

Overwritten back-
ups

in the series. You can't just use the last incremental backup because files that have changed since the global backup but not most recently will be recorded only in earlier incremental backup sessions.

The various backup programs handle incremental backups differently. Many keep a catalog of the backup on the hard disk itself. *Fastback*, for example, keeps a file named **FASTBACK.CAT.** It updates the file after every appended incremental backup, or, if the file doesn't exist or has been deleted or renamed, it writes the new incremental backup over the old one. Some programs, such as *Back-it*, create a new catalog file with each backup, resulting in many files that must be periodically culled.

The archive bit

The *archive bit* is at the heart of incremental backups. From Chapter 2, you may recall the *attribute byte* held in the directory entry of every file. The attribute byte sets various characteristics for the file, making it read-only, for example, or hiding it from directory listings. A byte consists of eight parts, or *bits*, with one of the bits devoted to telling whether the file has been changed since it was last backed up. This is the archive bit.

When DOS writes to a file, it sets the archive bit to "On." A backup program can scan directories for files with this attribute setting, copy the files over to backup media, and reset the archive bits to "Off." When you view a file but don't save it, the archive bit isn't set to "On." And when you use COPY or XCOPY to make backups, the archive bit is not turned "Off."

Special utilities can alter the archive bit setting of any file. DOS versions 3.2 and later offer the ATTRIB command for this purpose. Or you may use a utility package like the *Norton Utilities*. But fooling with archive bits isn't a very sensible way to manage backups. A good backup utility lets you quickly tag files you want to include or exclude from backups. Only a primitive backup program like DOS's BACKUP could give you reason to alter a file's archive bit.

Interference with the archive bit

It's important that other programs don't interfere with the archive bit. If the bit is turned off before a backup is made, you'll be left without a copy, and you probably won't notice. The **RENAME** command is notorious in this regard because it always turns the archive bit "Off" when it renames a file, even if the bit is set to "On" beforehand. If you want to ensure that a file is included in the next backup after it has been renamed, change the archive bit with a utility, or load the file into its parent software and then save it.

Archive bit settings may also be thrown into confusion when backup software crashes in the middle of a backup. A power outage, for example, may stop the backup in its tracks. Particularly with software that uses a proprietary format, some or all of the backup may be useless. But the archive bits for the files backed up before the interruption are turned "Off," leaving the software no way to find the changed files for a second copy. A global backup is the only safe recourse.

Because archive bits are switched "Off" after a backup, you can't make a second copy of an incremental backup directly from the hard disk. Duplicates are sometimes required for off-site storage. You'll need to copy the backup itself, which can be very inconvenient (if you've only one floppy drive of a given capacity) or downright impossible (tape-to-tape copying).

Simultaneous Backups

In *simultaneous backups,* two disk drives work in parallel. As data is written to disk, it is simultaneously written on both drives in the same sectors. No significant performance degradation occurs. When data is read, only one disk supplies the data. Special hardware is required. Tallgrass offers software for their dual-disk hard card that causes every diskwrite to the first drive to be repeated on the second. This facility is also available through a controller card that runs two hard disks in parallel, such as the one offered by Kolod Research.

This approach to backups is the most automatic of all. It performs silently, with no attention from the user *ever*. Indeed, the notion of "ease of use" doesn't apply because no action of any kind is required. Because the backups are constant, there's no problem of losing data entered since the last backup was made.

At first glance, the use of a second hard disk for backups seems ideal. The odds of both disks crashing at the same time are minuscule. Because hard disks have become so cheap, you could add a second drive to your existing controller for much less than the price of a tape drive or removable cartridge unit. But mirror-image backup units are vulnerable to theft, fire, and related mischief. Unless you're buying computer equipment for Fort Knox, you shouldn't regard your data as being "safe" until a copy of it exists well away from the hard disk it resides upon.

Temporary Backups

Temporary backups are fleeting copies of a file that are kept in the same subdirectory on the same disk, usually with the extension **.BAK**. Many programs, particularly text editors, create .BAK files as a matter of course. They protect you from damage you make to your own files. If you have a change of heart about your modifications to the file or if you create irreversible damage, as with an inadvertent deletion of part of the file, you need only copy the .BAK version over the original and you're back to squareone. Software that makes automatic .BAK files does so by erasing the previous .BAK file, renaming the current file with a .BAK extension, then writing the new version.

While temporary backups may hardly seem worth mentioning, they may be called upon more often than any other kind of backup. If your software cannot make them automatically, it may be worthwhile setting up a batch file to do it for you. For example, for the file **ACCOUNTS**, you could make a file named **BACKUP.BAT** containing only **COPY ACCOUNTS ACCOUNTS.BAK**. Update the copy every hour or so during a day of intense work on the file. It takes only a few seconds and it ensures that you won't lose a whole day's work to a moment's carelessness. When writing data to a RAM disk, the backup file should be directed to the hard disk. It's especially important to maintain .BAK files when writing computer programs or modifying programmable software. Any "improvement" can undermine your work up to that point, and you may not be able to return the file to its prior state.

Limitations

Of course, temporary backups don't help you in the event of a head crash or other hardware disaster. An incremental backup at the end of the day is needed. On the other hand, making incremental backups all day long would be a little too cautious—unless you've just written down the cure to cancer.

However, temporary backups are precarious for another reason. When software makes them automatically, it is very easy to overwrite the .BAK version. Many people fall into the habit of constantly saving a file, perhaps as often as every five minutes. It takes only a few keystrokes and a couple of seconds, and it guards against losing data to a power outage. But the .BAK file is not much of a backup when it updates only five minutes of work. If you're working with sensitive data, take care to protect the .BAK file until you're sure it won't be needed. Keep an eye on the size of the main file so that you'll spot accidental deletions. You may want to switch off the automatic .BaK feature and make the temporary backups manually.

Serial Backups

Our final form of backup is related to temporary backups, but it carries the process further. This form of backup has no customary name; we'll call it a "serial backup." Serial backups, a sequence of backups of the same file made at close intervals, allow you to recover work that has been accidentally ruined through modification. Computer programmers often have this problem. They'll make a change and save the file, make the next change and save it again, and so on. Only later does it become apparent that one of the many changes caused a serious bug that cannot be easily traced. It would be easier to abandon a few hours work and start anew, but the original condition of the file is lost forever. Had a separate copy of the file been made every half hour or so, it would be easy to find the point at which the bug was introduced and recommence with the file that preceded it.

The sequence of backups is kept on the hard disk in the same subdirectory as the original. The protection is against user failure, not disk failure. You can use COPY to make each copy of the file. The trick is to devise a sequence of filenames that indicate the backup order, make it easy to find the next filename in the series, and make possible bulk erasures of early portions of the queue. The simplest method is to tag the files with numerals, which DOS gladly accepts as filenames. Name the first file **10**, the next **11**, and so on, as in **COPY BIGPROG.PAS 10**. When you're ready to make the next copy in the series, an alphabetically sorted directory listing shows which number is last in the queue (**DIR I SORT**). To eliminate groups of ten files from the queue, use a wildcard deletion: **DEL 1?** erases files 10 through 19.

Making the backup

Maintaining a serial backup is a nuisance when you're trying to get a job done. But it can save several hours of work and reduces the likelihood that you'll need to fumble through your proper backups to restore a file you've trashed by good intentions and hard work. But be sure to eliminate the many duplicates when the work is finished and confirmed. A backup series can easily soak up a megabyte of disk space.

For large projects with a heavy investment of time, consider keeping a serial backup on backup media. Make a "snapshot" of the

project once a week or so, copying all related files. It may cost a
few hundred dollars for the media, but you'll have a safety net for
mistakes of all kinds. You'll be able to correct a wrong turn in the
project much more easily. Note that not all backup utilities let you
make a series of backups of the same file on the same diskette or
cartridge.

Diskette-Based Backup

Diskettes are the poor man's backup medium. These days you can
buy a hundred 360K diskettes at 25 cents each. But diskette-based
backups are much less convenient than using tape or removable
disk cartridges. The problem is not just the ennui of endlessly
swapping diskettes. You have got to *manage* the diskettes, keep
them properly labeled, ordered, and boxed. Otherwise, multiple
backups quickly fall into chaos, and there's a good chance that errors will occur when you restore data.

   Backups can be made using the DOS COPY command or its
more recent (and more sophisticated) cousin, XCOPY. Unless you
have exceptionally simple backup requirements, however, you'll
need to use a full-fledged backup utility. Your DOS diskette holds
the BACKUP program, which can do a passable job of backing up a
large hard disk—if you have the time to wait for it. As firm believ-
ers in frequent backups, we strongly recommend that you pass up
BACKUP and acquire one of the many backup programs available
on the market today. They are inexpensive, and the time they'll
save you will quickly repay your investment.

Backups Using COPY

Many people rely on nothing more than the DOS COPY command
for making backups. It may seem like a perfectly good way of protecting your data if you work on only a few files at a time. But we
advise against totally relying on COPY. With time, you'll have a gi-
gantic stack of disorganized backups, with little to indicate which
file versions are most recent. In the event of a major head crash,
restoring your data would be a nightmare. You'd have to re-create
the directory tree from scratch, reinstall all software, and reinstitute
keyboard macro files and other work that would likely be ex-
empted from the backup scheme.

The COPY command is the least flexible of all backup options. It's only really useful for making partial backups of files in a single subdirectory; when the files are related by filename or extension, wildcard characters ("*" or "?") can move the file by a single COPY command. Otherwise you are reduced to entering a separate COPY command for each file, constantly changing subdirectories or spelling out long path names.

COPY can locate files only by the characters in their filenames. It is oblivious to the file's time and date and to the setting of its archive bit. Sophisticated backup programs keep track of the subdirectory from which files were copied; COPY keeps no such records, so you must manually set up an identical directory structure on the target diskette. Files of the same name kept in separate subdirectories are easily confused.

Limitations

COPY is useless for backing-up files larger than the backup medium can hold. Nor can it handle bulk copies larger than diskette size. If you enter **COPY *.* A:** in a subdirectory containing 500K of files and drive A holds a 360K diskette, after awhile COPY issues a "disk full" message and quits. There's no way of specifying the remaining files after a disk change. Because the COPY command won't let you *exclude* files by a syntax that would mean, "copy all files except *.DOC," you can't move some files by wildcards, and then the remainder.

COPY does little to protect your data from corrupt media. You can use the /V switch to verify that data has been written correctly. After data is recorded on the floppy, it is read back and the error-checking information (CRC codes) from writing and reading are compared to be sure they are identical. This option doubles the time required and won't protect you from damage done to the floppies after the backup is made (unlike most backup utilities).

Error checking

Be aware that the COPY command in DOS 2.1 has a serious bug. When hundreds of files are copied by a single COPY statement, as in **COPY *.*A:**, every 256th file is skipped.

Although grossly inadequate for general backups, the COPY command works well for hour-to-hour backups of a project for which all files reside in one subdirectory. Tag the files with an identifying filename extension and use **COPY *.EXT**. Placing the line in a batch file makes life all the easier. When files can't be grouped by extensions, list them individually in a batch file to avoid retyping them repeatedly.

Applications

An alternative approach is to have COPY make copies only of those files that currently exist on the floppy diskette. Write a batch file containing this single line:

```
FOR %%F IN (*.*) DO IF EXIST A:%%F COPY C:%%F A:
```

This line is a modification of the command that would simply copy all files to floppy drive A:

```
FOR %%F IN (*.*) DO COPY C:%%F A:
```

By adding:

```
IF EXIST A:%%F
```

the floppy in drive A is searched for each file, and the copy from drive C is completed only if it is found. By placing this line in a file named, say, **SAVEDATA.BAT**, you need only type **SAVEDATA**, and the backup will be done for you. Of course, you'd want to keep the backup diskette in drive A, but probably no damage would arise if you tried to make the backup with the wrong diskette in the drive. To make the batch file friendlier, write:

```
CLS
REM . . .Backing up project files to diskette.
PAUSE . . .Place backup diskette in drive A:
ECHO OFF
FOR %%F IN (*.*) DO IF EXIST A:%%F COPY C:%%F A:
ECHO ON
```

Turning the DOS screen echo off prevents "file not found" messages from cluttering the display.

Backups Using XCOPY

The **XCOPY** command is unfamiliar to most DOS users since it was introduced only with version 3.2. Like COPY, it can move one or more files between disks. But it may operate on more than one subdirectory at once, and this feature makes it very useful for backups. XCOPY is designed for mass copying; if you omit the filename, it assumes *.*. As with COPY, you can specify a name for the new version of the file, renaming it as it is copied. For example:

```
XCOPY C:*.DOC A:*.BAK
```

copies files named *.DOC from the current directory to drive A, changing the filename extensions to BAK.

The syntax for XCOPY closely resembles COPY, but it uses eight switches to make use of XCOPY's advanced features. The most valuable of these is the /S switch, which causes XCOPY to extend its activity not to just the specified (or current) directory, but to all subdirectories below as well. When XCOPY does not find equivalent subdirectories on the target disk, it creates them. XCOPY does this is a particular way, and if you don't understand it clearly, you'll quickly find yourself confused.

The /S switch

When XCOPY copies files to an empty diskette, it treats the diskette's root directory as the equivalent of the *source* directory, which is parent to all other subdirectories from which files are copied. For example, Figure 8-1a shows a branch of a tree copied to a blank diskette; and Figure 8-1b shows the result. The copy is made by **XCOPY *.*A: /S**. You might instead expect that XCOPY would create the directory tree depicted in Figure 8-1c, but it doesn't.

Now, imagine that the diskette holds the same subdirectories, and that its *current* directory is the root directory. Figure 8-2a shows the source directories once again; 8-2b shows the tree on the target disk before XCOPY goes to work; and 8-2c shows the target disk afterward. XCOPY deposits the files from the source directory named **LEVEL1** into the root directory of the target diskette, even though the target diskette has a subdirectory by that name. Then XCOPY creates second instances of subdirectories named **LEVEL2A** and **LEVEL2B** in spite of the fact that they already exist as children of **LEVEL1**.

As you can see, XCOPY doesn't make an intelligent search of the target directory tree for the particular subdirectories it must match. In fairness to the designers of DOS, there's no obvious way to do this because any tree may have multiple subdirectories of the same name, and XCOPY would be forced to choose which to use. To make XCOPY move files to the proper subdirectory, you must name the target *parent* subdirectory in the XCOPY statement. For example:

Limitations

```
XCOPY *.* A:\LEVEL1 /S
```

causes XCOPY to copy files in source subdirectory **LEVEL1** to the target subdirectory **LEVEL1**, and so on with the subdirectories below.

The subdirectories copied to the target disk can be appended to that disk's directory tree at any point.

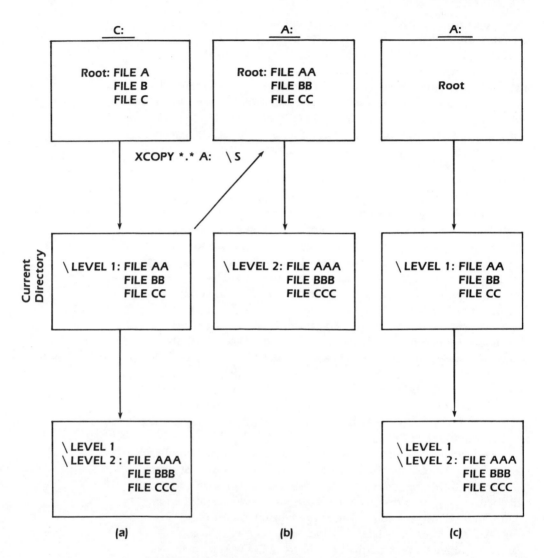

Figure 8-1 **Copying part of a tree using XCOPY**

The /S switch causes XCOPY to create subdirectories only if the target directory contains files. You may alternatively use the /E switch, which makes XCOPY create subdirectories even when the source subdirectory is empty.

/A and /M switches

If you've followed us so far, congratulations. The subdirectory naming conventions are the trickiest part of XCOPY; the rest is smooth sailing. XCOPY helps with backups not just because it can

scan directories; it also can test each file's archive bit and make a
copy only if it has been changed. This feature is activated by the /A
and /M switches, which are exactly alike except that /M turns off
the archive bit after the copy is made, while /A does not. The /A
feature is especially handy because you can use the archive bit to
make temporary backups while leaving the bit set for regular incremental backups.

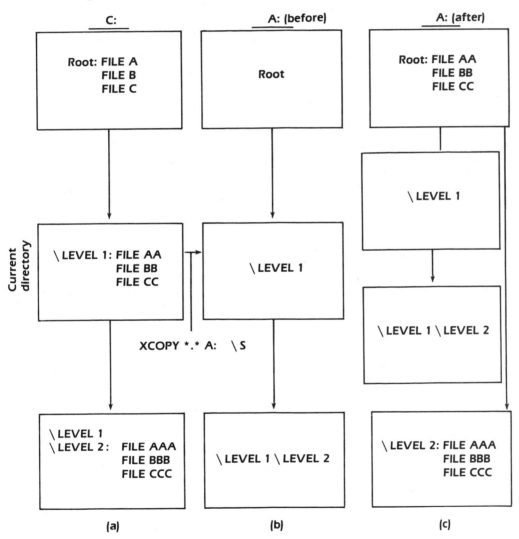

Figure 8-2 **Combining trees with XCOPY**

Unfortunately, XCOPY doesn't provide a switch for spanning many files across multiple diskettes. But the /M switch makes it possible, albeit clumsily. Combined with the /S switch, copies of all changed files are made until a disk fills, whereupon a "disk full" message occurs and XCOPY terminates. The archive bit remains set on the file for which there was insufficient space, but not on the others. So you can change diskettes and call XCOPY again, and it picks up where it left off. This approach is of no help with files for which the archive bit is turned off (set to 0).

The /P switch

XCOPY's other features include the /P switch, which displays a prompt for each file before it is copied, asking whether to copy it or not. The /W switch makes XCOPY wait for a press of a key before beginning. /D causes XCOPY to copy only files with a specified date (or later), as in /D:12-07-87. Finally, the familiar /V switch makes DOS verify the copies. Incidentally, XCOPY is not to be used when the APPEND command is in effect.

XCOPY has its uses, but it's confusing and inflexible. You're much better off acquiring a good backup utility, a good DOS shell, or both.

The DOS BACKUP and RESTORE Commands

The DOS BACKUP command is the most common backup utility, but not deservedly so. Like XCOPY, it is slow and inflexible. In the past it has also been unreliable, but the bugs seem finally to be removed (avoid versions before DOS 3.1). BACKUP can copy one, some, or all files from any or all directories to diskettes. It stores the data in a proprietary format, without embedded control codes. The only measure of error checking it allows is the use of the standard DOS VERIFY command, which roughly doubles the already-excessive time it takes to make a backup.

If we sound overly critical of the BACKUP program, it is not out of disrespect for Microsoft. When you buy DOS, you are buying an operating system. It's nice that a backup utility is thrown in, but it cannot be expected to compete with specialized programs that may fill a whole diskette and require a lengthy manual.

Syntax

The BACKUP command resembles other DOS commands, like COPY and XCOPY. You may list a source and a destination. For example:

```
BACKUP BIGFILE.DOC A:
```

backs up the file **BIGFILE.DOC** in the current directory onto the
diskette in drive A. Wildcards may be used. To back up all files
with a **.DOC** extension in the current directory, enter:

```
BACKUP *.DOC A:
```

Or, to back up all files in the directory:

```
BACKUP *.* A:
```

Of course, you may use full DOS paths:

```
BACKUP \LEVEL1\LEVEL2\LEVEL3\*.* A:
```

The BACKUP command's power arises from the /**S** switch, which
applies the command to the source subdirectory and all subdirectories below. To make a backup of all files on the disk, you merely
enter:

```
BACKUP \*.* A: /S
```

In DOS versions before 3.3, every file is backed up as a separate
file on the backup medium. However, a special **header field** is
placed at the start of the file to hold its DOS path and directory information. Each diskette also holds a file named **BACKUPID.@@@**
that contains reference information.

The format

Starting with DOS version 3.3, BACKUP writes the backups into
one giant file on the backup media. The file is named
BACKUP.XXX, where **XXX** is a number from 1 upward corresponding to the backup order. Each diskette also holds a file named
CONTROL.XXX, using the same format. It saves paths, filenames,
and other directory information for each file.

BACKUP creates a volume label on each diskette reading
BACKUP.XXX. If a diskette loses its label, you can easily identify it
by putting it in a drive and typing **LABEL**.

Tracking diskettes

When the diskette fills, it prompts you for a disk change, and
then continues writing. Hence, even small files may stretch across
two diskettes. Files larger than a diskette are readily copied. In fact,
the BACKUP command is the only way in DOS that you can copy a
file that exceeds diskette capacity to transport it to another machine.

Incremental backups are made via the /**M** and /**A** switches. The M
in /**M** stands for "modified," meaning that the file has been modi-

Incremental
backups

fied since the last backup, and its archive bit has been set. BACKUP automatically resets the archive bit to zero (turns it off) after the backup is made. Use the /A switch to make a sequential backup, where the newly copied files are *appended* to whatever data is already recorded on the backup diskette in the drive. Thus, to make an incremental backup of the entire disk, enter:

```
BACKUP \*.* /S /M
```

and to append the backups to earlier ones, enter:

```
BACKUP \*.* /S /M /A
```

Date and time Starting from DOS 3.3, you can specify files by their time of creation. Earlier versions can specify the date. The switches for these specifications are, appropriately enough, /D and /T. The expression:

```
BACKUP \*.* /S /D:1-10-88
```

backs up all files created *on* or *after* January 10, 1988. The /T switch works the same way. There's no flexibility in these commands. You can't back up files from earlier dates and times or from specific dates and times.

Logging the backup Also starting from DOS 3.3, the BACKUP program can be made to create a log file in the root directory of the hard disk (the source drive). It contains the date and time of the backup, names and paths of all backed up files, and their corresponding diskette numbers. When another backup is made, the log information is appended to that of the previous backup. Over time, the log file can grow quite large.

Diskette formatting A final improvement added to BACKUP in DOS 3.3 is the ability to format diskettes while the backup progresses. Earlier versions couldn't do this. If you ran out of diskettes, you had to terminate the backup session, go to DOS, and run the FORMAT program.

Performance The BACKUP program is unacceptably slow for general backup needs. A global backup of a 20-megabyte disk takes from one to two hours, depending on the number of files and complexity of the tree structure. The tedium has to be experienced to be believed. One saves so much time by instead using a sophisticated backup utility (which we'll discuss in a moment) that the cost of the software is repaid in only a few backup sessions.

The RESTORE command Because BACKUP uses a proprietary file format, you can only use the RESTORE command to reclaim your files. It prompts you for the appropriate diskettes and lets you know when you insert the wrong one. RESTORE basically uses the same syntax as BACKUP. For example, to restore all files in the subdirectory \LEVEL2, you must enter:

```
RESTORE A: C:\LEVEL1\LEVEL2\*.*
```

To additionally restore files belonging to the subdirectories below:

```
RESTORE A: C:\LEVEL1\LEVEL2\*.* /S
```

And to restore every file to a disk, re-creating the tree structure is required:

```
RESTORE A: C:\*.* /S
```

Features

Some of the switches differ between BACKUP and RESTORE. /B specifies the date, and (in DOS 3.3) /A specifies the time. /M causes only files that have been modified or deleted since they were last backed up to be restored. /N restores files that no longer exist on the hard disk (this switch must not be used with /A and /B).

Dangers

In DOS versions before 3.1, BACKUP and RESTORE had more than their share of bugs. There are reports of conflicts with memory-resident programs in versions 2.1 and 3.0. Files occasionally have been scrambled. And, most notoriously, RESTORE has refused to do its job in some cases, leaving you high and dry, with your backups in an otherwise unreadable form. The programs appear to have improved in recent versions. But they are still not nearly a match for even a second-rate full-scale backup utility.

Backup Utility Software

The computer software market is awash with backup programs. It's hard to distinguish between them—*Fastback, Flashbak, Fullback, BackTrack, Backup, KeepTrack*. Competition is keen, with "featuritis" rampant. Backup utilities tend to be a little pricier than the DOS shells discussed in Chapter 6. The average price is over $100, although many fine offerings are available in the $50 to $75 range. As with all software, there is no hard and fast relation between price and performance. The best-known may not be the best.

At any price, a good backup program pays for itself quickly: it pares down the time required for backups, helps avert mistakes, provides better error-correction, and creates records of the backup. While DOS shells have an (unwarranted) reputation as belonging to beginners, backup utilities are a tool for "power users." They can be customized to cut backup time to a few minutes.

Backup programs have been crossing boundaries with other utility software genres. Some have DOS shell features; others offer file-recovery features. The furious competition causes individual products to evolve constantly. The product that leads in spring may be left in the dust by fall. For this reason, we'll not make recommendations here. It's up to you to keep an eye out for reviews and recommendations. You'll learn here which features are important for your own backup needs. Keep a list of your requirements, and when you tentatively decide on a utility, call the maker and go down the list verifying that the product can do the job.

Performance

Backup programs tend to compete on speed rather than features. Because most users loathe making backups, the opportunity to get them over with more quickly seems irresistible. Performance is important, but you shouldn't regard the fastest program as necessarily the best. Ease of use may save you more time up front than rapid data transfer does during the backup. And *flexibility* is all important. Good software lets you easily specify particular kinds of files for backup so that your backups won't be filled with files that aren't required but can't be sorted out. Fewer files makes for faster backups; in this sense, a relatively slow backup program can outperform the supposed "winner."

Performance strategies

The *speed-demon* backup programs work by running two DMA channels at once. There are other strategies for speeding up backup utilities. Some read whole tracks or cylinders at once to avoid excessive head movements; afterward, they sort the data into files as it is written to floppies. Another ploy is to keep floppy drives spinning during disk changes. A disk change takes only about five seconds, and the fastest utilities, running in the fastest machines, can keep you continuously swapping floppies in and out of dual drives. Turning the drives on and off would slow down the backup because floppy drives take time to come up to speed. There's no harm in changing disks while the drives turn; the diskettes disengage when the drive door is opened. Floppy drives are normally shut off to save wear and tear on the diskettes, which are abraded by the floppy envelope.

The fastest backup programs can make astounding claims. Ten megabytes can be recorded on 1.2-megabyte diskettes in four minutes. Statistics like these are for ridiculously optimized conditions, however, rather like the EPA mileage ratings for automobiles.

They're often made using fast disk drives that hold a few large, completely defragmented files. Advanced error checking may be shut off. Be aware that data transfer is greatly slowed when formatting is done simultaneously. *Fastback* may fill a 360K diskette in 18 seconds, but it takes 47 when it simultaneously formats it.

Most backup utilities produce DOS-readable files, although more and more use proprietary formats. Disks that use a proprietary format elicit a "bad disk" error message from DOS. Even disks readable by DOS may not allow DOS access to the files backed up onto them. Sometimes the files are crammed into one giant file, with information about their subdirectory locations intermixed. Others may write a "map file" at the end of the backup (a potentially dangerous strategy if the final diskette becomes damaged).

Proprietary formats

But many utilities replicate the DOS format exactly. They copy from the source disk as much of the directory tree as is used by the files written on a given diskette. In a global backup, each diskette holds different parts of the tree. The same subdirectories tend to be created on several diskettes. For example, say that a hard disk's root directory has a child directory that holds many files—enough to fill two floppies. Two backup diskettes might each hold a corresponding subdirectory file, using the same name and location in relation to the root directory. But each will list only part of the files contained in the hard disk subdirectory. When the utility restores data, it *combines* the subdirectory listings to create a subdirectory matching the original.

That diskettes use the standard DOS directory format doesn't necessarily mean that backup programs employ DOS to make the copies. DOS is notoriously *slow*, and many programs directly control the hard disk and floppy disk hardware for faster data transfer. But DOS is also very *reliable*, and the backup software may be less so if it goes it alone.

Like all software, backup utilities may be *command driven* or *menu driven*. The DOS BACKUP program is an example of command driven-software. All specifications for the backup are given from the command line when the program is called. The advantage in this approach is that the program can easily be called from a batch file. You might set up one batch file named **FULBAKUP.BAT** and another named **QIKBAKUP.BAT**, placing the appropriate command lines for global and incremental backups in each. Then you'd have to type only FULBAKUP or QIKBAKUP, and the job would proceed. Menu-driven backups are much easier for beginners, because there's no complicated syntax to remember. This approach is especially useful during restore operations because they occur in-

Operation

frequently, and you're sure to forget the command structure. However, menu-driven programs are often more difficult to automate. Sometimes, command sequences may be captured as keyboard macros. More and more backup utilities tend to run *both* from the command line and from menus.

Some backup utilities let you create a *setup file* that tells the program exactly how to run the backup. Setup files can give much more exact specifications for a backup than can a single command line. You can specify particular filenames, extensions, subdirectories, file dates, and so on. *Backup Master* takes the interesting tack of letting you "record" a sequence of keystrokes through the menuing system, save them in a setup file, and play them back at a latter date. Different files may be tailored to your various kinds of backups.

Data restoration

Don't assume that a program that excels at flexible and speedy backups will necessarily do as well restoring data. Pushed to their limits, several programs have occasionally proven unable to reclaim data from backup diskettes. A reviewer of one utility found that it could span large files across several diskettes but could *never* restore them! Because restore facilities are seldom used, software may be widely recommended without full knowledge of its performance during a crisis.

Today, very few utilities follow DOS in requiring you to insert the first ten diskettes of a backup to recover a file from the eleventh. Some can scan the entire backup for multiple iterations of a file (held in separate directories) and let you choose which to restore. A valuable feature is being able to restore files to a different directory than that from which it was taken. Some utilities won't allow this, and their backups are especially unsuitable for transporting data to another machine. Only a few utilities create a report when data is restored, printing out the names of all directories and files created or overwritten.

Diskette requirements

The number of disks required for a global backup varies from program to program but not greatly. One survey found that a 10-megabyte backup takes 23 to 28 360K diskettes. Diskettes of other sizes require proportional quantities. Many utilities begin the backup by scanning the hard disk and telling how many disks are required. Not all can format disks on the fly, so you'll want to have more than enough ready to go.

Programs that use proprietary formats tend to fit more onto a disk. They may accomplish this by using larger disk sectors, so that less space is wasted between sectors. *Fastback* writes 421K on a 360K disk. Using a 1.2-megabyte drive, some programs can double the number of tracks on a standard 360K floppy, giving it a nominal 720K capacity, and actually cramming in about 800K. Superior error checking is supplied to make this scheme reliable. One program actually formats low-density diskettes for 1.2 megabytes and then marks many bad sectors off-bounds (some diskettes end up with *less* than 360K using this method).

Programs electronically mark each diskette so they can know its position in the backup sequence when data is restored. For your own convenience, you must carefully label the series of diskettes before its first use. Some utilities come packaged with special labels.

A variety of errors can occur during either backup or restore operations. Errors that occur during data restoration are obviously serious—your data is at stake. But even errors during backup can be very troublesome. Because incremental backups clear a file's archive bit once it has been copied, an interruption of the backup

Error checking

An Inside Look: Backups with COREfast

COREfast from CORE International is a full-featured backup utility that can make both file-by-file and image backups to diskette, both in DOS and proprietary formats. When started, the program displays the menu shown in Screen A. When you select the hard-disk-to-diskette backup option, it offers a "catalog" facility in which you can specify groups of files by wildcard characters or by tagging directory listings (the program includes a number of DOS shell-like features).

Choosing a simple file-by-file backup leads to the menu shown in screen B. The function keys are tied to various parameters. F2 names a file or wildcard combination, and F8 lets you extend the selection to all subdirectories below. F4 lets you tag the volume label of each diskette. Through F5 you can toggle between the DOS and proprietary formats, and F6 lets you specify the kind of diskette (this option is chosen in Screen B). F9 toggles *incremental backups* into effect, and F7 lets you specify a range of dates.

As the backup proceeds, each file is listed on the screen, and a summary is given at the end (as shown in Screen C). Diskettes may be automatically formatted. The program beeps when it requires a diskette change, and it continues the backup the second you close the drive door—no keystroke is necessary.

One of COREfast's great strengths is that file restoration uses a system of menus almost exactly like those used for backups. In the example given in Screen D, the single file SAMPLE.BAT is restored to drive D.

```
┌─────────────────────────────────────────────────────────────────────────┐
│ COREfast        Version 1.32   SN 00022560   Sunday, November 1, 1987    │
├─────────────────────────────────────────────────────────────────────────┤
│                              Main Menu                                    │
│                                                                           │
│          f1 - Help                                                        │
│          f2 - Backup data from disk to diskette                           │
│          f3 - Restore data from diskette to disk                          │
│          f4 - Display backup diskette directory                           │
│          f5 - Perform diskette utility functions                          │
│          f6 - Perform file management                                     │
│          f7 - Exit to DOS                                                 │
│                                                                           │
│                                                                           │
│                                                                           │
│                                                                           │
│ Press ESC to exit                                                         │
├─────────────────────────────────────────────────────────────────────────┤
│        (C) Copyright CORE International, Inc.  1985, 1986, 1987           │
└─────────────────────────────────────────────────────────────────────────┘
```

Screen A. **The Main Menu in COREfast.**

```
┌─────────────────────────────────────────────────────────────────────────┐
│ COREfast        Version 1.32   SN 00022560   Sunday, November 1, 1987    │
├─────────────────────────────────────────────────────────────────────────┤
│                         Backup Options Screen                             │
│                                                                           │
│   ┌───────────────────────────────────────────────────────────────────┐ │
│   │     Backup type selected: File-by-file                            │ │
│   │ f2 - File specification: \*.*                                     │ │
│   │ f3 - Backup diskette drive: A:      f8 - Include subdirectories: Yes│ │
│   │ f4 - Volume name: UNNAMED           f9 - Only modified files: No   │ │
│   │ f5 - Backup mode: High-speed      s-f1 - Read verify: No          │ │
│   │ f6 - Diskette capacity: 1.3MB (HD) s-f2 - Use error correction: Yes│ │
│   │ f7 - Date range: All              s-f3 - Update archive status: Yes│ │
│   └───────────────────────────────────────────────────────────────────┘ │
│                                                                           │
│   Chose diskette capacity to use in a 1.2MB diskette drive:              │
│       f1 - Help                                                           │
│       f2 - 1.3 MB floppy - (96 TPI, High Density)                         │
│       f3 - 800 KB floppy - (96 TPI, Quad Density)                         │
│       f4 - 400 KB floppy - (48 TPI, Double Density)                       │
│ Press ESC to exit                                                         │
├─────────────────────────────────────────────────────────────────────────┤
│        (C) Copyright CORE International, Inc.  1985, 1986, 1987           │
└─────────────────────────────────────────────────────────────────────────┘
```

Screen B. **Backup Options.**

```
COREfast Backup Program  Version 1.32   SN 00022560

D:\COREFAST\SCREEN04.CAP
D:\COREFAST\SCREEN05.CAP
D:\COREFAST\SCREEN06.CAP
D:\COREFAST\SCREEN07.CAP
Updating file status bits

Backup complete

   1601295 bytes backed up
       102 files backed up
         5 directories scanned
   1873920 bytes copied to backup media
Total backup time:  4 minutes,  0 seconds

Backup completed normally
Press ESC to return to menu

KBytes scanned: 1564K     Backup time : 3:59      Diskette % : 57
Files scanned : 102       Diskette # : 5 of 5     % Complete : 100

         (C) Copyright CORE International, Inc.  1985, 1986, 1987
```

Screen C. **The Summary Screen.**

```
COREfast           Version 1.32   SN 00022560    Sunday, November 1, 1987

                        Restore Options Screen


          Restore type selected: File-by-file
    f2 - File specification: SAMPLE.BAT
    f2 - Destination path: D:\
    f3 - Restore diskette drive: A:
    f4 - Volume name: UNNAMED        f7 - Include subdirectories: Yes
    f5 - Restore mode: High-speed    f8 - Overwrite read-only files: No
    f6 - Diskette capacity: 1.3MB (HD)



    f1  - Help
    f10 - Begin restore with selected options




Press ESC to exit

         (C) Copyright CORE International, Inc.  1985, 1986, 1987
```

Screen D. **Restore Options.**

can leave you with no way of restarting; you're forced to make a global backup the second time through. A good backup program can deal with many error conditions.

Backup programs deal with bad sectors on diskettes in varying ways. A few don't notice bad sectors at all and write data on top of them. A few abruptly stop the backup. DOS-oriented programs such as *KeepTrack Plus* can use the DOS VERIFY feature when data is recorded. But most programs check every sector before writing to it, and when they find a bad one, mark it off-bounds in the file allocation table and continue with the backup. The same responses apply to data restoration. Some utilities that check for bad sectors during backup seem to assume that no harm will befall the diskettes thereafter: they abruptly halt the backup when they encounter a bad sector on a floppy. When the program uses a proprietary format, your data is lost.

Error recovery

Fortunately, this failing is rare. Most utilities can recover from data loss and continue restoring files. Many programs that use proprietary formats write extensive error-correction code on the diskettes. Damaged data can often be restored using these codes. The makers of *Fastback* delight in advertising that their product can recover data from a diskette that's been stapled. *Backup Master* supposedly can recover from damage of "up to" 20% of the disk surface.

Bad sectors aren't the only gremlin that can interrupt a backup session. A program should be able to recognize when the diskette drive door is open and issue a message. And it should be able to identify a diskette in the backup series that has already been filled with data and has been inadvertently inserted into the drive a second time. Similarly, during data restoration, a program should be able to recognize instantly when the wrong diskette has been placed in the drive.

Flexibility

Be sure that a backup utility is coordinated with your computer hardware. The best programs can handle all floppy disk drive formats; owners of PS/2 machines should be watchful for utilities that have not been updated for the new 3½-inch formats. Programs that work through DOS should be able to handle any kind of drive, but remember that a DOS-like disk format doesn't necessarily indicate that DOS is used.

A critical advertising phrase to watch for is, "backs up any logical device." This expression means that the backup program operates through DOS, and it can copy to any size floppy drive, to any removable cartridge drive (including Bernoulli Boxes), to another hard disk, or to tape backup units that accept DOS commands.

Programs that can alternate backups between two floppy drives are preferable because work is done while you change diskettes. Many can run two drives, but don't expect them to be able to handle two drives of different capacity. Because many AT-class machines are equipped with one 1.2-megabyte and one 360K drive, dual-drive backups often aren't possible. This may be all for the better because mixing high- and low-density diskettes could lead to no end of confusion.

Keep in mind that a backup utility may make heavy demands on random access memory. Some programs may require a minimum of, say, 256K to back up a 10-megabyte disk, more for a 20-megabyte disk, and so on. Many programs work most efficiently when much memory is free. You may want to clear resident programs from memory before starting.

Memory require-
ments

It's important that a utility give constant feedback as the backup progresses. You can easily make a mistake in the specifications for the backup, and you won't know it if the program presents nothing more than a blank screen and occasional beeps to tell you to change diskettes. Some programs estimate how long the backup will require. They'll tell how many files are involved in the backup and list the results of wildcard searches. During the backup, they show the names and directories of files being copied and report what percentage of the total backup is complete.

Reporting

Tape Backup

To many, tape backup seems like a panacea for backup woes. What could be more convenient than pushing a button, walking away, and returning minutes later to a fully backed-up disk. In many situations, tape backup can be just this simple. But, like everything else in computerdom, there are many intricacies to tape backup; headaches (and even data-loss) can arise from choosing the wrong tape unit or from using it the wrong way.

Tape's weakness is its *linearity*. Any two bytes of data on a hard disk are separated by only a few inches; on tape they may be separated by hundreds of feet. Random access is a practical impossibility. That's why tape is used for archiving data on mainframe computers and seldom for direct access. Unlike a floppy disk drive or a removable cartridge disk drive, a tape unit serves no purpose other than backups. It does its job well, but does nothing else.

Fundamentals of Tape Technology

With few exceptions, all tape units use tape cartridges, which make handling tape as easy as handling a floppy. The tape is usually coated with a reddish-brown oxide much like that on audio tape. The surface is divided into a number of tracks—typically nine (the number varies by the standard the tape drive adheres to). Usually the tracks are read in *serpentine* fashion; rather than rewind the tape after each track is read or written, at the end of a track the drive motors reverse direction, and access continues on the adjacent track.

Tape formats

Tape formats vary from manufacturer to manufacturer. All disk sectors hold 512 bytes because DOS demands it; no similar standard exists for tape. Tracks are divided into logical units called **blocks**. A block may record a dozen disk sectors end to end and follow them with error-correction code. The format for numbering the blocks and laying out directories and file allocation tables varies considerably. Some formats require that the tape be preformatted, just as all disk drives are under DOS.

Technology

Tape units have a read/write head that in principle resembles the read/write head in a disk drive. The head creates a magnetic field across a gap, and that field affects, or is affected by, magnetic particles on the tape surface. Typical data densities run at 8,000 bits per inch. When the tape comes to an end, the head shifts to an adjacent track.

What makes tape units special is the rapid speed at which they move tape across the read/write head: usually 90 inches per second. This is a lot faster than audio cassette tape, but it's necessary to make backups at reasonable speed. By computer standards, it's not very fast at all; the read/write heads of a hard disk cover the circular tracks at roughly ten times this rate. A DC-600A cartridge is 600 feet long. Using nine tracks, the effective length of the tape is 5,400 feet, or 64,800 inches. At a thousand bytes per inch, the tape has an (unformatted) capacity of about 60 megabytes. At 90 inches per second, the tape could theoretically be filled in just twelve minutes. In reality, backups proceed more slowly.

Tape drives connect to the machine just like a hard disk. An interface board accompanies the drive and communicates with the computer through DMA (direct memory access), which moves data rapidly between the tape unit and system memory. Computers have several DMA channels, and most tape units use channels 1 or 2.

Data can simultaneously move from memory to tape as it moves from hard disk to memory.

Streaming

You'll often encounter the expression "streaming tape" in advertisements. Streaming is not a particular technology or tape format. It is an ideal for tape performance that all kinds of tape drives strive for, but seldom attain. "Streaming" refers to *continuous* data transfer to the tape. This condition is more easily achieved with image backups. Head movements in the disk drive are minimal so that there are few interruptions in the supply of data. But in file-by-file backups, data cannot always be transferred at the rate tape can absorb it; "underruns" occur.

Drives that use unformatted tape can continue turning during underruns; because the tape is unformatted, recording can recommence at any moment. But this approach wastes tape, possibly reducing a cartridge's effective capacity to below requirements. Formatted tapes, on the other hand, must stop when underruns occur. Repeated starts and stops are very time consuming, making for slower performance in these drives.

One study of tape drives found that most couldn't stream consistently. As with most aspects of tape drive performance, the ability to stream largely depends on the tape drive software; it must be very fast. Well-crafted software approaches a file-by-file backup by reading groups of files into memory, reading all in a single pass across the disk surface. Once the files are buffered in memory, the drive can embark upon a long period of streaming. When backup software has much RAM available, it can achieve streaming for longer periods. Some software tells how many underruns have occurred when it issues status reports.

While consistent streaming offers a certain theoretical satisfaction, it is of no real importance in itself. It is simply another factor in determining how long a backup will take. Optimal streaming occurs with image backups; as a result, it's tempting to think an image backup must be "best." But an image backup is simply faster.

It's interesting to note that streaming isn't limited to tape. Floppy disk backups that use two DMA channels (as described above) also stream, and the backup software may buffer files in memory to make the data transfer as continuous as possible. However, streaming is not perfect in these backups either. That the floppies never stop turning doesn't mean that data is constantly transferred.

Underruns

Benefits

Misconceptions about Tape Backup

Many users pay the hefty price of a tape backup unit in the fond hope that all the cares and woes of backup will magically disappear. The idea of solving all backup problems with the push of a button is irresistible. Unfortunately, life is not so simple. While you *can* buy a tape unit, plug it in, and start making daily image backups of the whole disk, you may be in for a rude awakening when you eventually lose some data. Tape backup is superior to floppy-disk backup in nearly all respects; nonetheless, it still requires careful forethought to be used adequately and safely.

Purchase criteria

Purchasing a tape backup unit is the most complicated of all equipment purchase decisions. When you buy a hard disk, a modem, or even a printer, the equipment follows standards set by IBM or other major players. But IBM didn't release a tape backup unit for any of its first generations of microcomputers, nor was one initially announced for the PS/2 machines. The first units came from relatively small companies, none of which succeeded in establishing dominance in the way that, say, Hayes set a communication standard for modems. The market was simply too small and scattered for a major marketing campaign that might have given us one tape format.

The result is chaos. Outwardly, tape units seem alike in that most use quarter-inch cartridges. But the way information is formatted on the tapes varies tremendously. Although manufacturers have banded together to formulate *QIC* ("quarter-inch compatibility") standards, many competing formats have been validated, and no single format has risen to prominence. The industry suffers from the contradiction of having *many* standards.

Hardware vs. software

The problem is that when you buy a tape unit, you are acquiring not just hardware but also a software package that may be every bit as elaborate as the software described above for backup to floppy disks. The software does for the tape what DOS does for disk drives: it finds its way around the tape, writes and retrieves data, provides error correction, and maintains directories. But disk drives all follow Microsoft's format for sector size, directory layout, and so on. Authors of software for tape drives are much less restricted. They can set up pretty much any scheme they like for laying out the data.

Generally speaking, the lack of standards means that you cannot record a tape on the machine of one manufacturer and read the tape on a machine made by another. Indeed, a single manufacturer may make incompatible tape units. If you intend to buy more than one tape unit for an office or to use for moving data between machines, they must all be the same. This means that if you select the wrong hardware for your needs, you'll be making that much greater a mistake.

The Lack of Standardization

In a moment, we'll look at the three primary tape standards: the *QIC* standard, the *PC/T* standard, and the *floppy tape* standard. We'll see that these standards are distinguished mostly by the tape formatting and error correction code. But they also vary in important ways that depend on hardware, such as the number of tracks on the tape.

Priorities

Given the lack of standards, you must be more concerned with *software* than *hardware* when you shop. Like hard disks, the bare tape drives are made by only a few manufacturers. The companies that make tape backup units buy the drives, add some control electronics, and write software to run the units. While the tape drives and control electronics are more or less equally capable and reliable, the quality of the software varies tremendously. Good software offers a convenient user interface, flexibility, good error checking, and high performance. Bad software can be very hard to use and can slow the drive to a snail's pace.

When advertisements tell you about this or that feature their drives offer, understand that almost always this is a *software* feature—one that may be implemented well or not. Like all software, the code that controls tape units may be constantly upgraded. The tape drive that seems least capable one month may have the hottest features of any when an upgrade appears. To some extent, the speed at which the drive can perform a backup is also software-dependent. Fancy algorithms for caching sectors and optimizing the order in which files are backed up can make a lot of difference.

Unfortunately, most tape drive makers are foremostly *hardware* manufacturers; they tend to write the software as an afterthought to designing the tape drive, and their in-house programmers often lack expertise in crafting a user-friendly interface. Tape-drive software tends to be a cut below the high polished packages we described for backups to floppy disks. Because the software is fitted to the particular hardware design, in most cases you cannot substitute more desirable software from other manufacturers if you don't like the program that comes with the machine. The problem, of course, is that you can't test the software until you've acquired the hardware.

The QIC Standard

Let's begin with the *QIC standard*, which refers to tape units that use the QIC-02 interface. As noted, QIC stands for "quarter-inch compatibility" and was formulated by the QIC industry committee, the largest and oldest industry group. It has set standards for a variety of tape formats in many cartridge sizes, including error correction, and interfacing with the computer. Virtually all tape formats are described in the QIC Committee specifications, even those that don't work with the QIC-02 interface. The two most common formats working under the QIC-02 interface are *QIC-11* and *QIC-24*, which write 20 and 60 megabytes on standard quarter-inch cartridges.

Specifications

The QIC standard does not require preformatted tape. Although this approach allows you to pack more data on to a tape, it means that no directory system can be instituted since positions on the tape are not demarcated. Directory information for each file is written in a *header* that immediately precedes the file. The QIC standard can make both image and file-by-file backups, but it can find a particular file only by searching the whole tape track by track until it reaches it. Successive incremental backups may be appended, but the tape is erased when track 0 is written upon; thus you cannot continue incremental backups indefinitely.

While many manufacturers use the QIC standard, you cannot usually share tapes between their machines. The differences lie entirely in software, however; so the incompatabilities could easily be corrected if only there were a will to do so.

Error checking

QIC handles error-checking in a very simple manner. Other formats process data as it is written to create an error-correction code, which is then laid down on the tape immediately after the data it was derived from. When the data is later read, the code tells if errors have occurred, and sometimes corrections can be made. In an entirely different approach, the QIC standard employs a two-gap read/write head. The first gap writes data, and, after the tape progresses a fraction of an inch, the second gap reads it to see that it was correctly recorded. When an error is found, the data is simply rewritten until it is done correctly. This form of error checking works well with errors that occur during data encoding, but it is

no help when defects develop later in the tape. In the view of manufacturers who use this format, you simply must buy a high-quality
tape cartridge.

The PC/T Standard

The PC/T ("personal computer/tape") standard, much less prevalent
than QIC-24, is the most DOS-like of all tape formats. The format
was developed for standard quarter-inch cartridges by 3M, Hewlett-
Packard, and Tallgrass, and it has been codified by the QIC com-
mitee as the QIC-100 specification. Tallgrass is the foremost maker
of PC/T drives. A miniaturized version for $3\frac{1}{2}$-inch minidrives is
available (as QIC-2000).

PC/T is more recently evolved than the other formats. Its developers had two goals in mind. First, they wanted the format to support very high data integrity so that the backup could survive
serious errors resulting from tape damage. Second, they wanted a
format sufficiently rigid that it could support the sorts of random-
access associated with disk drives. PC/T uses standard DOS commands, directories, and paths. Individual files can be located on
tape and overwritten, just like hard disk files. With proper software,
PC/T tape can be used as tertiary storage, much as mainframe computers use their large open-reel tape drives. In fact, a computer can
directly load and run software from tape using PC/T. (Whether
there is any point in doing this is another matter.)

PC/T achieves this flexibility by specially formatting the tape   *Formatting*
before use. As with a disk, the format is required only once and is
done by a special formatting utility that accompanies the tape drive
software. The formatting process carefully examines the tape for
imperfections; a high-capacity tape may take two hours to format
(some PC/T drives can format "in the background" so that you can
go on using your computer while the tape drive is at work).

The formatting utility divides the tape into 4-kilobyte blocks.   *Error-checking*
One block holds the data from one disk cluster under DOS 2.x or
two clusters under version 3.x. Every third block is a "parity block"
for error correction. The parity block contains error-correction
data for a pair of data blocks. When data in one block of the pair is
damaged, the tape drive software combines the parity block data
with the data in the second block of the pair to re-create the data
in the first. The parity block scheme is of no use when *both* data
blocks are damaged. Because damage to the tape tends to occur

along a continuous stretch, the PC/T format *interleaves* the data and parity blocks, keeping the three physically apart.

Using parity blocks increases tape requirements by 50%. PC/T compensates for this profligacy by increasing the number of tracks on the tape to eleven from the usual nine. Drives designed to read eleven tracks cannot read nine-track tapes at all—one reason why PC/T drives are completely incompatible with drives that use a different data format. Unlike the QIC standard, PC/T does not use a second head to read data immediately after writing.

Directories

PC/T partitions the tape into *volumes* that consist of one or more full tracks. Each may contain up to 256 files. Each volume begins with a directory that may be used for direct access to any file in the tape volume. This system lets control software find a given file relatively quickly. The worst-case search time on a 60-megabyte tape is a minute and a half.

The PC/T format has been touted as the ideal medium for transporting sensitive data between machines, because its error-correction scheme is considered especially robust against rough handling. Some reviewers, however, have questioned whether the error-rates achieved with PC/T are really any better than those of other tape formats. The price paid for the elaborate formatting is relatively slow operation in reading and writing data. This drawback may promote the greatest source of data insecurity: resistance to making backups at all.

The "Floppy Tape" Standard

The third major tape standard is "floppy tape," an appellation derived from its similarity to floppy disk operation. Floppy tape drives don't have a separate controller card. Rather, they connect to a standard floppy disk controller. From the computer's point of view, they function as just another floppy disk drive. Electronics on the drive convert disk-control commands into tape-control commands. Because tape control mimics DOS, many third-party backup utilities can work with floppy tape because they treat it as floppy-disk backup.

Formatting

Like PC/T, floppy tape requires preformatting of the tape by a special utility. Usually six tracks are used. In accordance with the DOS capacity limit, no more than 32 megabytes can be recorded in a single backup. The formatting pass constructs a bad-block table to mark damaged tape off-bounds. Every seventeenth block is set aside for error checking. If a single block of the preceding sixteen is

damaged, the error correction system can restore the data. However, when more than one block of the sixteen is corrupt, the
floppy tape format can alert you only to the fact that errors have
occurred and cannot correct them.

Floppy tape performs more quickly than the PC/T standard but is   **Performance**
slower than QIC. These relative performance levels grow out of sophistication of error checking and the degree to which formatting
enables random access to individual files. Like PC/T, floppy tape
doesn't follow the QIC standard in verifying that data has been
written correctly by rereading the tape immediately after writing.
But, because floppy tape is DOS-like, you may specify the standard
DOS /V (for *Verify*) switch in floppy tape commands, and the drive
will automatically make a second pass over the data to compare it
with the original disk data. This process is very time consuming
and required only for critical data.

A great advantage of floppy tape drives is that they may easily be
transported among machines. The floppy disk controller cards on
all IBM PCs or XTs present a D-connector in back for attaching an
external floppy drive; a floppy tape unit can plug into this connector. Hence, an entire office full of PCs can be easily serviced by
one drive. But the D-connector is not found on PC ATs, nor on various clones, such as Compaq portables. In these cases, an inexpensive adapter card is required, as for any other kind of tape drive.
Incidentally, to work with floppy tape, some floppy disk adapters
must have their main controller chip replaced with a more recent
version.

Miscellaneous Tape Standards

So far, we've discussed the three main tape backup standards. You
should be aware that there are many others, some of which get
good marks in comparative reviews. You'll even find open-reel tape
drives, which use self-threading reels resembling typewriter ribbons
(made by InterDyne). Because tape isn't usually used to transport
data between machines, there is less reason to adhere to a common
standard. But be sure to obtain a knowledgeable recommendation
for *any* drive before buying.

One unusual application of tape drives is the transfer of data between microcomputers and mainframes. While systems designers
slave away designing protocol converters for linking the machines
directly, several companies have simply created a tape drive with
electronics compatible with the half-inch, nine-track drive format

used by IBM mainframes. For example, the Emerald MTM 80-8000 Tape Subsystem can read and write 80,000 bits per second—much faster than the 9,600-bit per second transfer rates typical of terminal emulator boards. This approach isn't very elegant, but has the decided advantage that it works reliably.

VCR backup

Another interesting twist is the use of video cassette recorders for tape backup. VCRs are an analog technology, but they can be fed data as patterns of digital pulses. A special controller card plugs into the computer and connects directly to the VCR. To compensate for the low quality of the VCR hardware and tape cartridges, data is written several times along with error-detection codes. In spite of the redundancy, about 80 megabytes of data fit onto a cassette. Recording is slow, typically running at about a megabyte and a half per minute. There is no preformatting and no cataloging of files. Both image and file-by-file backups are possible, but searches for individual files are very slow because the entire backup must be scanned.

Supposedly, VCR backup saves money by letting you use a device you already own; you need only buy a controller card. But these cards are expensive ($600 and up in mid-1987). And you probably wouldn't enjoy moving your VCR back and forth between the television and the computer. One company, Alpha Micro, supports its *Videotrax* card with an enhanced VCR designed especially for backup; it can perform *background* backups while the computer is in use. Alpha Micro is researching ways of sending data to remote locations through video transmission channels, which have much higher data rates than modems.

Tape Cartridges

Tape cartridges descend from the world of minicomputers. Like VCR cartridges, they prevent contact between the tape and the outside world. This makes them vastly superior to audio-style cassettes. The cartridges contain aluminum base plates that facilitate very accurate positioning of the tape, making possible more tracks. And a special tape tensioning mechanism keeps the tape from stretching. Although you wouldn't know it to look at them, the cartridges are *high tech* and priced that way.

Cartridge formats

The 3M Company introduced quarter-inch cartridges in 1971; then they carried less than 3 megabytes. Many variants developed, but the DC-600A cartridge has long been the most prominent. These run in 300-, 450-, 600-, and 1,200-foot lengths, corresponding roughly to 30, 45, 60, and 120 megabytes of formatted capacity. Standards for 300- and 600-megabyte cartridges are under discussion by the QIC committee. The cartridges are four by six by five-eighths inches. A few manufacturers have managed to make *internal* tape units that use the cartridges, but most drives that use DC600A cartridges are *external*. More commonly, internal tape drives use DC1000 minicartridges, only two by three by one-half inches. They pack only 10 megabytes onto nine tracks, but the DC2000 version of the cartridges can fit 20 to 40 megabytes by squeezing up to 24 tracks onto wider tape.

Finally, several companies produce digital cassettes that closely resemble audio cassettes that can hold 20 megabytes in four tracks; they are said to be every bit as reliable as larger cartridges (these cassettes aren't to be confused with the true *audio* cassettes used in some low-end Apple and Commodore computers).

In spite of having few moving parts, cartridges can malfunction in many ways. So much data is packed into a small space that tiny inaccuracies make tapes unreadable. Many problems revolve around the tensioning of the tape. When the tape fails to maintain perfectly constant tension, it may begin to move laterally against the read/write head, or vertically, bouncing toward and away from the head. The lateral motion moves tracks away from the head gap. The bouncing motion moves the tape away from the head. When carried to extremes, either motion can move a track on the tape too far from the head for the head to do its work.

Quality

Inconstant tape tension leads to other problems. It can cause sections of the tape to stretch slightly. Particularly for preformatted tapes, the stretched sections can throw the read/write electronics out of sync. Poor tape tensioning also leads to minute instantaneous speed variations, which have much the same effect as tape stretching. These inaccuracies were not so problematic in the early days of tape backup when tapes ran at 30 inches per second with only 1,600 bits per inch. Today's 90-inch-per-second rate, with 8,000 bits per inch, makes for a 1,500% increase in transfer speed. The tiniest speed fluctuations lead to errors. In fact, much of the expense in designing and manufacturing tape drives lies in the fancy electronics that deal with the constantly changing tape conditions.

Tensioning

As if the tensioning problems were not enough, tape can also go bad through flaking. All tape rattles slightly between the guides that direct it across the read/write head. When the motion is severe, the tape edges become "scalloped" or "coined." In the extreme case, the outer tracks may become unreadable. More often, tiny particles

Flaking

of oxide coating separate from the tape surface. The loss of the oxide may not be a great problem in itself, because error correction facilities can compensate for the data loss. Rather, the flakes tend to scrape off against the read/write head, possibly contaminating it so that errors occur repeatedly. They may even build up to the point that the tape is held away from the head surface. Eventually the particles break free and are redeposited elsewhere on the tape, overwriting data after the drive electronics have certified it as being correct.

Tape Backup Performance

Tape drives are marked by a wide range of performance. Some are *very* slow, particularly in file-by-file backups. Most drives can transfer 25 to 90 kilobytes per second, with higher speeds typically accompanying larger-capacity drives. But poor software can severely hamper streaming. The drive may constantly stop and restart, or tape may be squandered on *inter-record gaps* (IRGs). It takes a drive roughly a third of a second to come up to speed so many stops quickly add up to minutes and even hours. A review of a drive produced by a premier electronics company found that 2.4 megabytes of small files required *two hours* to back up; the company promised it would soon release software that made the drive run 20 times faster! Software is that important in tape drives.

Manufacturers' claims

You must be cautious about manufacturers' claims for the performance of their drives. A typical advertising claim may state that a drive "backs up a 20-megabyte hard disk in four minutes flat!" Usually, statistics like this are for an image backup, done without optional read/write verification. Such backups bring a drive as close as it comes to streaming, so the statistics are for the best case. Depending on both hardware and software, file-by-file backups may be much slower. Claims for file-by-file backup performance are also suspect because tests are done on atypical disks. The disk is defragmented, filled with large files to avoid numerous directory accesses, and the directory tree may have only one level of subdirectories to shorten searches.

Comparative performance

Comparative reviews show quite a range in performance. Image backups of 10-megabyte hard disks may take from 1½ to 13 minutes. Image restores take about the same time as a backup. File-by-file backups for 10 megabytes range from 5 minutes to 35 minutes, with complete restorations taking two to four times longer (12 to 75 minutes). Some of the worst results occur with PC/T drives.

Generally speaking, you can expect a fast QIC drive to back up 20 megabytes in 6 minutes by image, or 12 minutes, file by file. A two-megabyte file-by-file *incremental* backup may take hardly a minute.

Increasingly, makers of tape drives are writing smarter software that undertakes an initial scan of the whole disk. The software copies groups of files into memory, sometimes going around the usual DOS facilities for extra speed. When available memory is filled, the tape starts turning; the files are disgorged onto it; and then the tape is stopped until the next group of files is loaded in memory. Faster computers may be able to move files into memory quickly enough to achieve sustained streaming. Running a file defragmentation utility before the backup begins helps greatly.

The ideal tape backup combines the speed of an image backup with the flexibility of a file-by-file backup. Indeed, some tape drive software can restore individual files from an image backup, although with difficulty. Because the image backup begins with cylinder 0 (the outermost cylinder on the disk), the disk's root directory and file allocation table is found at the start of the tape. The software reads the FAT and stores it in memory. Then it searches for the subdirectories leading to the desired file and finally searches for the file itself. All of this requires moving back and forth along the tape, making the restoration quite slow. The software speeds up the process by retrieving any clusters belonging to the file as they are first encountered, assembling the complete file once all clusters have been found.

The ideal

Restoring a file from an image backup can be painfully slow, particularly when the file was highly fragmented on the disk it was recorded from. But if the need is only occasional, the delay ought to be acceptable. Note that a tape standard like PC/T that uses formatted tapes can work more quickly during this kind of random access because it can use the format markings to skip more quickly to the locations on tape where the desired data is known to reside.

Restoring files

As tape drive software improves, some manufacturers are supplying software with their drives that performs *only* file-by-file backup, leaving image backups in the dust. Comparative tests show that the best software can achieve file-by-file backup times only marginally greater than those for an image backup. Such high performance is possible partly because the software ignores empty clusters during file-by-file backup, whereas it backs up *all* clusters during an image recording.

On nearly all available tape drives, file-by-file backup is limited to the files in DOS partitions. If you plan to partition the disk for a second operating system, you will need to contact the manufacturer about the availability of suitable backup software. Without this software, you will be limited to image backups, with all their attendant limitations.

Buying a Tape Drive

Buying a tape drive is harder on the nerves than buying a hard disk. Hard disks are much alike; but tape drives vary in many ways. Generally speaking, the same rules apply that were described for buying hard disk drives (Chapter 3). But, unlike a hard disk, you are buying both hardware *and* an elaborate software package. It's impossible to test the full range of features at a dealer's showroom, and you are all the more vulnerable buying through mail order.

Don't buy a tape drive until you have found a positive recommendation for the drive or have negotiated a return agreement so that you can experiment with the drive and return it if it proves unsuitable. Manufacturers may try to tempt you by offering free DOS shells, cache utilities, and other goodies. Don't be distracted from your real requirement: to be able to make fast, frequent, reliable backups with little effort or resistance. A cheap drive isn't cheap if you won't use it. Most have a one-year warranty; avoid those that offer only 90 days. If you have questions, call the manufacturer and ask for the support service—not a salesperson.

Capacity
requirements

When you finally buy, go for large capacity if you can afford it. A 60-megabyte unit costs only about a third more than a 20-megabyte unit. This is a good idea even if you have only a 20-megabyte drive to back up. You'll be able to append many incremental backups to a single tape. More important, you'll be ready to handle a larger disk drive when you inevitably acquire one. Although tape backup units will undoubtedly become faster, they are used infrequently enough that you'll want to go on using a drive for many years.

If you can't afford a high-capacity unit, you may find that a smaller one can do the job anyway. Some drives are accompanied by software that can *span* a backup across two or more cartridges. Or you may be able to back up part of a directory tree to one cartridge, and part to another. Of course, incremental backups should have no trouble fitting onto low-capacity cartridges.

Purchasing
considerations

Tape units share many of the concerns that accompany buying a hard disk drive. You must decide whether to opt for an internal or external unit, and sometimes must choose between full- and half-height drives. External units have their own fans, which may be noisy, and some drives can be very noisy when they wind tape at high speeds.

If you own an IBM clone, it's a good idea to phone the manufacturer to see if the drive has been tested with the model you own. Many reports of incompatibilities have arisen, so that if, you can't be certain, be sure to arrange a return agreement. Theoretically, tape units coupled with disk drives by the same manufacturer should give excellent performance, but, again, it depends a great deal on the quality of the software.

Sharing the unit

If you want to share a drive between several computers and won't be using floppy-tape drives on PCs, shop around for manufacturers that supply cheap adapter cards so that you'll have one for each machine. Maynard Electronics makes a special portable tape drive just for this purpose. Don't plan on swapping a single controller card between machines because you'll quickly wear out the contacts that plug into the slot. Besides, it would be so much trouble that you'd soon stop making backups.

Most tape drives come with various utility programs. Diagnostic software may check out the drive, and perhaps test the computer's DMA channels. **Certification utilities** test the integrity of blank tape cartridges by writing data and reading it back. Some PC/T drives may have a data verification program that scans the error-checking codes to find corrupted data. Some drives have tape erasure utilities. And most have a **retensioning utility** that steadily runs tape from reel to reel to equalize the tension; this measure helps avoid instantaneous speed variations that lead to errors; the utility is run after every 20 backups or so.

Utilities

We've mentioned many concerns about both tape hardware and software. Yet most advertisements for tape units mention the barest details. To avoid unpleasant surprises, we recommend that you follow these four rules when shopping for a tape drive.

Shop for software. Figure out the backup system you want and then buy a drive to fit it. Be sure that the software that accompanies the drive is powerful, flexible, and easy to use. Or find a drive that can be run by some of the backup programs offered by other companies.

Don't buy without a recommendation. Don't buy by brand name. One of the worst-performing drives ever released came from an internationally prominent electronics company. And don't buy the cheapest drive available on the assumption that it may be only a trifle less convenient. Remember that bad software can render a tape drive useless for some kinds of backup. Watch computer magazines for reviews, talk to people who use tape, or seek out informed advice at user-group meetings. The time spent on homework will be handsomely repaid over the years you use the drive.

Secure a return agreement. Unless you have a dependable good review of a drive, don't buy it without a return agreement. Ten days is adequate, but 30 is ideal, if you can find someone willing to agree to it. Some manufacturers have advertised 30-day money-back offers. Naturally, dealers don't like these arrangements, and they may try to hit you with a *restocking fee* of up to fifteen percent of the drive's price, plus shipping charges. The shipping fees ought to be your responsibility, but not the restocking fee; demand a *full* refund. Explain that you must examine the full range of software capabilities before agreeing to keep the unit. Sooner or later you'll find a dealer who will agree, provided that you maintain the packing materials in pristine condition.

Buy the unit when you have time to experiment with it. Once you've secured a return agreement, make use of it. Spend half a day putting the software through its paces in *all* kinds of backup and restore operations. If performance is too slow, send it back. Don't keep the drive out of inertia, thinking that its poor performance is unimportant because its use is only occasional. Any features that discourage your using the drive make your purchase that much less valuable.

Installing a Tape Drive

Installing a tape drive is much like installing a hard disk. Internal drives must be inserted into the machine, with all the attendant fiddling with guide rails (in ATs), bezels, screws, and power cables. The drive's controller card is inserted in a slot close enough to the drive to make cabling easy. And then the data and control cables are attached. All the principles discussed in Chapter 4 apply.

Device drivers

DOS doesn't control tape drives, so many tape units come with a device driver (others are directly controlled by their accompanying backup software). When a device driver is used, it is supplied as a small program that must be loaded into memory when the machine is booted. The loading is done automatically by listing the driver in the CONFIG.SYS file with the DEVICE command. If the driver file is called **TAPEDRV.COM**, the expression **DEVICE = TAPEDRV** must be placed in CONFIG.SYS. The documentation accompanying the drive will tell you exactly what to write if there is any confusion. Some tape units include an installation program on the floppy disk that automatically inserts the DEVICE command in CONFIG.SYS. You'll only need to call the program (perhaps by entering **INSTALL**), and the work is done for you.

Similarly, most drives require that you allocate a certain number of DOS buffers for the drive to perform optimally. This is done by the BUFFERS command, which we described in Chapter 7. A typical setting is **BUFFERS= 20**. This command is also placed in CONFIG.SYS.

Some installation programs completely replace the existing CONFIG.SYS file, wiping out other commands your system needs. This is bad software design but common nonetheless. If the drive's documentation doesn't expressly state that the installation program *modifies* CONFIG.SYS, it is best to play it safe and make a backup copy of CONFIG.SYS (for example, **COPY CONFIG.SYS KEEPCNFG.SYS**). This minor precaution could save you much grief trying to reconstruct the commands contained in your prior configuration file. (In fact, if you've read Chapter 5, recall that we advised you to make backups of both CONFIG.SYS and AUTOEXEC.BAT whenever changes are made.)

CONFIG.SYS

Once listed in CONFIG.SYS, the tape device driver is loaded whenever you start up your computer. It takes up memory (usually less than 20K) whether or not your tape drive is in use. While most of us can spare 20K, many other memory-resident programs may make demands on scarce memory. You may want to institute a system of flexible configuration files to load the tape device driver only during backups.

Besides changing CONFIG.SYS, installation programs move various files from the distribution floppy to your hard disk, including the device driver itself, the software to manage the backups, and various utility programs, such as formatting and retensioning utilities. Some installation programs move all of these files to the root directory. Others create their own subdirectory under the root directory. The name of the subdirectory is entirely at the manufacturer's discretion; if you don't like the name or position of the subdirectory, you may not be able to change it because the backup software may expect it to be present.

Auxiliary software

Of course, if no installation program is included, you will have to use COPY to move the files over to the hard disk. With luck, the backup software won't require that the files be placed in the root directory (which should contain as few files as possible). Note that the DEVICE command can use a path so that the device driver doesn't need to be in the root directory; you could place the driver in the subdirectory **TAPEUNIT** and write **DEVICE = \TAPEUNIT \TAPEDRV.COM** in CONFIG.SYS.

DMA and port addresses

Earlier, we talked about how tape drives use the various DMA channels. Some tape units let you set which channel is used. Similarly, there is a range of **port addresses** the tape drive may use. Ports are the gateways through which the device driver communicates with the tape drive. Because IBM hasn't issued its own tape drive, particular port addresses have not been reserved. While many addresses are available, other non-standard hardware may happen to select the same addresses, in which case conflicts occur and the system crashes. For the same reasons, drives may also have a selectable **interrupt vector**, a mechanism by which the tape unit exerts control over the computer.

All of these selections may be made through the backup software, or by changing dip switches or jumpers on the tape drive's controller board. Most tape drive owners need never concern themselves with these technicalities. The manufacturer makes settings at the factory that work in almost all machines. Problems arise in machines set up in a local-area network or equipped with special hardware such as a digitizer or plotter. If you have problems getting the tape drive working on a specially equipped machine, you'll need to check the documentation. It will tell the current settings, and (ideally) you can compare them to records you've kept of the port address and interrupt vectors used by other equipment (again, ideally).

With a measure of good fortune, you may be able to reconfigure the tape drive just by trying a few new settings at random. There's no intrinsic need to understand what the settings mean. You just have to hit on settings not currently used by other equipment. Unfortunately, the drive manufacturer's support people may be of only limited help because they can't know the configuration used by unusual equipment installed in your machine. In the worst case, you may find it necessary to seek help from a dealer or a consultant.

Tape formatting

The final step in installation is formatting tapes. As we explained above, formatting is required only for some tape formats. The format is a *single-pass* operation; the concepts of low-level and high-level formatting don't apply as they do to hard disk formatting. Some machines make a second, verification pass over the newly formatted tape, however. Because the DOS FORMAT command isn't used, there are no standard commands or procedures for initiating the formatting; the software for each tape unit has its own command interface (although some imitate DOS). You'll have to consult the documentation to get going. Some manufacturers sell preformatted tapes for their drives.

The Future of Tape Backup

Ironically, just as tape backup has overcome serious technical obstacles and evolved into a mass-market product, it is threatened with extinction. Most observers believe that sooner or later erasable optical disks will completely supplant tape backup units. Laser disks are an ideal backup medium because they are inherently cheap and permit random access at high data-transfer rates. The relatively slow average seek times of optical disk drives are no impediment when used for backups. It is easy to imagine an inexpensive *fixed* laser disk that would constantly back up the slightest changes made on hard disks. Tape could not do this practically. But tape manufacturers are fighting back. Tape units with capacities measured in *billions of bytes* have appeared (albeit at very high cost).

In any case, it will be well into the 1990s before erasable laser technology becomes cheap. The write-once laser drives now appearing carry a high price for both the units and the disposable cartridges they use. While we're waiting for inexpensive laser technology, tape drives continue to be the most reliable and convenient way to back up data.

Instituting a Backup System

In devising a backup system, you must learn to think clearly about the different kinds of information on the disk. Which data files change and which do not? You must decide what sorts of backups will accompany particular kinds of work, how often the backups are to be performed, and how the backup media are to be organized. When the backup scheme encompasses many computers, you must also determine *who* is to look after backups and how backup records are to be kept. This may sound a little excessive—particularly if you're planning for yourself alone. But without a schedule, backups are likely to be neglected. Buying hardware is only half the battle.

Deciding among Backup Options

We've looked at four kinds of backup media: diskettes, high-capacity removable disks, a mirror-image second hard disk, and streaming tape. Each technology has its strengths and weaknesses:

Ease of use A mirror-image second hard disk is easiest, with tape and removable disks running second, and diskette backups far behind.

Flexibility Diskette backups may be best of all because you have such a broad choice of backup software, and diskettes are completely portable between machines. Removable disks and mirror-image disks have the advantage of directly substituting for a badly damaged hard disk. Owing to its linearity, tape is the least flexible medium.

Price Diskette-based backups are very cheap. Mirror-image hard disk systems and streaming tape units cost roughly the same. Removable cartridge drives are most expensive.

For small hard disks, **removable high-capacity cartridges** are the ideal backup medium. The backup may proceed unattended; any file is instantly accessible; the backup medium may substitute for the drive itself; and the cartridges may be transported to a safe location. But removable cartridge drives are very expensive, and it is hard to justify buying one for backups alone. Today, most cartridges hold 20 megabytes, and soon they will hold 30 or 40; backing-up a very large hard disk may require several cartridges, and this defeats some of the advantages of the medium.

Mirror-image
backup

Mirror-image hard disk systems would be the ideal backup system were it not for a fatal flaw: the backups don't protect against all kinds of data loss. You could lose everything if the machine is stolen or somehow destroyed. There's limited protection from user error or vandalism. And there's always the possibility that *both* disks could crash simultaneously during, say, an earthquake.

Mirror-image systems are ideal when input data is unrecoverable as in an online reservation system. The on-going backups ensure that no more than one data record will be lost. But the disk still requires external backups, either on diskette, removable cartridge, or tape. These backups may be made infrequently, since risk is spread across two kinds of backup. The proper frequency depends on how you evaluate the risk of data loss through theft, fire, and so on. Tape is ideal for these backups because global backups make most sense, and because a fast image backup is adequate (file-by-file recovery is performed by the mirror-image hard disk).

These reservations also apply to the use of a second, ordinary hard disk for backups, employing one of the disk-based backup utilities that can copy over the entire subdirectory structure. The situation is much the same, but you lose the automaticity. Vendors report that this approach is becoming quite common, because a bare drive is relatively inexpensive and can readily be connected to the existing controller. There's danger in this approach, but perhaps the degree of risk from theft or destruction is no greater than other risks businesses undertake.

Second hard disks

Like removable disk cartridges, **streaming tape backup** is expensive but convenient. Tape units are cheaper than removable disk cartridge units, but less flexible. If the hard disk fails, it must be repaired before work can continue. Finding and restoring individual files is slow. And tape is not a particularly good way of moving data between machines. On the other hand, tapes can make unattended backups of much larger hard disks. When backing up very high-capacity drives, tape is much cheaper than buying a second mirror-image drive. But tape drives serve no purpose other than backup. A removable cartridge drive, although more expensive, also lets you archive data.

Streaming tape

As we've seen, tape backup can be made cheaper by buying interface cards for several computers and sharing one drive among them. This approach tends to undermine tape's advantage in ease of use, however. It discourages frequent incremental backups; it may create a confusion of tape cartridges; and it makes it difficult to quickly restore an individual file. But it may be the cheapest solution to backup in offices where many computers require frequent backups. This approach is easily managed; the cost of the tape unit is spread over many machines; and relatively little time is spent making backups.

Diskettes are the most inconvenient backup medium. Even high-speed utilities are onerous when the whole hard disk must be backed up, and they are liable to discourage people from making backups at all. Diskette backup is unsuitable for very high-capacity disks. A 250-megabyte hard disk needs *two hundred* 1.2-megabyte floppies (or, heaven forbid!, *seven hundred* 360K floppies). And diskette backups require exceptional organization if multiple series of diskettes are to be kept in proper order.

Diskettes

But diskette backups can offer flexibility. Utilities that store files in DOS format make searching through backups easy. And the diskettes can be read by any machine, anywhere. The backups can double as a means of moving work between office and home.

Those who ordinarily access only a small portion of their hard disk's data may find that diskette backup is no less convenient than any other approach. If global backups are required infrequently, the disadvantages of diskettes in large backups become unimportant. Most people who own a 1.2-megabyte floppy drive would find that a daily incremental backup can be performed in hardly a minute without a disk change. For those with simple needs, spending hundreds of dollars on a tape backup system would be wasteful.

In the end, you must pay whatever it costs to get the backups made. But keep in mind that not everyone's backup requirements are equal. The *best* backup system is the one that meets *your* requirements most cheaply in terms of both money invested in hardware and time invested in its use. To make the right choice, you must first think clearly about how much you will be backing up, and how often. And that is our next topic.

Backup Frequency

Backups must be multiple. If you use a single series of diskettes for all your backups or a single tape cartridge, you take the risk that a disk crash *during* the backup will wipe out both the original files and the prior backup copy. You would lose everything. Besides, backup media can be defective, and multiple copies are a wise precaution, as we'll explain in a moment.

Standard
procedures

Many corporations maintain sufficient backups that they can financially "restart" the company on any previous day of the preceding month. This is an extreme case: these companies are using *serial global backups*. More generally, the MIS (management information systems) world maintains three generations of global backups, known respectively as the grandfather, father, and son. As time passes, the son becomes the father, the father becomes the grandfather, and the grandfather media is rerecorded as the new son. Global backups are made weekly. A second series of global backups may be kept at one-month intervals, usually made at the end of the month. Hence the company keeps end-of-month backups for the three prior months, and end-of-week backups for the three prior weeks, with some overlap. Copies of the most recent weekly and monthly backups are kept off-site. In addition, many companies warehouse the source documents for the data for long periods.

Earlier in this chapter, we described six kinds of backups: *global*; *partial* (project-specific global backups); *incremental*; *simultaneous* (as by a mirror-image hard disk system); *temporary* (such as .BAK files, to protect you from minute-to-minute errors in your work); and *serial* (a backup series that lets you backtrack in your work).

Most backup schemes consist of periodic global backups followed by frequent incremental backups, and we'll confine our discussion to this common system. The remaining four approaches are specialized. Recall that partial backups are useful when files are intricately interrelated, such as the code modules of a computer program; simultaneous backups are useful for unrecoverable input data, as in reservation systems; and temporary and serial backups are useful for recovering from user errors made within one working session.

The frequency of incremental backups may be proportional to the amount of work done on the machine. But the schedule for global backups should be strictly observed. If a global backup is scheduled for the first and third Mondays of each month, the backup should be made even if the computer has been used very little during the preceding two-week period. This rigidity is justified because global backups are the *base point* for reconstructing data after total data loss.

Extra global backups are a good idea on certain occasions. It's a good idea to follow heavy editing of the directory tree with a global backup. You could spend hours rationalizing the subdirectory system and moving files, only to have your last global backup restore the previous state of affairs. Keep in mind that files *erased* since the last global backup will reappear. An extra global backup is also a good idea immediately before you introduce potentially dangerous software to the disk, such as a public domain disk utility. Bad software can do much damage. Be equally careful if you are learning to program and plan to experiment with DOS disk-access functions (*don't*) use the absolute sector write function on the hard disk; confine your experiments to floppies).

Always follow at least a two-generation model for global backups. Keep the prior backup on hand. If you do need to make a global restoration and something has gone wrong with the most recent global backup, you have something to fall back on. A good plan is to move the prior global backup off-site to guard against catastrophes like fire and theft. You'll need only two sets of diskettes or

Scheduling global backups

two cartridges. Take the current backup to the off-site location, bring back the old one, and use it for the new backup.

Excluding files

Some backup software lets you exclude certain kinds of files from global backups, particularly program files, which are easily identified by the .EXE and .COM filename extensions. The rationale is that you already have backups of these files because you own the original distribution diskettes. Program files may take up several megabytes of disk space, so excluding them may save many disk changes in backups made to floppies. But it's not a good idea to exclude files from a global backup. The great value in a global backup is that, after data restoration, work can begin again *immediately*. You may have to spend hours reinstalling software if it is excluded from the backups.

One kind of file virtually never requires backing up at any time. These are **.BAK** files automatically made by software. As backups of backups, they are redundant. There's no harm in recording the files if it doesn't inconvenience you. But if there are many, you should either delete them or see to it that they are excluded from incremental backups. Without doing so, incremental backups may be doubled in length as many files are copied twice. Find out how your backup software can be made to ignore files with .BAK filename extensions. Or use the DOS ATTRIB command to clear the files' archive bit: **ATTRIB *.BAK -A**.

Disk maintenance

A global backup is a good opportunity to perform various disk maintenance tasks. Take a little extra time. Delete unnecessary files, including .BAK files. Run a utility that checks for bad sectors and damaged files (we'll discuss these in Chapter 9). Most important, take time to run a defragmentation utility (also explained in Chapter 9) so that your files will be compacted into as few cylinders as possible. All of these tasks need to be carried out about once a month on a moderately to heavily used disk.

The ideal order for these tasks is disputable. Ideally, the backup should be made of a disk cleared of unnecessary files and free of defects. In addition, having the disk defragmented beforehand helps the backup run faster. But housecleaning is a rather dangerous activity; files are often purposely destroyed when they are mistakenly thought obsolete. And disk utilities have often been known to damage the disks they are supposed to protect. Defragmenters, in particular, have a checkered history. Hence it can be argued that you should back up *before* doing housecleaning and running utilities. This is certainly a good plan until you have used a defragmenter successfully many times. (If a utility scrambles your data and then

you copy it onto your backup media, you'll be very glad to have
kept that second global backup.)

Earlier, we explained how incremental backups may be either
written over the prior incremental backup, or *appended* to it.
When incremental backups are appended and are frequent, two
problems arise. First, much backup media may be required to hold
incremental backups; you won't be able to recycle the media until
after the next global backup. Second, restoring all data to a disk is
much more work with appended incremental backups, because
each backup must be restored in sequence to ensure that the most
recent file versions will be returned to the hard disk.

Appended backups

It's for these reasons that it's impractical to continue with incremental backups *indefinitely* after an initial global backup. Even
when incremental backups are written over one other, with time
the incremental backup becomes very large and many diskettes or
many feet of tape must be gone through to complete the backup.
As the cumulative incremental backup approaches the size of a
global backup, it begins to take as long as a global backup (possibly
longer, depending on the software). Hence global backups must be
made often enough to keep incremental backups quick and possibly
to hold down the amount of backup media involved.

While the frequency of global backups depends in part on how
often incremental backups are made, the frequency of incremental
backups is entirely a matter of judgment. It all depends on the
value of your data, and on how great a risk you want to take. Backups are so widely neglected that it is tempting to go to the opposite extreme and say that no amount of backing up is excessive.
But hard disks are more reliable than is popularly believed. When a
disk is brand new, more frequent backups are a good idea because
manufacturing problems will appear early on. But after a few
months of good service, a drive is very likely to perform for several
years without problems, just like a quality automobile. As a drive
ages, more frequent backups become advisable. Of course, most
drives in existence today are still in adolescence, and many will
probably be discarded before they wear out.

Scheduling incre-
mental backups

Incremental backups ought to be made at least once a week (on
machines used all week long). Twice a week would be wiser, and a
daily incremental backup is a good idea when the work that goes
into files cannot be reproduced (you can always re-enter data into
a spreadsheet, but an inspired sonnet may come your way only
once). If you make daily incremental backups, they will probably
need to be *overwritten* if you use diskette backups, unless very few
files are changed. Otherwise scores of diskettes will be required.

Organizing Backup Media

Whether you make your backups on disk or tape, you must carefully label and organize the media. Failure to do so leads to all sorts of confusion. You'll lose track of which backups have become dated and should be overwritten. You won't know which disk or cartridge to insert for an *append* backup. You'll forget whether all backups have been made. Worst of all, when catastrophe strikes and it's time to restore data to your hard disk, you may be unable to locate the most recent backups. This problem is particularly acute when you must sort out the newest versions of files from several incremental backups.

Alas, we don't like to make an already onerous task more complicated. But there are four steps to organizing your media, each leading to its own brand of confusion when it is omitted. The steps are:

Labeling. Each diskette or cartridge must be labeled using a simple code showing where it belongs in the backup system.

Record keeping. Each diskette or cartridge needs some kind of written record of what was recorded on it and when.

Storage. Groups of diskettes and sometimes cartridges must be kept in their own marked containers, each with its own labels and records.

Rotation. Procedures and record keeping must be instituted to ensure that backups are performed on the proper media, and that crucial backups have been sent off-site.

Labeling media

Always keep global and incremental backups on separate media. If possible, use different color labels for the two kinds of backups. Mark the media clearly, indicating both the backup's generation and, if multiple diskettes or cartridges are involved, with a sequence number. For example, you might have media marked **Global A** and **Global B** for a two-generation global backup, plus other media marked **Incremental**. Perhaps labels for the two global backups could be colored red and yellow, respectively, and blue labels could mark the incremental backups. Even this simple measure helps avoid mistakes.

Using diskettes, each series of labels should have a number from 1 upward. Be sure to have more than enough diskettes to handle the worst case, and preformat them if your backup utility requires it. Some backup programs cannot format diskettes on the fly, and you may have to interrupt the backup if you run out of diskettes. *Never* make backups on unlabeled diskettes, thinking that you'll sort through them if they're ever needed. Restoring a hard disk properly can be difficult enough without adding to the confusion.

Second backups

When data is critical and irreplaceable, you may want to keep a second backup. It's best to perform a second backup onto a second set of media, rather than copy the first backup. This approach avoids duplicating undetected errors made in the first backup. And a direct backup is often faster than a diskette-to-diskette copy because the data source operates at hard disk speed. Those who use tape drives or haven't a matching floppy drive have no choice in this matter. Remember that backups made with proprietary diskette formats can't be copied by DOS.

File Catalogs

Most backup programs keep some kind of catalog of each backup session. A few can create a catalog retroactively by scanning the backup media. Some catalogs are readable only by the backup program. You may be able to ask the program to display information from the file, but you can't read it directly or print it out. These files are often kept on the hard disk in the subdirectory in which the backup program resides; others write the catalog on the backup medium when the backup is finished. Catalogs slow down backups because the read/write heads on the hard disk must constantly move from the files they're reading to the catalog file. This is particularly true when the hard disk contains many small files.

A printed listing of the backup may be invaluable when files are lost. When backups are incomplete or disorganized, a catalog can help you reconstruct the directory tree and assess the damage. When backup programs keep a catalog of all files on the hard disk itself, the catalog may be destroyed by a disk failure. It's a good idea to print out the catalog file after every global backup.

Some backup programs can be made to print out a catalog as the backup is made. The MS DOS version of BACKUP does this with the /L switch. The same can be accomplished in PC DOS by *redirecting* screen output to the printer, as in **BACKUP C: A: /S >PRN**.

Off-site Data Storage

Giant corporations rely so much on their computers that they plan for the most extreme form of data loss: destruction of the entire computer system. Besides shipping daily backups to an off-site location, they maintain stand-by hardware. While most of us can afford to live without a computer for a few days until the insurance company replaces it, recovering from total data loss is another matter. Yet many who religiously make backups leave the backups open to destruction by fire, flood, or thorough-going thieves.

This sort of catastrophic data loss is much less likely than loss to a drive failure or user error. But it is a serious possibility. Many who would not *think* of leaving $10,000 of computer equipment uninsured leave several times that value in data completely at the mercy of the Fates. Now that computer theft is sharply on the rise, it's particularly worthwhile becoming more concerned about crime. Those with modest backup needs often find it easiest to keep a sole copy of crucial files on a single floppy disk or tape cartridge, never removing the media from the drives. The backups may be of no value to a thief, but he'll carry it away with the equipment nonetheless.

Choosing a site

Keeping a backup off-site is the obvious countermeasure. How often the off-site backup needs renewing depends on just how precious the data is to you. What's most important is that you choose an off-site location that is easily accessible. Otherwise you'll only be encouraging resistance to your own backup system. While nothing feels quite so secure as a safe deposit box, getting to the bank by 3 p.m. is a tremendous hassle. If the hard disk is in an office, it's much simpler to just take a copy of the backups home.

The ideal off-site location is cool, dry, and stationary, but a less favorable environment may do the job. Floppy disks, at least, are much more rugged than they appear (in spite of what advertisements may imply). *PC* magazine once sponsored a study of floppy disk durability, subjecting diskettes to high humidity, corrosive gases, microwave ovens, thermal shock, X-ray units, and airport security machines. The disks also were exposed to a variety of magnetic sources, including welding machines, fluorescent light ballasts, color televisions, calculators, and the insides of telephones. Of all the tests, only directly rubbing a bar magnet on the diskettes led to loss of data (a magnet held two inches away had no effect).

Those who work at home and lack an obvious second location should consider keeping the off-site backup in their car. Experience has shown that floppies weather extremes of temperature, humidity, and motion quite well. So long as they're kept out of direct sunlight or moisture, they should be all right. Although storing floppies in an automobile breaks all the rules, it's a far sight safer than having no off-site backup at all.

This brings us to the end of our discussion of backups. We've gone on at such length because the topic is so very important. Talking with disk repair services, we've found that they constantly encounter hysterical people who have lost one or two years' work or whose small businesses may have been destroyed for want of a few backups. The question is, can *you* learn from the experience of others?

Chapter 9

Surviving Hard Disk Disasters

When your best efforts fail and a file, or a whole disk full of files, fly off to never never land, there's still hope of reclaiming your beloved data. Utility programs can unerase files, reassemble accidentally formatted disks, and repair damaged directories, file allocation tables, boot records, bad sectors, and format markings. None of these utilities can do the job every time, and you must *never* neglect backups because you have a shelf full of recovery tools. Adequate backups are your best defense against the data gremlins.

Two kinds of disasters threaten a disk. In one case, files are lost owing to operator negligence, but the disk itself is undamaged. In the second case, the disk malfunctions and requires repairs; "repair" can mean anything from running the DOS CHKDSK program to sending the drive to the shop (in the later case, "repair" usually means "replacement"). Of course, files may be lost in the second case, too. Sometimes, a very small defect can stop you from using the disk at all. You'll encounter one of the much feared DOS error messages:

```
DISK ERROR READING DRIVE C:, GENERAL FAILURE,
ERROR READING, WRITE FAULT, BAD SECTOR,
SECTOR NOT FOUND, FILE ALLOCATION TABLE BAD,
DISK ERROR READING FAT, DISK NOT READY,
INVALID DRIVE SPECIFICATION, DATA ERROR,
NON-SYSTEM DISK OR DISK ERROR, READ FAULT,
BAD DATA, ABORT, RETRY, IGNORE?
```

You can do *much* to avert these disasters and to recover from them when they occur, by investing a little money and time. To do this intelligently, you must understand the diffent ways in which a disk can fail; that is where we shall begin.

How Disks Fail

Equipment failures may be *mechanical* or *electronic*. Most of us tend to visualize any drive malfunction as a "crash" where the read/write heads dive-bomb into the disk surface. Some people exhibit a near-hysterical anxiety about head crashes, as if every disk is poised to self-destruct at any moment and that few live for very long. In fact, head crashes account for only about 1% of the hard disk drives sent in for repairs. The hysteria is a measure not of the imminence of a head crash, but of the consequences when the disk hasn't been backed up. Drives fail in many other ways and in some

cases you can recover some or all of your data (if you are willing
to hand over a lot of money to a special repair service—more on
this later).

Mechanical failures generally center on the motor that turns the
platters or the actuator that moves the read/write heads back and
forth. The head actuator is by far the more complicated of the two,
but until recently many problems developed in drive motors. Sometimes the motor burned out, or, if it used a drive belt, the belt
broke or became slack. More often, the bearings in the motor or
the spindle that supports the platters wore out. When this happens,
a squealing noise emanates from the drive. It is a clear signal that
the drive is in trouble and that it should be sent in for repairs at
once. You should make global backups *immediately* when you encounter this condition. Alas, disks sometimes squeal during a major
head crash, so it may be too late.

Electronic failures occur in the circuitry on the disk drive or on   Electronic failures
the controller board. Simple components may burn out. Compli-
cated ones may malfunction because of design flaws. It appears that
a faulty chip on the controller board of early IBM ATs partly account for their notorious disk failures. Electronic failures damage
data only when the drive is writing data; the damage tends to be
local. But a long time may pass before you first discover an instance of the damage, and in that time the faulty components may
work their mischief again and again. The worst outcome occurs
when a directory or file allocation table is the victim of a faulty
write operation. This silent error can destroy all your data just as
surely as an all-out head crash.

Other problems arise from **soft errors**. These result from   Soft errors
changes in the drive's magnetic medium or in its mechanical alignment. In a soft error, the drive continues to function mechanically
and electronically. But, for various reasons, it fails to read a given
bit of information the first time it tries. It may succeed the second
time or perhaps the third. In fact, soft errors are a normal part of a
disk drive's operation. Even on a spanking new, healthy drive, minor electrical surges may throw off a read operation. If an operation fails, the disk controller automatically makes nine more
attempts, each time waiting for the platter to spin around once
more.

The designers of DOS didn't consider this precaution sufficient.
When the disk controller reports that it was unable to complete a
request, DOS tells it to try again, and once more still if the second
request also ends in failure. Hence, 30 tries are made before DOS
finally gives up and reports a disk "failure." If it prompts you with

the "Abort, Retry, Ignore?" message, the answer "Retry" may send DOS back for 30 more tries. Sometimes, numerous tries end in a success. There should be no reassurance in this outcome. The disk is breathing a last gasp.

Kinds of failure

With this understanding, let's look at what can go wrong:

Magnetic fade Magnetic markings on the disk surface slowly fade. Files tend to be rewritten periodically so that they stay intact. But the format markings that define sectors are written only when the disk is given its low-level formatting. Similarly, boot records and some directory information are written only once. After some years, the disk controller may be unable to read some of the markings, or soft errors may increase to unacceptable levels.

Media degeneration The magnetic coating on the platters very slowly disintegrates. Recall that, even when a disk drive is new, some points on it's platters have relatively low *magnetic retentivity*, and they can barely act as magnetic domains. As the medium deteriorates, these points become ineffective, soft errors increase, and new bad sectors form.

Track misalignment The actuator that pushes and pulls the read/write heads across the platters may gradually pull out of alignment, especially on drives that use stepper motors. Depending on the nature of the misalignment, the heads will stray to the sides of tracks at either the inner or outer edge of the platters, and this may vary as the temperature rises. More and more soft errors occur, and gradually the heads are pushed too far from the track to be able to read it at all.

Platter wobble With time, the bearings in the spindle that supports the platters begin to wear. A platter may begin to very slightly wobble. With each revolution, the wobble increases and then decreases the distance between the heads and the disk surface. Again, soft errors increase.

Controller malfunctions Sometimes the electronic components on controller cards stray outside acceptable tolerances. The result is a slight misalignment of magnetic domains that throws off timing in read/write operations.

Electrical pulses A strong voltage spike may find its way past your surge protector and the computer's in built protection cir-

cuitry. It can result in a blast of magnetism striking the platter surfaces. The result is rather like a mechanical head crash—a stretch
of data is totally destoyed, including the format markings that sur-
round sectors. But the drive is physically unharmed. "Repair" consists of restoring damaged format markings.

Head crash A head touches down on the disk surface. In the best
case, only a tiny stretch of a track is affected, and the disk may be
returned to service by reformatting it so that the affected areas are
set aside from further use. In the worst case, several heads crash on
cylinder 0, where DOS keeps the partition table, root directory,
and file allocation tables. The medium may be damaged to the
point that the disk cannot support the DOS area after the disk is
reformatted. Or the read/write heads may be fatally damaged. Even
when damage is slight, particles of the medium may break loose
and fly around inside the disk drive casing, ready to cause another
crash at any time.

Software error "Freeware," possibly written by an aspiring nine-
year old, may run amuck and erase files right and left. Even software from reputable companies may sometimes commit murder. In
the worst case, the software will inadvertently overwrite FAT sectors held in DOS buffers, and these will be written to both copies
of the FAT kept on the disk; all data may be lost.

Operator error Besides accidentally erasing files or reformatting
the disk, an inexperienced user can damage data by rebooting during a disk operation. The directory entries of individual files aren't
updated until the file is completely written. Directories themselves
may be damaged. *Don't use Ctrl-Alt-Del as a panic button!*

Of course, sometimes components just blow out. The drive motor may burn out, or a capacitor may short-circuit. But more often
a drive gradually descends into decrepitude. As it does so, soft errors occur with greater frequency. Unfortunately, this process is invisible until it is too late. DOS doesn't notify you until the drive
fails 30 times in a row. When deterioration is widespread across
the disk surface, performance may be compromised as many extra
turns of the platters are inserted into read and write operations.
This is particularly true when the problems lie upon the crucial
DOS structures on cylinder 0.

Recovering Erased Files

In Chapter 2 we explained how DOS organizes files by directories
and file allocation tables. A file's directory listing contains its name,
size, and other information, including the number of the first cluster it occupies (recall that a *cluster* is the unit in which DOS allocates sectors—four sectors in later DOS versions). The file
allocation table keeps track of each additional cluster the file occupies, each position in the table telling which cluster is next.

How DOS Erases Files

When DOS "erases" a file, it does two things. First, it changes the
first character of the file's directory listing to the Greek *sigma*
character. In subsequent directory searches, the character indicates
to DOS that the directory slot is "empty" and open for insertion of
a new file. Still, all information from the previous file remains intact
except for the first character of the filename, which is overwritten
by the sigma character.

Second, DOS goes through the file allocation table and *deallo-
cates* clusters given to the file. That is, it changes the markings that
keep track of the file to markings that show that the clusters are
free for use by other files.

What DOS doesn't do is actually erase the information in the
clusters occupied by the file. It would be easy enough to do this,
but there is no point in it. When the clusters are required for another file, they can be allocated even with old information in them.
The old information is destroyed only when a new file overwrites
it. Even if the new file is shorter than the one previously occupying
a cluster, DOS keeps track of the file length, so data from old files
doesn't creep into new ones.

Unerasing the File

Because the file is intact, it should be an easy job to recover it. But
often problems arise. Losing the file's information in the FAT is
pretty disastrous. After all, there are thousands of clusters on the
disk, and the FAT is the only way of knowing which is linked to
which. The *starting cluster* of the file is recorded in its directory
entry so that we can always be sure where it is. But subsequent

clusters may be anywhere on the disk. To recover a file, we not only have to find its clusters, we have to get them in the right order.

In the simplest case, a file occupies only one cluster. To unerase it, a utility has to find its entry in the directory, using the former filename and extension, minus the first character. It asks the person who erased the file to enter the deleted first character of the filename, and it replaces it. Then it looks up the *starting cluster* in the entry and goes to the FAT to reallocate the cluster to the file. That's all there is to it.

The simplest case

When the file stretches across several contiguous clusters, the utility has a bit more work to do, but not much. After restoring the directory entry, it goes to the FAT and reallocates as many successive *unallocated* clusters as the file requires. It knows how many clusters are needed, because the file size is recorded in the directory. Figure 9-1 diagrams this scheme.

Multicluster files

(1) Find entry in directory   **(2) Adjust file allocation tables**

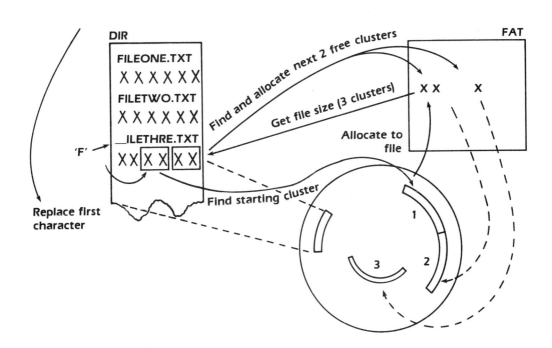

Figure 9-1 **Automatic unerase**

Actually, the unerase utility reallocates *successive* clusters only when it finds that those clusters aren't currently in use by other files. If successive clusters are free, there's a good chance they belong to the erased file. Otherwise, odds are that the file is dispersed across the disk, making recovery much more difficult and perhaps impossible.

Dispersed files

Unerase utilities deal with the latter case in two ways. They may go ahead and gather together as many nearby clusters as are required. This "automatic recovery," is based on blind hope. Once the file is resurrected, you can look into it and see if the correct clusters were chosen. Or unerase utilities offer a "manual mode" in which cluster after cluster is shown on the screen, and the user strikes one key or another to include or reject the cluster in the rehabilitated file. There are some serious drawbacks to the latter approach. To understand them, let's first take a look at how files become fragmented.

The Origins of File Fragmentation

In Chapter 7 we learned about file fragmentation and defragmentation utilities that physically unify files so that they may be read with minimal head movement. In DOS versions 2.x, when DOS allocates space to a file, it scans the file allocation table from its beginning, and allocates the first it finds. On a freshly formatted disk, this system is very efficient, and the first files placed on the disk are entirely contiguous. But once files are erased, problems begin.

How DOS fills the disk

DOS fills the disk from the outer edge inward. Imagine that a small file is placed on cylinder 1 and that many more follow. Then the file is erased, opening up a single cluster on cylinder 1. Thereafter, a new file is copied to the disk, and it requires *two* clusters. DOS searches the FAT, finds the open cluster in cylinder 1, and allocates it to the file. Then it goes on looking for a second cluster and finds one farther inward on the disk, perhaps in cylinder 10. The new file is fragmented.

Ideally, DOS would scan the file allocation table for a free block of clusters large enough to fill the file. But that would be slow, and as the disk fills, it would become impossible. To do the job right, DOS would need to take on the role of a defragmenter. Some operating systems do this job, but DOS is not one of them.

An improved method

Still, starting from DOS version 3.0, a change was made to discourage fragmentation. As the disk fills, DOS keeps track of the position in the FAT from which it last allocated a cluster. When another cluster is required, it begins its search from that location in the FAT. This is to say that DOS allocates every cluster *once* before it goes back and *re*allocates clusters freed by file erasures. If the last allocated cluster was on cylinder 600, DOS starts its next search for a free cluster at this same cylinder, rather than seek out *freed* clusters closer to the outer edge of the disk. Once every cluster on the disk has been allocated once, DOS reverts to its 2.x-style mode of allocating whatever cluster is closest to cylinder 0. This state of affairs continues indefinitely thereafter. But, for awhile, it does quite a bit to discourage file fragmentation.

Manual File Recovery

Now, let's reconsider what goes on during a manual file recovery. This process is diagrammed in Figure 9-2. The clusters belonging to a file may be widely dispersed across the disk. This is most likely to happen when the disk is nearly full, or the file is very large. If many files have been deleted (say, in a general housecleaning), hundreds of open clusters may lie between the clusters given to a particular file. It's a long haul looking through all these clusters.

Worse, the file's clusters may get out of order. When a file gradually grows over months and even years, DOS may allocate new clusters from any point on the disk. A file can begin on cylinder 200, continue at cylinder 400, then 300, then 100, then 500, and so on. This is often the case with very large files, and it makes them extremely difficult to recover. Not only is it hard to find the clusters, but it becomes difficult to arrange the reclaimed clusters in the proper order.

Cluster order

This problem leads us to the greatest impediment to manual file recovery of all. Many files cannot be visually inspected. Program files, in particular, appear as so much gobbledygook when they are displayed. If you accidentally erase a program file and then attempt to undelete it, you can use only automatic recovery. If the recovery was successful, the program will run. If it wasn't, you'll know quickly, because the machine will "hang" and you'll need to reboot to get going again (no harm is done).

Inspecting the clusters

Most data files, other than simple word processor files, are also difficult to reclaim manually. True, files for databases, spreadsheets, and outliners are likely to have intelligible English written amid the gobbledygook, but figuring out the proper sequence for the clusters is often next to impossible. If one cluster is out of order, the

(1) Find (or replace) entry in directory **(2) View unallocated clusters** **(3) Adjust file allocation tables**

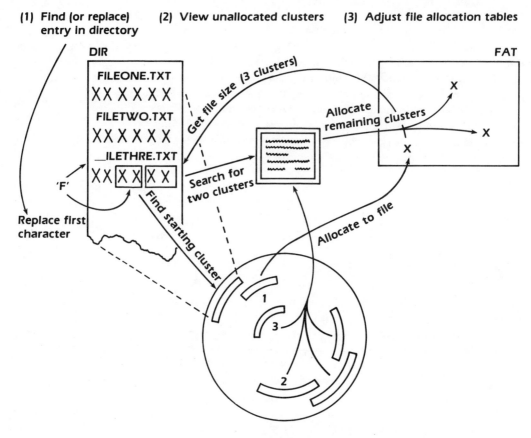

Figure 9-2 **Manual unerase**

software that uses the file will almost definitely freeze up—and that means the data is as good as lost.

Other problems

So far we've spoken about an erased file as if nothing had happened on the disk from the moment of its accidental erasure. Often, the person who deleted the file recognizes the error immediately and runs straight for the unerase utility. But sometimes hours or days may pass before you realize that valuable data is missing. During that time, DOS may hand over to a new file the directory slot formerly occupied by the file. Or DOS may allocate to another file some (or all) of the erased file's clusters. When this happens, you've got Big Trouble on your hands.

Directory entries

When the directory slot is taken over by another file, two crucial pieces of information are lost. The number of the starting cluster is gone. And the file size is no longer available to tell how many clusters are involved. But the file may still be recovered. It's done by searching every unallocated cluster on the disk.

When a file's former clusters have been given over to another file, the data is obliterated permanently. It may be possible to partially recover the file. After all, it's better to rewrite only *part* of the *Great American Novel*. But generally only text files are useful after a partial recovery. When a sector is missing from a database, the alignment of all the records is thrown off, and the database program reads the surviving data improperly. (Certain popular programs have their own file recovery tools, however. For example, the *Mace Utilities* include recovery programs for dBASE files.)

Incidentally, if you've erased a file and wonder what's happened to it, *don't* use file-recovery utilities until you've tried an unerase program. In DOS, both the *CHKDSK* and *RECOVER* programs create large temporary files that may overwrite the deallocated clusters of the file(s) you wish to reclaim. Other utilities may do the same.

When many files have been unerased, perhaps by using the DEL command with wildcard characters, problems are compounded. A utility attempts to recover them by repeating the procedure for recovering a single file. But if the files are fragmented, a cluster belonging to one erased file may easily be incorporated into another. Hence, a failure to correctly reclaim one file can cause a failure to reclaim a second. If you attempt to manually reassemble the files, sorting through the numerous deallocated clusters can be overwhelming.

Lost clusters

Multiple erasures

Unerase Utilities

We've seen that unerase utilities have *automatic* or *manual* modes. In the *Norton Utilities*, the approaches are divided between separate programs. The *Quick UnErase* (QU) program automatically reassembles single files or groups of files. It works in two modes, dubbed "interactive" and "automatic."

In interactive mode, the program scans a directory and displays all information remaining from erased files, including its name (except the first letter), its size, and its time and date stamp. From this listing you can select one or more files to unerase. You're asked to supply the first letter of the filename. Alternatively, in automatic mode you can enter the name of a file, or a group of files (using wildcard characters), and the *Quick UnErase* program does its best at recovery.

Automatic unerase

An Inside Look: Recovering Erased Files
with *Norton UnErase*

NU, the main *Norton Utilities* program, contains a detailed, versatile unerase program, (Another program, *Quick UnErase*, attempts best-case automatic file recovery.) *NU* begins by scanning a specified directory for all slots that hold entries for erased files. It lists these, as shown in Screen A.

```
Menu 2 part 1
                        Select Erased File or Sub-Directory
                     Create file                ?t000000.50%
                     ?$qcnt1.50%                ?t000001.50%
                     ?ample.fil
                     ?creen00.cap
                     ?creen01.cap
                     ?creen02.cap
                     ?creen03.cap
                     ?creen04.cap
                     ?creen05.cap
                     ?creen06.cap
                     ?creen07.cap
                     ?ead.me
                     ?elp.50%
                     ?isplay.50%

                     15 entries to choose from
                  Speed search:

  Item type    Drive   Directory name                           File name
  Erased file  D:      \                                        ?ead.me
```

Screen A. **Erased Files Listed in the Directory.**

Once you select an erased file from the listing, the program checks whether its starting cluster has since been allocated to another file. If not, it reports that recovery is "probable" and gives complete directory information on the file, including the number of clusters it occupies. It then asks that you type in the first character of the filename, which had been overwritten when the file was deleted (Screen B).

Next, the *UnErase* program offers a number of ways of gathering and examining the clusters that may contain the file's data. You may first call for an automatic undeletion to see if it will be successful. Or you can look at each available cluster in turn. You may ask to see clusters or sectors by number, or you can go into **zoom mode**, in which the program selects free clusters within a specified range. Finally, you can specify a string that the program searches for throughout the disk. Screen C shows a menu of these features.

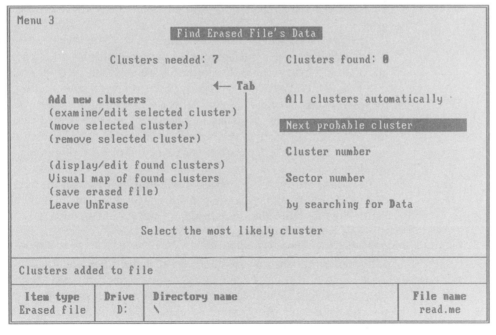

```
Menu 2 part 2
                    ┌─────────────────────────────────────┐
                    │ Complete Selected Erased File Name   │
                    └─────────────────────────────────────┘

                       Name: ?ead.me
                 Attributes: Archive
              Date and time: Sunday, November 3, 1985, 9:33 am
     Starting cluster number: 502 (sector number 2,115)
                       Size: 12,928 bytes, occupying 7 clusters


           Successful UnErase: Probable
           The first cluster of this file is not used by another file.


                            ?ead.me


                  To restore the missing first character
                     press any letter or number key

┌───────────┬───────┬───────────────────────────────┬───────────────┐
│ Item type │ Drive │ Directory name                │ File name     │
│ Erased file│  D:  │ \                             │ ?ead.me       │
└───────────┴───────┴───────────────────────────────┴───────────────┘
```

Screen B. **Status Report for the Erased File.**

```
Menu 3
                    ┌─────────────────────────────────┐
                    │  Find Erased File's Data         │
                    └─────────────────────────────────┘

           Clusters needed: 7           Clusters found: 0

                         ◄── Tab
     Add new clusters                   All clusters automatically
     (examine/edit selected cluster)
     (move selected cluster)            ┌──────────────────────────┐
     (remove selected cluster)          │ Next probable cluster    │
                                        └──────────────────────────┘
     (display/edit found clusters)      Cluster number
     Visual map of found clusters
     (save erased file)                 Sector number
     Leave UnErase                      by searching for Data

                  Select the most likely cluster

Clusters added to file

┌───────────┬───────┬───────────────────────────────┬───────────────┐
│ Item type │ Drive │ Directory name                │ File name     │
│ Erased file│  D:  │ \                             │ read.me       │
└───────────┴───────┴───────────────────────────────┴───────────────┘
```

Screen C. **Menu of Cluster Recovery Options.**

When you choose to view clusters one by one, a special editor presents the data in various formats. You may view it as text, as hexadecimal codes, or in the format of a directory, FAT, or partition table.

Manual unerase

Searching for
clusters

Unremoving
subdirectories

If it includes clusters in a file that do not belong to it, you'll know it only by trying to use the file.

UnErase, the manual unerase program in the *Norton Utilities*, is more complicated. Like *Quick UnErase*, it presents a list of erased files, but with an additional feature. If the directory entry for the file has been overwritten, you can make a new entry in the directory to try to re-create the file.

The point behind a manual unerase program is that it allows you to easily search for clusters, view them, and juggle them into the correct order. *UnErase* gives you the option of running an initial automatic search to see what the program can find on its own. This selection serves as a base to which to add and subtract clusters. Various features let you find your way to remote points on the disk. It lets you step through unused clusters to quickly view them. In the "zoom" mode, it will track down open clusters in a specified range. Or you may use the "data" option to search for particular data values *within* open clusters anywhere on the disk.

Many disk toolkits also include a utility that "unremoves" subdirectories. Because subdirectories are nothing but files with a special attribute byte setting, these utilities are very similar to unerase programs. Once given the DOS path of the removed subdirectory, these programs do their best to recover it, searching for clusters that they can identify as having belonged to a subdirectory. Then they display the names of the erased files found in the clusters (all files must necessarily have been erased to remove the directory, so all filenames lack a first character).

The utility may not be able to tell when it has reached the end of a subdirectory. Before using the utility, it's important to make a list of any files from the directory that can be remembered. This measure helps you figure out when the recovery is complete so that you can call it to a close.

Unerase programs are a bit more popular than they really ought to be. If you follow the rules given in Chapter 5, you can avoid accidental erasures. And, if you make frequent backups, you can avoid unerasing files altogether. Still, a good unerase utility is an essential part of any software library. When you purchase one, practice using it a little bit. You'll quickly learn the limitations of unerase utilities, and you'll be better prepared to deal with a crisis when it comes.

Recovering from an Accidental Reformatting

The accidental reformatting of a hard disk holds a special terror all its own: with a few false keystrokes, every byte of data is lost. It's difficult to take precautions against this disaster, because its perpetrator, the DOS *FORMAT* program, is often required for formatting floppies. Computer novices—who have trouble getting *any* DOS command right the first time—can easily direct *FORMAT* to drive C: instead of drive A:. And even experienced users can make the Great Mistake in a moment of foggy-headedness.

In Chapter 5 we pointed out several ways of avoiding accidental reformatting. It's worth briefly reviewing them. Keep your low-level formatting program (if you have one) and the *FDISK* partitioning program away from the hard disk. Place FORMAT.COM in its own subdirectory and don't give automatic access through the PATH command. Consider renaming the program and calling it through a batch file that always directs it toward drive A:. If, after all this, you still worry that employees or others will break through your defenses, keep FORMAT.COM off the hard disk, buy preformatted floppies, and lock away the DOS diskette.

Because good advice is as often ignored as taken, you'd better know about "unformatting" hard disks. The very notion of unformatting a disk seems a logical impossibility. After all, "formatting" lays down sector markings on every track on the disk, and these overwrite any recorded data. But recall that there are *two* levels of formatting, and it is *low-level formatting* that defines sectors. The DOS FORMAT command performs only *high-level formatting* on hard disks. Hence your data is accidentally damaged only if you inadvertently run a low-level formatting program.

Many people buy hard disks that are preformatted at low level, and they don't own a low-level formatting program. But even those with a program can easily avoid an accidental low-level formatting. Just keep the program off the hard disk and the diskette that holds it out of reach. After all, it makes no sense to store a low-level format program on the hard disk it operates on; the program would erase itself when used.

If you read Chapter 4 closely, you'll remember that a high-level format writes the DOS root directory and the file allocation tables. When the /S option makes the disk bootable, the system files

Avoiding the problem

How FORMAT works

(IBMBIO.COM and IBMDOS.COM) are also written. That's all. Data
previously recorded on the disk is untouched, including all subdirectory files. But the data is as good as lost, because without a
root directory, there's no way to find the subdirectories, and without a file allocation table, there's no knowing which sectors are
linked together to form files.

An Inside Look: Unformatting a Hard Disk with the *Mace Utilities*

To install the "unformat" feature onto your hard disk, you need only move a file
named **RXBAK.EXE** to the drive and install the line **RXBAK** in AUTOEXEC.BAT.
Thereafter, whenever the drive is booted, RXBAK makes a snapshot of the crucial
DOS structures destroyed during a high-level format. RXBAK does its job in only a
few seconds, creating or updating a file named **BACKUP.M_U**.

When the evil deed is done and the disk has been reformatted, the **Mace Utilities**
diskette is placed in drive A and you type **UNFORMAT**. The program asks which drive
and then presents screen A, which enquires whether RXBAK has been installed. If it
has, the unformat program immediately goes to work scanning the disk for the
BACKUP.M_U file; otherwise it begins the precarious task of attempting a partial recovery.

```
A)unformat c:


Was MACE installed            y = yes...BACKUP.M_U created.>
    prior to FORMAT?          n = no...BACKUP.M_U did not exist.>_
```

Screen A. **Choosing the Kind of Recovery.**

```
Boot Restored

FAT 1 restored!
FAT 2 restored!

Directories restored.

Disk is as it was when BACKUP.M_U was last updated.
Files not modified since then will be intact.
Modified files may contain invalid information.
Consult manual.
Press any key....
```

Screen B. **The Report Following Unformatting.**

The unformat program scans the disk from the innermost cylinder outward. It may take a half hour to find the snapshot file, or much longer on a high capacity drive—it depends on where the file happens to have been located. Once the file is found, recovery is over in seconds. As a final precaution, the program stops and tells the name of the snapshot file (for safety's sake, you're allowed to keep new and old versions) and asks if it is the one to be used during recovery. If you answer "Yes," you'll instantly see screen B, and the unformatting will be complete.

The "Snapshot" Approach

There are two approaches to "unformatting" an accidentally reformatted hard disk. The most effective approach works by keeping a utility on the disk that takes a "snapshot" of the root directory, file allocation table, and other DOS information. It stores the information in a file with contiguous clusters (clusters from other files are relocated to make room). The utility may be executed at any time, but usually it is called from AUTOEXEC.BAT so that a snapshot is made automatically at least once a day when the computer is booted.

If the disk is accidentally reformatted, a companion utility is loaded into the newly created root directory. This program seeks out the snapshot and replaces the new root directory, FAT, and other files with the old ones—the disk is "unformatted." But there may still be problems. Changes probably were made to files between the times the last snapshot was taken and the reformatting occurred. Parts of files may be lost, or nonsense may be inserted. New subdirectories, and all the files they contain, vanish without a trace. Still, compared with losing everything, these problems seem small.

The Recovery Approach

The *Mace Utilities* include a recovery program that attempts to recover as much data as possible from a hard disk that has been reformatted, and that hasn't been protected by a "snapshot" utility. This is the *ultimate* recovery utility; it valiantly faces overwhelming odds, and you can't expect too much from it. It starts by searching for old directories by seeking out sectors that contain the dot (".") and double-dot ("..") entries. If the directory is unfragmented, the program can find its way to the subdirectory's end and then scan it for the starting clusters of other subdirectories. With luck, the directory tree will at least partially reemerge from the ashes. Subdirectories highest in the tree are listed in the root directory.

Once the directory tree is reestablished, the utility learns the starting clusters for each file listed in the subdirectories and begins the familiar "unerase" procedure for each file. The lengths of the files are known from the directory listings, so the utility knows how many sectors to look for. Files located in the root directory are lost for good, since their names and pointers to their starting clusters were lost during the format operation.

If the disk has been very recently defragmented, practically everything can be recovered. More typically, fragmentation makes it impossible for the utility to effectively unerase many of the files. Without a file allocation table to tell the program which sectors are incorporated in *other* files, thousands of sectors present themselves as possibly being part of any given file. It is the most chilling nightmare ever to fill a computer screen.

Dangers

Incidentally, the *FORMAT* program performs *both* low- and high-level formatting on floppies, so your data really *is* lost forever if you mistakenly reformat a floppy. Some versions of FORMAT.COM supplied with clones (including Compaq computers) perform both levels of formatting even on hard disks. Be very careful.

In a world of widespread computer illiteracy, "unformat" utilities provide a welcome safeguard against Murphy's Law. But they should not be adopted in lieu of good management. The *FORMAT* program is dangerous even in the hands of experienced computer users. Care and training in its use shouldn't be neglected just because a partial recovery can be made when mistakes occur. Above all, an "unformat" utility must not be allowed to allay anxieties about insufficient backups. Frequent backups remain the most effective defense against *all* kinds of data damage—accidental formatting included.

Data Recovery

Earlier in this chapter, we discussed the myriad ways in which data can be corrupted. A wide variety of data recovery tools are available, and none fulfill every requirement. Some perform intricate surgery on the disk formatting. Others are specialized for recovering damaged files. Still others allow the technically adept to edit directories, file allocation tables, and even the boot record. You'll find that most commercially available tools operate only in DOS partitions; they can't help you with other parts of the disk. They also will probably fail if you've used special software (as described in Chapter 4) that creates partitions over 32 megabytes or that combines two disks into one logical drive.

Bit-level Recovery

A fascinating approach to disk maintenance and repair is offered in *Disk Technician* from Prime Solutions. While most recovery programs operate byte by byte, ignoring the formatting information between sectors, this elaborate program tests the disk bit by bit. The process can be very time consuming. During a first pass, the program minutely examines the integrity of every magnetic domain. When a soft error occurs, it makes a note of it in a *history file* it keeps on the disk. Thereafter, the program is to be executed every day when the system is booted. As problems arise, the program notices them and compares them to the prior state of the disk. The manufacturer claims that using artificial intelligence techniques, the program can spot the gradual development of serious mechanical defects. When it does so, it issues the message: "Call Your Computer Hardware Service Repair Technician."

Taking the trouble to run such a program comes as close as you can to "maintaining" a hard disk. When format markings decay, the program lifts all data on the track into memory, reformats the single track, and then rewrites the data. If "marginal bytes" produce

Testing as maintenance

too many soft errors, it relocates data held in the corresponding sector and marks the sector off bounds. The program does its best to repair damaged files, and when it fails, it reports which files must be restored from backups.

All this doesn't come without a little care. There are daily tests, weekly tests, and monthly tests. On a 20-megabyte disk in an AT, these require 1 to 20 minutes, 10 minutes to 3 hours, and 40 minutes to 22 hours, respectively. The longer tests write on the disk and read back. The tests are restricted to DOS partitions, and they must be within the 32-megabyte limit.

Head Seek Tests

Some disk test programs perform head seek tests. These ensure that the read/write heads move accurately between tracks, no matter the pattern of movement. Many utilities that check the integrity of the disk surface simply step the heads track by track across the surface. This approach may be too tame. A track that is barely readable under such tranquil conditions may be completely unreadable when the heads fly back and forth across the disk surface.

Head seek tests are usually hidden inside general-purpose diagnostics. The disk-installation utility *SpeedStor*, which we discussed in Chapter 4, includes a worst case "butterfly" test in its *HARD-PREP* program. The *HTEST* program in the advanced edition of the *Mace Utilities* includes "accordion" and "stagger" tests. The names of these tests give some idea of their vigor. They ensure that tracking is uniform throughout the range of motions. Such tests may provide an early-warning signal for hardware failure.

Recovering Damaged Files

Most "file recovery" programs are designed to piece together what remains of a file after one or more sectors go bad or are somehow damaged. Generally, one turns to such a program when application software refuses to load a file, or crashes when it does. Often the program is split into a *test* portion and a *recovery* portion. Sometimes the two portions are broken into separate programs, one of which just looks and reports, one of which looks and corrects.

Most mainframe computers constantly watch their hard disks for new bad sectors. Perhaps such utilities will arise for IBM microcomputers as OS/2 spreads. Until then, one does well to regularly survey the disk for damage. When many bad sectors arise, it's a sure warning that you are about to encounter a serious failure.

DOS includes the *RECOVER* program for this purpose. Like most such utilities, *RECOVER* can operate on one specified file, or it can scan the whole disk. It does not work very well in the latter role, and you'll want to use it only for individual files. This job is done simply by naming the file on the command line, as in **RECOVER MYFILE.DOC**. Wildcards are accepted in the filename.

When loaded without a filename, *RECOVER* automatically works on every file in the current directory. Whether or not a file is damaged, it renames it in the format **FILE0001.REC, FILE0002.REC**, and so on. When a file contains a bad sector, it is broken in two, with each part placed in its own file. The result is a complete mess; be very careful.

The *RECOVER* command gives you no control over file recovery. You can either take it or leave it. Most other utilities are more flexible. For example, in the *Disk Test* program of the *Norton Utilities*, you can test either files or the entire disk for damage, can automatically scan subdirectories, can have files moved away from borderline sectors, and can have the entire process logged. Groups of files may be tested using wildcards. Thus, you could check the integrity of every *Lotus 1-2-3* file on the disk simply by entering **DT *WKS**.

Unlike *RECOVER*, a utility like *Disk Test* doesn't break a damaged file into pieces, and it does not rename it. Rather, it marks the bad sector off-bounds and inserts a new sector into the file as a replacement. Because a "bad sector" may still occasionally be readable, many attempts are made to recapture the data and transfer it to the replacement sector. When the data cannot be recovered, the new sector is arbitrarily filled with a character, such as an asterisk. These characters don't interfere with text files. But many other kinds of data files may be rendered useless. When program files are recovered this way, they will crash when run. Hence, "file recovery" isn't a sure thing, and owning a good recovery utility is no substitute for frequent backups.

The RECOVER command

Alternative utilities

Orphaned Clusters

Orphaned clusters are clusters that appear to be occupied by a file, but aren't linked to any file listed in a directory. In Chapter 2 we described how each position in the file allocation table gives the number of the next cluster in a file, and that cluster's corresponding position in the FAT gives the number of the next cluster still. Special codes are inserted in the table when the cluster is free or when it is marked off-bounds because of media damage.

CHKDSK

When you run *CHKDSK*, DOS traces every file through the FAT, keeping track of which clusters are occupied. Then it checks all remaining FAT positions to see that they are either free or discarded. When *CHKDSK* finds clusters that are marked as belonging to a file, but in fact don't, it announces "xx lost clusters in xx chains—convert to files?" If you answer "Yes," *CHKDSK* places the clusters into files in the root directory, using the names **FILE0000.CHK**, **FILE0001.CHK**, and so on. *CHKDSK* automatically makes these files when you call *CHKDSK* using the /**F** switch: **CHKDSK /F**.

How orphaned
clusters originate

Orphaned clusters are often linked into chains, where one orphaned cluster points to another, which in turn points to another. This is the case because orphaned clusters are nearly always parts of files that have fallen apart. Most originate when software is abruptly terminated while it is in the midst of file operations. Sometimes this happens because of a power outage, but more often it results when a novice user employs Ctrl-Alt-Del as a panic button. In file operations, DOS fills in directory entries last. When the machine reboots between the time the file is mapped in the FAT and the time it is listed in the directory, the clusters are orphaned.

When *CHKDSK* retrieves orphaned clusters, it places them in files that have no date or time stamp. A directory listing gives a file size, but, in fact, DOS cannot know exactly where in the clusters the data ends, so the value is only approximate. Generally, the data you'll find in recovered clusters is useless. Often it comes from temporary work files set up by your software; these files are normally erased when the program terminates. After visually inspecting the files, you can delete them all by entering **DEL FILE*.CHK**.

Using orphaned
clusters

Occasionally you'll want to keep the orphaned clusters. It sometimes happens that a work file mysteriously disappears after it is loaded and a power outage suddenly occurs. The file will continue to be listed in the directory, but with a file size of 0 bytes. What has happened is that DOS has prepared to rewrite the entire file, and it has temporarily set the file size to 0 until it has finished writing it. This is the time to run *CHKDSK* and recover the orphaned clusters best you can. Text data may be easily recovered this way, since you can easily rename the files *CHKDSK* creates and load them into a word processor. But when the file is full of binary gibberish, it may be impossible to reconstitute a usable file. Orphaned clusters may also be used to rebuild *cross-linked files*, our next topic.

Cross-linked Files

Sometimes an error creeps into the file allocation table and two files become *cross-linked*. Consider two files that each stretch across five clusters. The first might cover clusters 101 through 105, and second, clusters 201 to 205. Now, say that somehow an error is made when the file allocation table is written (perhaps because of an electrical transient), and the third cluster of the first file is recorded as 203 instead of 103. When DOS reads the file, it will load sectors 101, 102, 203, 204, and 205. The chains of FAT entries that track the files have become *cross-linked*, and clusters 103 through 105 have become orphaned clusters. Figure 9-3 diagrams this phenomenon. Only the first file is damaged in this case. The FAT entries for the second file continue to point from clusters 201 to 205. Incidentally, there are rare occasions when a file becomes cross linked to itself. In the worst case, the linkage forms a loop, and *total* confusion results.

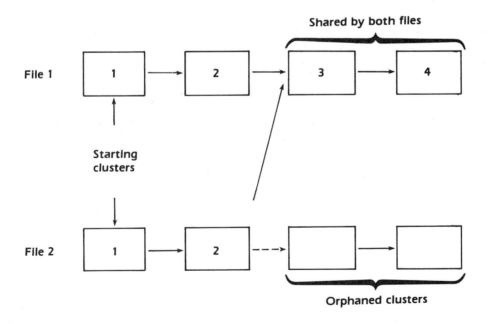

Figure 9-3 **Cross-linked files**

The DOS *CHKDSK* command can detect cross-linked files, but cannot do anything about them. DOS has no way of knowing which file is damaged, because it has no knowledge of the files contents. Besides, repairing the damaged file entails finding the orphaned clusters that belong to it. When more than one string of orphaned clusters is found, DOS wouldn't know which to reattach to the damaged file.

Fixing the files

Although DOS is helpless in this regard, you can sometimes solve the problem quite easily. First, you must inspect the two files to see which is damaged. If it is a data file, load it into the application software and see that everything is all right. Often, when the file is damaged, the software refuses to load it or it crashes when it loads, and you'll have to reboot the machine. A cross-linked text file may suddenly change topic as it shifts into the contents of the second file; or the latter part of the file may be nothing but gobbledygook.

Once you've decided which file is the damaged one, you have several tasks. You must reclaim the orphaned clusters, perform surgery on the damaged file, and then reconnect the orphaned clusters to the end of the file. Generally, this process can be performed only for text files. Surgery on most other kinds of data files requires technical sophistication and an insider's knowledge of the file structure.

Text files

To recover a cross-linked text file, make copies of both files involved, and operate upon these copies. Erase the originals. This action makes each file independent of the other in the file allocation table. Load the damaged file into your word processor. The file may have been cross-linked to a file that contains characters that confuse your word processor. You may have to try a variety of editors before you find one that can load the program. Often, the simplest editors, such as *notepad* editors, are the most accepting. Then delete the unwanted part of the file. Next, run *CHKDSK* to organize the orphaned clusters into files, and look through the files using the DOS TYPE command. Finally, combine the two files using the COPY command. Say that the damaged file is named **GOODBYE.TXT**, and *CHKDSK* has named the orphaned clusters **FILE0003.CHK**. The files are combined by entering:

```
COPY GOODBYE.TXT+FILE0003.CHK GOODBYE.TXT
```

If you truncate **GOODBYE.TXT** just right, the original file will be exactly reconstituted. Otherwise, you may have to do a little surgery at the junction between the two files using your word processor. Figure 9-4 diagrams the procedure.

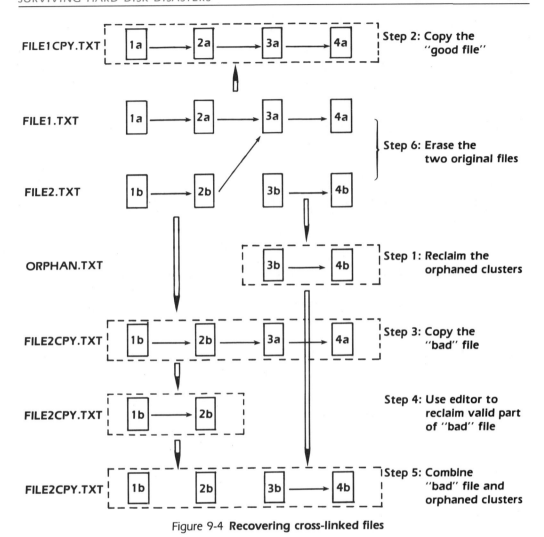

Figure 9-4 **Recovering cross-linked files**

Recovering Damaged Boot Records, Directories, and FATs

If you've read Chapter 2 closely, you'll understand that the worst place a disk can sustain damage is on the master boot record, directories, or file allocation tables. When the partition table in the master boot record is harmed, there's no way for the computer (the fixed-disk BIOS) to find its way to the beginning of the DOS partition (the "Invalid drive specification" message results). A damaged DOS boot record is less serious—it merely prevents you from booting from the hard disk, but you can still use it after booting from drive A. Damage to directories means the loss of filenames and starting clusters and possibly the loss of a chain of subdirectories.

Damaged FATs

Finally, damage to file allocation tables means that DOS can't find most of the clusters that make up a file. You may recall that the FAT is so precious to DOS that it keeps a second copy, and updates both copies every time a change is made. When one copy is damaged so that a sector cannot be read, DOS uses the second, and tries to copy it over the first. But *logical* damage can be done to FATs. In this case, the FAT sectors are readable, but the numbers they contain are scrambled. As with damaged directories, many files may be lost.

Making repairs

What can you do? One solution is to keep an unformat utility installed in the machine. When DOS structures on cylinder 0 are damaged, you can treat the disk as if it had been reformatted. The recovery program will replace the damaged structures. Of course, you'll encounter the usual problem of dealing with changes on the disk that have occurred since the format program last took a "snapshot."

A similar solution is open to you when subdirectories are damaged. When DOS cannot read the subdirectory and valuable files are gone, consider running the program in the *Mace Utilities* that attempts to recover from an accidental formatting without the benefit of a copy of cylinder 0. This program attempts to piece together subdirectories and can deal with damaged sectors in subdirectories. This solution is hardly ideal, but it may be better than nothing. Be sure to back up the disk thoroughly before trying it.

Performing Microsurgery on the Disk

When standard disk-recovery utilities won't do the job, the only remaining option is to perform microsurgery directly upon the surface of the disk. For example, if a subdirectory is damaged, you can trace its location through the root directory and other subdirectories, read individual sectors from it, make changes, and then rewrite the sectors to disk. It's not very hard getting at the disk. The problem lies in making sense of the data held in the disk sectors. Obviously, this approach is open only to the knowledgeable and the patient.

Traditionally, hackers have used *debuggers* to modify disk sectors. DOS includes the DEBUG program for this purpose. Debuggers present the contents of a disk sector as a series of 512 numbers—one for every byte. To double the confusion, the numbers are often presented in *hexadecimal* form (base-16 numbers). Sometimes the equivalent ASCII character is displayed, but these are mostly odd symbols and graphics characters.

Debuggers

To make matters easier, software houses have devised utilities specialized for viewing particular DOS structures on the disk. These include partition table editors, FAT editors, and directory editors. Such tools go straight to the desired structures and present them on the screen in an easily understood format. For example, the four-byte *file size* is represented as a decimal number; you can edit the number as easily as if it were in a spreadsheet, and then write it back to the disk. A tremendous amount of work is saved by having a utility make such conversions automatically. In older DOS versions, each FAT entry took up a byte and a half. Using a conventional debugger, it took a lot of work to calculate one cluster number. With a FAT editor, the work is done for you.

Disk toolkits

You'll find disk toolkits advertised in technical magazines. Some, like *Disk Mechanic* from MLI Microsystems, can deal with non-standard floppy disk formats, including fancy copy-protection schemes. Another is *Disk ToolKit* from Morgan Computing, which includes a full-screen FAT editor. The *Norton Utilities* offers a complete disk surveillance program. You can explore and edit any area of the disk. When a sector is displayed, you may specify whether it is to be displayed as hexadecimal numbers, as ASCII characters, as directory entries, as FAT entries, or as partition table data. It can approach the disk either through the directory tree (showing a file's clusters) or by absolute sector numbers (side 3, track 231, sector 5). No matter how information is displayed, it can be overwritten on the screen, and the new values are written to the disk.

As all else in life, when it comes to hard disk disasters, you must never say, "it can't get any worse." Even a thoroughly discombobulated disk can be made worse by a disk toolkit. If you have a tape backup unit available, make an image backup before starting work. Go slow. And be especially careful of the partition table because the most horrendous event of all is to lose track of the beginning and end of the DOS partition.

Dangers

One final bit of advice. As you work, stop every ten minutes. Breathe a deep sigh. Then think about how much more pleasant life would be if only you would keep decent backups.

Guarding against Hard Disk Disasters

You can do much to avoid hard disk disasters. Earlier in this chapter, we looked at utilities that keep an eye on soft error rates to warn you about incipient problems. We also saw how "unformat" programs regularly take a "snapshot" of crucial DOS information as a precaution against accidental reformatting. In Chapter 5, we discussed a number of techniques for protecting your files from inadvertent erasures and formattings. And in Chapter 7 we presented a number of optimization techniques that reduce the movement of the read/write heads, lengthening the disk's life.

These precautions guard against operator error and equipment failure. Alas, there is more to the demonology of hard disks. In this section, we'll look at some other important hazards and what you can do about them.

Locating the Machine

You can do much to protect your hard disk just by putting the computer where it won't be knocked about. The machine should rest on a sturdy table or desk. The more massive the furniture, the better it can absorb shocks rather than pass them onto the hard disk. Tables pose particular risks, since they are apt to sway when nudged. If the movement is toward an adjacent wall, a collision could send a shock wave back toward the machine. In this situation, always buttress the table firmly against the wall.

Vibrations

Never place impact printers on the same surface as the computer. In particular, daisy-wheel printers send out fearsome vibrations. Although these disturbances won't by themselves overwhelm a hard disk, they contribute to the general seismic climate and help to push both hard disk drives and floppy drives out of alignment.

Ventilation

Position the machine in a way that avoids heat buildup—the foremost cause of erratic hard disk failures. Avoid pushing the machine flush against a wall, blocking the rear ventilating fans. And try not to place the machine in the outflow of the room heating system. If the machine must be used in a sweltering environment, consider implementing some of the heat-reduction techniques discussed later.

Sideways
installation

Be especially careful about standing the machine upright on its side using one of the special floor stands designed to support it. This approach is wonderful for freeing desk space, but it leaves the machine out of the line of sight, making it easy to kick or bump. Perhaps the worst danger is a heavy office chair careening into a free-standing system unit. Be aware that some hard disk drives aren't designed to operate on their sides (or even upside down). It's a good idea to check with the manufacturer.

Finally, the most important measure of all is to thoroughly edu- cate the people who will be around the computer about the dam- age caused by physical shocks. While the system manager's usual problem is getting people to *not* be afraid of computers, here is an exception. When a desk or table supports a computer, one does not sit on it, lolling one's legs; one doesn't drop piles of law books onto it and one doesn't shove aside the machine to make room for something else. Offices that fail to instruct every new employee in these matters can lose a $1,000 piece of hardware (and $100,000 of data!) in a fraction of a second.

Educating others

Power-line Protection

Power-line interruptions can damage data in several ways. Most ob- viously, work that hasn't yet been saved may be lost when the power goes out. This is the *least* serious outcome. When power goes out while the file is written, a prior version of the file stored on the disk may be lost along with the version in memory. This happens with text files or other *sequential files*, which are com- pletely rewritten to disk when they are saved. In *random-access files*, where only a small part of the file is written each time, dam- age may be limited to one record (however, if power goes out while critical index tables are written, a whole database may be un- dermined, even though most of the data remains intact).

Power-line disturbances create their greatest damage when they occur as the disk writes to the DOS system area on cylinder 0. DOS cannot deal with a damaged root directory, which means that all your data is stranded. Voltage spikes that barge through a disk drive's protective circuitry may spray magnetism down at the disk surface, damaging format markings as well as data. Again, DOS can- not recover from the resulting error.

There are three levels of protection against power-line interrup- tions. At the lowest level, you may add a power-line filter that "clamps" high-speed, high-voltage transients. This service is per- formed by the familiar **surge protectors** that most machines are equipped with. Contrary to what many will tell you, not all are the same. Surge protectors have two tasks—to "grab" a spike and to

Surge protectors

diffuse it. The best designs combine devices called *metal-oxide varistors* and *avalanche diodes* to respond to spikes within billionths of a second, and a *gas discharge tube* to diffuse the excess power. When you buy one, be sure that it is UL (Underwriter's Laboratory) tested, and that its specifications allow for a clamping level of at least 50 to 100 joules; ideally it will meet the IEEE-587 standard. (Sorry to throw gobbledygook at you about this, but there's no simple explanation.)

Voltage regulators

The next level of protection comes through **voltage regulators** and **line protectors**. Besides intercepting voltage spikes, these constantly filter and regulate power to supply optimal, "noise-free" electricity to your machine. They are much more expensive than surge protectors, and you must take care to buy one large enough to meet your current and future needs. This entails adding up the total wattage of all your components, or simply buying one with as great a capacity as your computer's power supply. Ratings are often given in *amps*, which may be multiplied by the usual 110-volt line current to obtain the equivalent wattage (for example, 2.0 amps multiplied by 110 volts equals 220 watts). Add at least 10% extra capacity for the startup ("inrush") current.

Standby power supplies

Finally, the ultimate in power-line protection is afforded by a **standby power supply** (SPS) or an **uninterrupted power supply** (UPS). In addition to voltage regulation, these provide battery backup that takes over when power is lost. Standby units quickly switch over to battery power—they have less than 15 milliseconds to do so—while the more expensive UPS units always supply power through the batteries (which are constantly recharged). This equipment costs several hundred dollars. The backup power lasts from about five minutes to a few hours, depending on the supply and your system's power requirements. Five minutes may not sound very long, but it's plenty of time to save your work and turn off the machine. Most come with an alarm that rings when the power goes off.

Guarding against Theft

An all-too-common way of losing all one's data is by having the computer stolen. Used floppies or tape cartridges aren't usually a thief's target, so your backups ought to be safe. But a tape backup unit will surely disappear along with the computer, and if the cartridge holding the recent backups is inside the unit well, you know the rest.

Several companies make devices that can make it very difficult to steal a PC without doing considerable damage to it. The Anchor Pad Company makes *anchor pads*, large plates that fit between the computer and the desk it rests on and between the monitor and the top of the computer case. They use adhesive mats that cling to the equipment using 6,000 pounds of force. Similar devices are made to hold down printers. Also, some computer furniture has been designed so that you can easily lock away the machine and peripherals.

Anchoring equipment

The next line of defense is to stop someone from opening the cabinet and stealing the drive. It is, after all, much easier to leave a guarded building with a drive and a few adapter cards than to exit carrying an AT and monitor. Qualtec Systems makes *PC-LOK*, which makes it impossible to take the cover off a computer without the proper key. IBM ATs already have a lock, of course, although it's been reported that you can get into a locked AT using a crowbar and a lot of brawn. To stop people from booting the system, the same company makes *FILE-LOK*, a device that locks into the front of a floppy disk drive.

Finally, some drives are specially designed for daily removal. When you're done with work, you can lock it away. Perhaps more important, you can transport the drive to another computer and start up work just as you left it. Sysdyne makes a portable hard drive that uses a special "docking port" installed either outside the system or as an internal half-height drive. Microcomputer Memories Inc. makes the *Transpc* hard disk card that's specialized for constant removal and transport; it even comes with a soft carrying case. Of course, if you're going to consider removing the media, one of the removable cartridge drives discussed in Chapter 3 may be just the candidate.

Removable drives

Don't overlook the possibility of the *intentional* destruction of data. A disgruntled employee (or ex-employee) may take revenge in a big way. Little knowledge is required to enter **FORMAT C:**. And your *unformat* program will offer no protection if the perpetrator knows enough to erase the utility's special "snap shot" file before firing up the format program. Even if you have an elaborate security system in place, it may be possible for a well-informed employee (one who has read this book, for example) to run a low-level format program from drive A to decimate every sector on the hard disk. A person inclined to commit these crimes may be all the more encouraged by the knowledge that it will be next to impossible to prove that he or she is the culprit.

If this calamity ever happens to you, you can be sure that your first thought will be, "the backups! where are the backups?" There's much to be said for locking away backups—at least the monthly global backup that we discussed in Chapter 8. Locking away both low- and high-level formatting programs is also a good idea.

Worms and Trojan horses

If you're the only person having access to a machine, you may feel that vandalism is of no concern. But no treatment of hard disk disasters is complete without a discussion of **worms, Trojan horses**, and other pathological designs. These are bits of code inserted into software which, at an appointed moment, attack your hard disk and erase everything in sight. Such programs are created by adolescents, or adults with adolescent minds, whose particular brand of moral imbecility leaves them unable to feel guilty about destroying something so abstract as thousands and thousands of hours of labor.

Worms are generally found in mainframe computers that are never turned off. The software migrates around the system like a worm, hiding itself here and there. *Trojan horses* are nested inside an application program, where they may sit quietly for months until one day something activates the destructive code. Trojan horses are a threat to many people because they may be placed inside public domain software.

A highly respected shareware word processor was the victim of such an intrusion. Someone quietly downloaded the program from an electronic bulletin board and inserted destructive code in a seldom-used section of the program. The program was then uploaded to the bulletin board. Thereafter, dozens of people downloaded the altered copy and happily used it until suddenly the hidden demon awoke and erased their hard disks.

Happily, such intrusions are extremely rare. There's no reason to lie awake at night worrying about them. But you should know about such things. Because much public domain software is very poorly programmed, you ought to keep especially thorough backups in any case.

Repairs

If faulty, most computer equipment fails within the first 90 days. Thereafter, you're likely to have two or three years of carefree service before decrepitude slowly sets in. As they gain experience, manufacturers are making equipment more and more reliable. Unfortunately, two trends work in the opposite direction. The technology changes so rapidly that experience quickly becomes obsolete. And the cutthroat competition at the low end of the computer market has tempted many manufacturers to create products that aren't nearly so good as they might be. It often pays to buy quality. Repairs tend to be very expensive, and a single trip to the shop may cost you more than you saved by bargain-hunting. When a mechanical failure damages your data, the cost may be far greater still.

Before turning to the ins and outs of repair services, let's look at what you can do on your own.

Dealing with Sporadic Failures

Sporadic failures are the most exasperating of all hard disk problems. Suddenly the computer "locks up"—the screen freezes, the keyboard refuses all keystrokes (even Ctrl-Alt-Del), and floppy disk drives go on spinning. Sometimes, turning off the machine and then starting it up immediately sets everything right; then you can pick up the pieces and continue your work. Often, the machine won't run again until some hours later. In either case, you can expect the machine to crash again, perhaps in an hour, perhaps in a month.

Erratic failures are especially vexing because you cannot be sure   *Analysis*
what part of the machine caused the crash. When your system suffers a complete hard disk failure, you need only disconnect the drive, reconfigure the machine, and reboot to see if the machine works fine without it. But when the problem is erratic, you have no way of knowing whether the faulty component has been removed from the machine or whether the next failure just hasn't arrived yet.

Such occurrences are a surprise in a *digital* computer, where things tend to work either completely or not at all. There are two very common culprits—heat and power insufficiency—and you should consider whether they are responsible for your problems before seeking professional help.

Heat is everybody's business. Like the oil in an automobile, it is   *Overheating*
one of the very few aspects of a complicated device that anyone can easily comprehend and look after. Every time you add another board or disk drive to your machine, you should make a mental note that you have changed the heat load in the machine. Months

later, when your machine abruptly crashes on a mid-August afternoon, one of the first questions you should ask is, "too hot at last?"

Heat interferes with hard disks when some parts expand more than others, throwing off the alignment between disk and read/write heads. No permanent damage is done to the drive, although data may be destroyed if the heads are writing when the drive fails. Turning off the machine and waiting for a half hour or so is usually enough to return the machine to working order—for awhile. Unless the machine is suffering through atypically hot weather, you'll need to add some cooling to the machine. We explained how to do this in Chapter 4. Remember that *you must not leave openings in the back of the machine*. When you fail to replace a plate after removing a card from a slot, you are undermining the machine's cooling system.

Insufficient power

Another cause of sporadic failures is insufficient power. This topic was also covered in Chapter 4, so we won't dwell on it here. However, we want to reiterate that a *barely sufficient* power supply may become *insufficient* in hot weather. Higher temperatures raise the resistance of all electrical circuits, so slightly more power is required to run the machine. Power insufficiency is generally only a problem on standard IBM PCs, which have a meager 63.5-watt supply (most PC clones have more). When sporadic system crashes may be attributable to *either* the power supply or to an overheated disk, diagnosis is difficult. If you remove the drive to see if the machine works all right without it, you're also unburdening the power supply. Try running the machine with the cover off, directing the flow of a small room fan into the cabinet. If the machine doesn't crash, you'll know that added cooling will probably solve your problems.

Getting the drive started

When the drive has suffered a crisis of some kind, it often refuses to respond to DOS. An "Invalid Drive Specification" error message may result. Sometimes you can get it going one last time by turning the drive in various orientations. There's value in this because you may need to make last minute backups, and you may be able to park the heads before sending the drive to a repair service.

Open the machine and carefully remove the drive, leaving the cables connected (or remove it and reattach the cables). Place a book or magazine on top of the power supply and place the drive on it. Absolutely do not let any part of the drive electronics touch any part of the machine or any conducting surface. Next, place the DOS diskette in drive A and boot from it. Then try for a directory reading from drive C (**DIR C:**). No good? Keep trying, holding the drive in various orientations. Be ready with your backup software for the moment the drive comes through. Be very careful of vibrations once you get it going.

Many people respond to erratic hard disk failures by pretending that they haven't occurred. It is *so* much easier to hope that the machine crashed because of an errant cosmic ray than to acknowledge that you have a serious problem on your hands, one that could take up a lot of your time and energy. There's no joy in the prospect of running the computer from floppy disks while the hard disk is away at the repair shop. Sorry. You can have the tooth fixed now, or you can have it pulled later. It's time for a trip to the dentist.

Facing the music

Kinds of Repairs

Although head crashes are widely feared, they actually occur very rarely. Disk repair services report that only about 1% of their business comes from repairing crashed heads (in fact, they more frequently receive drives that have been intentionally opened by curious users!). This is good news. When your drive will run no more, most likely it has failed in a way that can be repaired without loss of data.

After all our talk about spinning cylinders and flying heads, it may surprise you to hear that most drive failures are electronic. One of the chips or other components mounted on the outside of the drive gives up the ghost. This means that the drive can be repaired without opening it up. If you've kept an eye on the disk, testing it periodically for incipient problems, it's unlikely that the faulty components damaged much data before.

Electronic failures

When the drive mechanics have failed, repair is more serious. The repair service must be equipped with a **clean room**. The drive is meticulously cleaned before it is passed into the room, and employees dress with face masks and caps. Various parts may be replaced, including a platter scratched by a serious head crash. Repair services report that it's not always easy to get replacement parts for drives, and that often they are stripped from "rejects." They tend to consider some of the cheaper drives as "throwaway" drives—it makes more sense to buy a new one than to repair it.

Mechanical failures

When you take a drive in for repair, the service may ask whether you want the data on the drive saved or not. If so, they'll do their best to keep it intact. They are unlikely to be able to do any more for your data than can the utilities discussed in this chapter. For them, "saving data" means that they won't reformat the drive which

Data preservation

means that they won't be able to test it very thoroughly. The usual 90-day warranty on repairs may be waived when data is "saved." Incidentally, when the servo markings on the platters of voice-coil drives have been damaged, they can usually be remedied only by the manufacturer.

Repair charges

Because most repairs are electrical and do not require opening the drive, the average repair takes only about half an hour. The base price for the repair usually runs from $80 to $100. To this basic fee, a charge may be added for every megabyte of drive capacity—typically $1. This may seem like a soak-the-rich scheme, but it actually reflects the time required to format and test the drive.

Deciding on a Repair Service

Services that specialize in hard-disk-drive repair have sprung up in large metropolitan areas. If one of these shops is near you, take your drive straight to it. The base charge may be a little higher than that at a general-purpose repair service, but it's much more likely that the repairs will be made within cost overruns. General repair shops often must forward damaged drives to one of these services in any case, since they haven't a clean room (or the expertise) to do the job themselves. They'll bill you generously for this delay.

Locating a repair service

You can find out about specialty repairs in the yellow pages—if one is nearby. Otherwise, you'll need to hunt around. Ads often appear in computer magazines. Or try asking around an electronic bulletin board, or contact a local user's group. We've included the names of two Silicon Valley specialty repair services in our appendix of manufacturers' names and addresses.

Of course, if the drive is under warranty, you won't have any choice about where it goes for repair. You may have no say about saving the data in this case. Rather than blindly return the drive to the vendor, find out where it is going and see if you can't save time by sending it directly to the manufacturer or repair service.

If you can't drive to the service, try to send the drive through the gentlest form of conveyance you can find. Be sure to repack it in its original container (you *did* set it aside as we advised, didn't you?). And try to park the heads before shipment. Drives that won't work in any other respect will sometimes obey the *SHIPDISK* program.

Afterword

If you've stayed with us from cover to cover, congratulations! You're now in a position to understand just about anything you'll encounter concerning hard disks. In the introduction we explained that your hard disk is the control center of your machine. You may have found this claim a bit hyperbolic, but by now you ought to understand why it is so—or why it *should* be so.

We hope you'll put what we've taught you to work. The first priority is a backup system. Then get the tree organized and do a thorough housecleaning. Install some productivity tools for zipping around the disk and automating tasks that you've performed hundreds (even thousands) of times by hand. Then turn your attention to optimizing disk performance; minimally, install a defragmentation utility and take a serious look at caching. Finally, get into the habit of running a disk diagnostic tool periodically. If you'll follow the most important rules we've taught you about disk backup and maintenance, you are almost certain to avoid a catastrophic failure, and you'll never lose more than a few hours work (even when others are doing their best to lose it for you).

We'd like to propose that you set an immodest goal for yourself: that you strive to increase the speed of the average disk access in your machine by 500%. By this, we mean the time it takes to load a program or file, to make a backup, or to copy or move around files, measuring the event from the first keystroke you make to initiate it, to the moment the disk drive stops blinking. You certainly have the knowledge to do this now, and in many cases a 1,000% improvement is in store. Make it a game. You can only win.

Glossary

8088   The microprocessor in the IBM PC, XT, and compatibles.

80286   The microprocessor in the IBM AT and compatibles.

80386   The microprocessor in the IBM PS/2 model 80 and various high-speed AT compatibles.

A

accelerator board   An add-in board that replaces the computer's CPU with a faster model.

actuator   The device that moves a disk drive's read/write heads across the platter surfaces.

APPEND   A DOS command that causes DOS to seek data files and program files in other directories when the file isn't found in the current directory.

archive attribute   A setting in a file's attribute byte that tells whether the file has been changed since it was last backed up.

archive bit   The bit in a file's attribute byte that sets the archive attribute.

archive medium   A storage medium—floppy disk, tape cartridge, removable cartridge—that holds files kept as records but that need not be instantly accessible from a hard disk.

ASCII character   A one-byte character from the ASCII character set, including alphabetic and numeric characters, punctuation symbols, and various graphic characters.

ASSIGN   A DOS command that can assign a different drive specifier to a disk drive.

ATTRIB   A DOS command that can read and set file attributes.

attribute byte   A byte of information, held in the directory entry of any file, that describes various attributes of the file, such as whether it is a read-only file or has been backed up since it was last changed.

AUTOEXEC.BAT   A file read by DOS when the machine is booted. It contains any number of DOS commands which are automatically executed.

automatic data compression   A technique in which data is automatically compressed and decompressed as files are written and read from disk.

automatic head parking   Head parking performed automatically whenever the machine is turned off.

average latency   The average time required for any byte of data to rotate to a read/write head—one half rotation of a platter.

average seek time   The average time required for a disk drive's read/write heads to move from one track to another.

B

background backup   A hard disk backup that proceeds *in the background* as the computer is simultaneously used for other purposes.

bad sector   A disk sector that cannot reliably hold data because of a media flaw or damaged format markings.

bad track table   A label affixed to the casing of a hard disk drive that tells which tracks are flawed and cannot hold data. The listing is entered into the low-level formatting program.

bare drive   A disk drive sold without a controller card.

batch file   A file that contains a series of commands that DOS executes when the file is called. All batch files have a *.BAT* extension.

bay   An opening in the computer cabinet that holds disk drives.

Bernoulli Box   A removable-cartridge, semi-floppy disk drive made by Iomega Corporation.

Bernoulli principle   A physical principle that causes a floppy disk to become rigid like a hard disk, making possible higher data densities.

bezel   A plastic panel that extends the face of a half-height drive so that it covers a full-height drive bay.

BIOS   The "Basic Input-Output System" that is the part of the computer's operating system built into the machine on read-only memory (ROM) chips.

bit   One of the eight On/Off settings that make up a byte of data.

blank   An aluminum disk coated or plated to make a hard disk platter.

block   In tape backup, a "block" is a number of sectors written in succession and followed by various identifiers and error-correction codes.

block-line memory   A highly advanced form of memory storage, still in the laboratory, which allows extremely high data densities.

boot record   A one-sector record that tells the computer's inbuilt operating system (BIOS) the most fundamental facts about a disk and DOS. The information it supplies lets the computer load COMMAND.COM into memory, thus booting the machine.

boot security   The ability of security software to circumvent a break-in made by re-booting the machine from a floppy disk (so that the security software isn't loaded).

bpi   Bits per inch. A measure of data density along a track.

bubble memory   A special form of high-density, relatively slow memory chip that continues to hold data after power is removed.

buffer   A temporary storage area for data passing from one point in a computer system to another. Most buffers are created in system memory.

byte   The basic unit of computer memory, large enough to hold one character of alphabetic data.

C

caching   See *sector caching* and *memory caching*.

CD-I   "Compact Disk—Interactive." A special laser disk standard, devised by Sony and Philips, which combines program code, data, photographic stills, moving video, and sound on a compact disk.

CD ROM   "Compact Disk Read-Only Memory." A compact disk that holds reference materials, such as a dictionary or business statistics.

central processing unit   The microprocessor chip that performs the bulk of data processing in a computer.

certification utility   Utility software that certifies that a tape or disk cartridge is free of flaws.

CHDIR   Change Directory—the DOS command that changes the current directory.

child directory   A subdirectory that is named by a particular directory. In *MAMMALS/PRIMATES/APES, APES* is a child of *PRIMATES*, and *PRIMATES* is a child of *MAMMALS*.

CHKDSK   A DOS program that analyzes disk directories and file allocation tables for errors.

clean room   A dust-free repair facility in which hard disk drives can be opened for servicing.

cluster   A group of one or more sectors that is the basic unit in which DOS allocated disk space. The number of sectors in a cluster varies by disk type and DOS version.

CMOS chip   The battery-powered memory chip in ATs that holds the clock setting and system configuration information.

coated media   Hard disk platters coated with a reddish iron-oxide medium upon which data is recorded.

COMMAND.COM   The main operating system file, which is loaded last when the computer is booted and remains in memory throughout the time the machine is in operation.

CONFIG.SYS   A file that may be created to tell DOS how to configure itself when the machine starts up. CONFIG.SYS can load device drivers, set the number of DOS buffers, and so on.

configuration file   A file kept by application software to record various aspects of the software's configuration, such as the printer it uses.

control cable   The wider of two cables that connects a hard disk drive to a controller card.

controller   The electronics that control a hard disk drive and intermediate the passage of data between the drive and the computer.

controller card   An adapter holding the control electronics for one or more hard disks. Ordinarily, it takes up one of the computer's slots.

CPU   See *central processing unit*.

CPU speed See *processor speed*.

crash A malfunction that brings work to a halt. A *system crash* is usually caused by a software malfunction, and it can ordinarily be remedied by rebooting the machine. However, a *head crash* or *disk crash* entails physical damage to the disk, and probable data loss.

CRC See *cyclic redundancy check*.

cross-linked files Files that have come to share disk sectors as the result of an error in the file allocation table.

current directory The directory DOS directs its operations to *by default* unless some other directory is specified.

cyclic redundancy check An error-checking system in which the pattern of a sequence of data is analyzed and represented as a number. The number may be recorded beside each sector on disk or each data block on tape. When the data is subsequently read back, the calculation is repeated and the result compared to the one derived when the data was first written.

cylinder The group of all tracks located at a given head position.

cylinder 0 The outermost cylinder on a disk. It holds the root directory, file allocation tables, and other critical DOS structures.

cylinder density The number of sectors held by a cylinder. It is the measure of the maximum amount of data that can be recorded at any one head position.

D

data cable The narrower of two cables that connects a hard disk drive to a controller card.

data compression A group of techniques whereby data is compressed into smaller files on a disk.

data density The density at which data is recorded along a track, usually expressed as "bits per inch."

data-transfer rate The maximum rate at which data can be transferred from the disk surface to system memory. It cannot be greater than the rate at which data passes beneath a read/write head.

DC600A The standard quarter-inch tape cartridge.

deallocated cluster   A cluster of disk space marked in the file allocation table as "available" after the file that used it has been erased.

dedicated servo surface   In multiplatter voice-coil drives, a dedicated servo surface is a whole platter side given over to *servo data* that is used to fine-position the read/write heads.

defragmentation   See *file defragmentation*.

defragmenter   A software utility that defragments files.

DEVICE   A DOS command (placed in CONFIG.SYS) that causes DOS to load a device driver into memory.

device driver   A memory-resident program, loaded by CONFIG.SYS, that controls an unusual device, such as a plotter or expanded memory board.

dip switch   A tiny switch (or group of switches) found on a circuit board. Dip switches configure the circuitry to act in a particular way.

direct memory access   A process by which data moves directly between a disk drive (or other device) and system memory without passing through the central processing unit.

directory entry   The 32-byte record, held in a directory, that tells a file's name, size, time and data, starting cluster, and other pertinent information.

disk caching   See *sector caching*.

DMA   See *direct memory access*.

DMA channel   One of several independent DMA facilities in a computer. DMA channels may work simultaneously.

DOS buffers   Holding areas in memory where DOS keeps disk sectors that are in transit between the disk surface and the locations in memory where the data is manipulated. Each buffer holds one 512-byte sector.

DOS shell   A utility program that makes DOS easier to use by supplying a graphic directory tree, scrollable directory listings, and many other features.

drive geometry   The dimensions of a drive in terms of the number of platter sides, tracks, and sectors per track.

drive specifier   The identifying letter DOS gives to a drive, such as **A:** or **C:**.

DSS   See *dedicated servo surface*.

DV-I   A video compression technique devised by RCA that allows over an hour of moving video to be written on a compact disk.

dynamic linking   A technique in advanced operating systems (including OS/2) in which parts of a program are constantly swapped in and out of memory as they are required.

E

embedded servo data   Magnetic markings embedded between tracks on disk drives that use voice-coil actuators. The markings allow the actuator to fine-tune the position of the read/write heads.

encoding   The protocol by which data is laid down on the disk surface as a pattern of "Ons" and "Offs."

encryption   The translation of data into unreadable codes to maintain security.

extended boot record   A "boot record" that begins each volume in an extended DOS partition (under DOS 3.3). The machine doesn't actually use these records for booting.

extended partition   Starting with DOS 3.3, a hard disk may have two partitions that serve DOS—an ordinary, bootable partition (called the *primary partition*) and an *extended partition*, which may contain any number of *volumes* of up to 32 megabytes each.

external command   In DOS, an external command is one that is served by a file separate from COMMAND.COM. CHKDSK and RECOVER are two examples.

external drive   A disk or tape drive mounted in a separate cabinet with its own power supply and fan.

F

FASTOPEN   A DOS command (starting with version 3.3) that records in memory the location of a file the first time it is opened so that a subdirectory search may be avoided when the file is subsequently reopened.

FAT   See *file allocation table*.

FCB   See *file control block*.

FCBS   A DOS command (placed in CONFIG.SYS) that sets the maximum number of file control blocks that may be used simultaneously.

FDISK   The DOS disk-partitioning program.

file allocation table   A table held on the outer edge of a disk that tells which sectors are allocated to each file and in what order.

file attribute   Information held in the attribute byte of a file's directory entry.

file control block   A small block of memory used by DOS to manage files. File control blocks are now obsolete but occasionally appear in older software.

file defragmentation   The process of rearranging disk sectors so that files are compacted onto consecutive sectors in adjacent tracks.

file recovery   Techniques for repairing and reassembling files that have incurred one or more bad sectors.

FIND   A DOS command that searches for strings within files.

flaw density   A measure of the number of flaws on the platters in a hard disk drive.

floppy tape   A tape standard using drives that connect to an ordinary floppy disk controller.

FM encoding   See *frequency modulation encoding*.

FORMAT.COM   The DOS format program that performs both low- and high-level formatting on floppy diskettes but only high-level formatting on hard disks.

formatted capacity   The total number of bytes of data that could be fit onto a disk after it has been formatted. The *unformatted capacity* is higher because space is lost defining the boundaries between sectors.

form factor   The physical dimensions of a device. For example, a half-height drive that fits into a PC drive bay uses a "5¼-inch half-height form factor."

frequency modulation encoding   An outdated method of encoding data on the disk surface that wastes half the disk space.

full track buffer   A buffer, usually located on a disk controller card, that is filled with the contents of an entire track when a sector is requested from the track. Subsequent requests for other sectors on the track can then be met instantly.

geometry   See *drive geometry*.

gigabyte   One billion bytes (a thousand megabytes).

global backup   A backup of all information on a hard disk, including the directory tree structure.

guide rails   Plastic strips attached to the sides of disk drives mounted in IBM ATs and compatibles so that they may slide into place.

hard disk card   A miniaturized hard disk built into a controller card and installed in one of a computer's slots.

hard error   An error reading or writing data caused by damaged hardware.

head   See *read/write head*.

head actuator   The device that moves read/write heads across a disk drive's platters. Drives use a stepper-motor actuator or a voice-coil actuator.

head crash   A rare occurrence in which a read/write head strikes a platter surface, gouging the magnetic medium.

head parking   A procedure in which a disk drive's read/write heads move to an unused track so that they won't damage data in the event of a head crash or other failure.

head seek   The movement of a drive's read/write heads to a particular track.

head seek test   A rigorous test that checks the accuracy of head seek operations.

hexadecimal number   A number encoded in base-16, such that digits include the letters A through F as well as the numerals 0 to 9 (for example, 8BF3).

hidden file   A file that isn't displayed in DOS directory listings because its attribute byte holds a special setting.

high-capacity drive   A drive of 100 megabytes or more.

high-level formatting   Formatting performed by the DOS FOR-
MAT program. Among other things, it creates the root directory
and file allocation tables.

history file   A file created by utility software to keep track of earlier use of the software. For example, many backup programs
keep history files describing earlier backup sessions.

I

IBMBIO.COM   One of the DOS system files required to boot the
machine. The first file loaded, it enables the machine to read
IBMDOS.COM.

IBMDOS.COM   One of the DOS system files required to boot the
machine. Loaded by IBMBIO.COM, it in turn loads COM-
MAND.COM.

incremental backup   A backup of all files that have changed
since the last backup.

interface   A protocol, embodied in the electronics of the disk
controller and disk electronics, that intermediates the exchange
of data between the drive and computer.

interleave   The numbering of sectors on a track so that the
"next" sector arrives at the read/write heads just as the computer
is ready to access it.

interleave factor   The number of sectors that pass beneath the
read/write heads before the "next" numbered sector arrives. For
example, when the interleave factor is 3:1, a sector is read, two
pass by, and then the next is read.

internal command   In DOS, an internal command is one contained in COMMAND.COM, so that no other file must be loaded
to perform the command. DIR and COPY are two examples.

internal drive   A disk or tape drive mounted inside one of a computer's disk drive bays (or a hard disk card, which is installed in
one of the computer's slots).

inter-record gaps   In tape backup, sections of wasted tape that
occur when the disk cannot supply data as quickly as the tape
drive can write it.

interrupt vector A mechanism by which an external device can take control of the computer's microprocessor.

JOIN A DOS command that can link the subdirectory of one drive into that of another.

jumper A tiny box that slips over two pins that protrude from a circuit board. When in place, the jumper connects the pins electrically. By doing so, it connects the two terminals of a switch, turning it "on."

keyboard macro A series of keystrokes automatically input when a single key is pressed. For example, Alt-A could be made to enter **DIR A:**. Keyboard macros require special utility software.

key disk In software copy protection, a key disk is distribution diskette that must be present in a floppy disk drive for an application program to run.

kilobyte One thousand bytes.

kit All components required to install a hard disk in an IBM PC or compatible: drive, controller card, cables, and various attachments.

landing strip An unused track that the read/write heads land on when power is shut off.

laser disk A disk that encodes data as a series of reflective pits that are read (and sometimes written) by a laser beam.

level-one subdirectory A subdirectory that is directly below the root directory (that is, it is a child directory of the root directory).

logical drive A "drive" as named by a DOS drive specifier, such as **C:** or **D:**. Under DOS 3.3, a single *physical drive* may act as several *logical drives*, each with its own specifier.

low-level formatting   Formatting that creates sectors on the platter surfaces.

M

magnetic domain   A tiny segment of a track just large enough to hold one of the magnetic flux reversals that encode data on a disk surface.

magneto-optical recording   An erasable laser-disk recording technique that uses a laser beam to heat pits on the disk surface to the point that a magnet can make flux changes.

master boot record   On hard disks, a one-sector table that gives essential information about the disk and tells the starting locations of the various partitions.

Mb   "Megabit."

MB   "Megabyte."

mean time between failure   A statistically derived measure of the probable time a drive will operate before a hardware failure occurs.

medium   The magnetic coating or plating that covers a disk or tape.

megabyte   One million bytes.

memory caching   A service provided by extremely fast memory chips that keeps copies of the most recent memory accesses. When the CPU makes a subsequent access, the value is supplied by the fast memory, rather than from relatively slow system memory. Memory caching is found on some accelerator boards.

memory-resident program   A program that remains in memory once it has been loaded, consuming memory that might otherwise be used by application software.

menu software   Utility software that makes a computer easier to use by replacing DOS commands with a series of menu selections.

MFM   See *modified frequency modulation encoding.*

MHz   Megahertz—Millions of cycles per second.

microprocessor   The integrated circuit chip that performs the bulk of data processing in a computer.

millisecond   One-thousandth of a second.

MKDIR   Make Directory—The DOS command that creates a new subdirectory.

modified frequency modulation encoding   The method of encoding data on the disk surface that is most widely used today. The coding of a bit of data varies by the coding of the previous bit.

MORE   A DOS command that causes DOS to pause after displaying a screenful of information (say, in a directory listing); the next screen is shown when a key is pressed.

ms   "millisecond"—one-thousandth of a second.

MTBF   See *mean time between failure*.

multitasking   Running several programs simultaneously.

multiuser system   A system in which several computer terminals share the same central processing unit (CPU).

N

network   A system in which a number of independent computers are linked together to share data and peripherals, such as hard disks and printers.

nonvolatile RAM disk   A RAM disk powered by a battery supply so that it continues to hold its data during a power outage.

O

off-hours backup   Backups made automatically when the computer isn't in use.

orphaned clusters   Clusters that have accidentally been marked as "unavailable" in the file allocation table even though they belong to no file listed in a directory.

OS/2   IBM's multitasking operating system for ATs and most PS/2 machines.

overlay   Part of a program that is loaded into memory only at the times it is required.

overrun   A situation in which data moves from one device faster than a second device can accept it.

overwrite   To write data on top of existing data, erasing it.

P

PATH   A DOS command that causes DOS to seek program files in other directories when the program isn't found in the current directory.

path program   A utility program that extends the operating system so that it searches for files in other subdirectories when the files aren't present in the current directory.

parent directory   The directory that holds the entry for a subdirectory file. In *MAMMALS/PRIMATES/APES*, *MAMMALS* is parent to *PRIMATES*, and *PRIMATES* is parent to *APES*.

partial backup   A backup of all files related to a particular project to maintain the state of the project at a given time.

partition   A section of a hard disk devoted to a particular operating system. Most hard disks have only one partition, devoted to DOS.

PC/T   A tape format that uses a scheme in which every two blocks of data are followed by a block for error checking.

perpendicular recording   A recording technique in which magnetic domains are created perpendicular to rather than parallel to the disk surface, making possible much higher data densities.

physical drive   A single disk drive. DOS defines *logical drives*, which are given a specifier, such as **C:** or **D:**. A single physical drive may be divided in multiple logical drives. Conversely, special software can *span* a single logical drive across two physical drives.

plated media   Hard disk platters plated with a metal film upon which data is recorded.

platter   A disk contained in a hard disk drive. Most drives have two or more platters, each with data recorded on both sides.

port address   One of a system of addresses used by the computer to access devices such as disk drives or printer ports. You may need to specify an unused port address when installing a tape backup unit.

power supply   A metal box, found inside any computer, which converts line current into the voltages required by the computer.

presentation manager   The graphical, icon- and window-based software interface offered with OS/2.

primary partition   Starting with DOS 3.3, a hard disk may have two partitions that serve DOS—a *primary partition*, which is an ordinary, bootable partition, and an *extended partition*, which may contain any number of *volumes* of up to 32 megabytes each.

primary storage   System memory—the 640K available to DOS, or 16 megabytes available under OS/2.

processor speed   The clock rate at which a microprocessor processes data. For example, a standard IBM PC operates at 4.77 MHz (4.77 million cycles per second).

proprietary format   In backups, a format in which data and error-correction codes are compressed on diskettes, sometimes without using ordinary DOS sectors. The format is entirely the creation of the backup utility's manufacturer.

Q

QIC   The most common tape-backup standard, which uses unformatted tape and minimal error-checking.

QIC Committee   An industry association that sets hardware and (increasingly) software standards for tape backup units.

R

rails   See *guide rails*.

RAM disk   A "phantom disk drive" for which a section of system memory (RAM) is set aside to hold data, just as if it were a number of disk sectors. To DOS, a RAM disk looks like, and functions like, any other drive.

random-access file   A file in which all data elements (or records) are of equal length. They are written in the file end to end, without delimiting characters between. Any element (or record) in the file can be found directly by calculating its offset in the file.

read-only file   A file in which a setting has been made in the attribute byte of its directory listing so that DOS won't allow software to write into the file.

read/write head   A tiny magnet that reads and writes data on a track. Each side of each platter has its own read/write head.

RECOVER   The file-recovery program included with DOS.

removable cartridge drive   A hard disk drive in which the platters are contained in a cartridge that may be removed and replaced with another. Some removable cartridge drives include the head actuator in the cartridge.

restocking fee   A fee charged by mail-order vendors when goods are returned for reasons that aren't the vendors' fault.

retensioning utility   A software utility that runs a tape cartridge through a drive to equalize the tension throughout the cartridge.

RLL   See *run length limited encoding*.

RMA number   Return Merchandise Authorization—A number given to you by a vendor when you arrange to ship a drive for repairs.

RMDIR   Remove directory—the DOS command that deletes a subdirectory from a disk. The directory must be empty.

ROM BIOS   See *BIOS*.

root directory   The main directory of any hard disk or floppy diskette. It always resides in a fixed number of sectors on the outer edge of the disk.

run-length limited encoding   A data encoding method in which patterns in the data are translated into codes. The technique can increase data densities by 50 to 100% over conventional encoding methods.

S

secondary storage   Disk storage—storage immediately online for the computer to load into memory without human intervention.

sector   A section of one track, defined with identification markings and an identification number from 0 to 65,535. In DOS, all sectors hold 512 bytes of data.

sector caching   A procedure in which frequently read (or recently read) disk sectors are stored in memory in anticipation that they will be required again. By keeping them on hand, time-consuming disk accesses are avoided.

sector size The number of bytes in a sector—normally 512 in DOS, but alterable by special utility software.

security software Utility software that uses a system of passwords and other devices to restrict an individual's access to subdirectories and files.

sequential file A file in which varying-length data elements are recorded end to end, with delimiting characters placed between each element. To find a particular element, the whole file up to that element must be read.

settling time The time required for read/write heads to stop vibrating once they have been moved to a new track.

serial backup A sequence of backups of a file or group of files that acts as a series of "snapshots" of the state of a project at different points in time.

servo data Magnetic markings written on disk platters that guide the read/write heads in drives that use voice-coil actuators.

shell Utility software that operates "on top of" DOS, providing an easy-to-use powerful interface.

SHIPDISK A program that parks a drive's read/write heads (moves them over an unused track).

shock rating A rating (expressed in Gs) of how much shock a disk drive can sustain without damage.

simultaneous backup Backups automatically written to a second hard disk whenever data is written to a first hard disk.

soft error An error in reading or writing data that occurs sporadically, usually because of a transient problem, such as a power fluctuation.

SORT A DOS command that can sort directory listings or sort the contents of a text file.

spindle The post upon which a disk drive's platters are mounted.

SRR See *stretch-surface recording*.

ST506/412 The standard 5-megabit per second interface used by most hard disk drives in IBM microcomputers.

standby power supply A backup power supply that very quickly switches into operation during a power outage.

starting cluster The number of the first cluster occupied by a file. Starting clusters are listed in each file's directory entry.

stepper band   A notched band that marks the track positions traveled by the read/write heads in drives that use a stepper-motor actuator.

stepper-motor actuator   An assembly that moves read/write heads across platters by a sequence of small turns of a special kind of motor.

streaming   In tape backup, a condition in which data is transferred from the hard disk as quickly as the tape drive can record it so that the drive does not start and stop or waste tape.

stretch-surface recording   An experimental recording technology that stretches a magnetic film above a platter's surface.

string   A sequence of characters. *A gray cat* is a 10-byte string in which two of the characters are spaces.

subdirectory   A directory listed in another directory. Subdirectories exist as variable-length files.

subdirectory attribute   A setting in a directory entry's attribute byte that marks the entry as representing a subdirectory file.

subdirectory file   A file that holds a subdirectory (all subdirectories exist as files of arbitrary size that may be located anywhere on a disk).

SUBST   A DOS command that can assign a drive specifier to a subdirectory.

surge protector   A device that provides minimal protection against voltage spikes and other transients in the power line that feeds the computer.

SYS   A DOS command that transfers the two hidden system files (IBMBIO.COM and IBMDOS.COM) to a particular position on a floppy or hard disk so that it can be used for booting the machine.

system crash   A situation in which the computer seizes up and refuses to proceed without rebooting. Systems crashes are usually caused by faulty software. Unlike a "hard disk crash," no permanent physical damage occurs.

system files   Three files required by PC-DOS to boot the machine: COMMAND.COM, IBMBIO.COM, and IBMDOS.COM (the latter two are hidden files).

system memory   The computer's random-access memory (limited to 640K under DOS).

system integrator   A computer consultant/vendor who tests available products and combines them into highly optimized systems.

T

tagging   A technique in many DOS shells that lets you use the cursor to "tag" files in a directory listing. The files may then be copied, erased, and so on, as a group.

tape format   The way in which data is laid out in tape backups. The various tape formats differ in the number of tracks on the tape, the kind of error checking performed, and directory layout.

temporary backup   A second copy of a work file, usually named with the extension .BAK. Application software creates these files so that you can easily return to a previous version of your work.

temporary file   A file temporarily (and invisibly) created by a program for its own use.

thin-film media   See *plated media*.

tpi   Tracks per inch—a measure of track density.

track   One of the many concentric circles that hold data on a disk surface. A track consists of a single line of magnetic flux changes.

track buffer   See *full track buffer*.

track density   The number of tracks that can be fit on a platter side.

track-to-track seek time   The time required for read/write heads to move between adjacent tracks.

tree diagram   A graphical display of a directory tree. Many DOS shells present a tree diagram and let you operate on the tree by moving a cursor across the diagram.

Trojan horse   Destructive code hidden in programs by vandals. The code remains inoperative until a particular event occurs, whereupon it destroys as much data as it can, usually by erasing the hard disk.

TYPE   A DOS command that displays files.

U

underrun   In tape backup, underruns occur when data cannot be delivered from the hard disk as quickly as the tape drive can record it.

"unerase" utility   A utility that can sometimes restore a file that has been deleted by the DOS DEL or ERASE commands.

"unformat" utility   A utility that, using prior precautions, can largely restore a hard disk to its former state after the DOS FORMAT command has been accidentally applied to the disk, destroying access to its data.

unformatted capacity   The total number of bytes of data that could be fit onto a disk. The *formatted capacity* is lower because space is lost defining the boundaries between sectors.

uninterrupted power supply   A device that supplies power to the computer from batteries so that current isn't lost, even momentarily, during a power outage. The batteries are constantly recharged from a wall socket.

V

virtual disk   See *RAM disk*.

virtual memory   A technique by which operating systems (including OS/2) load more programs and data into memory than there is system memory to hold them. Parts of the programs and data are kept on disk and constantly swapped back and forth into system memory.

voice-coil actuator   A device that moves read/write heads across hard disk platters by pushing and pulling at a bar inserted through a coil.

voltage regulator   A device that smooths out voltage irregularities in the power fed to the computer.

volume   (1) In tape backup, a volume is one or more tape tracks organized as a unit. (2) In diskette-based backup, a volume is one of the diskettes that hold a backup. (3) Under DOS 3.3, a single hard disk may be partitioned into several volumes of up to 32 megabytes, each with its own logical drive specifier (C:, D:, E:, and so on).

volume label   An identifier of up to eleven characters that names a disk; a volume label may be written on a hard disk, but they are intended for floppy diskettes or removable cartridges.

volume label attribute   A setting in the attribute byte of a directory entry that specifies that the entry is to be interpreted as the disk's volume label. This attribute occurs only in the root directory.

W

Whitney technology   An advanced suspension system for read/write heads.

Winchester drive   An ordinary, nonremovable disk drive.

worm   A destructive program sometimes loaded into mainframe computers by vandals. It constantly shifts its own location in the system.

WORM drive   A "write-once, read-many" laser disk drive. It uses cartridge disks on which any sector may be written upon only once, but that can be read back any number of times.

X

XCOPY   A DOS command that can search multiple subdirectories and even the entire directory tree, when it copies files.

Y

Y-connector   A Y-shaped cable that divides a power supply cable into two cables so that two drives may be connected.

Product Manufacturers

1DIR+   Bourbaki Inc.
Box 2867
Boise, ID. 83701
(208) 342–5849

Awesome I/O Card   CSSL, Inc.
909 Electric Avenue, Suite 202
Seal Beach, CA 90740
(213) 493–2471

Back-it   Gazelle Systems
42 Norton University Avenue, Suite 10
Provo, UT 84601
(800) 233–0383

Backup Master   Intersection Concepts, Inc.
80 Long Court, Ste 1A
Thousand Oaks, CA 91360
(805) 373–3900

Bernoulli Box   IOMEGA Corporation
1821 West 4000
South Roy, UT 84067
(408) 436–4922

BIOS upgrade chip (for early PCs)   Diagsoft, Inc.
6001 Butler Lane, Suite 2
Scotts Valley, CA 95066
(408) 438–8247

Breakthru 286   Personal Computer Support Group
                 11035 Harry Hines Boulevard, #207
                 Dallas, TX 75229
                 (214) 351–0564

Command Plus   ESP Software Systems Inc.
                 11965 Venice Boulevard, #309
                 Los Angeles, CA 90066
                 (800) 992–4ESP

Copy II PC   Central Point Software, Inc.
                 9700 SW Capitor Highway, #100
                 Portland, OR 97219
                 (503) 244–5782

Corefast   CORE International
                 7171 North Federal Highway
                 Boca Raton, FL 33431
                 (305) 997–6055

Cubit   SoftLogic Solutions, Inc.
                 530 Chestnut Street
                 Manchester, NH 03101
                 (800) 272–9900

Data Pac   Tandon Computer Corporation
                 405 Science Drive
                 Moorpark, CA 93021
                 (805) 378–6104

Dayflo   DayFlo Software
                 17701 Mitchell Avenue North
                 Irvine, CA 92714
                 (800) 367–5369

Disk Mechanic   MLI Microsystems
                 PO Box 825
                 Framingham, MA 01701
                 (617) 926–2055

Disk Optimizer   SoftLogic Solutions, Inc.
                 530 Chestnut Street
                 Manchester, NH 03101
                 (800) 272–9900

Disk Technician   Prime Solutions Inc.
1940 Garnet Avenue
San Diego, CA 92109
(619) 274–5000

Disk Tool Kit   Morgan Computing Co., Inc
PO Box 112730
Carrollton, TX 75011
(214) 245–4763

DPATH+Plus   Persoanl Business Solutions
PO Box 757
Frederick, MD 21701
(301) 865–3376

Dub-14   Golden Bow Systems
See Vfeature Deluxe

Electra-Find   O'Neill Software
PO Box 26111
San Francisco, CA 94126
(415) 398–2255

Fastback   Fifth Generation Systems
11200 Industriplex Boulevard
Baton Rouge, LA 70809
(714) 553–0111

FILE-LOK   *See* PC-LOK

FilePaq   *See* FilePath

FilePath   SDA Associates
PO Box 36152
San Jose, CA 95158
(408) 281–7747

Flash   Software Masters, Inc.
6352 Guilford Avenue
Indianapolis, IN 46220
(317) 253–8088

HardCard   Plus Development Corporation
1778 McCarthy Boulevard
Milpitas, CA 95035
(408) 946–3700

HARDPREP   *See* SpeedStor

HFORMAT   *See* HTEST

HOPTIMUM   *See* HTEST

Hot!   *See* XTREE

HTEST   Paul Mace Software
400 Williamson Way
Ashland, OR 97520
(503) 488–0224

JDISKETTE   Tall Tree Systems
1120 San Antonio Road
Palo Alto, CA 94303
(415) 964–1980

KeepTrackPlus   The Finot Group
2390 El Camino Real, Suite 3
Palo Alto, CA 94303
(415) 856–2020

Mace Utilities   Mace Software
400 Willison Way
Ashland, OR
950(503) 488–0224

Megafunction Board   Tecmar Inc.
6225 Cochran Road
Solon, OH 44139
(216) 349–0600

MTM 80–8000 Tape Subsystem   Emerald Systems Corp.
4757 Morena Boulevard
San Diego, CA 92117
(619) 270–1994

Norton Commander   Peter Norton Computing Incorporated
2210 Wilshire Boulevard, #186
Santa Monica, CA 90403
(213) 453–2361

Norton Utilities   Peter Norton Computing Incorporated
See Norton Commander

Novo Drive 1000   Kapak Designs
18784 Cox Ave.
Saratoga, CA 95070
(408) 378–4444

PC-LOK   Qualtec Security Products, Inc.
1400 Coleman Avenue
Santa Clara, CA 95050

PC Tools   *See* Copy II PC

Q-DOS II   *See* Back-it

Repair services   (specializing in hard disks)
Rotating Memory Service
473 Sapena Court, #26
Santa Clara, CA 95054
(408) 988-2334

California Disk Drive Repair
3350 Scott, Building 59
Santa Clara, CA 95054
(408) 727-2475

SafePark   *See* Disk Technician

SafetyNet   WestLake Data
PO Box 1711
Austin, TX 78767
(512) 474-4666

SDADEL   *See* FilePath

Silencer   PC Cooling Systems
31510 Via Ararat
Bonsall, CA 92003
(619) 723-9513

SmartPath   Software Research Technologies
3757 Wilshire Boulevard, Suite 211
Los Angeles, CA 90010
(213) 384-5430

SpeedStor   Storage Dimensions
981 University Avenue
Los Gatos, CA 95030
(408) 395-2688

Squish   SunDog Software Corporation
264 Court Street
Brooklyn, NY 11231
(718) 855-9141

SQZ	Turner Hall Publishing 10201 Torre Avenue Cupertino, CA 95014 (408) 253–9600
SuperKey	Borland International 4585 Scotts Valley Drive Scotts Valley, CA 95066 (800) 255–8008
TheEMCEE	Command Software Systems, Inc. 28990 Pacific Coast Highway, Suite 208 Malibu, CA 90265 213–457–1789
Transpc	Microcomputer Memories Inc. 9340 Owensmouth Ave. Chatsworth, CA 91311 (818) 700–8000
Turbo-Cool	*See* Silencer
Vfeature Deluxe	Golden Bow Systems PO Box 3039 San Diego, CA 92103 (619) 298–9349
Videotrax	Alpha Micro PO Box 25059 Santa Ana, CA 92799 (800) 992–9779
X2C	ABMComputer Systems 24605 Charlton Drive Laguna Hills, CA 92653 (714) 859–6531
XTREE Executive Systems, Inc.	15300 Ventura Boulevard, Suite 305 Sherman Oaks, CA 91403 (818) 990–3457
Zoo Keeper	Polaris Software 613 West Valley Parkway, Suite 323 Escondido, CA 92025 (619) 743–7800

Index

About the Authors

Peter Norton is well known in the personal computing field as "the Guru of personal computers." He is the author of a number of best-selling Brady books and utilities, including *Inside the IBM PC, Revised and Enlarged, Peter Norton's DOS Guide, PC-DOS: The Guide to High Performance Computing*, and *Peter Norton's Assembly Language Book*. Additionally, Mr. Norton is the CEO of a successful software manufacturing and publishing company, Peter Norton Computing, Inc., located in Santa Monica, Ca. *The Norton Utilities* is famous for saving the "derrieres" of many computer users. Other products include *The Norton Editor, The Norton Commander* and the newest product, *The Norton Guides*, an on-line help system for programming languages and software commands. Peter grew up in Seattle, Washington, attended Reed College in Portland, Oregon, and graduated from the University of California at Berkeley. He now lives in Santa Monica, California with his wife and daughter.

Robert Jourdain is a professional programmer and author of the best-selling *Programmer's Problem Solver for the IBM PC, XT & AT*, a general hardware reference for IBM PC programmers. He has also written a library of 250 assembly language routines, *Turbo Pascal Express*. Both books are published by Brady. His software includes an authoring system for animated graphics presentations and a text database for researchers and writers. He attended Berkeley, the University of London, and Kyoto University.

Inside the IBM PC

Access to Advanced Features and Programming, Revised and Expanded
by Peter Norton

The most widely recognized book about the IBM PC written by the most highly acclaimed IBM PC expert. Covers the IBM PC, XT and AT, every version of DOS from 1.1 to 3.0.

The classic work includes:
- The fundamentals of the 8088 and 80286 microprocessors, DOS and BIOS
- Programming examples to show how the machine works, in BASIC, Pascal, and Assembly Language
- How ROM is allocated
- A detailed look at disk data storage

Your only source for understanding and using the hardware and software that make up your IBM PC system.

ISBN: 0-89303-583-1 • $21.95 (book)
ISBN: 0-13-467325-5 • $39.95
(book/disk, includes 15 programs)

The Norton Portfolio

From Brady Books

Peter Norton's Assembly Language Book for the IBM PC

by Peter Norton and John Socha

Learn to write efficient, full-scale assembly language programs that double and even triple your programs' speed. To learn techniques and enhance your knowledge, you'll build a program step-by-step.

The book is divided into three parts:
- Part 1 focuses on the mysteries of the 8088 microprocessor
- Part 2 guides you into assembly language
- Part 3 tackles the PC's more advanced features and debugging techniques

The book disk package includes a fully integrated, powerful disk for instant, hands-on experience in assembly language. The disk contains all the examples discussed in the book, and advanced professional version of the program you build.

With the expertise of Peter Norton and John Socha to guide you, you're guaranteed an experience that's both informative and practical.

ISBN: 0-13-661901-0 • $21.95 (book)
ISBN: 0-13-662149-X • $39.95 (book/disk)
Requires: IBM PC, AT, XT or compatible

Peter Norton's DOS Guide

Revised and Expanded
by Peter Norton

Here's tried and true instruction from the true-blue friend of PC users everywhere. Newly updated with coverage of DOS 3.3, this best-seller is distinguished by Norton's easy-to-follow style and honestly factual approach. Includes advice on hard disk management and discussions of batch files for DOS customization.

Topic-by-topic organization make this manual not only a lively tutorial, but also a long-lasting reference.

ISBN: 0-13-662073-6 • $19.95

To Order:
Complete and mail the form following these advertisements

Turbo Pascal Express

250 Ready-to-Run Assembly Language Routines that Make Turbo Pascal Faster, More Powerful and Easier to Use

Learn to substitute lightning-fast assembly language routines for critical parts of your Turbo Pascal programs with this book/disk package.

Programmers know all too well that 20% of a program takes 80% of the run time. Now run time is pushed into fast forward, thanks to this package. Its two disks are chock-full of more than 250 assembly language routines to manipulate data structures; process strings; handle screens; exploit disk operations; and streamline the fundamental routines that chew up valuable compile time.

The book offers extensive documentation, including details on how each routine functions; specifics on coupling each module to existing programs; hints on avoiding potential trouble spots; and abundant examples of the program modules in action.

ISBN: 0-13-535337-8 • $39.95
Requires: IBM PC, XT, AT or compatible, 256K RAM, 2 disk drives and Turbo Pascal v. 3.0

More From Robert Jourdain

Programmer's Problem Solver

For the IBM PC, XT & AT

The total IBM programming book you absolutely need. Brady's most comprehensive and insightful complete reference guide to the facts, numbers and procedures you need to achieve program control over PC hardware.

- For programmers in BASIC, Pascal, C and other languages—you'll find disk directory access, keyboard macros, scrolling, paging on the monochrome card, advanced video, and sound control.
- For assembly language programmers—it includes overlays, device drivers, error diagnosis and recovery, COM files, DOS access, and real-time operations.
- For everyone—it explores graphics on the EGA, control of serial and parallel ports and modems, proportional spacing and printer graphics, file operation of all kinds, and assessment of what equipment is installed.

Every section begins with a review of the fundamentals and includes cross-referencing. You'll also find helpful appendices for brand-new programmers, a detailed index, all standard data tables, and an advanced-level glossary. This ultimate reference book is an excellent source of ideas, a valuable tutor, and a tremendous time-saver.
ISBN: 0-89303-787-7 • $22.95

To Order:
Complete and mail the form following these advertisements

///Brady

Inside the Norton Utilities™

The Official Guide.

by Rob Krumm
with an Introduction by Peter Norton

More than a million PC users depend on the Norton Utilities to make their computers reliable, efficient tools. The official guide to these best-selling programs, *Inside the Norton Utilities* shows you the most efficient way to use:

- Norton Utilities—the original
- Norton Utilities Advanced Edition—faster, and with new features
- Norton Commander—for high speed computer management
- Norton Editor—a programmer's tool in the Norton tradition

With this book you'll learn to fill the gaps in DOS's functionality. You'll explore memory and hard disk organization. You'll learn how to use the Norton Utilities, and, more importantly, how the Norton Utilities work with your data.

Inside the Norton Utilities covers formatting disks and erasing and copying files and disks. Then it shows you how to undo it all using UnErase and other Norton Utility functions. Working with Inside the Norton Utilities you'll learn how DOS stores data and gain greater control over your files. You'll stop losing data accidentally, and you'll stop disasters before they happen.

Rob Krumm runs a computer school in Walnut Creek, California. He is the author of *Getting The Most Out Of Utilities On IBM PC* and *Understanding and Using dBASE III Plus*. His columns and commentaries regularly appear in the *San Francisco Examiner* and Computer Currents.

ISBN: 0-13-467887-7 • $19.95

Order Form

Indicate the titles and quantities desired below.
Enclose Check or Money order or use your credit card for payment:

☐ Enclosed is a check for $_____

☐ Charge my   ☐ MasterCard   Account # _____
                     ☐ VISA   Exp. Date _____

Signature _____

Name _____
Address _____
City _____ State _____ Zip _____

(New Jersey residents please add applicable sales tax.)
Dept. 3

Return to: PH Mail Order Billing
                    Route 59 at Brook Hill Drive
                    West Nyack, NY 10994

Title	Code	Quantity	Price	Total
Utilities				
Hard Disk Manager	38377		$39.95	
dBASE III Plus To Go	19621		$39.95	
1-2-3 Ready-to-Run	93988		$39.95	
1-2-3 Power Pack	63540		$39.95	
Instant Ventura Publisher	46779		$39.95	
Also by Peter Norton				
Inside the IBM PC	03583		$21.95	
Inside the IBM PC book/disk	46732		$39.95	
Peter Norton's Assembly Language Book for the IBM PC				
Book	66190		$21.95	
Book/Disk	66214		$39.95	
Peter Norton's DOS Guide	66207		$19.95	
Also by Robert Jourdain				
Programmer's Problem Solver	03787		$22.95	
Turbo Pascal Express	53533		$39.95	
Inside the Norton Utilities	46788		$19.95	

- -

Place
Postage
Here

PH Mail Order Billing
Route 59 at Brook Hill Drive
West Nyack, NY 10994

- -

⫴*Brady Line*

Insights into tomorrow's technology from the authors and editors of Brady Books.

You rely on Brady's bestselling computer books for up-to-date information about high technology. Now turn to the *Brady Line* for the details behind the titles.

Find out what new trends in current technology spark Brady's authors. Read about what they're working on, and predicting, for the future. Learn what technologies Brady's editors are watching—what software will be hot, what new systems are sure winners. Get to know the authors through interviews and profiles, and get to know each other through your questions and comments.

Brady Line keeps you ahead of the trends with the stories behind the latest computer developments. Informative previews of forthcoming books and excerpts from new publications keep you apprised of what's going on in the fields that interest you most.

- Peter Norton on operating systems
- Jim Seymour on business productivity
- Jerry Daniels, Robert Eckhardt, and Cynthia Harriman on Macintosh development, productivity, and connectivity

Get the Spark. Get Brady Line.

Published quarterly beginning with the Spring 1988 issue. Free exclusively to our customers. Just fill out and mail the coupon below to begin your subscription.

F

R

E

E

Name_____

Address_____

City_____ State_____ Zip_____

Name of Book Purchased_____

Date of Purchase_____

Where was this book purchased?

Retail Store   Computer Store   Mail Order

Fold and mail this form for your free subscription to Brady Line

Fold along dotted lines and staple

Place
Postage
Here

Brady Books
16th Floor
1 Gulf + Western Plaza
New York, NY 10023